D0952114

the

HIDDEN
LIFE

of

OTTO
FRANK

ALSO BY
CAROL ANN LEE

Anne Frank's Story

*Roses from the Earth: The Biography of
Anne Frank*

Carol Ann Lee

WILLIAM MORROW
An Imprint of HarperCollins*Publishers*

the HIDDEN LIFE of OTTO FRANK

FIRST U.S. EDITION

Book design by Shubhani Sarkar

Printed on acid-free paper

Library of Congress Cataloging-in-Publication Data
Lee, Carol Ann.
    The hidden life of Otto Frank / Carol Ann Lee.
      p. cm.
    Includes bibliographical references and index.
    ISBN 0-06-052082-5
    1. Frank, Otto, 1889–1980. 2. Jews—Germany—Biography. 3. Jews, German—Netherlands—Amsterdam—Biography. 4. Holocaust, Jewish (1939–1945)—Netherlands—Amsterdam. 5. World War, 1939–1945—Collaborationists—Netherlands—Amsterdam. 6. Ahlers, Tonny, d. 2000. 7. Holocaust survivors—Netherlands—Biography. 8. Frank, Anne, 1929–1945. Achterhuis. 9. Amsterdam (Netherlands)—Biography. I. Title.
DS135.G5 F58455 2003
940.53'18'092—dc21
[B]

2002038941

03 04 05 06 07 BVG/BVG 10 9 8 7 6 5 4 3 2 1

In memory of
my father,
Raymond Lee

Contents

Acknowledgments

The idea to write this book came from Swiss publisher Thomas Meyer. He suggested it to me after a talk I gave in Basel about my biography of Anne Frank, *Roses from the Earth*. I thought about it at length, remembering how intrigued I had been by Otto Frank's letters from the Western Front during the First World War, which I had not been able to include in my book about his daughter, and by his determination to have the diary published in an era when the Holocaust (not referred to then as such) was an inaccessible subject in literature. I was also fascinated by the dichotomy between Otto Frank fighting for his country in the First World War and his persecution by his country in the Second, and how he reconciled himself to the appalling contrast in his circumstances. His life was divided in two in another way: after 1945 and the loss of his first wife and children in the Holocaust, Otto Frank embarked upon a mission to bring Anne's diary to as wide a public as possible. Her book became one of his primary reasons for living.

Generally speaking, only the barest details of his life have been public knowledge. Otto Frank was famous for the last thirty years of his life, but even then, few interviewers thought to ask him about himself. He wrote thousands of replies to readers of his daughter's diary who wished for some communication with him, but rarely deviated from a set response. When he did, with a remark seemingly thrown in as an afterthought—"I was liberated from Auschwitz at the end of January, two days after I had faced an execution squad. I returned to Amsterdam . . ."—it raised many questions, most of which remained unanswered.

Otto Frank was ninety-one years old when he died in 1980. By any standards, it is a long life to study in depth. During the winter of 1999, I examined some of my old notes, read Otto Frank's intriguing letters, spoke to a few of his relatives and friends, and walked through the streets in Amsterdam, close to my own home, where Otto's life had at first been good and was then torn apart. I realized how much I wanted to write about this hidden, haunted life.

In order to do so, I had to consult many people who generously gave their time and shared their knowledge. I must first of all thank Yt Stoker, whose patient and expert guidance through the archives of the Anne Frank Stichting and in other areas of research was invaluable and contributed much to the final form of the book. I would also like to thank Jan Erik Dubbelman, Teresien da Silva, and Dienke Hondius of the Stichting. Dienke's loan of the English translation of *Terugkeer*, her intelligent and scrupulous study of Jewish concentration camp survivors returning to the Netherlands, is gratefully acknowledged; it illuminated a particularly dark era in Otto Frank's life for me.

I received help from a number of other archives and institutions and wish to single out for particular thanks Sierk Plantinga at the Rijksarchief in The Hague; Johannes van der Vos, Hubert Berkhout, and David Barnouw at NIOD; Verola de Weert at the Amsterdam Bevolkingsregister; and Peter Kroesen of the Gemeente Archief in Amsterdam. The staffs of the Jewish Historical Museum of Amsterdam, the Koninklijke Bibliotheek in

The Hague, the Auschwitz-Birkenau Museum, the United States Holocaust Museum, and the Simon Wiesenthal Center in Los Angeles were also very helpful, and I must thank Gillian Walnes of the Anne Frank Educational Trust for providing advice and contacts.

I received excellent ideas for further research from Susan Massotty, Simone Schroth, and Elma Verhey. Francoise Gaarlandt-Kist of my Dutch publisher, Balans, provided expert guidance on how to improve an initially unwieldy manuscript, and Jan Michael helped me not to despair about the work that entailed, but to see it as a surmountable challenge. My agent, Eva Koralnik of Liepman AG, Switzerland, has been a great support and a source of invaluable advice, and I am very grateful to her husband, Pierre Koralnik, for bringing us together. I also offer my sincere thanks to Marion Nietfeld, who set me on a trail that had never been followed before, and to Paul van Maaren, who provided material that helped light the way.

Grateful acknowledgment is made to all those authors and publishers who allowed me to quote from their works, and to those people named below who permitted me to quote from their private letters. (The citations within the text appear at the end of the book.) Quotations from Anne's diary, and the personal correspondence of the Frank and Elias families—used by the kind permission of Buddy Elias—are under the copyright of the Anne Frank-Fonds, Basel.

I offer my heartfelt gratitude to those who shared personal and often deeply painful memories with me: Anton Ahlers and his wife (who does not wish to be named), Cas Ahlers, Ilse Blitz, Angus Cameron, Barbara Mooyart-Doubleday, Annette Duke, Barbara Epstein, Vincent Frank-Steiner, Jack Furth, Hilde Goldberg (many thanks to her sister-in-law, Bea, for providing the initial contact), Edith Gordon, Stephan van Hoeve, Dola de Jong (thanks to Pauline Micheels for putting me in touch with her), Bee Klug, xiv Gabriel Levin, Rose and Sal de Liema, Lillian Marks, Father John Neiman, Laureen Nussbaum, Katja Olszewska, Hanneli Pick-Goslar, Alfred Radley, Tony van Renterghem, Judith and Henk Salomon, Jacqueline Sanders–van Maarsen, Eva and Zvi Schloss, Rabbi David Soetendorp, Franzi Spronz, Anneke Steenmeijer, Cor Suijk, and Thesy Nebel. I regret that it was not possible to speak to Miep Gies, who no longer grants interviews after enduring a bout of severe ill health. The questions I would have liked to ask Mrs. Gies were answered on her behalf by Cor Suijk initially, but through her son Paul and his friend Gerlof Langerijs, I was able to learn more about certain aspects of the past that interested me. My thanks go out to all of them.

Gusta Krusemeyer and Henri Beerman translated scores of documents from German and Dutch into English for me, even though they had their own work to do. I thank them deeply for that, and for their kindness, generosity, and amiability, which made working with them such a pleasure. Thanks, too, to Maarten Fagh, for putting me in touch with them, and to Hendrik Wilhelm Reiters, for additional help with German translations.

The following group of people have supported my work in ways too numerous to mention and are very close to my heart: Buddy and Gerti Elias, Jan Michael and Paul Clark, and Alison Davies. My love and respect go out to all of them and to my mother, my brother and his wife, and my husband's sister, who have all been instrumental in the completion of this book.

Finally, as any writer who also happens to be a mother knows, the most basic necessity before settling down to write is not only a room of one's own but the certainty that one's child is in the safest possible hands. For this, and for countless other things, I thank my beloved husband, Ronnie, and my parents-in-law, Dick and Truus Cornelisz. They shared the care of my son, River, during the often peculiar writing hours I kept, and I want to dedicate this book to them.

PREFACE

"I HAVE TO TELL YOU THAT THE IDEA PUT
forward in your book was wrong. My father did not 'probably' betray Otto Frank and his family—he most certainly *did* betray
them."[1] With these words, Anton Ahlers confirmed the possibility
put forward in these pages that his father, Tonny Ahlers, had managed to evade justice for over half a century for the betrayal at 263
Prinsengracht. When this book was first published in the
Netherlands in March 2002, I fully expected someone who had
known Tonny Ahlers to come forward and say that he or she had
more information about him. What I did not anticipate was that
family members would contact my publishers and the press to ver-
ify that Ahlers had indeed betrayed the Franks and their friends on
August 4, 1944. But that is what happened.

It was never my intention to raise the matter of the betrayal of
Otto Frank and his family again. There had already been so much
speculation on the subject, and although I wrote at length about the
case against Wilhelm van Maaren (the main suspect) in my biography of Anne Frank, *Roses from the Earth*, ultimately I felt that there
was no decisive evidence.

Then, in September 2000, I was given a letter written by Otto Frank that had never been published before.[2] It told an incredible story that had been kept secret for decades and centered on one man: Tonny Ahlers, a member of the NSB (Dutch Nazi Party). By chance, two months later, I was given a letter written by Ahlers that contained facts about Otto's life during the Second World War that at the time were unknown to anyone else outside the small circle of the eight fugitives and their helpers.[3] Deeply unpleasant in tone, it heavily contradicted some of the statements made in Frank's letter and made several accusations that I thought could not be true. Ahlers referred to other letters he had written in defense of Karl Josef Silberbauer, the man who arrested the Frank family and with whom he had corresponded. In the archives of the Nederlands Instituut voor Oorlogsdocumentatie (NIOD—Netherlands Institute for War Documentation), I found two more of Ahlers's letters, a summary of his wartime activities by a member of the SD (Sicherheitsdienst—the Security and Intelligence Service of the German SS), and a report by the authorities investigating Silberbauer in 1963–64.[4] Why hadn't this person been interrogated in regard to the betrayal? It took months of research—tracing names and sifting through layer upon layer of documentation—before I found the answer.

Meanwhile, I set out to discover what had happened to Ahlers. I learned that he had been imprisoned after the war on suspicion of betraying people to the SD. I found small strands of information, such as dates and addresses, and followed these leads. Sometimes I came up against a wall, but occasionally a gap in the wall allowed a glimpse of something relevant and I would keep going. A break-through came when I was able to consult Ahlers's collaborator files in The Hague; among the papers was an attestation by Otto Frank and further references to the relationship between the two.[5] I knew by then that Ahlers was no longer alive; he had died six weeks before I first heard of him. But I spoke twice, briefly, to his wife, who still lives in Amsterdam.

My search continued in archives that have never been consulted

in reference to the betrayal at 263 Prinsengracht yet contain material relating directly to it. When all the strands had been extracted,
a disturbing chain of events came to light. At last I understood why
the story had remained hidden and, perhaps, why the informant
was never brought to justice. I also came to understand just how
easily one very ordinary, not particularly intelligent young man
with anti-Semitic leanings could be drawn into the colossal Nazi
machine, which alienated him from his family and had a profound
impact upon the lives of everyone around him.

The publication of this book in the Netherlands caused a furor,
with most of the press coverage focusing on the subject of the
Frank family's betrayal. Following an article in the newspaper *De
Volkskrant,* Tonny Ahlers's brother Casper (Cas) called the newspaper and spoke to a journalist there.[6] Cas said that he had known
for many years that his brother was the Franks' betrayer and
claimed to have in his possession a candlestick that had been taken
from the secret annex. A couple of days after his telephone call, I
visited Cas's home in the quiet countryside of Emmen.[7] Not far
away lay Kamp Westerbork, where the Franks and their friends
were sent to await the train that would take them to Auschwitz
and the eventual death of them all except Otto Frank. I came away
from the meeting feeling that I knew much more about Tonny
Ahlers; the results of the interview with Cas are documented here.

In the meantime, my Dutch publisher also received a call, this
time from Tonny Ahlers's daughter-in-law, who suggested that I
speak to her husband, Anton, Tonny's youngest son. After meeting
Anton Ahlers, I saw little reason to suspect his motives in coming
forward. He is an intelligent man whose integrity those who know
him do not doubt. He has nothing to gain from admitting himself to
be the son of the Frank family's betrayer and wants to retain his
anonymity as far as possible. Over the course of several meetings, he
told me what he remembered of his father—with whom he had largely
avoided contact as soon as he was old enough to do so—and explained
his reasons for believing his father to be behind the call to the

Gestapo. Surprisingly, he bears no grudge at having had his background made public. "It's a relief," he says. "Of course, it was a terrible shock to see my father's face on the news, but I've lived with this secret for a long time. I could never have told people voluntarily that my father betrayed Otto Frank, but now that it has been made public, I feel it's my duty to tell what I know and to prevent any lies and half-truths going into the papers. I just want to set everything straight and get rid of this burden that I've lived with most of my life."[8]

Since the initial publication of this book and the revelations by members of the Ahlers family, a considerable amount of information has come to light, including one very startling new fact. Together with a few minor corrections to the previous editions published in the Netherlands and the United Kingdom, this information appears here for the first time. Regarding how this material reflects upon the person of Otto Frank, I hope that these discoveries will be seen in context and that readers will realize for themselves just how terrible Otto Frank's wartime situation was and how he, and others like him, had no choice but to make decisions that were difficult and had consequences no one could have foreseen.

As a result of the earlier material published in this book, the Dutch government is funding a new investigation into the betrayal of the Frank family, conducted by NIOD, publishers of *The Diaries of Anne Frank: The Critical Edition,* an entire chapter of which was devoted to the subject of the betrayal. The historians at NIOD must have seen the documents about Tonny Ahlers in their archives but failed to consider their significance to the case. It was a sizable error of judgment; Ahlers was then alive, could have been interviewed, and perhaps even could have been made accountable for the crime of betraying the Franks. It is too late for that now, but at the very least Tonny Ahlers will finally take his place among the usual suspects.

Ahlers liked to tell people that where he had been, "no grass shall ever grow."[9] He failed to realize that his footprints might still be visible upon the scorched earth.

the

HIDDEN
LIFE

of

OTTO
FRANK

prologue THE LETTER

THE YOUNG MAN RIDING HIS BICYCLE
along the busy streets of Amsterdam passes unnoticed among the
city center crowds. On this clear April day in 1941, he pedals with a
sense of purpose, his mind on the extraordinary task that lies
ahead. Within the folds of his light, white raincoat are confidential
letters concerning some of Amsterdam's many Jewish inhabitants,
and those people who persist in listening to the illegal radio broadcasts from the Dutch government-in-exile in London. He has several addresses to visit today; the first is on the Prinsengracht.[1]

Having spent many of his twenty-four years in the city, he
knows the narrow streets intersecting the canals well, and within
minutes he is leaving the main roads where trams hurtle through,
bells clanging, and turning his bicycle toward the Westerkerk. In
the shadow of the church's tall and ornate steeple, the old merchants' houses slouch against one another like cards ready to top-
ple. Halfway down the row, he stops and leans his bicycle against a
wall. He takes a step back, to read the numbers, and sees it immediately: 263 Prinsengracht. A large warehouse, with the name of
the company upon the door: Opekta, Spice Merchants. He looks up
at the silent building and rings the bell.[2]

■

THE SOUND OF THE DOORBELL IS LOUD-
est in the main office, overlooking the canal. One of the four secretaries gets up and presses a buzzer. She waits patiently for the
visitor to climb the unnerving, almost vertical stairs that lead up
from the front door to the confined, damp hallway on the first
floor.[3] There is no access beyond for visitors until they state their
business.[4] A moment later, she sees the caller silhouetted against
the opaque square window with its black lettering, REPORT HERE.
She slides the window open.

The handsome young man waiting on the other side is tall, slender, and dark-haired, with pronounced cheekbones and light-
colored, friendly eyes. His clothes, although somewhat shabby, are
clean and neat.

The secretary asks what they can do for him.

"I want to see Otto Frank," he says.[5]

"Do you have an appointment?"

The friendly eyes go suddenly cold. He answers with a sneer,
"I'm a member of the NSB."

A Dutch Nazi . . . it is as though the temperature in the building
has dropped. One of the office girls pushes a button to allow the
young man into the room. The secretary motions him to follow her.
Together they walk along the hallway and up a short flight of stairs,
in silence. In front of them are closed, diamond-patterned doors.
She knocks on one of the glass panes. The handle creaks as she
opens it.

The young man pushes past, leaving her motionless in the corridor, and closes the door so that no one can hear what he is about
to say.

■

OTTO FRANK EMIGRATED FROM GERMANY
in 1933 with his wife and two small daughters to escape the Nazis
and their persecution of Jews. Since his arrival in Amsterdam, he

has worked hard to build up the Opekta business, and the move to the Prinsengracht premises at the end of 1940 should have signified a bright outlook for the company. But the occupation of the Netherlands by the German army has thrown everything into jeopardy, and not just the future of the business. He thought he had found a safe haven for his family, but it was not to be. The Nazis have caught up with them. His sole aim now is to maintain a low profile, not to draw attention to himself, to fall in with whatever rules and regulations are thrown at them, and to keep the business ticking over. As long as he and his family are left alone, that is what matters most. He has to be invisible.

Today has been quiet and unremarkable, the kind of day for which he must be grateful. Orders dispatched and goods received, advertising campaigns thought out, and possible new clients targeted. He is not expecting callers; the knock on the glass pane surprises him.

The young man who enters is not familiar, despite the air of cocky self-assurance with which he shuts the doors and approaches the desk. Otto rises to his feet, partly out of ingrained courtesy but also owing to instinctive apprehension.

The young man stands squarely in front of the desk and, without offering his hand, introduces himself: "Tonny Ahlers. I work as a courier between the NSB and the Gestapo."[6] Ever on the lookout for an opportunity, Ahlers cannot fail to notice his surroundings: tasteful decoration, dark rich furniture, advertising posters neatly framed on the walls, organized files, lots of leather-bound German classics—and a large safe. An elegant office in a fine old building.

Ahlers makes his demand quickly: "Twenty guilders from you, now."

Otto takes out his wallet immediately and hands over the money. Ahlers pockets it, asking, "Do you know a man named Jansen?"

Otto's mind races. Jansen is such a common Dutch name. He shakes his head slightly. "There are lots of Jansens. Whom do you mean?"[7]

4

Ahlers reaches inside his coat. He pulls out a letter, unfolds it, and holds it up. "I took it from the file of incoming reports."

The first thing Otto sees is the signature, "Joseph M. Jansen," followed by the customary greeting of the Dutch Nazis, "Hou-zee," and then a number, "Member 29992."[8] He looks at the handwriting and draws in a deep breath. He recognizes it. He swallows and holds out his hand: "May I?"

Ahlers passes the letter to him.

Otto takes it; the paper trembles slightly in his grasp. He hardly dares to read the spidery black scrawl but knows he must. Years later, he will recall what led up to this cataclysmic event when he sends a letter describing the incident to the BNV (Bureau Nationale Veiligheid—Netherlands Bureau of National Security):

> In March 1941 I was on the Rokin when I met a certain Mr. Jansen, the husband of one of my demonstrators who worked earlier for my firm Opekta, now at Prinsengracht 263, Amsterdam. Mr. Jansen's son also worked in my warehouse. Mr. Jansen helped to build exhibition stands for my company, and thus the family was well known to me and of good conduct. In March when we met, Mr. Jansen and I had a short conversation, and Mr. Jansen asked me if I was still able to get goods from Germany because I was Jewish. I said that I did and that I had no difficulties and after we spoke about other things, Jansen said, "The war will be over soon," to which I answered that I was convinced that it wouldn't, and that the Germans were still having a tough time of it. Then we split up.[9]

Jansen. Otto never did like him very much. Now Jansen has written to the leaders of the NSB, alleging that Otto expressed doubt about the German victory and attempted to influence him. In addition, wrote Jansen, Otto had insulted the German Wehrmacht and made other derogatory remarks about the Nazis. Jansen requested that the SS be informed of these matters and that "the Jew Frank" be arrested.[10]

Otto looks up and meets Ahlers's curious pale eyes. "I know the man," he says.

Silence.

Ahlers glances away. "I don't earn much . . ."

Otto speaks quickly, urgently: "Please, come back. I can give you more money—"[11]

Ahlers nods. His gaze is direct now, the muscles in his long jaw tightened. "You can keep the letter. Or tear it up, whatever you prefer." He pauses. "You're not the only one in trouble." He holds up another letter, which Otto scans, but it has nothing to do with his personal situation; it is from a maid who wants to inform the SS that her employers listen regularly to the illegal English wireless broadcasts.

Ahlers folds the letter and replaces it inside his white raincoat.

Otto's voice is soft and measured. "I can pay you more next time."

"Oh, it's not the money," Ahlers replies airily. Otto almost believes him—clearly this young man enjoys the power he has over his fellow citizens. Amsterdam has become a jungle, with Jews and people against the Nazi regime providing fair game for men like Ahlers.

"I'll see you out." Otto moves across to the diamond-patterned doors and opens them slowly.

Ahlers stands at the foot of the short flight of stairs while the older man closes the doors to his office. In a second, he can see that this building, like many old canal houses, is divided into two: a front house and a rear house, or annex, linked by a single block. He is standing on the first floor of the connecting corridor. In front of him is a winding wooden staircase that passes over the lower part of a long window with opaque panes. The stairs curve away at the top, and the last few steps cannot be seen. They must lead to the upper floors of the annex. He recognizes it instantly; he used to live with his mother and stepfather in a house built exactly like this one, only five doors away at 253 Prinsengracht. He

6   remembers it well; a few months after leaving the house, he was sentenced to jail for street violence.[13]

Otto escorts him to the ladderlike steps that lead to the front door. Ahlers steps into the sunlight. His bicycle is still there, but before climbing onto it he takes out the maid's letter from his inside pocket and checks the address. He replaces it, and then jumps onto his bicycle, planning his next speech as he rides along. His new job with the SS is to confiscate wirelesses from people who listen to the forbidden broadcasts. For this, he receives fifty guilders a week and five guilders' commission for every appropriated wireless.[14] To that he can add Otto Frank's twenty guilders—and whatever he can extract from him in the future.

Ahlers cycles along the tree-lined street. The canal sparkles below him, as though someone has thrown diamonds into the water.

■

OTTO FRANK SITS DOWN BEHIND HIS desk. The poisonous letter rests, accusingly, on the green blotter. Behind him, through the long window onto the courtyard, the chestnut tree is beginning to grow new leaves. Next week he will see Tonny Ahlers again, and shortly afterward, he will begin to make preparations to go into hiding with his wife, Edith, and his beloved daughters, Margot and Anne. A year from now they will be living, like hunted animals, in the annex above the office.

On his orderly desk, the date on the calendar reads April 18, 1941: the date on which Otto Frank was led into an enigma that has never been documented, and into a maze of blackmail, terror—and betrayal.[15]

one GERMANY

Before the Second World War and
the Holocaust, Otto Frank had little interest in his Jewish heritage.
He was neither proud nor ashamed of being born a Jew; it was a
matter of indifference to him. During the Great War, when he was
serving in the German army, he made a rare comment in a letter
home: "I often get the feeling that mothers, brothers and sisters
are the only trustworthy people. At least, that's how it is in Jewish
families like ours."[1] His otherwise nonchalant attitude was typical
of the German Liberal Jewish bourgeoisie, particularly in
Frankfurt where he grew up. He declared that, at the time, "assim-
ilation was very, very strong. Many turned to baptism just to get
higher positions. My grandmother never went to synagogue, except once, to be married. And in all her life she never set foot in a
synagogue again."[2]

Otto Heinrich Frank, born on May 12, 1889, and his brothers,
Robert (1886) and Herbert (1891), and sister, Helene (1893),
studied several languages during their childhood and youth, but
Hebrew was not one of them.[3] Like most assimilated German Jews
of the time, the Frank family opposed Zionism, feeling that

8   Germany was their homeland. Alice Stern, Otto's mother, could trace her ancestors back through the city archives to the sixteenth century. However, Michael Frank, Otto's father, was not native to Frankfurt; he had moved there from rural Landau in 1879 at the age of twenty-eight. Michael and Alice were married in 1885, by which time Michael was already pursuing a career in banking. As the nineteenth century drew to a close, Michael became a stockbroker and invested in two health farms and a company producing cough and cold lozenges. In 1901, he set up his own bank specializing in foreign currency exchange. The considerable success of this business enabled the family to move into their own home: a new, semi-detached house at 4 Mertonstrasse in Frankfurt's Westend.[4] The house, with its three front-facing balconies, center tower, and landscaped garden, had a separate entrance for the Franks' staff.

Exquisitely dressed, young Otto and his siblings visited a riding school on a regular basis until they were proficient on horseback, called upon neighbors at the correct hour in the afternoon, had private music lessons, and accompanied their parents on outings to the opera, where they had their own box. Edith Oppenheimer, a much younger relative of Otto's who lived in the same area of Frankfurt, recalls, "Otto used to tell me about the wonderful family parties that were held often, some costume balls. There were special parties for children."[5] Michael and Alice Frank were not remote parents by any means; despite the emphasis on manners and comportment, judging from the surviving letters of Otto and his older brother Robert the house on Mertonstrasse rang regularly with laughter, stories, poetry, and singing.

After attending a private prep school, Otto was sent to the Lessing Gymnasium not far from home. He entered into the spirit of the school's credo: tolerance. His nature ("aware and curious, warm and friendly")[6] made him popular, and his classmates paid no attention to the fact that he was the only Jewish pupil in their form. In his old age, however, Otto received a book about the

Lessing Gymnasium written by a former classmate. Otto's response to this man was icy:

> I can imagine how much work you had, doing research into the lives of all the graduates. I was unpleasantly struck by your apparently knowing nothing about the concentration camps and gas chambers, because there is no mention of my Jewish comrades dying in the gas chambers. Since I am the only member of my family who survived Auschwitz, as you may know from my daughter Anne's diary, you should understand my feelings.[7]

In Otto's youth, however, religion played no part in his life. He recalled, "We were very, very liberal. I was not barmitzvahed."[8] His relative Edith Oppenheimer explains, "The formal exercise of the Jewish religion was not important to Otto. It was not an issue in middle-class Germany before the Great War. Otto was very outgoing, and a lot of fun. Everyone in the family thought he had a great future."[9] Otto enjoyed his school days and wrote regularly for the Lessing Gymnasium newspaper. During the holidays, however, he became restless: "I could not bear staying at home very long after school."[10] In Frankfurt, life was too organized, and the "parties every week, balls, festivities, beautiful girls, waltzing, dinners . . . etc.," had begun to bore him.[11] When his parents sent him to Spain for the 1907 Easter break, the trip sparked an interest in foreign travel.[12] In June 1908, Otto received his Abitur (graduation certificate) and enrolled in an economics course at Heidelberg University. He then left for a long vacation in England.

■

UNIVERSITY EDUCATION IN GERMANY IN the early years of the twentieth century did not come cheaply. Most young scholars were Gymnasium graduates, like Otto Frank, or wealthy students from abroad, like Charles Webster Straus, who arrived in Heidelberg to complete a year's foreign study as part of his course at Princeton University in the United States. Charles, or "Charlie" as Otto was soon calling him, was born in the same month and year as Otto.[13] In a 1957 letter to Eleanor Roosevelt, Straus recalled:

> At Heidelberg University, through members of my mother's family living in Mannheim who knew the Frank family intimately, I met Otto. . . . Over the following months, Otto and I became close friends. He had matriculated at the same time as I had at Heidelberg and we not only attended many courses together, but he spent many evenings with my parents and me at our hotel as I spent many evenings, and indeed, many weekends with his family who owned a country place near Frankfurt. Otto was not only my closest friend during the three semesters we both studied at the university but he was the one that my parents liked best.[14]

Having decided that his economics course contained too much theory, Otto left Heidelberg and returned to Frankfurt, where he began a year's training with a bank. Straus also cut short his studies, and upon his arrival home, "my father asked me to invite Otto to come with me and have a year's experience working at Macy's, of which my father at that time was half owner. My father added that, if Otto decided on the basis of that experience to remain at Macy's, a good future awaited him. I urged Otto to accept this invitation—which he did. He started working at Macy's in 1909 along with me."[15] Otto's family were divided about the move to New York: his father encouraged him, seeing it as an opportunity to learn about foreign commerce and to improve his English, but Otto's sister Helene (Leni) was upset, especially so because Otto would miss her sixteenth birthday. There was someone else, too, who did not want Otto to leave: his fiancée.

Only Michael Frank accompanied Otto to Hamburg, where the

luxury German liner *Kaiser Wilhelm Der Grosse* awaited him in
September 1909. It was raining when father and son said farewell,
and by the time the ship had reached the open sea, the weather had
worsened, leaving most of the neo-baroque public rooms empty as
passengers took to their cabins. Otto headed for the deserted writing room and, amid "endless rolling from side to side," wrote a
quick letter to Leni: "Since I don't want to write a postcard for such
an important event as your birthday, I decided to write this, and
send the card on later. A sixteenth birthday is not an easy thing
and only comes once in a lifetime. So celebrate it accordingly, and
don't let my absence spoil it for you, be really happy." He had little
to say about himself, other than,

> I'm still feeling fine here, touch wood (I'm knocking three times
> underneath the table now). The boat is magnificently appointed
> and offers all one can dream of—it's really luxurious. I can't tell
> you a lot because as you can imagine since I left Father, not much
> has happened. I haven't made any friends yet, but I'm not con-
> cerned. My companion must be coming aboard later, which is
> agreeable to me, because I have my peace and quiet to arrange the
> cabin. Just now, 5:30, it's pouring cats and dogs, but that doesn't
> affect me here in the writing room.[16]

Otto had received a number of good-luck telegrams from family and friends before boarding the ship, but within days of arriving in New York he was frantically booking a passage home. His
father was dead, and his engagement had been broken off in spec-
tacular fashion.[17]

■

MICHAEL FRANK'S SUDDEN DEATH ON
September 17, 1909, brought his widow's strength of will, which
she had kept hidden under an outward show of serenity, to the

fore. Alice immediately took over the management of the bank while her sons pursued their own concerns. Otto's younger brother, Herbert, continued with his studies, while his older brother, Robert, whom everyone regarded as the intellectual one of the family, remained deputy manager of Ricard, a fine arts dealership in which his father had invested. Otto was uncertain of his own future, having been diverted from his career path in New York by the dramatic end of his engagement.

Otto's youthful love affair was the subject of much speculation eighty years later when previously unpublished pages of Anne's diary were discovered. Otto had apparently deliberately withheld them because they focused on his marriage to Anne's mother and raised the possibility that he was still in love with another woman. In a diary entry dated February 8, 1944, Anne had written: "I know a few things about Daddy's past, and what I don't know, I've made up. . . . It can't be easy for a loving wife to know she'll never be first in her husband's affections, and Mummy did know that. . . . [Daddy's] ideals had been shattered."[18] Anne had already alluded to her father's lost love in her entry for Christmas Eve 1943: "During these days, now that Christmas is here, I find myself thinking all the time about Pim [Otto's nickname], and what he told me last year. . . . Poor Pim, he can't make me think that he has forgotten her. He will never forget. He has become very tolerant, for he too sees Mummy's faults."[19] Otto made curious changes to this passage for the published diary. The version edited by him reads: "I find myself thinking all the time about Pim, and what he told me about the love of his youth. . . . Poor Pim, he can't make *me* think that he has forgotten everything. He will never forget this. He has become very tolerant."[20] Otto seems to have been compelled both to reveal and conceal the meaning behind Anne's words, on the one hand adding "the love of his youth" while on the other substituting "forgotten everything" for "forgotten her."

In a 1994 letter written by Otto's cousin and close confidante

Milly Stanfield, the truth about the affair is unveiled at last, although Milly does not name the woman involved: "Actually Otto was engaged to her when he was about eighteen, just before he went to the States for a year and was very serious about her, but when he got back found she had not waited for him and married someone else. He was very upset, of course, but years later (1922, I think) met her and her husband at the same hotel on holiday. He told me it didn't worry him and rather amused him."[21] Another of Otto's relatives, Edith Oppenheimer, heard the story from Milly: "Otto was due to come to America to apprentice in business, and he asked his love to wait for him. According to Milly, she promised but she did not. In any case, he took the break-up very hard."[22]

Otto himself later told a friend about "the young love he had experienced when he was nineteen," which Anne "actually wrote a novel about."[23] This was *Cady's Life*. In her diary on May 11, 1944, Anne outlined the story and how the two main characters, Hans and Cady, "draw apart" after their romance ends, but meet by chance while they are on holiday in the same hotel. Hans is married by then, as he explains to Cady. A few years later, Cady herself marries "a well-to-do farmer" by whom she has two daughters and a son. Cady is still in love with Hans, until "one night she took her leave of him in a dream."[24] There is a sense of closure in both novel and fact; Cady resigns herself to her loss after a dream, and Otto apparently did the same after the encounter in the hotel. In her diary, Anne noted defensively: "It isn't sentimental nonsense for it's modeled on the story of Daddy's life."[25] In the diary edited by Otto, these lines about the novel are omitted and replaced by two vague sentences that were published in the Dutch edition but are not to be found in Anne's actual diary.

Otto returned to the United States quickly, putting the emotional upheaval of the autumn of 1909 behind him. On December 19, he wrote to his sister from New York, where he was lodging with family acquaintances: "You cannot imagine how often I think of you and how I feel here. It seems I don't know how lucky I am, to live in this house and feel so at home. Marly is very kind, and I get along with Eugenie B. too. She is a nice girl, not very clever, but pretty." In a reference perhaps to his broken engagement, Otto confessed wryly, "You know how I get along with girls: good, but apparently not very good." Reflecting the general view of the time that female passions must be kept firmly under control, he warned Leni not to read too many "forbidden" novels because "it's too exciting. You have to be sensible and know your limitations." A more suitable sort of reading for a young girl was Mörike, "an excellent writer. I have all his works in my cupboard." Otto concluded his letter with an older brother's admonition not "to dirty [the books], because they're bound in white, and keep them in order."[26]

The glamorous world Otto inhabited in New York was more exclusively Jewish than the one he was used to in Frankfurt, but it was not without tension.[27] The numbers of Jewish immigrants, particularly from Russia and Poland, had escalated after the pogroms at the turn of the twentieth century. New York's German Jews were embarrassed by the new arrivals and attempted to "remold" them. Intense programs of philanthropy were initiated, led by the Strauses among others. Otto's evenings were frequently spent at charity balls in the Strauses' home at 27 West Seventy-second Street. Such events were generally held in the lavishly decorated front parlor known as the Pompeian or Egyptian Room. Otto's great friend Charles Straus, aged twenty-one, had changed his name to Nathan Straus Jr. in preparation for a future in politics. He gave everyone three months to get used to his new moniker. His sister-in-law insisted on calling him Charlie to annoy him; Otto also did so, yet Straus seems to have found that endearing.[28]

During his months in New York, Otto switched from one department to another at Macy's in an effort to understand how such a large corporation operated before he transferred to a city bank.

The Franks were still very wealthy then; Otto returned to Frankfurt on several occasions although travel by liner was expensive. Sometimes he stopped briefly in London, where his brother Herbert was living at 40 Threadneedle Street while also working in a bank, and he visited his cousin Milly Stanfield in Hampstead when he could.[29]

Milly was ten years younger than Otto. She grew up to become a talented teacher, writer, and musician, although as a child she would hide under the piano when she was supposed to be practicing. Milly recalled vividly the first time she saw Otto. It was at the family home in Hampstead in 1908: "Otto played the cello in his youth and the first time he visited us in London I had just started on my three quarter baby instrument and he took it up and played a solo on it."[30] Milly came to regard Otto as "a big brother: he talked to me very freely and felt I knew him well."[31] Later that same year, Milly and her parents visited the Continent and traveled to Frankfurt, where she met Otto's family. She was impressed by their home and lifestyle: "The Franks had a big luncheon with an enormous ice-cream gateau decorated with fairytale figures, and Aunt Toni [another relative] invited us all to the circus."[32]

Otto returned to this life in Frankfurt in early 1910, but by summer he was again in New York, where he stayed until the following year. In mid-1911, he took a full-time administrative position with a metal engineering company in Dusseldorf.[33] He traveled to Frankfurt regularly and enjoyed a holiday in Switzerland in 1912 with his family, Milly, and her parents. The Stanfields visited the Franks again in July 1914, shortly before war broke out in Europe. Otto and his brothers told the Stanfields they were mad to travel when "Alsace was practically under siege."[34] Other relatives from Paris joined them in the house on Mertonstrasse: Otto's Uncle Leon and Aunt Nanette and their three sons, Oscar, Georges, and Jean-Michel. They suffered extreme anti-Semitism in Paris, especially Jean-Michel, who was bullied by his contemporaries not only because he was Jewish but also on account of his effeminacy and "oriental doll look."[35] These highly strung guests created a stir, which Milly missed but heard about later: "The Paris Franks were sure there would be war and were almost hysterical. They had sons of military age and remembered the Franco-Prussian War of 1870 . . . their two elder sons [were] both brilliant young men."[36]

At the beginning of August, the Stanfields were advised by the British consulate to go back to England. They found Frankfurt's Hauptbahnhof in uproar and their train was delayed for two hours: "The Franks . . . came to the station in relays, bringing us goodies, keeping us company." At home in London, Milly felt her loyalties torn as she worried about Otto and his family in Frankfurt: "It seemed as if a wall of fire separated Germany from the Allies of the West."[37]

■

UNTIL 1914, GERMAN MILITARY ACADE-mies made enrollment by Jews extremely difficult and excluded them from certain regiments. In the national crisis of the Great War, German anti-Semitism increased and Jewish men were accused of shirking war service and profiting from the black market. The literature of the period makes this explicit: "Don't fool yourselves, you are and will remain Germany's pariahs."[38]

Otto Frank was one of 100,000 Jews who fought for Germany in the Great War. In 1914, his Dusseldorf employer loaned him out to a company that did important war work, and he stayed with that firm until August 1915, when both he and Robert were called up. Milly remembered, "Robert fared better [than Otto]. He had volunteered as a stretcher-bearer, in the German equivalent of our Royal Army Medical Corps. As dangerous as fighting, it was a most essential service and far better suited to Robert's personal beliefs. Herbert, the youngest of the brothers, was not robust enough to join the army and was given a desk job."[39] On August 7, 1915,

"Kanonier Otto Frank" wrote to his family from the training depot in Mainz that he was "quite content" and "happy to be here, since this was apparently the last transport, everything else was canceled. Everyone wants to join in the victory!"[40]

Otto was sent to the Western Front shortly after writing the letter. His unit contained mostly surveyors and mathematicians: he was a range-finder attached to the infantry. Although his early letters were hopeful, he soon learned that his Parisian cousins Oscar and Georges, who had visited his family in Frankfurt the year before, had been killed in action. It was precisely what their parents, Leon and Nanette, had feared most. Otto's uncle Leon killed himself in November 1915 by jumping from a window, and his aunt Nanette was committed to a mental hospital. Jean-Michel, then twenty, was left alone in the family home.[41] At Otto's suggestion, Herbert went to stay with him.

Otto was determined to remain optimistic, and in February 1916, he wrote to Leni in a whimsical mood: "If you stay unmarried, then I'll stay unmarried too, and we'll head a wonderful household together, what? Silly boy. Why do I think about such things now? I believe my life here is better than yours at home. I miss nothing here and the danger I am in is only in your imagination. It's really not that bad."[42] A few days later, he wrote to Leni again, repeating his gentle reprimand not to worry about him: "You do not have to be afraid for me—really. It would be sheer accident if anything happened, although accidents do occur."[43]

Five months later, he must have wondered at his own words. On July 1, 1916, the Battle of the Somme began. At 6:30 that morning, the guns of thirteen British divisions opened over the German trenches. An hour later, German troops responded, and what followed was one of the fiercest battles in world history. Otto was in the thick of it yet escaped injury "by a miracle."[44] The First World War records of the German army were destroyed by bombing in the Second, and Otto's surviving letters to Leni from the period refer only in passing to his experiences; clearly he wanted to save his sister from the true horrors of the front line. On December 24, 1916, he ventured the heartfelt hope that "this cannot last much longer, surely."[45]

When the Somme offensive was over, thousands of troops on both sides were dead, maimed, or suffering shell shock. Morale, especially among German troops, deteriorated toward the end of 1917, and it was up to the officers to boost soldiers' spirits.[46] That year Otto became an officer himself after demonstrating his bravery in a reconnaissance action. He "tried to treat my men in the same liberal way" as his chief, "a decent, enlightened man who handled his unit with the utmost fairness—a democratic man who would have no officers' mess or officers' orderlies in his unit."[47] Despite the constant danger, it is clear from his letters that Otto thought often about his mother and sister, who worked together as volunteer nurses in a Red Cross military hospital. Leni was earnest in her work but also enjoyed the attention it brought her from the soldiers recuperating under her care. Otto patiently answered her questions about love while ruminating on his own future: "The language of the heart and the emotions it makes are the most important of all. . . . You're the kind of person who acts on emotion, needs love in order to flourish, and is able to give love. I am very similar in this respect."[48]

Otto, who also wrote frequently to his brothers, was pleased with how Bitz (Herbert) was beginning to show initiative with the family bank business, which was in difficulty, and happy that Robert was going to be stationed nearby, close enough for them to meet. He admitted to his mother that he was finding the war "debilitating,"[49] but "we're not living in an ideal world."[50] He was concerned about their dwindling funds and felt that the sale of a number of paintings from their home on Mertonstrasse was necessary: "In these times you have to be happy with any cash because you don't know what's around the corner."[51]

■

On November 20, 1917, Otto's unit
moved up to Cambrai, just as the British launched their tank attack
on the Hindenburg line, and became the first range-finding unit
to deal with this new kind of warfare. The British success was
short-lived; ten days later, they were forced back to where they began. Earlier that year, Otto had been optimistic about Germany's
success in the field of battle: "I'm salivating at the newspapers and
hoping that the Russians get bushed, because Russia can't survive
another winter again and so I'm still optimistic."[52]

In the summer of 1918, after his promotion to lieutenant, Otto
wrote to Leni that he was depressed:

> You can't imagine the feelings that our loneliness and isolation
> from culture and women awaken in us out here. We think of a
> thousand, old, treasured things and are only too happy to lose our-
> selves in dreams. We all have it so good at home that we aren't es-
> pecially eager to have homes of our own, strong as the impulse to
> do so may be in us. . . . It is not just immediate happiness but the
> future that one's thoughts return to time and again, and the mo-
> ments when one does not think of the future are few indeed.

He was beginning to feel that the war would go on forever: "My
hope that this year we will force an ending to all this conflict pre-
vails even though I find it difficult to believe peace will come this
year. The pre-conditions for it still need to be set."[53] When he
wrote on July 31, it was to announce that they were being transferred to the city of St. Quentin. Otto was billeted with a large
farming family there. His cousin Milly recalled that they "all loved
him and nicknamed him 'Le Grand Brun.' He went back—I think
with Edith in the late 1920s—and they treated him as a long
lost son."[54]

The war did end, in November 1918, and Otto's mother, Alice,

20 and sister, Leni, began to prepare excitedly for Otto and Robert's homecoming, but only Robert returned. For a full month, the family in Frankfurt agonized over what could have happened to Otto. It was a dark afternoon in January 1919 when he finally stepped through the door at Mertonstrasse, thin and seemingly taller than ever.[55] His black hair was thin on the crown, and his pale eyes were tinged with tiredness, but he smiled at his over-joyed family. When they had all composed themselves and were sitting together around the dining room table with cups of tea, Otto explained why he was so late. His unit had borrowed two horses from a Belgian farmer, who was distraught to see them go. Otto promised he would bring both horses back personally, and as a German officer, his word was his honor. When fighting ceased, he returned the horses, and the farmer received them with amazed gratitude. Otto then told them about his excruciating journey home. Milly remembered that he told her family the same story: "Otto had had to walk the whole way back from France after Germany capitulated. It took him three weeks; he arrived looking like a ghost."[56]

When Otto stopped talking, Alice started to shout. Furious with her son for prolonging his homecoming over a couple of mangy horses, she was not to be placated, even when Otto insisted that he had sent her a letter that must have gone astray. She drew herself up regally to her full height, although she was very small, and threw the china teapot straight at her astonished son.[57]

■

IN THE AFTERMATH OF THE GREAT WAR, approximately 490,000 Jews lived in Germany. During the 1918 Revolution, Jews were attacked by angry crowds who blamed them for the shortage of food, inflation, and all that was deplorable in Weimar's early years. There were frenzied fights on the streets of Berlin, witnessed by a correspondent for *The Times* of London. On

August 14, 1919, he noted cautiously, "indications of growing anti-Semitism are becoming frequent."[58]

The Franks had more pressing problems; their bank business was plainly in trouble, mainly owing to Alice's investment in war loans, which proved worthless. A large fraction of their wealth had been lost, and in 1919, Otto took over the running of the bank in an attempt to salvage what was left. He was reluctant to assume his new role, however, and did so "more from necessity than by choice,"[59] assuming management of the business in cough and cold lozenges at the same time. His cousin Milly remembered that because "Robert was interested in Fine Arts and their father had died when they were in their teens, it fell to Otto to manage the family bank in the period of chaos that marked the first year after Peace was signed. . . . His younger brother, Herbert, was devoted to him, but he was never a leader."[60] Milly and her mother visited Frankfurt in October 1920, and Milly spoke to Otto about the political situation: "He pointed out the weakness of the government in power and the existence of two fringe parties, the Nationalists and the Communists. Both were potentially dangerous, especially those of the Right. Otto, a middle-of-the-road Liberal, was worried."[61]

While he was working for the bank, Otto became friendly with Erich Elias at the Frankfurt Stock Exchange. Erich worked for the Heichelheim Bank as an agent and stockbroker, but left at the end of 1920 and joined the Michael Frank bank as a full partner on February 3, 1921. In that same month, Erich and Otto's sister, Leni, were married. They lived in the house on Mertonstrasse, where their first child, Stephan, was born at the end of the year. There were two more weddings in the family the following year. In April 1922, Herbert married Hortense Schott, an American who lived in Aachen. It was a turbulent relationship, and no one expected the marriage to last. In July, Robert married Charlotte (Lottie) Witt, a policeman's daughter and his secretary at Ricard.

Lottie was not Jewish and wanted to convert, but Robert told her it was not necessary; there were no objections within his family to the fact that Charlotte was a Gentile. Alice was against the wedding initially simply because she felt that Lottie was not good enough for her son. Robert ignored his mother, and eventually Alice accepted Lottie as part of the family. Her one remaining wish was that Otto would find himself a suitable wife.

■

POLICE REPORTS FROM THE EARLY 1920S show that anti-Semitism in Germany was continuing to rise: "The mood for Jewish pogroms is spreading systematically in all parts of the country," said one, while another concluded: "The fact cannot be denied that the anti-Semitic idea has penetrated the widest levels of the middle class, even far into the working class."[62] Although aware of the growing menace, Otto's anxiety about the bank business was far greater. Herbert had resigned from the board in the autumn of 1921, finding the business too dull, but Otto persuaded him to resume his position in 1923. Hoping to lift the bank out of the rut it had fallen into, Otto and Erich decided to open a branch in Amsterdam, then the center of foreign currency trading. It was a great risk; many other German banks that had taken the same route found themselves in a complicated situation owing to the rule preventing them from attracting Dutch clients and the stipulation that they had to concentrate solely on German flight capital. Nonetheless, Otto and Erich could see no other way forward.[63]

In late 1923, Otto opened the Michael M. Frank & Sons Bank at 604 Keizersgracht in Amsterdam. The following year, Otto took on Johannes Kleiman as an employee and had him registered as a proxy with the Amsterdam chamber of commerce. Kleiman, born in Koog aan de Zaan on August 17, 1896, had known Otto since the spring of 1923, when Otto was traveling between Amsterdam, Berlin, and Frankfurt in order to establish the bank business. He liked Otto ("lively and full of energy") from the moment they met, and was intrigued by his fleeting visits to Amsterdam. Their "long, unreserved friendship,"[64] however, did not begin until 1933, and for the time being, Kleiman's authority within the company was limited.

The bank venture failed. On December 15, 1924, the bank went into liquidation, presumably as a result of "speculative activity, perhaps involving the French franc, a currency that was being traded with considerable losses in Amsterdam in the summer of 1925." The business moved to Kleiman's address in the city, and he was then granted full powers, remaining "Otto's confidant and mainstay in Amsterdam until the dissolution of the business,"[65] which took over four years. Kleiman eventually went to work for his brother's disinfectant manufacturing business.

Otto returned to Frankfurt in early 1925. He was almost thirty-six years old and had to find some way of getting rid of the family's growing list of debts. On a personal level, he desperately wanted a home of his own and children, as he had written to Leni seven years before: "We can't wait too long after the war if we want to be young for the children we hope to have. For children are, after all, the be-all and end-all of a healthy marriage."[66] There was only one solution to all these problems, and on April 5, 1925, Otto Frank became engaged to Edith Holländer of Aachen. Her dowry included a substantial sum of money.

To family and friends, the announcement came "like a bombshell." Otto's relative Edith Oppenheimer recalls, "No one knew her. She lived far away, and she was much more religious than Otto." Later, to his second wife and her daughter, and to his immediate family at the time, Otto admitted that his marriage to Edith Holländer was, plainly put, "a business arrangement."[67]

■

"I HAVE THE IMPRESSION THAT DADDY married Mummy because he felt she would be a suitable wife. I have to admit I admire Mummy for the way she assumed the role of his wife and has never, as far as I know, complained or been jealous. . . . Daddy certainly admired Mummy's attitude and thought she had an excellent character. . . . What kind of marriage has it turned out to be? No quarrels or differences of opinion—but hardly an ideal marriage. Daddy respects Mummy and loves her, but not with the kind of love I envision for a marriage. . . . Daddy's not in love. He kisses her the way he kisses us. . . . One day Daddy is bound to realize that while, on the outside, she has never demanded his total love, on the inside, she has slowly but surely been crumbling away. She loves him more than anyone, and it's hard to see this kind of love not being returned."[68]

Anne's observation of her parents' marriage, hidden away for more than fifty years until its publication in a Dutch newspaper in 1998, was unforgiving, perceptive—and truthful.[69] Otto confessed to his second wife and her daughter that he had never loved Edith Holländer but had great respect for her intelligence and skills as a mother. He said little about his first marriage apart from that, although he told a number of people that it was an arranged union that appeared to suit them both. Today some members of the Holländer family believe that Otto benefited the most, using Edith's considerable dowry to "clean up long-standing debts. . . . Edith was known to be a clever person, faithful to the family tradition which believed in true values. . . . Otto Frank was obviously the master of that household." This view extends to the diary; the same family member asserts that the Holländers were "grossly neglected in all editions of Anne's books . . . after corrections, editions and self-serving additions by Anne's father who was by then the one living family member, Otto had become Anne's mentor, role-model and undisputed influence in her life. This may sound like sour grapes now, but it is common family knowledge— of a family who has by now no voice in this world anymore."[70]

Nonetheless, arranged marriages among Jewish families at that time were the norm; in certain circles, they were held in more esteem than actual romances. Edith's parents were aware that their daughter's suitor was far from wealthy, and that a large dowry was viewed as a definite advantage. Their greatest misgiving was probably their future son-in-law's apathy toward his religion. The Holländers were prominent in Aachen's Jewish community; they observed the Sabbath and festivals, and Edith's mother kept a kosher household. Otto later recalled that Edith was "very religious. Not Orthodox, but she was kosher. . . . Of course, when my mother-in-law came we never had anything from a pig. We adjusted."[71]

The Holländer family fortune originated from Edith's grandfather, Benjamin Holländer, who started an industrial supplies and scrap metal business in 1858 under his own name.[72] Edith's father, Abraham, was born in Eschweiler in 1860, one of nine children. After his marriage to Rosa Stern of Langenschwalbach and the birth of their first child, Julius, in 1894, Abraham took his wife, son, and parents to Aachen, where he expanded the family business. Abraham gained control of the firm and quickly made his fortune. Three more children were born in the Holländer home on Liebfrauenstrasse: Walter (1897), Bettina (Betti; 1898), and Edith, born on January 16, 1900.

Edith was a shy girl, family-oriented, and academic. In 1906, she began as a pupil at the Evangelische Victoriaschule, a private Protestant school for girls that also accepted students of other religions. She learned English, French, and Hebrew alongside the five cousins with whom she was good friends: Meta, Frieda, Irma, Ilse, and Elsbeth. In her diary, Anne marveled at her mother's privileged upbringing: "We listen open-mouthed to the stories of engagement parties of two hundred and fifty people, private balls and dinners."[73] The end of this carefree life coincided with the Great War. Edith's sister Betti, only sixteen, died suddenly from appendicitis on September 22, 1914; Edith would later name her first child Margot Betti in memory of her. Two further family tragedies occurred: Edith's uncle Karl died on December 28, 1915, while serving in the German army, and her eldest brother, Julius, was shot in the arm during a battle, leaving him permanently handicapped. In the midst of all this, in 1916, Edith graduated from school. Both Julius and Walter intended to help their father in the family business, and to prepare for this they took a course in business with a professor from the Institute of Technology. Unfortunately, Abraham Holländer preferred to keep his position at the helm of his firm; dominating his sons, he allowed them "only filial rights, not equal to his own."[74] They compensated for this rejection by enrolling in various Jewish-run charities, and they also joined football and gymnastic teams.

By contrast, Edith had a good relationship with her mother and adored her brothers. She overcame her shyness once she got to know people, and had many friends with whom she played tennis and went swimming in the waters of the Frisian Islands, driven there by her cousin Irene, one of the first women in Germany to own a car. Edith dressed stylishly, wearing "flapper" dresses and pearls, and had her hair cut in a neat bob. She learned to do the Charleston and bought herself a gramophone player and a selection of boxed records that still exist today, with Edith's distinctive handwriting upon the inventory.[75]

Edith was the only one of the Holländer children to marry. Her introduction to Otto Frank may have occurred through the bank business, or through Herbert Frank's wife, Hortense, who had once lived in Aachen. Edith's cousins were envious of the marriage, which took place on Otto's thirty-sixth birthday, May 12, 1925. Edith wore a fashionable white gown embroidered with fresh flowers and a long, diaphanous train, while Otto dressed in a dark suit and bow tie. After the wedding, there was a celebration at the city's Grosser Monarch Hotel, and then the couple departed to tour Italy, accompanied on their honeymoon by Edith's parents.

Anne's lines about her parents' marriage imply that Otto told

Edith he had been deeply in love with another woman when he was younger ("It can't be easy for a loving wife to know she'll never be first in her husband's affections, and Mummy did know that," Anne had written),[76] but Edith had apparently never experienced the emotions she felt for Otto before, and she hoped at first that he would reciprocate. It was not to be, however, and Edith had to settle, unhappily, for a passionless but steadfast union. Otto cannot have been satisfied either; his letters from the Western Front portray him as a romantic and an idealist. "The longing for love is human nature," he had written in 1918,[77] believing then that marrying someone for reasons other than love resulted in "half a life."[78] Otto's marriage to Edith Holländer, according to their watchful daughter, occurred when "his ideals had been shattered and his youth was over,"[79] although we do not know whether Anne's observations were based on her own impressions of her parents' relationship or on her father's confidences. Nonetheless, there can be little doubt that neither Otto nor Edith found in the other the soulmate for whom they both evidently longed.

On the fourteenth anniversary of their wedding, Otto wrote an introspective letter to Edith that clearly outlines how their relationship evolved:

> Our marriage hasn't been lacking in whims of fate and looking back at the time from San Remo until now, only then do you actually realize how much everything has changed. Yet the most difficult situations haven't disrupted the harmony between us. From the beginning you have shown spirit, such as one seldom sees, a solidarity which gave you the strength to carry on through thick and thin. Apart from having a talent for this, upbringing and the parental home also play a constant role in this and we have to be thankful for that which we have received from home. Thus we should also strive to pass on to our children this feeling of solidarity, tolerance and of dedication to the other. What is still to come,

nobody knows, but that we will not make life miserable for each other through little arguments and fights, that we do know. May the coming years of our marriage be as harmonious as the previous ones.[80]

As Edith cannot have failed to notice, in his sermonlike portrait of their marriage, her husband talked at length about unity and endurance but said nothing about love.

two FATHERHOOD
AND EXILE

FOR THE FIRST YEAR OF THEIR MARRIED
life, Otto and Edith lived with his mother in Frankfurt. Leni and
Erich were also living there still, and on June 2, 1925, Leni gave
birth to her second child, Bernhard (Buddy). With a toddler and a
baby in the house already, Otto and Edith had some idea of what to
expect when, on February 16, 1926, their daughter Margot Betti
was born. The Holländers immediately visited the new arrival; as
soon as she was out of the hospital, Edith began to keep notes of
this and other events in her daughter's life in a baby book.[1] In May,
when Edith traveled alone on the sleeper-train to Aachen with
Margot, she was pleased by her daughter's good behavior. There
were many visits to Aachen for Margot, ensuring that both the
Holländers and Alice were given equal amounts of time with their
granddaughter. On December 21, Leni accompanied Margot to
Aachen again so that Otto and Edith could take a holiday alone together in Switzerland. Two days after Julius brought Margot home
to Frankfurt in his car, on January 17, 1927, Abraham Holländer
died at the age of sixty-six. Edith recorded in Margot's baby book:
"I am going home for fourteen days. Margot has given her grandfather much sunshine and happiness."[2]

Edith now ate only kosher food when she stayed with her mother in Aachen, but she attended the Westend synagogue regularly while living on Mertonstrasse and continued to do so after October 1927, when she, Otto, and Margot moved into their own home at 307 Marbachweg, in a neighborhood where there were few Jewish families. Their apartment, in one half of a large yellow house with green shutters, was spacious; Margot had her own bedroom, and there was a guest room with a balcony overlooking the garden at the rear. Gertrud Naumann, who lived next door, was ten years old but mature for her age and often baby-sat Margot. Below the Franks, in the other half of the house, lived the landlord, Otto Könitzer, and his family. Otto and Edith had little to do with him; they knew that he was a follower of the Nazi Party.

In June 1928, Otto and Edith enjoyed a holiday with Nathan Straus and his family at Villa Larêt in Sils-Maria, a luxury home in Switzerland belonging to one of Otto's cousins. At the end of the year, Otto, Edith, and Margot traveled by train to Aachen and celebrated Hanukkah with Edith's mother and brothers. Edith was pregnant; she gave birth on June 12, 1929. "It's a girl again," Otto told Kathi Stilgenbauer, their housekeeper, when he rang from the hospital where he had spent the entire night during his wife's complicated labor. Annelies Marie was born at 7:30 A.M. and recorded by the exhausted nurse in charge as "a male child."[3] Edith started a new baby book for this second daughter and recorded that "Mother and Margot visit the baby sister on 14 June. Margot is completely delighted."[4]

■

OTTO FRANK LOVED BOTH HIS CHILDREN, but from the very beginning, he had a special bond with his youngest daughter.[5] Her boldness made him laugh and brought him out of himself in a way that Margot's tranquillity could never reach. It was on her father that Anne bestowed her first smiles, it was Otto to whom she ran when she was hurt or uncertain, and it was he who tucked her into bed at night and then sat with her until she fell asleep. After Anne's birth, Margot drew closer to her mother, out of instinct or for comfort, which in turn brought Edith a joy and companionship she lacked elsewhere. Otto later admitted that Anne was "a little rebel with a will of her own. She was often wakeful at night," and he recalled "going in to her many times, petting her and singing nursery songs to quieten her."[6] Anne also became the favorite of her uncle Julius, who had been a tempestuous child himself and would recognize something of his own character in Anne. Julius and Walter visited Frankfurt soon after Anne's birth, and in August the Franks traveled to Aachen so that Rosa Holländer could meet her new granddaughter. Julius, suffering from the depression that always threatened to engulf him, managed to wake early each day to clown around for Anne.[7]

In the middle of the hot summer of 1929, Otto's brother-in-law Erich Elias left Frankfurt for Switzerland, where he had been invited to open a branch of Opekta. Erich was a founding member of Opekta, which was part of the Frankfurt-based company Pomosin-Werke, manufacturers of pectin, a preservative and gelling agent most commonly used in jam preparation. Otto's sister, Leni, and her four-year-old son Buddy remained part of the Mertonstrasse household for another year, and seven-year-old Stephan stayed behind until 1931. In Switzerland, the Eliases lived in a boarding-house until they could afford their own home in the city of Basel.

Otto, Edith, and the children returned to Frankfurt from Aachen in September, and Edith gave up trying to breast-feed Anne, who immediately began to gain weight normally—something which had worried them before. Margot also experienced health problems, and her parents had been advised by doctors to sit her under a sunlamp every week; this was thought to improve the constitution. Edith cared lovingly for the girls through the day, but in the evening when he had finished work, Otto would bathe and play with them, telling them stories he had invented himself about two sisters, both named Paula, one who was good and one who was bad. Margot and Anne loved his tales, and Anne even used the character of Bad Paula in a story of her own years later when she was in hiding.

In October, the fortunes of the Frank family bank plummeted in the wake of the Wall Street crash. The trade in throat lozenges was also adversely affected, and with Edith's dowry money gone, Otto saw no alternative but to move both businesses into one office in a much less expensive building. The address was shared with another firm to keep costs down even further. It was not the only difficulty in their lives that year: Otto's cousin Milly visited them and found "conditions in Germany just impossible. . . . I remember talking to Otto about politics. He said, 'I don't like it. I don't know what's going to happen. I'm scared of the Right.' He saw it coming—at a time when I don't think many of the Jews were particularly worried."[8] Nonetheless, Otto remained in Germany, hoping that the danger would somehow pass by.

The Franks' housekeeper, Kathi Stilgenbauer, gave them her notice in 1929 after accepting a proposal of marriage. Before she left, Kathi asked Otto who the Brownshirts were; these uniformed men had begun to make a nuisance of themselves in the neighborhood for the Jewish families living there. She recalled: "Mr. Frank just laughed and tried to make a joke of the whole thing. . . . But Mrs. Frank looked up from her plate and she fixed her eyes on us and said, 'We'll find out soon enough who they are, Kathi.' "[9] Matters came to a head in March 1931, when Otto Könitzer decided he could no longer bear having Jews living in his house and told the Franks they would have to find alternative accommodation. They moved into a five-room apartment at 24 Ganghoferstrasse, which was smaller but had the welcome compensations of a garden and more "child-friendly" surroundings. The children's old friends from Marbachweg continued to call every day, and the new neighbors were welcoming.

The bank business, however, damaged further by the closure of the Frankfurt Stock Exchange in the summer of 1931 and the strict laws imposed upon companies dealing in foreign currency, continued to fail. In April 1932, it suffered another blow, and one from which it never recovered: Herbert Frank was arrested by income tax officials on grounds of breaching the 1931 Regulation Governing the Trade in Securities with Foreign Countries Act. A few months before, Herbert had offered to act as an agent to a stockbroker from Karlsruhe who had over one million reichsmarks of foreign shares in German industrial companies to sell. Such negotiations were illegal, but Herbert sold the shares, acting in good faith. He kept a record of the transactions and the commission he earned, which stood in his favor during the court case that followed. The newspapers reported the affair, and Otto was quoted in the *Frankfurter Zeitung*. He defended his brother, "the proprietor with the controlling interest in the bank,"[10] insisting that Herbert had trusted the man from Karlsruhe, who had not told Herbert the shares had been issued abroad and who had since disappeared. When Herbert was jailed, the Franks immediately filed an appeal against his arrest. Otto was able to talk to him by telephone and later wrote to Leni that their brother seemed "well enough. He has a lot of courage and won't be bought out." Otto had lost some of his usual optimism: "Business is poor. You can't think straight when nothing seems to be going right. Only the children are enjoying themselves, as no doubt your children are too."[11] Herbert was released on May 14 and told that his trial was set for October 1932.

The eldest Frank brother, Robert, tried to find another solution to the family's financial problems. He traveled frequently to Paris and London, hoping to make some beneficial new connections in the business of art dealership. The situation was more serious than ever; it was beginning to look as though they would lose the family home on Mertonstrasse, something that none of them wanted to happen. In June, Otto's mother, Alice, took the train to Paris, aiming to borrow money from her nephew Jean-Michel, who had been left a fortune by his mother after she died in the asylum. He had already used part of his inheritance to set up a partnership in furniture design, and in his studio in rue Montauban he worked with artists such as the Giacometti brothers and Salvador Dali. His clinical style was already highly collectible, though Coco Chanel said it made her feel as though she were "passing a cemetery."[12] To outsiders and society, Jean-Michel was a flamboyant Communist homosexual who dabbled in drugs "to disturb his friends"[13] and always dressed in the same gray London suit. His family knew him as he really was: witty and compassionate. He worshiped Leni, in whom he found a kindred spirit, and would do anything to help her. Otto had already described the crisis to him over the telephone ("ongoing expenses, outstanding debts, and mortgage payments . . . the situation has become impossible"),[14] and in a letter to Alice wrote of his desperation:

> My pessimism and worries of the last few months were only too well-founded. . . . Herbie will try to get away from Frankfurt and find a job elsewhere. There isn't much he can do here but he needs something to live on even if it isn't much. Erich has work. We have no idea where we will end up, but the main thing is that we stay healthy and that you have an income. We're younger and better able to deal with adversity. It is important to see things as they are and to act accordingly. We'll try to hold on to the business as long as we can. We'll have to discuss later what the solution should be. Apart from H, we have no customers who can keep us from sinking. But to dissolve the firm seems pointless at this time. . . . We keep our courage up as always.[15]

Jean-Michel was eventually stirred into action when he received a letter from Leni, who enclosed a copy of Otto's latest, dispirited letter to her. Alice sent Otto a telegram to say that their

Parisian cousin had given her enough money to meet the next
month's mortgage payments on the Mertonstrasse house. Otto was
greatly relieved:

> Jean has behaved admirably, and we cannot thank him enough. I
> spoke briefly to Robert. He's still so overwrought that you can
> hardly hold a conversation with him. . . . I don't know quite how
> everything can be arranged. But it's obvious that everyone is keen
> to keep the house and optimistic, so I get my courage from that.
> Hopefully things will start looking up financially but at the mo-
> ment there's no way forward. . . . I always tried to sweep problems
> under the carpet but that's no longer viable, and the sooner and
> more openly we discuss the situation, the better. . . . I don't have
> much to tell you about us. Margot is an angel, she had a school out-
> ing today. She was thrilled. . . . I'm anxious to hear more from you
> and hope you're not too stressed.[16]

On October 1, 1932, Herbert resigned from the bank and
headed for Paris himself. His wife, Hortense, had left him in
September 1930, and in August 1932, they were divorced. She
moved to Zurich, and the Franks never saw her again. Herbert refused to attend his trial in Frankfurt, claiming "material and mental injury,"[17] and asked Otto to represent him. Otto told the court
that the bank had trusted the stockbroker because he was German
and therefore assumed he understood the German laws on dealing
in foreign currency. Herbert won an appeal and avoided a fine, but
the incident had upset him, and he decided against returning to
Frankfurt. Despite Herbert's legal victory and the money from
Jean-Michel, the bank business continued to flounder, and in
December 1932, "as a result of changes in the economic situation,"[18] Otto informed the owner of the Ganghoferstrasse apartment that they would be leaving in the new year. Otto, Edith,
Margot, and Anne moved into the house on Mertonstrasse in

March 1933, but Otto knew that this was only a temporary measure until the difficulties with paying the mortgage resurfaced.

■

THE RISE OF THE NAZI PARTY WAS AN even greater worry than the Franks' financial problems, and Otto began to consider leaving the country he had been prepared to die for in the Great War. On July 31, 1932, almost 14 million Germans had voted for Hitler in the national elections, giving the Nazis 230 seats in the Reichstag. The party's promises of a new era of national pride and German domination in world business affairs, coupled with Hitler's mesmerizing personality, proved irresistible to the majority of the country's voters. Their open anti-Semitism created no obstacles either; they did not have to persuade the German people that the Jews were their "misfortune"—most of Germany's non-Jews either agreed with the sentiment or did not feel strongly enough about it to vote against the Nazi Party.

In January 1933, Otto and Edith were visiting friends when they heard on the radio that Hitler had been elected chancellor. As the cheers from Berlin mounted, Otto glanced across at Edith and saw her sitting "as if turned to stone." When their host—presumably not Jewish himself—said cheerfully, "Well, let's see what the man can do!" Otto was unable to respond.[19] The hatred that had been seething for decades was about to burst forth, as Otto knew: "As early as 1932, groups of Stormtroopers (Brownshirts) [Nazi followers] came marching by singing: 'When Jewish blood splatters off the knife.' That made it more than clear to everyone. I immediately discussed it with my wife: 'How can we leave here?' but eventually there is of course the question: How will you be able to support yourself if you go away and give up more or less everything?"[20] He was aware that many of their friends were no longer calling upon them: "My family had lived in Germany for centuries and we had many friends and acquaintances not only Jewish but also Christian ones, but by and by many of the latter deserted us, incited by the National Socialistic propaganda."[21]

Otto's relative Edith Oppenheimer remembers how life changed that year: "My father always told us that one weekend in 1933 a friend of his handed him a book and said, 'I think you should read this.' It was *Mein Kampf* [Hitler's autobiography and vision of a new Germany]. Father stayed up all night reading, and the next morning announced that we were going to America. There was a family conference, and he tried to persuade the other members of the family that it was dangerous to stay, but my Opa Stern, who was manager of a leather factory, felt obligated to stay. He was later arrested and tortured, and committed suicide in prison." Edith Oppenheimer's grandmother, her parents, and her other grandparents emigrated to the United States, "greatly bewildered that 'their' Germany could have turned against them in this way."[22]

Otto's efforts in establishing a business abroad had failed before; in order to try again with a wife and two children depending on him, he had to feel sure that he could make it succeed.[23] His mind was made up by a law forcing Jewish and non-Jewish children to remain apart from each other in school. Margot had at first attended the Ludwig Richter School, where, although she was one of only five Jewish children in a class of forty-two and had lessons in Judaism, as her mother insisted, she had never felt different from her fellow pupils. Her first report card praised her intelligence and hard work. However, Margot's head teacher and form tutor were dismissed from their posts by Nazi officials who considered them "political opponents." After leaving Ganghoferstrasse, Margot had begun to attend the Varrentrapp School, which was closer to the Mertonstrasse, but when the new decree was passed, she had to sit apart from her non-Jewish classmates with all the other Jewish children.

Otto was resolute that he would not raise his daughters "like horses with blinkers, ignorant of the social landscape outside their

38   small group,"[24] and turned to his brother-in-law, Erich Elias in Switzerland, for advice about work elsewhere. Erich was eager to help and informed Otto that the Opekta company was hoping to "expand the international market for pectin,"[25] and he could probably find Otto employment abroad. In early 1933, Otto was appointed manager of Pomosin Utrecht in the Netherlands, which had supplied jam manufacturers with pectin since 1928. Unfortunately, the managing director of the company in Utrecht was so disagreeable that Otto asked Erich if he could find him something else. Erich suggested that Otto set up as an independent pectin supplier in Amsterdam, a city Otto already knew well and where he had friends. Otto gladly agreed, and Erich, who was now manager of the Swiss branch of Opekta, provided him with an interest-free loan of 15,000 guilders to begin the enterprise. The loan was repayable over ten years, and shares in Opketa-Amsterdam served as security against it; Otto could repay the debt at any time by surrendering his shares. Otto decided that his business would concentrate on selling pectin to housewives, leaving the factory market free to Pomosin Utrecht.

Gertrud Naumann, who used to baby-sit for Margot when the Franks lived at Marbachweg, had always stayed in contact with the family and was upset to learn that they were emigrating. She recalls that her last visit to the Franks was very subdued, and Otto was evidently apprehensive about the future. "Mr. Frank never spoke about anything that troubled him. But . . . you could see the way it was worrying him and working inside him."[26] Otto captured his family's last visit to the town center of Frankfurt on his favorite Leica camera in March 1933; in the photograph, taken on the city's Hauptwache Square, Edith and her daughters are holding hands; both young girls wear serious expressions, and Edith's own smile has an understandable sadness to it. They had already made plans to stay in Aachen while Otto established the business and found them a home in Amsterdam.

On April 1, 1933, three weeks after the photograph was taken, there was a nationwide boycott of all Jewish businesses in Germany, and that was followed by the passage of numerous laws expelling Jews from business and social life. Since Hitler's seizure of the Reich chancellorship on January 30, the democratic state lay in ruins, leaving the path clear for the elimination of all who opposed the Nazi government. The Communist Party was almost wiped out, along with every other political group, until only the Nazi Party remained. Mass arrests, imprisonment in jails and concentration camps, and the murder of anyone who spoke publicly against the Nazi Party became commonplace.

At the beginning of August 1933, Otto Frank boarded a train to Amsterdam. Whatever his fears for the future, he had no doubt that he was pursuing the only option available to him: "The world around me had collapsed. When most of the people of my country turned into hordes of nationalist, cruel anti-Semitic criminals, I had to face the consequences, and though this hurt me deeply I realized that Germany was not the world and I left forever."[27]

■

EDITH AND THE CHILDREN STAYED IN Aachen until December 1933, sharing the large town house the Holländers had begun renting the year before. Anne's lively personality made her Oma Holländer both laugh and despair; when they were out together one day and had just boarded a busy tram, three-year-old Anne looked around and then asked loudly, "Won't someone offer a seat to this old lady?"[28] Such incidents were typical of Anne.

Edith traveled often to Amsterdam between August and December 1933 to view apartments with her husband. On November 16, Otto sent a postcard to Gertrud Naumann in Frankfurt: "We'll soon have a place to live. Winter will pass and perhaps we'll see you here sometime next year. I have a lot of work and am tired and nervous

40 but otherwise, thank God, in good health."[29] On December 5, Otto and Edith moved into their new home at 37 Merwedeplein in Amsterdam-Zuid's Rivierenbuurt (River Quarter). The apartment was large and light, with a spacious room on the floor above that they could rent out for extra income. A wide balcony at the rear overlooked their neighbors' gardens. Hundreds of Jews in flight were settling into the area; their German, Austrian, and Polish voices rang in the air. One Dutch newspaper that was unsympathetic toward the refugees issued them a warning on how to behave: "Do not speak German on the street. Do not attract attention by speaking loudly and dressing loudly. Study and follow the ways of the land."[30] Other instructions would follow.

Edith wrote to Gertrud a few days after her official immigration: "We have so much to do. You are right: how well I could use your help with unpacking and clearing up. Aunt Hedi has been here for a week, without her I would not finish at all. Tomorrow both uncles will bring Margot and will stay for Christmas. Anne also wants to come. Rosa will have a hard time to keep her there for another couple of weeks."[31] When the apartment was furnished with their belongings shipped over from Germany, Edith's brothers, Julius and Walter, brought Margot by car to Amsterdam. Anne remained in Aachen with Oma Holländer so that Margot could settle into the unfamiliar surroundings in peace. On January 4, 1934, Margot began her new school on Jekerstraat, which was only a two-minute walk from home, and Anne arrived in Amsterdam a month later, on Margot's birthday.

In the meantime, other relatives had fled from Germany. Robert Frank and his wife, Lottie, emigrated from Frankfurt to London in the summer of 1933 and opened their own art dealership in a basement on St. James's Street. They entered into London life with enthusiasm: Robert bought himself a bowler hat and umbrella, and Lottie liked to invite friends to afternoon tea at Fortnum & Mason. Their house in Kensington became a popular meeting place for people in the art world. In October 1933, the house on Mertonstrasse was repossessed, and Alice Frank emigrated to Basel. Leni and Erich, together with their sons Stephan and Buddy, settled Alice into a four-room apartment of her own until they found a larger home where she could join them. Although the area in which she lived was pleasantly quiet, Alice found it difficult to adjust, and she had trouble understanding Swiss German. Edith confided to Gertrud the real problem: "Omi still suffers from homesickness in Basel and from being separated from her other children."[32] Edith could understand her mother-in-law's homesickness only too well: she was suffering from the same complaint and had to remind herself: "One must not lose courage."[33]

■

DURING HIS MONTHS OF LIVING ALONE IN Amsterdam, Otto had rented a room at 24II Stadionkade in the south of the city and traveled to work by tram. It stopped just short of the Opekta office at 120–126 Nieuwe Zijds Voorburgwal. Although the centrally located offices were in a tall, modern building, the premises rented by Opekta were small: two rooms and a claustrophobic kitchen. Otto's aim was to convince as many housewives as possible to use pectin in their jam-making. Sales occurred mainly through pharmacists, although there were also some transactions to wholesalers.

Working alongside Otto was Victor Gustav Kugler, who had previously worked for Pomosin Utrecht. Kugler was born in June 1900 in the (then) Austro-Hungarian town of Hohenelbe. His mother was single when she gave birth to him, and relied on support from her parents. Kugler was baptized a Catholic and attended a Catholic school. In 1917, he joined the Austrian Navy, but an injury led to his exemption from active duty. After the Great War, he worked for the Deutsche Maschinenfabrik as an electrician and was transferred to Utrecht, where he married a local woman. By 1923, he was assistant to the director of Pomosin Utrecht and should have had Otto's job in Amsterdam, but the Opekta company ultimately decided he was unsuitable for the position and gave him the task of being Otto's right-hand man instead. Otto admired Kugler's no-nonsense approach and sensed the compassion and integrity beneath his serious attitude. Kugler was committed to his work and made the sixteen-mile trip from his home in Hilversum on his motorized bike every day.

Apart from a junior clerk whose main duty was packaging the products, Otto employed only one other full-time member of the staff. When this secretary fell ill, another Austrian-born worker was recommended to him: Hermine (Miep) Santrouschitz, born in 1909 in Vienna. Miep had arrived in the Netherlands as a starving child, sent by a welfare organization to live with a Dutch family until she recuperated. It was always intended that she would return to her parents in Austria, but she settled in so well with her foster family, the Nieuwenhuises, who called her Miep, that she stayed in the Netherlands permanently.[34] In late 1933, a friend told her there was a job available with Opekta, and she applied for it, not knowing what it was exactly. Her first two weeks were spent in the tiny office kitchen making jam. Once she had perfected that, Otto promoted her to dealing with customer complaints and information, typing, and bookkeeping.

Miep's attraction to Otto was instant: "In a shy but gentlemanly way this slim, smiling man introduced himself. . . . His dark eyes held my eyes to him, and I felt immediately his kind and gentle nature, stiffened somewhat by shyness and a slightly nervous demeanor. . . . He apologized for his poor Dutch. . . . I gladly spoke German. . . . He wore a mustache and when he smiled, which was often, he revealed quite uneven teeth." They shared the same passionate political views and promptly became close friends: "I called him Mr. Frank and he called me Miss Santrouschitz, as

Northern Europeans of our generation did not use first names with each other. Feeling at ease with him quite quickly, I threw formality aside and demanded, 'Please call me Miep.' Mr. Frank did as I asked."[35]

Otto found that he had a talent for advertising, and together with Miep, he devised a series of ideas for convincing housewives that Opekta was the best product on the market for fun, quick, and easy jam-making. There were regular, lively ads in newspapers and magazines, an *Opekta Journal,* and even a promotional film in which Miep starred. Otto experimented with various recipes, including jam for diabetics, tomato jam, and chocolate jam. Although their first year was not their best—the company was established "just too late to be able to profit from the 1933 harvest (and hence from the preserving season)"[36]—it did provide Otto with a small income. This was even more welcome in January 1934, when the family bank in Frankfurt ceased all trading. On September 26, 1938, the business was officially struck off the German register.

■

THREE WAVES OF GERMAN JEWISH refugees, approximately thirty thousand in total, entered the Netherlands before war broke out: in 1933, after Hitler came to power; in 1935, following enactment of the Nuremberg Laws; and in 1938, in the wake of "Crystal Night." The majority settled in Amsterdam. Reactions from Dutch Jews and Gentiles ranged from outright rejection to expressions of solidarity. After 1934 and again in 1938, the Dutch government placed restrictions on the number of refugees permitted entry to the Netherlands. The justice minister, Goseling, referred to these desperate, harassed people as "undesirable aliens" who would do better to return to Germany and Austria. Dutch aid committees encouraged them to go elsewhere and promoted Britain and the United States as

44   desirable locations. Many refugees were sent straight back to Germany, where they ended their days in concentration camps and prisons. Many of those whose emigration was approved were placed in refugee camps because the Dutch government felt that all refugees should receive assistance wholly from private Dutch Jewish organizations. The government's first choice for a large refugee camp was close to Elspeet and not far from the home of Queen Wilhelmina, who made plain her disapproval. In 1939, construction began at another site: Drenthe in the flat and barren northeast region of the Netherlands, far away from the main cities and towns. Strict instructions were given for Kamp Westerbork: it was not allowed to be any more comfortable or attractive than the poor housing occupied by Dutch residents nearby. Freedom of movement within the camp, even then, was limited.

German Jews able to rent or buy their own homes in the Netherlands found that prejudice from the Dutch was due more to their nationality than to their Jewishness. Hilde Goldberg, who emigrated from Berlin to Amsterdam in 1929 with her parents, Walter and Betty Jacobsthal, and her brother Joachim, remembers: "We didn't speak German at all, not even at home because of what the Nazis had come to represent, and we wouldn't dream of speaking German on the streets. That would have caused us great trouble."[37] Laureen Nussbaum (née Klein), whose parents had known Otto and Edith in Frankfurt before they, too, settled in the River Quarter in 1936, remembers: "It was not about anti-Semitism in the 1930s. The anger and dislike arose because we were German. It didn't matter that we were Jewish Germans arriving in the country in fear of our lives; we were simply Germans to the Dutch."[38]

Most of the German Jewish refugees found their homes in the River Quarter and in the area around Beethovenstraat. Their appearance in these pleasant neighborhoods caused great jealousy, as Laureen recalls. "The Dutch Jews, and many of the non-Jewish Dutch, could not afford to rent apartments in the south like the

German Jews. These houses were very lovely: large, modern, and expensive. They had central heating—an absolute luxury then. There was a lot of envy. Dutch Jews covered the whole spectrum from the very poor to the very wealthy, but in the main, the German Jews were wealthy, which bred resentment."[39]

Dutch Jews were also fearful that, with so many refugees arriving, anti-Semitism would erupt in the Netherlands, as it had in Germany. There had been some racism toward Jews in the Netherlands before the 1930s, but it was always contained: "Mild forms of anti-Semitism increased from the end of the nineteenth century, but never gave rise to pogroms as in Eastern Europe. It was, for instance, not possible for a Jew to advance to a high post in the civil service; in this, Holland was not different from other European countries. Some restaurants and dance-halls made it plain that Jews were not welcome on their premises, a form of exclusion also applicable to black Dutchmen from Surinam."[40]

Among those Jewish refugees who desperately missed Germany was Edith Frank. Miep recalls that Edith longed for her homeland "much more than Mr. Frank. Very often in conversation she would refer with melancholy to their life in Frankfurt, the superiority of some kinds of German sweets and the quality of German clothing."[41] Hilde Goldberg agrees:

We got to know Otto when he was setting up Opekta. He got on with life in Amsterdam, but Edith found the adjustment very hard. She came from a very protective, very middle-class background, and in Amsterdam life was more easygoing. She was always beautifully dressed, with her hair set just so, and she dressed her children beautifully, too—their dresses, although casual enough to play in, were always well-made. She was a good mother, very conscientious, but she never really made friends with people because she had such reserve. I think the problems between her and Anne before they went into hiding were due to her reticence to mix with

46   people. The neighborhood was very friendly and everyone knew
      each other, but she held herself back, and I think that irritated
      Anne.[42]

Edith tried to find positive elements in her new life: "Our home
is similar to that in Ganghoferstrasse, only much smaller. In our
bedrooms there is room only for the beds. There is no cellar, no
pantry, but everything is light, comfortable and warm, so I can
manage without a help."[43] She had great problems learning the
Dutch language and asked a neighbor to give her private lessons,
but she was so discouraged by her early attempts that she abandoned the classes and tried to learn it purely by ear. Otto and the
children came into constant contact with the language and picked
it up quickly, conversing with one another before long in a mixture
of German and Dutch, perhaps alienating Edith further.

Edith's weekly visit to the Liberal synagogue became even more
important to her in these circumstances. Otto attended occasionally, but for him it was a social rather than a spiritual experience.
In his ignorance, however, Otto tried to register his family with the
Orthodox community. He was astonished to be told that he would
"have to have a new marriage ceremony"[44] because the Orthodox
rabbinate did not recognize Liberal Jewish marriages. There was
then no Liberal Jewish congregation in Amsterdam, only an
Orthodox one. Hilde Goldberg recalls: "Otto and my father got together a committee to establish somewhere for the Liberal Jewish
congregation. It was just a hall at first, but later it became a proper
organization."[45]

Throughout the summer of 1934, one of Otto's uncles who lived
in Luxembourg sent him money to help with the ongoing expenses
of the Opekta company. Otto wrote each time to thank him, adding
on July 9 that Edith and Anne had gone to Aachen for a few days.
Margot stayed behind in Amsterdam; she was finding life in a new
country more difficult than Anne, who enjoyed attending the local

Montessori school. Edith informed Gertrud, "Both children speak Dutch well and have nice friends."[46] In the autumn of 1934, Otto wrote to his uncle: "Though my income remains fairly modest, one must be satisfied to have found some way of earning a living and getting on."[47] In a more open letter to Gertrud, he admitted: "I am traveling almost every day, and only get home in the evening. It's not like in Frankfurt, where one eats at home at lunchtime—and where one can relax a little, too. It goes on all day. . . ."[48] The business was picking up; at the end of 1934, Otto rented larger offices at 400 Singel, three stories above a warehouse and overlooking the canal. Otto had to work harder than ever, since two other companies were promoting a similar product. He often acted as his own sales representative, visiting housewives and wholesalers across the country. He was sometimes away from home for a week or more, and Edith wrote to Gertrud, "Mr. Frank doesn't relax at all and looks thin and tired."[49] The children were happy, however: "During the holidays I was by the sea with the girls, because Anne has not fully recovered [from a recent illness], but she will go to stay in a children's holiday home and will miss school for another three weeks. Margot is tall, tanned and strong and has great joy in learning."[50]

Business improved in 1935 when Otto managed to persuade a number of small wholesalers to stock pectin, but his profits really depended upon the strawberry harvest. He was at least able to employ more staff. In January, a thirty-four-year-old Amsterdam lawyer, Anton Dunselman, was appointed supervisory director of the company. A young man named Henk van Beusekom worked in the warehouse, Otto's friend Isa Cauvern helped with secretarial duties, and there were at least two demonstrators, one of whom was a Jewish refugee from Frankfurt, Renee Wolfe Manola. She was employed by Opekta for six months before emigrating to the United States. At some point in 1935, probably after Renee departed, the Jansen family began to work for Otto.[51]

48   Jetje Jansen was engaged at Opekta throughout 1935 and 1936 as a full-time demonstrator, while her husband, Joseph (a professional theater actor who once had aspirations to become a Roman Catholic priest), worked for Otto on a casual basis building display stands for trade exhibitions. Their son helped with the packing and dispatch duties in the warehouse. The Jansens were a deeply unhappy family: Jetje was Jewish, and since 1932 she and her husband had begun to draw apart; that year Joseph Jansen joined the Dutch Nazi Party (NSB). Later he claimed to have become a member because "I was convinced that democracy needed to be renewed," and his wife gave him "a feeling of inferiority . . . if our relationship had been good, it would never have come so far with me and I would never have resorted to the NSB."[52] He later became a member of the Nazi Weerafdeling, the unarmed defense section of the Dutch National Socialist movement, and eventually joined the Schutzstaffel, the NSDAP's security organization, under the command of Heinrich Himmler, leaving Jetje for a baker's widow who supported the NSB. In 1935, however, he was a jealous husband, and over the course of his wife's employment at Opekta he convinced himself that she and Otto were having an affair. There were no apparent grounds for his suspicion, but it sparked in Joseph Jansen a deep and lasting hatred of Otto Frank. Otto's uncomplicated decision in 1935 to employ the Jansens would lead him into a situation that has never previously been documented—a maze of blackmail, terror, and despair.

It was through Jansen that Tonny Ahlers would enter the life of Otto Frank.

three ENTRAPMENT

IN THE EARLY SUMMER OF 1935, OTTO'S
mother, Alice, arrived in Amsterdam for a long holiday. Anne accompanied her back to Basel; she had been pestering her parents
for some time to visit her cousins, Stephan and Buddy. In
December, it was Otto and Margot's turn to travel to Basel, leaving
Anne at home with her mother, and then with Oma Holländer in
Aachen, recuperating from the influenza she had had since
October. Because Anne also had a heart condition, she was sometimes confined to bed in order to rest, which she hated. In
Switzerland, under Buddy's expert tuition, Margot learned to
skate; when she heard about this, Anne immediately wanted lessons, too. Otto later explained the differences between his two
daughters:

> Anne was a normal, lively child who needed much tenderness and
> attention, and who delighted us and frequently upset us. When she
> entered a room, there was always a fuss. Anne never stopped
> asking questions. When we had visitors, she was so interested in
> them that it was hard to get rid of her. At school she was never a

particularly brilliant pupil. She hated arithmetic, and I used to practice her multiplication tables with her. She did well only in the subjects she was interested in. . . . Margot was the bright one. Everybody admired her. She got along with everybody. . . . She was a wonderful person.[1]

The Franks' social circle was beginning to expand. Otto and Edith had become close friends with their neighbors, Hans and Ruth Goslar, German Jewish refugees like themselves. Hans Goslar had been director of the press office in Berlin for years until the Nazis dismissed him. He and his wife, Ruth, together with their young daughter Hanneli, tried to settle in England, where Hans had been offered a job, but the company for which he worked would not allow him to take the Sabbath day off. The family moved on to Amsterdam, intending to emigrate to Palestine eventually. Hans began advising Jewish refugees on legal and financial matters, using his home as his office. Through the Goslars, Edith was able to enjoy her religion more: Hans, a founding member of the German Zionist group Mizrachi, invited the Franks to share their Friday night celebration, and Edith and Ruth often attended the synagogue together. Following her mother's example, Margot developed a firm interest in Judaism and looked forward to her weekly Hebrew classes. Hanneli Goslar, who was Anne Frank's best friend at the time, recalls, "Margot always said that after the war she wanted to be a nurse in Palestine. Otto had no interest in attending the synagogue for worship. Anne was like him in that sense, and he may have influenced her decision. He was such a wonderful father, and I loved him, too. Every night at home, Otto would have a beer. He would tip the glass up and up and up, and Anne and I would sit, open-mouthed, waiting for him to spill it. But of course he never did—he did it to tease us!"[2]

In the summer of 1936, Edith took the children to Otto's cousin's Swiss villa in Sils-Maria. In September, Alice and

Stephan arrived in Amsterdam while Edith's mother was also there. Stephan complained on a postcard home that the weather was "dreadful. We drove here with the car. I [Alice's nickname, pronounced *ee*] has a cold and is in bed. If she isn't better by Saturday then she will come home with me. . . . I'm sight-seeing in Amsterdam with great interest and have already been to the Rijksmuseum. . . . I'll be sorry when these wonderful days are over but glad to come home to Basel too. I send greetings from her bed."[3] His second card gives a small glimpse of family life: "Yesterday I was with Ottel [one of Otto's nicknames] in his office. There wasn't much to see of Opekta. . . . I sleep very well in my fold-up bed. Anne is already up at six o'clock every morning and then we sit and chat. Otto crawls into her bed and then Margot jumps down from the top bunk."[4]

When their visitors had gone, Edith holidayed alone in Aachen and traveled briefly to Frankfurt. Upon her return, she wrote to Gertrud in October: "I found the children in good spirits and they are happy to have me back again. Papi left on Monday again for a week. . . . We have at least seen each other and had a chance to talk. Let's hope we'll have another chance soon."[5] The following year, the Franks received a letter from Kathi Stilgenbauer, their former housekeeper in Frankfurt, informing them that her husband had been arrested and imprisoned by the Nazis. Edith wrote: "We think often of you and your grief."[6] Later that year, Otto visited Germany on business; it was the last time he was in the country before the war. Meeting Gertrud, he told her, "If they saw us together now they would arrest us."[7] When Edith wrote to Gertrud again, she did so in a mood of dejection: "My husband is hardly ever at home. Work is getting harder and harder."[8]

Otto's friend Johannes Kleiman had joined Opekta as book-keeper, but the Jansens had gone and new representatives were taken on, together with another full-time typist, Bep Voskuijl. Tall, kind, and rather shy, Bep was Dutch, born in 1919, the eldest child

in a large family. After finishing school, she worked briefly as a domestic help and as a seamstress before taking evening courses to
qualify as a secretary. In the summer of 1937, she began working
for Opekta: "I was under Isa Cauvern. Miep, who was ten years
older, was more or less my boss. . . . The relationship between
Frank and Kleiman was not just business but also friendship; they
used to play cards every week, I believe. Otto Frank and Ab Cauvern
[Isa's husband] were also good friends."[9] She remembered Otto as
"affectionate, unsparing with himself and keenly sensitive . . . a
soft word always made far more impression than any shouting."[10]
Bep obtained a position for her father at Opekta; Johan Voskuijl
was a trained bookkeeper but worked for Otto as warehouse manager. He and Otto became close friends, and he confided in Otto
that he had stomach cancer. Despite the painful treatments, he
continued to work at his own insistence.

By 1937, Miep was a regular visitor to the Franks' home, together with her future husband, Jan Gies. Jan, then thirty-two,
worked for the Social Services Authority and lived on Rijnstraat in
the River Quarter. Miep saw many similarities between Jan and
Otto, not only in their appearance but also in their character: "Men
of few words with high principles and ironic senses of humor."[11]
They had dinner with the Franks on an almost weekly basis and
discussed politics frequently; they shared the same views about the
Nazi Party and spoke vigorously about Germany, where Jews had
lost all their rights and were subject to harsh, intensifying regulations. The Nuremberg Laws, in force since September 1935,
stripped Jews of their nationality and banned them from sexual relationships and marriages with non-Jews.

On October 29, 1937, Otto began two months of continual traveling. He had plans for "something in England," as Edith wrote to
friends, adding, "whether it will turn out is uncertain. Unfortunately we are not satisfied with how the business is going and need
to supplement it somehow."[12] Otto's travels covered Basel, Paris,

London, and Bristol. There was a brief respite at home before he left again, with Anne, on December 17 for Luxembourg and then Basel, where they stayed until December 25. Edith wrote to Gertrud that Anne was thrilled to accompany her father to Switzerland: "For two years she had hoped for a trip with her Papi. I don't know whether Omi came back with her. Since Uncle Robert and Uncle Herbert are also there at the moment she was very fortunate indeed. Margot traveled to Oma today, where I hope she has a good time. . . . My husband is overly tired and really needs a few days off. The business is tough, but apart from that we live quietly."[13]

Otto's plans might also have included emigration to England if he could have established a business there, since Edith was worried about their safety in the Netherlands. After Hitler occupied the Rhineland in 1936, invasion had become even more probable. The Dutch government was eager to maintain relations with both Germany and Britain, since it needed Germany's support for its economy and Britain's for security. Hitler had two valuable allies in Italy and Japan, and in 1938, his domination of Europe began. On March 12, German troops occupied Vienna, and Austria was incorporated into the Reich. Miep recalls how "the whole [Opekta] office stood together listening to Mr. Frank's wireless, as the dramatic voice announced Hitler's triumphant entry into the city of his youth, Vienna."[14] The humiliations and restrictions that had befallen Germany's Jews now swept through Austria.

Julianne Duke, a former neighbor of the Franks' in Amsterdam whose family had emigrated to the United States, remembers that her parents asked the Franks to join them: "Mrs. Frank wrote that she wanted to emigrate, but Mr. Frank saw no need to leave Holland. He trusted in man's basic goodness, rather than focusing on the darker, irrational side of human nature."[15] Otto himself later recalled: "In the Netherlands, after those experiences in Germany, it was as if our life was restored to us. Our children went to school and at least in the beginning our lives proceeded normally. In those days it was possible for us to start over and feel free."[16] Miep noticed that Otto's attitude was in sharp contrast to his wife's views: "Mrs. Frank was particularly vocal in her bitter response [to Germany's actions]. . . . Mr. Frank, with his usual nervous, quiet manner, kept shaking his head, expressing hope."[17] Although Edith was distressed about the current situation in Germany, she still missed her old life there, confiding to Gertrud that "for us the years at Marbachweg were also among the best. . . . That I cannot travel home more often annoys me."[18] Edith still regarded Germany as home, even after five years of living in Amsterdam.

Unfortunately, Otto's plans for "something in England" had fallen through, and he put all his efforts into a new business venture in Amsterdam. To compensate for the loss of profits during the winter months, when fruit was scarcer, Otto set up Pectacon, which dealt in herbs, spices, and seasonings. Goods were imported from Hungary and Belgium and sold to butchers throughout the Netherlands and Belgium. Otto had little experience as far as seasonings and recipes were concerned and engaged a German Jewish refugee as his adviser. Hermann van Pels, who was an expert, was born in Germany in 1890 to a Dutch couple. In December 1925, he married Auguste (Gusti) Röttgen, ten years his junior. For ten years they lived in Osnabrück, where their son, Peter, was born in November 1926. As the persecutions in Germany escalated, the van Pelses fled to Amsterdam, renting an apartment at 34 Zuider Amstellaan, directly behind the Frank family. Hermann van Pels was a valuable addition to Otto's staff. He invented recipes that were then made up at Pectacon, and he checked the orders taken from the sales representatives. He passed on his knowledge to Victor Kugler—who became something of an expert himself on spices—and acted as an intermediary between the management and the warehouse staff who milled and packed the goods.

Hermann van Pels and his wife, Gusti, were quick-thinking, gregarious, and extremely temperamental. Although Otto liked them, he was very critical of the way they treated their shy, unacademic son: "Peter's parents were absolutely no good for him. They hit him and threw him out. Peter didn't have the backing of his parents at all."[19] The van Pels family became part of Otto and Edith's social circle, which rapidly increased after the grim events of November 1938. That month, a young Jewish Polish student shot the third secretary of the German embassy in Paris, Ernst von Rath, in protest of his elderly parents being thrown out of Germany. The Nazis used the incident to unleash a pogrom: during the night of November 9–10 (Crystal Night), the Nazis and their followers attacked Jewish communities throughout Germany, destroying thousands of synagogues, businesses, and homes, killing almost a hundred Jews, and sending many more to concentration camps. Seven thousand Jews who gained entry to the Netherlands in the aftermath were the last refugees to cross the Dutch border legally before the war.

On November 12, amid the ongoing repercussions of Crystal Night, Walter and Julius Holländer were arrested. Julius was freed immediately because of his war wound, but Walter was sent to Sachsenhausen concentration camp, not far from Berlin. The authorities would release him if he could prove he had the means to leave Germany. Walter and Julius had already considered emigrating to the United States but needed an affidavit from a relative living there before they could leave. On December 1, Walter was transferred to the Dutch refugee camp at Zeeburg, where the internees, under constant police supervision, were forbidden to have contact with the outside world. Although they were not allowed to earn an income, the internees had to pay for their stay. Walter was able to leave the camp on several occasions, but only with written permission, and then simply to visit the Huize Oosteinde, a popular meeting place for refugees. While Walter was

56   in Zeeburg, his mother and brother remained at home in Aachen. The Holländer business had been liquidated under new Nazi laws.

At the end of 1938, another recent Jewish refugee from Berlin, Fritz Pfeffer, and his Gentile girlfriend, Lotte Kaletta, became part of the group who met every Saturday afternoon at the Franks' apartment. Pfeffer was born in 1889, in the German town of Giessen, where his father owned a clothing store. Pfeffer trained as a dentist and went into business in Berlin. In 1921, he married Vera Bythiner, many years his junior, with whom he had a son, Werner Peter, born in 1927. The marriage ended in divorce six years later, and Pfeffer was granted custody of his son, whom he adored. In 1936, at the age of thirty-seven, he met Martha Charlotte (Lotte) Kaletta, who was then nineteen. Lotte's first marriage to a Jewish dentist had fallen apart after the birth of her son, who was also in the custody of his father. Lotte moved into Pfeffer's home and lavished all the love she was unable to give to her own son onto Werner Peter. Crystal Night tore their lives apart. Pfeffer sent his son to live in London with his brother Ernst, unable to join them himself because he had neither the funds nor a grasp of the English language. In December 1938, Pfeffer and Lotte emigrated to Amsterdam, leaving Lotte's son behind with his father. Both father and son were later killed by the Nazis, as was Pfeffer's first wife.

Pfeffer found work in a friend's surgery in the River Quarter. He and Lotte hoped to wed in the Netherlands or Belgium, but Pfeffer's status as a German Jew, even before the implementation of the Nuremberg Laws that followed the invasion of the Low Countries, created difficulties. To avoid further trouble, in 1940 the couple registered themselves as living in separate houses. Hilde Goldberg's family already knew Pfeffer from Berlin, where he and Hilde's father had been members of the same rowing club. She recalls: "Fritz Pfeffer came to our house every evening. He would always ring the bell, then come in and say, 'Well, what's new?' And when we heard the bell go in the evening, we would all cry, 'Well, what's new!' He was a good man, and very intelligent. Lotte was beautiful, kind, and thoughtful. She had a terrific sense of humor."[20]

Only Edith Frank seemed to believe Pfeffer and Lotte's stories about the terrors they had endured in Germany; other guests at the Saturday gatherings merely shook their heads in puzzlement. Among the usual guests were the German Baschwitz family, who had lived in the Netherlands since 1933 but had known Otto much longer. Isa Baschwitz recalls: "In Frankfurt, my father [Kurt Baschwitz] was a school-friend of the older, intellectual brother of Otto, Robert Frank. In Amsterdam, Otto made contact. The family used to visit each other for morning coffee. I used to go around mainly with Margot, who was three years younger than I. Anne was a very vivacious girl who, because she had a heart condition, was rather pampered and spoiled and always got her own way."[21]

Despite all the tensions, at the end of the year, Otto sent a spirited letter to his mother: "What can one say in a birthday letter in times like these? We have to be grateful for what we still have—and not give up hope! It is miserably cold here, too, and we think constantly of those who, unlike ourselves, have no warm place to stay."[22]

■

THERE HAD BEEN FEW INSTANCES OF anti-Semitic violence in the Netherlands before the German invasion. Jews were seen as "different," and anti-Semitic literature was a regular feature in Amsterdam cafés, but prejudice was more likely to be expressed verbally than physically. For example, after a large Zionist meeting in the Dutch seaside town of Zandvoort had ended, a woman stood up and inquired, "Gentlemen, once you have all left for Palestine, may we have Zandvoort back?"[23] Incidents such as the 1938 attack on Jews in Amsterdam's Bijenkorf department store were rare.

In the wake of that particular episode, a youth who had

participated in the riot was sentenced to eight months in the Leeuwarden prison. Tonny Ahlers, whom the authorities recorded as "1.82m tall, lean, with dark blond hair and a snub nose," had been in trouble most of his life.[24] Born in 1917 to working-class parents in Amsterdam, and lame in one leg due to polio, Ahlers had been a difficult child whose behavior became markedly worse following his parents' divorce in 1928.[25] Tonny and his younger siblings—two brothers and three sisters—were placed in a Salvation Army children's home and then split up. Tonny and his brother Cas managed to remain together throughout a series of foster homes in and around Apeldoorn but never stayed long in any of them because Tonny's behavior was not only disruptive but also cruel. Cas Ahlers recalls how his brother waited for the newspapers to be delivered, and then, as the man pushed the papers through the letterbox, Tonny would grab his hands and pull them back and forth until they were badly grazed on the metal of the opening. "He liked to hurt people," Cas explains.[26] His only friend was a local architect who believed himself to be God's messenger. The man's wife had left him, taking their child with her, and for some reason, Tonny befriended him, protecting him from the town's youths, who ridiculed the man at every opportunity.

After a nine-month spell in a sanatorium—presumably related to his polio—Tonny worked as a hairdresser's assistant, switching from one salon to another. His aggression made his working life, like his home life, perennially unstable. At nineteen, he decided to switch to another trade, but he convinced himself that nothing would earn him the sort of money he dreamed of having, so he took off suddenly for France on a whim. For three months he worked for a firm producing radios and similar appliances, but when his visa ran out, he was forced to return to Apeldoorn. Three months of being unemployed convinced him that the town was no good for him; he moved to Amsterdam, where his mother had married again and was living at 253 Prinsengracht, a substantial property with a front house and a large annex. He lived with her for several months, but their relationship was poor. Later she described Tonny, her eldest son, as having "always been a misfit" with "a naturally bad character," dishonest but capable of charming his way out of any situation. Tonny's father, on the other hand, lived in the same neighborhood and seemed to find his son's contemptuous manner, bragging, and petty thievery amusing.[27]

In March 1939, Tonny Ahlers wound up in jail again. This time he had been caught committing violence against the NSB, but upon his release in October, his anti-Semitism was fueled by the same Dutch Nazis he had been jailed for attacking. Only a week into his freedom, he was cautioned along with other members of the NSB for smashing the windows of Jewish-owned property. His social services file describes him as "a very difficult young man who is constantly in trouble. . . . His personality is shaped by the fact that he feels as though the world is against him. . . . Did he allow his friends to draw him into anti-Jewish violence? This got him a prison sentence. . . . He admits himself that he has a troublesome character, just like all the Ahlers, he says."[28]

As the 1930s drew to a close, Tonny Ahlers's hatred of Jews began to manifest itself in an increasingly aggressive form. Shattering synagogue windows and breaking the nose off the statue of the Jewish playwright Herman Heijermans were only the beginning.[29] What began in his teenage years as mindless acts of vandalism was starting to turn into something far more destructive. As Nazi violence against Jews in Germany intensified, and the power of the SS breached all ordinary societal limits, Tonny Ahlers let his family know that his interest in the Third Reich was something far more than juvenile curiosity: it was the map of his future.

■

AT THE BEGINNING OF 1939, JULIUS Holländer received an affidavit from his cousin, Ernst Holländer, guaranteeing work and support in the United States. Rosa Holländer would spend the rest of her life with Edith in

Amsterdam. In March, she arrived, and her luggage consisted only of some cutlery and food. In a 1954 interview, Otto recalled, "My wife's mother always paid more attention to Anne's character, as Margot was very easy to handle. Oma spoiled the girls, but not unreasonably."[30] The interviewer, Otto's friend Jean Grossman, continued on the same theme: "To other members of the family, Edith Frank's gentle mother sometimes had to defend her soft treatment of Anne. She had a son, Anne's uncle [Julius], who as a child was also highly-strung and stormy, and who was considered a 'rather peculiar person' in later years. The grandmother often said, 'If we had known more of the psychology of children when my son was Anne's age, he might have developed differently.' "[31]

In April, alone in Aachen, Julius sent some antique furniture that Edith had wanted on to Amsterdam. Everything else was left behind in the apartment, and what remained of the Holländer business was later sold at auction. Julius then took the boat from Rotterdam to New York and traveled on to Massachusetts. Walter was freed from Zeeburg on December 14 and departed for the United States two days later. For over a year, both brothers were unable to find employment and had to rely on their cousin Ernst for everything.

In the spring of 1939, Edith and Margot had a short holiday in Luxembourg with some of Otto's relatives. In May, when Otto himself was absent from home on a business trip, he sent a loving letter to Anne, who kept it to serve "as a support to me all my life."[32] It included Otto's gentle reminder to "educate yourself. We have agreed the 'controls' with each other and you yourself are doing a great deal to swallow the 'buts.' And yet you like to spoil yourself and like even more to be spoiled by others. All that isn't bad, if deep in your little heart you remain as loveable as you always have been. I have told you that as a child, I, too, often rushed into things without thinking twice and made many mistakes. But the main thing is to reflect a little bit and then to find one's way back to the right path."[33] He signed the letter "Pim," the nickname Anne and Margot had given him. Asked later how it originated, Otto laughed: "I don't know. *Père*—father—Pim?"[34]

His friend Jean Grossman wrote about the relationship between the girls and their parents and made it clear that Edith and Otto played equal roles in their children's lives:

> In his courteous, quiet voice, Otto told me of the education of his daughters. Books and the sources of knowledge were always accessible to them. When he could not answer their questions himself, he went with them to find out. . . . I was keenly aware of Otto's own feeling for the wonders of the universe, his awareness of how much life is enriched by the knowledge of the world and its peoples past and present, their literature and art and what lies behind their actions. . . . As for discipline: "The system is patience," Anne's father said. Anne was sometimes difficult. Her parents tried to be fair and reasonable, and their reproofs were always gentle: a mild deprivation of privilege and occasionally, when she was little, a quick spank. They were not afraid to be firm, to say, "This you cannot do," and hold to it. They held to their word in promises, too, earning their children's trust and reliance. . . . Edith and Otto understood the differences between their two daughters and their individual needs. They chose different schools for the girls . . . everyone helped with the housework, and they rented out rooms. Edith went about the city with her daughters, to the shops, to concerts, to museums.[35]

Otto's time was taken up more and more by the business. Working all the hours he could to ensure the success of Pectacon/Opekta, he was suffering from nervous exhaustion. In a July 1939 letter, Edith told Gertrud: "My husband is in desperate need of a few days' rest. The business is a constant struggle but otherwise things are going smoothly for us."[36]

On August 23, 1939, Germany and Russia signed a nonaggression pact agreeing to the eventual partition of Poland between them. On September 1, 1939, Germany invaded Poland. Two days later, France and Great Britain declared war on Germany. Russian troops stormed Poland's eastern territories on September 17 and two weeks later gained control of seven cities. Poland surrendered and was divided between Germany and Russia. Hitler's Einsatzgruppen began a systematic program of murder in the country in 1941, killing thousands of intellectuals, officials, and priests. The occupying forces in Poland issued crippling anti-Semitic decrees through specially formed Judenräte (Jewish councils). In Austria, Jews were made to wear a prominent yellow star and leave their homes for squalid ghettos. In Poland, they were forced to emigrate if they could afford to do so, but in 1941 the borders closed. Many of those who wanted to emigrate to Palestine had their dreams shattered by opposition from the Arabs and from the British, who were reluctant to do anything to upset the oil trade.

On April 9, 1940, Denmark and Norway fell to the German army. Most Dutch people were shocked and confused at the speed of events around them, though many still believed they would remain on the sidelines of another world war, just as they had been able to do during the 1914–18 war. The German author Konrad Merz had written that "often it seems to me that a flight to Holland is like a flight into past decades,"[37] but suddenly Dutch neutrality was under significant threat.

Otto had finally faced the truth of their situation, but it was too late. His cousin Milly Stanfield, who lived in London, recalled: "During the first months of the war, Otto was virtually our only link to the Continent. We couldn't write to relations in Germany for England was at war with Germany. But Otto could write to Germany because he was doing so from neutral Holland. I got a letter from him saying how terribly unhappy he was because he was sure that Germany was going to attack. He said, 'I don't know what to do about the children. I can't talk to Edith about it. There's no use worrying her before she has to be worried. Forgive me, but I just had to write it.' " Milly suggested that they send the children to her in England. Otto wrote back: "Edith and I discussed your letter. We both feel we simply can't do it. We couldn't bear to part with the girls. They mean too much to us. But if it's any comfort to you, you are the people we would have trusted."[38]

In the early hours of May 10, 1940, Germany invaded Belgium, Luxembourg, France—and the Netherlands. On the day of the invasion, most people went to work as usual, though little was achieved. Miep remembers: "The mood in the office was forlorn and shocked. Mr. Frank's face was white. We crowded around the wireless in Mr. Frank's office and listened through the day for developments."[39] The country was in the grip of hysteria, which deepened with the news that the Dutch royal family and the government had escaped to London. In the midst of large-scale battles by Dutch forces to defend their country, the Germans called for surrender, threatening to bomb the port of Rotterdam. Before the deadline expired, the Germans attacked, and Rotterdam was virtually destroyed. The Netherlands capitulated on May 15 (Belgium on May 28). The Austrian-born Reich commissioner Arthur Seyss-Inquart now presided over the country. His direct staff were all Austrian or German SS officers, men who regarded the persecution of the Jews as an important task.

The Germans entered Amsterdam aglow with victory, watched grimly by some and greeted as heroes by others. There were 140,000 Jews then resident in the country; 60 percent of them lived in Amsterdam. When night fell, bonfires were lit throughout the city as people burned English books and anti-Nazi literature. Jewish families laden down with belongings hurried to the harbor to see if they could board boats to England. The evening wore on, and the streets kept filling up; people ran from house to house, asking advice, making plans. There were rumors that convoys of

64   ships waited in the harbor for Jews, and that people pushing through the screaming crowds in their rush to climb aboard had fallen into the sea and drowned. Many Jews committed suicide that night.

The Dutch Nazi Party, formed in 1931 by Anton Mussert, was at first free of anti-Semitism. Gradually introduced, the party had proved unpopular, and in 1933 there were only 1,000 official NSB members. On the eve of invasion, however, this figure had leapt to 32,000. After the occupation of the Netherlands, anti-Semitism became a driving force, acting like a magnet for young men like Tonny Ahlers, who joined the party in the summer of 1940.[40] Ahlers's mother confirmed that "before the war, he was already anti-Semitic. . . . After the capitulation of the Netherlands this trait showed itself more clearly."[41] Ahlers also joined the more extreme Nationaal Socialistische Nederlandse Arbeiders Partij (NSNAP) in October 1940, on the invitation of two neighbors who were Party leaders.

The aim of the Dutch National Socialist Workers' Party was to reproduce the ideology and operations of the NSDAP in Germany. The organization swiftly gained a reputation for violence against Jews and acts of robbery in general. Ahlers became a familiar face at the Sicherheitspolizei headquarters, a branch of the German security police (Sipo), which later employed people to hunt down Jews. There he spent most of his time in the company of three officials: Martin Brückner, Pieter Grimm, and Louis Schieffer, all of whom were tried after the war and imprisoned for their crimes. Ahlers and his friend Peters delivered "progress reports about the situation in the city to Schieffer for him to forward to the German commander in The Hague."[42] (Peters eventually worked for the Zentralstelle für Jüdische Auswanderung [Central Agency for Jewish Emigration], which was run by the German Sipo and SD in Amsterdam and charged with the administration of Jewish deportations from the Netherlands.) Ahlers's brother Huibert later gave a statement recalling how, "after the May days of 1940, Tonny wore a swastika armband right away. The few times he came home he always paraded contacts and papers from the SD. . . . He also used these papers to commit various frauds."[43]

Within a few weeks of the invasion, NSB members had taken over the press and clerical positions left by Jews who were forced to resign. The WA (paramilitary section of the NSB) began to attack Jews in the streets. Despite this, the only incident Otto noticed that summer was in his neighborhood: "It was very quiet in Amsterdam. But at the beginning of June, I once saw a German Army car coming down Scheldestraat and into Noorder-Amstellaan. At the corner it stopped and the driver asked the flower-seller, who had his stand there, some question. Then they drove on. But at the next corner the car turned around, returned, stopped again at the Scheldestraat corner, and a soldier jumped out and slapped the flower-seller's face. That was how it began."[44]

■

IN THE SUMMER OF 1940, ROBERT FRANK was among hundreds of Germans living in Britain who were arrested "in the interests of national security."[45] It took his wife, Lottie, weeks to find out what was happening to him; she knew only that an "R. Frank" was listed for deportation, in a shipment of those considered dangerous, to Australia. Eventually, Lottie was notified that it was not her husband on the list, and she was able to visit him at a refugee camp on the Isle of Man. After a few months, Robert was released and returned to work in London. In the United States, Walter and Julius had found employment with the E. F. Dodge Paper Box Company in Leominster, Massachusetts, and become good friends with their employer, who offered to sign an affidavit that would have allowed Edith and the family to emigrate to the United States. But, as Otto recalled, "time was too short and after Hitler had invaded Holland in May 1940 it was not possible

66   anymore to leave the country."[46] France signed armistices with
Germany and Italy on June 22, and the French government, in control of the south of the country and led by Marshal Pétain, cooperated with the German invaders.

On October 22, 1940, a law was passed in the Netherlands that
demanded: "All industrial or commercial firms owned by Jews or
having Jewish partners are to be reported. Failure to report will be
punishable by up to five years' imprisonment or fines of up to
100,000 guilders."[47] Those companies affected by the ruling had
to report to the Wirtschaftsprüfstelle (Bureau of Economic Investigation, or BEI). The day after the law was passed, Otto registered
a new company, La Synthèse N.V., in Hilversum. This was a cover
for Pectacon, which Otto hoped to prevent from falling into
German hands. Otto admitted to owning 2,000 guilders of the
company's 10,000 guilders' total share of capital and said that the
remaining shares had not been issued. With Jan Gies named as supervisory director and Victor Kugler as managing director, Otto
(who was the actual owner) had made it appear that the business
was 100 percent "Aryan," or non-Jewish. As far as Opekta was concerned, Otto registered the company with the BEI but acknowledged himself as the sole proprietor and declared his investment
of 10,000 guilders in capital.

In December 1940, Otto's companies moved into new premises
that years later would become one of the world's most famous addresses: 263 Prinsengracht. The building, like many Dutch canal
houses, was actually two buildings connected by a corridor: a
seventeenth-century front house and an eighteenth-century annex. The building had been empty for over a year before Otto began to rent it. There was a large warehouse on the ground floor, and
Otto had the open-plan first floor of the annex divided into two
rooms to provide him with an office and a kitchen. The other offices, where Kleiman, Miep, Bep, Kugler, and Hermann van Pels
worked, were on the first floor of the front house. Goods were

stored on the floor above, while spices were kept in a dark room at the back overlooking the annex. The rest of the building stayed empty. At that point, six people worked for Opekta and five for Pectacon, including the sales representatives but not the temporary staff who came and went on a regular basis.

Otto put his business concerns aside on February 16, 1941, the day his eldest daughter, Margot, became fifteen. Otto wrote "Mutz" (Margot's nickname) a poem, which was a family tradition at times of celebration. In addition to her Hebrew classes, Margot had also enrolled in a Zionist youth organization. Otto wanted to interest Margot in German literature and paid his friend Anneliese Schütz, a Berlin journalist who could find no work in Amsterdam, to give Margot and other local Jewish teenagers weekly lessons in the classics. The tutorials were hosted each week by a different family. Anneliese started them off with Goethe and Schiller, Otto's own favorites. Laureen Nussbaum also attended the classes: "Those lessons were very good for us, but we felt awkward because we had such mixed emotions about all things German. We hated what had happened to us there, and what was happening still, of course, but our parents talked constantly with great nostalgia about Germany before Hitler. Our Dutch friends didn't have these problems; they simply hated all things German."[48]

On March 12, 1941, another law was passed affecting Otto's businesses. This demanded that any changes made to Jewish-owned or Jewish-managed companies before the October law that had allowed those companies to avoid registration at that time had to be reported. It also included changes made since then. Otto had been able to evade registering Pectacon as a Jewish-owned company by keeping quiet about the remaining shares, but now he had to act. He informed the BEI that a meeting had been held on February 13, 1941, during which the remaining shares of 8,000 guilders had been issued to Johannes Kleiman and Anton Dunselman, the lawyer. At the meeting, Otto announced he would

68   keep 2,000 guilders' worth of shares (as was permitted) and then resigned from the company. Kleiman replaced him, thus making the business wholly Aryan. The meeting had never actually taken place: it was simply a device to fool the Nazi government further.

In early March, Otto was devastated by the news that his cousin Jean-Michel Frank had committed suicide. Jean-Michel fled Paris in the winter of 1940, having heard "accounts from refugees in Paris about the persecution of homosexuals and Jews." He emigrated to Buenos Aires, where he made a deep impression upon the director of the Museum of Decorative Arts and gained "a whole circle of rich clients."[49] He moved on to New York, where he gave lectures at the School of Fine and Applied Arts and was feted by society. Then, on March 8, 1941, in imitation of his father's own suicide, he threw himself from the window of his Manhattan apartment. He was forty-six years old. His friend Jean Cocteau mourned: "His death was the prologue of the play, the final curtain run down between a world of light and a world of darkness."[50]

■

THE MEASURES AGAINST THE JEWS IN THE Netherlands were slow to surface at first—a deliberate tactic on the part of the occupying forces—but gradually law upon law was implemented, each new one worse than the last. In time, they were all issued through the Jewish weekly newspaper, the *Joodse Weekblad*. The Germans appealed to the Amsterdam Bevolkingsregister for a map showing where Jews lived and how many of them there were ("one dot = ten Jews"). From October 1940, no one was allowed on the streets between midnight and four o'clock in the morning. There was no travel beyond the Dutch border, and various goods became impossible to find. The Dutch government in exile, headed by Professor Pieter Gerbrandy, and the royal family in exile began making wireless broadcasts; together with the speeches of Britain's prime minister Winston Churchill, these helped maintain morale among the anti-German Dutch.

On February 11 and 12, 1941, fights broke out between Nazis and Jews at the markets on Waterlooplein and Amstelveld. Hendrik Koot, a member of the WA, was fatally injured, and Höhere SS und Polizeiführer (Higher SS and Police Leader) Hans Rauter ordered the Jewish quarter to be closed off. The Joodse Raad voor Amsterdam (Jewish Council for Amsterdam) was established in February 1941 and headed by Abraham Asscher and David Cohen; it served as liaison with the German authorities, kept order in the area, and passed on the discriminatory decrees to the Jewish community. Much has been written about the Joodse Raad, which was both instrument and victim. The council cooperated with the Germans but did so in the belief that resistance would only lead to further problems and violence. Hendrik Koot died three days after the market riots. *Volk en Vaderland*, the Dutch Nazi weekly newspaper, reacted to his death: "Judah has dropped its mask at last. Murdered? No, cut down with sadistic lust. Crushed under the heel by a nomadic race of alien blood."[51] On February 17, 1941, Koot's funeral took place in Amsterdam's Zorgvlied cemetery. In the photograph of the ceremony that appeared in *De Telegraaf* the following day, a young man appears, prominent in a white raincoat and standing next to Mussert, the leader of the NSB: Tonny Ahlers. Koot's funeral was filmed to be shown at NSB gatherings, and Ahlers can be seen in the first few grainy shots, holding his camera and leaning over the railings of an old canal house, trying to get the best shots of the hearse. His swastika armband is clearly visible.[52]

Ahlers was present, too, at another landmark event in the history of the German occupation of the Netherlands. Koco was a popular café in Amsterdam-Zuid run by two German Jewish refugees, Ernst Kohn and A. Cahn. After several confrontations with the Nazis, some of the customers handed the owners a number of crudely made weapons, including a flask of ammonia, which hung on a wall in the café. On February 19, 1941, members of the Grüne Polizei[53] and the NSB—among them Tonny Ahlers—entered the café. They were attacked and sprayed with ammonia but recovered quickly enough to start shooting. The owners, together with the customers present, were arrested. Cahn was tortured and killed by a firing squad; he became the first person to be executed during the occupation. The Koco affair led to further reprisals: "The Germans had only been waiting for a pretext and now they had it. On February 22 and 23, they descended on the Jewish quarter en masse." What followed were scenes of absolute horror as 425 Jewish men and boys were dragged from their homes and from the streets, steered under blows onto the Jonas Daniel Meijerplein square, and then sent, beaten and bloody, to the concentration camps of Buchenwald and Mauthausen. The Dutch protested against these events with a strike, mainly organized by the Communist Party, on February 25. In Amsterdam, Hilversum, and Zaandam, everything came to a standstill for three days, until martial law and the threat of severe punishment brought the action to an end.

During the strike, Ahlers and his friend Peters used their knowledge of the city and its inhabitants to help the WA root out and arrest those involved. Ahlers also began working at the Fokker factory as an inspector. The job was given to him by Untersturmführer Kurt Döring of the SD, who employed him as an informant, with special instructions to watch out for Communists working at the factory. Döring recalled: "When I was sent to Amsterdam in 1940 Ahlers was already a regular visitor to the SD office on the Herengracht. Originally he was not in the active service of the SD but he kept pressing me for active employment."[54] Apart from his work at Fokker, Ahlers had a profitable sideline photographing fights that broke out between Nazis and Jews and selling the pictures to the SS; postwar witnesses claimed that he often started the fights so that he could then take photographs. According to his brother Cas, Tonny Ahlers often turned up at Café Heck to harass the Jewish clientele who liked to drink coffee there with friends. Ahlers was incensed by the presence of these particular customers, whom he claimed only ever bought one coffee and made it last all day ("typical Jewish behavior," he told his family); he would upset the tables and throw the coffee cups to the ground. Ahlers was also involved in a riot that broke out on the Thorbeckeplein, very close to Rembrandtplein. Members of the NSB began hurling chairs through the windows of the Jewish-owned Café Alcazar on the square. Ahlers captured these disturbing images on film and took part in the violence himself. His family dismissed this incident as more evidence of "Tonny's troublemaking."[55] Ahlers was then still living in a small room on the Haarlemmerweg, but his landlady hoped to get rid of him: "Ahlers was definitely pro-German. I did not completely trust him, and when I glanced into one of his cupboards, I saw a uniform hanging in there with the insignia of the SS. He also had a flag with the swastika upon it in his room."[56] When Ahlers bragged to her about the work he was doing for the SD, she gave him notice to leave her house.

Around that time, Ahlers came into contact with Josef van Poppel, a Dutchman who worked for the Reichssicherheitshauptamt (RSHA), or the Reich Security Main Office, in Berlin, which controlled intelligence, security, and criminal police work, and the Abwehr, the Wehrmacht counterintelligence organization in Scheveningen. Van Poppel published the anti-Semitic weekly *Doodsklok* and in one issue ridiculed the father of Otto's closest friend, Nathan Straus. He and Ahlers met through their local NSNAP group. Van Poppel had already heard of Ahlers: "I knew that Ahlers was working for the SD. The German Döring was his direct superior. In those days there was a Café Trip on Rembrandtplein owned by the former *souteneur* van den Brink. He had his own SD." Ahlers worked for van den Brink and told van Poppel that one of his tasks was to convince young men to join anti-German groups and then inform the SD. Van Poppel recalled that Ahlers's work as an agent provocateur was well paid: "He operated mainly in cafés such as Ruttens and Heck. For the same purpose, he frequented a café on Kalverstraat. I think it was called the Storchnest. He was quite wealthy then and spent entire days lounging in Café Trip." Eventually, Ahlers became a secret agent himself, working within van Poppel's ring of spies. Van Poppel admitted after the war that Tonny Ahlers was the most anti-Semitic of his men and "had everybody arrested whom he wanted to be arrested, because his superior, Döring, covered him completely."

Van Poppel added one final damning remark in his statements about his former friend's wartime past: "With a lot of Jewish arrests, Ahlers was the instigator."[57]

It was at this point, while Tonny Ahlers was working his way through the Dutch Nazi network and showing his aggression toward Jews at any opportunity, that he and Otto Frank met.

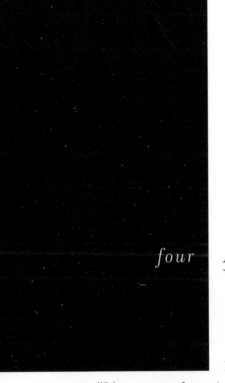

four   A VERY DANGEROUS
YOUNG MAN

IN HER DIARY, ON MAY 7, 1944, ANNE
wrote: "I have never been in such a state as Daddy, who once ran
out onto the street with a knife in his hand to put an end to it all."[1]
The line was from Anne's original version, and Otto edited it out
from the published diary. The date and circumstances of his im-
pulse to commit suicide are not known, but clearly, before the
Frank family went into hiding, Otto was deeply traumatized by
something.

In March and April 1941, catastrophic events occurred in Otto
Frank's life. In a letter sent to Scheveningen's Bureau Nationale
Veiligheid (Bureau of National Security, or BNV) on August 21,
1945, Otto described the crisis:

In March 1941 I was on the Rokin when I met a certain Mr. Jansen,
the husband of one of my demonstrators who worked earlier in my
firm Nederlandse Opekta, 263 Prinsengracht, Amsterdam. The
son of Mr. Jansen also worked in my warehouse. Mr. Jansen
helped to build exhibition stands for my company, and thus the
family was well known to me and of good conduct. In March when

we met, Mr. Jansen and I had a short conversation, and Mr. Jansen asked me if I was still able to get goods from Germany because I was Jewish. I said that I did and that I had no difficulties and after we spoke about other things, Jansen said, "The war will be over soon," to which I answered that I was convinced that it wouldn't, and that the Germans were still having a tough time of it. Then we split up.[2]

Jansen was, of course, Joseph Jansen, the husband of Otto's former sales representative Jetje, with whom Jansen believed Otto had enjoyed an affair. In another account, Otto added, "I did not like him very much."[3] Otto gave several versions of the disturbing incident that followed his conversation with Jansen; most are official declarations given to the Dutch police in the late 1940s, and one is a vague anecdote given to Anne Frank's first biographer, Ernst Schnabel, in 1957. All differ from each other in minor ways, which is understandable given the scale of events unfolding at that time, but all fail, ultimately, to tell the startling story of what really happened.

April 18, 1941, was a quiet day at the Prinsengracht. The doorbell rang, and one of the office staff buzzed it open. There were footsteps on the stairs, and then the visitor appeared at the office window: a good-looking young man, in his early twenties, tall, slender, and dark-haired, with pronounced cheekbones and light-colored, friendly eyes. One of the secretaries asked what they could do for him. "I want to see Otto Frank," he said. When asked what his business was, he answered with a sneer: "I'm a member of the NSB."[4]

In his office on the first floor of the annex, Otto glanced up from his desk as the diamond-patterned double doors opened. The young man entered and closed the doors behind him so that no one else could hear what he was about to say. Then he introduced himself: "Tonny Ahlers."[5]

IN HIS DECLARATION TO THE BNV, OTTO
recounted that Ahlers "asked me if I knew a certain man named
Jansen, to which I answered that there were a lot of Jansens and I
didn't know which one he meant. He showed me a signature on a
letter in which I read, 'Hou-zee, Jansen' ["Hou-zee" was the greeting used by the NSB] and then: 'member 29992.' I recognized the
handwriting and said I knew who it was and asked for the letter to
read. He gave it to me and I read it and saw that it was addressed to
the leaders of the NSB and they had to pass it on to the SS. In this
letter, it was announced that Mr. Jansen had met me, the director
of Opekta, and that I was saying insulting things against the
German Wehrmacht and other accusatory things."[6]

It is at this point that Otto's accounts of the meeting with Ahlers
begin to differ. In his letter to the BNV, Otto writes: "[Ahlers] said
that he was working as a courier between the NSB and the SS and
that he had intercepted the letter. He did not ask for a reward but
anyway I voluntarily gave him ten guilders. I asked him to come
back again . . . he came back, so I gave him another five or ten
guilders."[7] In his 1946 declaration about Jansen, Otto stated something similar, but in 1957 he told Ernst Schnabel that Ahlers had
demanded twenty guilders from him there and then.[8] Otto ends his
letter to the BNV with the statement: "I asked him to come back
again but he made it clear that it was not the money for him [that he
was not doing it for the money], although he didn't earn much."[9]

Given what we already know of Tonny Ahlers's character, several factors here do not make sense: matters become clear only
when we learn what happened after this meeting. Of course, it is
possible that Otto could not recall whether money was demanded
or offered, and how much changed hands, but other questions
need to be asked at this stage. For instance, in his 1945 letter to the
BNV, Otto was able to remember Ahlers's initials, full name, and
address. If they met only on that one occasion (and before Otto's

horrific experiences in the camps), how was Otto able to recall such details? Curiously, Otto could not remember Jansen's forename, despite having known him for a much longer period. In the letter to the BNV, Otto states that Ahlers gave him Jansen's letter, thus saving him from being arrested by the SS, and then walked out of his life forever. This does not have the ring of truth: why would the highly anti-Semitic Ahlers save the Jewish Otto Frank? They did not even know each other. According to both Ahlers and Otto, this was the first time they ever met; presumably, Ahlers only knew of Otto's existence from Jansen's letter, which he had somehow "intercepted."[10]

There are further surprises in Otto's 1945 account: "I didn't know what kind of other things the young man did. But I do remember that he showed me some other letters. One of them was about a maid who wrote that the people for whom she worked listened to the English wireless. I can't remember to whom this letter was addressed."[11] What was Ahlers going to do with these other letters? In this instance, we have the answer. Ahlers's former landlady on the Haarlemmerweg declared in 1946 that her extenant had told her that he was unemployed but receiving benefits. However, one month before Ahlers met Otto Frank, he told his landlady that he had found a job that paid fifty guilders per week: "He said he had to confiscate the wirelesses of people who listened to the forbidden broadcasts from England. He would also receive five guilders' commission for every wireless he handed in."[12] Ahlers was not about to play guardian angel to someone else with the letter he showed to Otto that day. Clearly, he was on his way to seize the wireless from the household whose maid had written to the SS.

The final surprise is this: in all versions of the events of April 18, 1941, Otto remained firm that after one or possibly two encounters with Ahlers, he "did not see or speak to the young man again."[13] But according to Ahlers and other witnesses, that first meeting in Otto's private office was the start of regular visits. Furthermore, Otto's 1945 agenda features the name "Ahlers" on several occasions, and in a letter dated November 27, 1945, Otto writes that he and Ahlers met again that summer.

From all the available documents, it would appear that their purpose was to come to an agreement on their story.

■

WHEN TONNY AHLERS CLOSED THE DOORS to Otto's private office that April day in 1941, he left by the long corridor in which the stairs to the upper floors of the annex were clearly visible. "The Jew Frank," as Ahlers called him, was probably not what Ahlers had expected.[14] In his elegant office on the Prinsengracht, Otto was taller than the younger man, well dressed, courteous, and spoke Dutch in the voice of a wealthy and educated German. Ahlers, always on the lookout for an easy means of making money and with a need to dominate people, knew an opportunity when he saw one.

Initially, Ahlers received cash from Otto Frank in return for his silence over Jansen's letter.[15] Even though he apparently allowed Otto to keep the letter, he knew what it contained and could have used that information against Otto at any point. By Ahlers's own admission, after that first meeting, he began to watch Otto Frank and took a keen interest in his business affairs. He soon discovered, for instance, that Otto was delivering to the Wehrmacht (German army). In a 1966 letter, Ahlers writes that Otto was "selling Pectin products to the German-Wehrmacht. . . . He had no problems in getting his raw materials. In my opinion Frank got his raw materials straight from Berlin . . . he felt completely sure and safe in the situation [that the materials would keep coming]. The only way he could feel safe, surely, is because he was delivering to the Wehrmacht."[16] On this issue, Ahlers was correct. One such order for the German army in the Pectacon delivery book reads:

"5 June 1940. Sold to the Sunda Company, The Hague, by order of the Armee Oberkommando, Berlin. Various goods. 5 June 1940. From the Sunda Company, The Hague. Bought. By order of the Armee Oberkommando, Berlin. The buyer safeguards the seller against all objections, by whatever authority, which might endanger the execution of this contract."[17] The deliveries to the Wehrmacht (via brokers) ensured the survival of Otto's business. More than 80 percent of Dutch firms delivered to the Wehrmacht during the war, and one can hardly be shocked by the statistics or the fact that Otto did the same; the Nazis were in supreme control of the country, and it would have been almost impossible to avoid this sort of contact. Refusal to do so would have resulted in disaster for Otto Frank; merely speaking ill of the Germans could result in arrest, as he was aware.

In an unpublished interview with the Netherlands Institute for War Documentation (NIOD), Miep Gies admitted that during the war they had sold to the Wehrmacht and that a "trusted Wehrmacht cook" came into the business with Kleiman.[18] On the author's behalf, a close friend of the Gies family asked Miep about these transactions: "With no hesitation, she said: yes, there were deliveries. The agreements were made by Kleiman, and with this, the circumstances of the company in wartime should be kept in mind. There was no choice—no delivery could mean the closing down of the company."[19] In another unpublished interview with the Dutch authorities in 1964, Otto acknowledged that his company had done business with the German occupying forces,[20] and a 1948 letter written by the former warehouseman at 263 Prinsengracht during the war divulges: "The company supplied a lot of goods to the Wehrmacht during the occupation, by way of brokers." One of these was "Mr. van Keulen from Haarlem, a supplier of canned goods and buyer of goods for the Germans. . . . A lot of people visited the business, among others van Keulen."[21] Miep Gies later insisted that she had never heard of him, but in fact, van Keulen *was* one of the buyers and suppliers to the business during the war, and sometime after the liberation, Otto called upon him in Haarlem, for reasons unknown.[22] In his 1966 letter, Ahlers continues: "This pectin was a conserve product which was used in the German war industry. There were many other Dutch businesses doing this as well."[23] Pectin was a preservative that could be put to many uses, depending upon the type of pectin it was. All pectin was useful for food production, but certain kinds could be applied as a balm for wounds and as a thickener for raising blood volume in blood transfusions. Other types of pectin were used in the steel industry as a hardener and in the oil industry as an emulsifier. Therefore, it is possible that the Wehrmacht used the pectin they bought from Otto Frank's company for the war industry, but it is highly unlikely that even if this was the case, Otto would have known for what purpose the supplies were intended.

Ahlers clearly knew a great deal about Otto's business affairs, and for one very good reason: Ahlers himself was involved in these transactions. Two and a half months into his work at the Fokker factory in Amsterdam-North, Ahlers was fired for undisclosed reasons.[24] He then established his own company, Petoma, in the spring of 1942 to manufacture surrogates. It was based on the Jan van Galenstraat, a few minutes' walk from the Prinsengracht.[25] The business proved a success, which was fortunate for Ahlers, since by then he had responsibilities. In early 1941, he had met a Dutch girl named Martha, who was four years younger than he was, at a dance.[26] They began dating, and in June she told him she was pregnant. Martha still lived with her parents at the time, but the morning after she had confided in them that she was expecting a baby, she got up to find two suitcases waiting for her at the foot of the stairs. Her mother told her, "Your cases are packed, now get out. You've brought shame on the family."[27] Martha and Tonny were married on July 23, 1941, and their son was born the following year. Their relationship was tempestuous and violent from the start, but she loved him; having never traveled anywhere, Martha felt that her husband was a man of the world and looked up to him because of that.[28]

In an interview with the author, Martha confirmed that her husband and Otto Frank "did business together. My husband had his own company during the war and Otto Frank made deliveries to him."[29] Other family members confirm this. Ahlers's son remembers his father explaining that pectin was sold in bottles, but during the war they sometimes had to use special paper, "the type that holds in water. My father sold this paper to Otto Frank, and he got a nice profit from it because he got the price of the contents along with their packaging."[30] Tonny Ahlers's brother Cas learned only after the war that there had been a relationship between Tonny and Otto Frank: "But it was not a friendship, no. Tonny always referred to it as business, plain and simple."[31] Questioned by a family friend about the matter, Miep Gies said she did not have any contact with Otto's business associates, but she admitted it was very possible that one of their clients was Ahlers, if the transactions were for surrogates—and Petoma was a company dealing in surrogates.[32]

The arrangement between Otto and Ahlers must have begun before the hiding period, but how long it lasted is not clear. In 1943 (when the Franks were already in hiding), Ahlers began a second company, PTM, which was a buying agency for the Wehrmacht; Ahlers acted as a broker for the German army, buying goods from various companies and selling them on. He also manufactured products for the Wehrmacht. The head of another business that worked with Ahlers's company declared, "My goal was to become a supplier for the Wehrmacht, with all the attendant advantages like Arbeitseinsatz, allocation of raw materials, etc."[33] In the same way, through his association with the Wehrmacht, Otto was able to receive commodities for longer than usual, and then good-quality substitutes. At the offices on the Prinsengracht, "a marked business revival" took place after the occupation.[34]

Otto Frank had made a pact with the devil, but the price can scarcely be imagined. In working with the enemy, Otto hoped to protect not only his company but also himself and his family, for by then most Jewish people realized something of the immense danger that faced them. Throughout the war years, Otto was to all intents and purposes leading a double life. It was not just the business associations but the ever-present specter of Ahlers that haunted him—a man less than half his age who had saved his life but whose hold over him was profound; Jansen's terrible letter ensured that Otto remained in Ahlers's debt. Ten years after the end of the war, in an unrelated matter. Otto wrote to his lawyer Myer Mermin that "no good comes from giving way to blackmail."[35] Mermin could not have guessed the depth to which Otto knew it to be true.

■

ACCORDING TO OTTO'S 1946 DECLARATION, when Tonny Ahlers left his office on April 18, 1941, Otto showed Jansen's accusatory letter to Kugler and Miep. They were horrified; Miep already knew about the meeting with Jansen and after the war told police investigating the matter: "Mr. Frank read me [Jansen's] letter and I still remember that the letter said that the Jew Frank was still tied to his company and had expressed himself in an anti-German fashion during a conversation. I cannot say for sure who signed the letter in question, but I deduced from its content that it had been written by the Jansen I knew."[36] Kugler added in his statement to the police, "As far as I can tell, there was not a single motive for Jansen wanting to expose Mr. Frank to prosecution."[37] After the war, it became clear that Jansen had done so in revenge for the affair he imagined Otto had had with his wife, Jetje.

Otto told two other people about the letter: his friend Gerard Oeverhaus, a Dutch detective with the Aliens Police who understood Otto's anger about the anti-Jewish legislation, and his lawyer, Anton Dunselman, who had been involved in Otto's businesses since the 1920s. Dunselman read the letter at his office on the Keizersgracht, took some notes from it, and locked it away. He later destroyed it, fearing that his own safety would be in danger "during a possible arrest of Mr. Frank."[38] Otto said nothing about the letter at home: "I did not want to tell my wife about the incident and frighten her. Because of Jansen's letter, I was afraid for months that if I met him in the street, Jansen would file a new complaint against me."[39] The damage Jansen wanted to inflict upon Otto had not been stopped, however; it had merely been diverted.[40]

■

TONNY AHLERS'S APPEARANCE AT OTTO'S office had another consequence: shortly after his first meeting with Ahlers, Otto decided he needed to prepare a place for himself and his family to hide. Danger was too close. Jan Gies recalled: "The initiative to go into hiding, to find a hiding place, to organize everything for it, came from Otto Frank. He had thought it all out . . . and he had already divided certain different tasks for his staff members when he asked them to help him and his family."[41] Kleiman was the first to be taken into Otto's confidence. Otto then approached Kugler, Miep, Jan, and Bep to ask whether they would "be willing to take full responsibility for everything connected with our hiding."[42] When they answered yes, Otto told them what he would require from each of them. Questioned recently as to whether she had understood the extent of those responsibilities, Miep replied: "The shopping, yes. I did not ask any further. At that time you did not ask questions. You would not ask so many things. You just did what was asked of you and nothing more." Miep and Bep viewed it as an extension to their work: "We were the office ladies. We would get instructions, and we understood very well that that was the way it should be. There was no other way. We did not feel wronged or restricted by that. . . . That was normal, wasn't it? It was just the same as work."[43] To refuse would have been unthinkable in that context. Kugler felt no different: "I didn't think about the dangers it would have for me. . . . We knew that if we didn't hide them, it would be like committing them to death. So we had very little choice."[44]

Hermann van Pels was brought into the discussions between Kleiman and Otto, and he and his family were invited to share the Franks' ill-fated hiding place, rather than the Goslars, who had a baby and were expecting a third child. Otto quickly realized "that the best solution would be to hide in the annex of our office, 263 Prinsengracht."[45] There was one problem: Otto allowed his friend, the pharmacist Arthur Levinson, to prepare ointments and perform experiments in the annex. Levinson was told that those quarters were now required by the business for storage, and he was given the office kitchen for use as a laboratory instead. An employee of Kleiman's brother (who was also informed about the plan to hide) cleared and cleaned the annex. Then, using the subterfuge of requiring specialist cleaning or repair, large items of furniture were taken to Kleiman's home, where they were picked up in his brother's van and ferried to the annex. Dried and canned food, linen, clothing, and utensils were easy to move without suspicion over a long period. The preparations to turn the annex into a relatively comfortable hiding place were always made after office hours or on the weekend. As a future precaution, the windows of the front house facing the annex were painted blue, and those in the connecting corridor were pasted over with semitransparent paper. Such caution was essential to prevent outsiders from calculating what was happening at 263 Prinsengracht. But without being aware of it, Otto Frank was already under surveillance. In private postwar letters to Silberbauer (the Gestapo officer who arrested the Franks in 1944), Ahlers writes that he had known the truth about the secret annex from the time that the Franks went into hiding there.[46]

■

IN APRIL 1941, GREECE SURRENDERED
to Italy, and Germany took control of Yugoslavia. On June 22,
Hitler's army invaded Russia, prompting Britain to offer aid to the
Russians. As the year wore on, the terrible weather stilled the
German advance and killed thousands of German soldiers.

In May, Pectacon was renamed Gies & Co. There were no further changes to the company, and Otto remained director. On July
16, Miep and Jan Gies were married, although they had been living
together since 1940. Otto and Anne, Kleiman, Kugler, Bep, and
Hermann and Gusti van Pels were among the guests. Margot and
Oma Holländer were unable to attend owing to illness, and Edith
stayed at home to care for them. The sun shone before and after the
ceremony, and a surprise reception, hosted by Otto, was held at the
Prinsengracht offices the next day. Present on both occasions was
an attractive young Jewish woman named Esther, who was then
working for Otto as a secretary. He later had to dismiss her under
new laws regarding Jews in employment. Miep remembers:

> That's the way things were. She did not come back, I think. She did
> not survive the war. . . . She was the only one in the office who was
> Jewish. She said good-bye, and we wished her the best. She stayed
> in Amsterdam, but could not find work anywhere else. . . . It was
> all so painful, you see. You heard about her dismissal [from other
> jobs] but did not talk about it further. You did not know what was
> going to happen. You gave in to that. Had to accept it. The Germans
> were the boss and you were scared—frightened to death.[47]

Otto also employed two men who were members of the NSB.
Miep recalls a conversation she had with Otto about one of them, a
sales rep named Daatselaar: "Mr. Frank had been aware of his
membership in the Dutch Nazi Party before he'd gone into hiding,
because the man had worn his NSB pin on his lapel. I remembered

that Mr. Frank had commented, 'This man you can trust. I know
he's not a Nazi at heart. He must have joined the NSB because he
was hanging around with a bunch of young men who joined. Being
a bachelor and needing a social life, that's why he joined too.' "[48]

Although he trusted Daatselaar, Otto did not tell him about the
hiding plan, but he did use the man as an example to Anne when
she became upset that the mother of one of her friends was a
staunch supporter of the NSB. Otto's close relationship with his
youngest daughter was still strong, despite Anne's early adolescent
rebellion. When she and her friend Sanne Ledermann left
Amsterdam for a holiday with Sanne's aunt in Beekbergen, she
wrote to her father often, addressing him as "My most beloved
Hunny Kungha" (one of several nonsense names Anne used to address her father), and confessed that she missed him terribly and
longed for the day when he, Edith, and Margot would arrive to collect her. The one consolation was the stillness in Beekbergen;
there were no air raids, and Anne told her grandmother in
Switzerland that despite the bad weather, "we sleep a lot better
at night here than in Amsterdam. There's nothing at all to disturb us."[49]

An eruption of new laws passed in 1941 resulted in Jews being
excluded from almost all areas of public entertainment, sport, and
education in the Netherlands. In his memoir, Otto wrote: "When I
think back to the time when a lot of laws were introduced due to the
occupying power, which made our lives much harder, I have to say
that my wife and I did everything we could to stop the children
noticing the trouble we would go to, to make sure this was still a
trouble-free time for them." He recalled how, following the decree
that separated Jewish children from non-Jews in special schools, it
became difficult for his daughters to "keep up their friendships
with non-Jewish children, particularly now that it was also forbidden for Christians to visit Jewish families and vice versa."[50] After
the war, Otto told a friend how Edith protected her children "as the

86 anti-Jewish regulations narrowed their world. . . . She continued to make their friends welcome, to give parties for them. She and Oma Holländer set the children daily examples of generosity and concern for others. When war brought privation to Amsterdam, no poor person who came to their door went away empty-handed. Edith used to send Margot and Anne down the steep stairs with food and gifts, to save the old or enfeebled the difficult climb."[51]

Otto was aware that his youngest daughter was developing more quickly than normal under the new, difficult circumstances: "Through Margot, Anne got to know pupils in the higher classes of the new school. Soon boys started to notice her. She was rather attractive and knew how to use her charms."[52] Anne became fascinated with the subject of sex, something her mother refused to discuss with her. Otto was more open, though he tried to keep information to a minimum, as Anne's best friend at the Jewish Lyceum, Jacqueline van Maarsen, recalls: "She was extremely curious about sexual relations between men and women and pumped her father constantly for information. He invented all sorts of subterfuge, which she then told me and which really made me laugh."[53]

In September, when Otto allowed himself a break from work, it was Anne who accompanied him to a hotel in Arnhem he had booked. Edith, again, stayed at home with her mother and Margot. In a postcard to his own mother in Switzerland, Otto explained: "We're not staying long, I just wanted to have a bit more peace and quiet, but didn't want to go off completely on my own. Anne is always good, dear company and she was able to have a few days off school. Everything is well."[54] Upon his return to work, Otto learned that everything was far from well: Pectacon had been earmarked for liquidation. The BEI had received a German report that accurately described Otto's changes to the business as "intended to create the impression that most of the capital as well as the directorship of the business are in Aryan hands." The report condemned the changes: "They are not approved and therefore have no legal validity." On the basis of these findings, the BEI appointed Karel Wolters, a Nazi-approved lawyer, as "trustee of the company" and charged him with Pectacon's liquidation.[55] On September 22, 1941, Otto Frank and Johannes Kleiman visited Wolters at his offices on Rokin.

Karel Wolters, born in Venlo in 1909, was a successful lawyer and public prosecutor. He joined the NSB in 1933 and during the occupation became a member of the Nazi-affiliated Rechtsfront (Legal Front), the Economisch Front (Economic Front), and the Nederlandsch-Duitsche Kultuurgemeenschap (Dutch-German Cultural Union). Questioned specifically about Pectacon after the war, Wolters replied: "I know that I acted as liquidator of Pectacon, but I cannot remember any more details. Possibly the business was sold through me. I do not know the salary."[56] The documents relating to Wolters's dealings with Otto Frank make for curious reading. It was widely accepted that the men working as Verwalters (in charge of liquidating companies) were mostly crooks, but the statements made about Wolters by the nineteen Jewish businessmen and their personnel who came under his control describe him as protective. His attitude toward Otto was extraordinary: he wanted Pectacon to continue as usual, according to Kleiman's declaration.

Kleiman refused Wolters's suggestion: "We were not in favor, because it was very well possible that a member of the NSB or a German would take charge of the business and that is why I proposed to Wolters to liquidate the business. I asked for a period of eight to ten days' time. Wolters agreed to this. In practice, we were in charge of the liquidation."[57] In his declaration, Otto outlined how they were able "to transfer the entire store of goods and the machinery" to the smokescreen for the business, La Synthèse N.V., which had been renamed Gies & Co.: "I also owned shares in this firm, which I never reported and still own at present. The firm Gies & Co., then registered itself at our address 263 Prinsengracht

88 and Pectacon at Wolters's office, 6 Rokin. The amount of the liquidation was 18,000 guilders, of which as non-Jewish capital an
amount of 5,000 guilders was paid to Kleiman and to Dunselman
3,000 guilders. The remaining amount of 10,000 guilders (minus
2,300 guilders for the Wirtschaftsprüfstelle) was deposited at the
Lippmann-Rosenthal Bank in Amsterdam."[58] Pectacon's books
from 1940 are missing, but those available reveal irregularities between the entries previous to the invasion and those from the period of liquidation, leading one to speculate that there were
extensive negotiations between Kleiman and Wolters. The German
authorities in charge referred to the proceedings as "very unfavor-
able," having expected to rake in a substantial amount of money
from the liquidation. They described Kleiman's explanation of the
poor revenue from supplies sold "unsatisfactory."[59] Wolters finished his dealings with Pectacon on April 15, 1942. He evidently
did his best, under the circumstances, to help Otto Frank maintain
the company.[60]

Aside from Otto, his staff, and Karel Wolters, one other person
was aware that Gies & Co. was a smokescreen for Pectacon. Tonny
Ahlers sometimes worked as a Verwalter's assistant and learned
through his contacts how Otto had been able to save his business
from German takeover. In his 1966 letter to a Dutch journalist,
Ahlers wrote, "I knew about [Otto Frank's] little game with Gies."[61]
Whether he told Otto that he knew is no longer possible to deter-
mine. What is certain, however, is that this was just the latest frag-
ment in an increasingly dangerous arsenal of knowledge that
Ahlers was building up against Otto Frank.

■

MORE PROBLEMS AROSE AT THE PRINSEN-
gracht offices in October 1941, during the ongoing liquidation of
Pectacon. Otto's brother-in-law Erich Elias was dismissed as
manager of Rovag, the Swiss subsidiary of Pomosin-Werke. The

new manager wanted to know what was happening with the loan Erich had made to Otto in 1933, which provided the capital for Opekta Amsterdam. Otto explained that he had paid back 5,000 guilders of the original 15,000 guilders of the loan and the rest had been taken over by Dunselman, a move approved by two officials at the Pomosin-Werke headquarters in Frankfurt. The Frankfurt officials had written to the BEI, stating that owing to the agreement made in 1933 between Erich and Otto, Pomosin-Werke owned the Opekta-Amsterdam shares. While awaiting the BEI's decision, the Frankfurt officials suggested depositing Otto's shares in the company with a bank often used by German administrators of liquidated Jewish businesses.

Although Otto was worried that Pomosin-Werke might pursue its claim to his business after the war, the actions of the Frankfurt officials helped to save the company. When the BEI decided to "Aryanize" Opekta fully by giving it to one of the company's competitors, the judgment was never executed—presumably because of an appeal by Pomosin. Whatever the reasons behind it, Pomosin's early intervention, together with the help of Dunselman, Kleiman, and Wolters, served to enable Otto to stay in charge of Opekta. Miep recalls how this worked: "Mr. Frank would remain in the capacity of adviser, but in reality would continue to run the business as usual. The only real change would be from the legal standpoint. . . . Mr. Frank came to work every day. He sat at his desk in his private office and made all the decisions and gave all the orders. Nothing changed except when a check had been made out, or a letter had been typed. Mr. Frank would then pass whatever it was that needed signing over to Kleiman or Kugler for a totally Christian signature."[62]

Given all the business problems Otto was encountering at that time, it was hardly unexpected when Anne wrote to her relatives in Basel that her father was not well and suffering "rheumatism in his back." He remained the same as ever at work, Miep remembers:

90 "He was always himself, never missed work, never complained, and kept his private life at home."[63] Matters only worsened in November when, along with all German Jews in occupied territories, the Franks lost their German citizenship and had to report to the Zentralstelle für Jüdische Auswanderung (Central Agency for Jewish Emigration) with a list of their possessions. Otto recalled: "We tried our best to keep these things from obtruding on the children. . . . The children were scarcely aware of it when we had to register. I went alone. The Dutch official who was in charge of the list did not say a word when he saw me."[64] On December 5, all non-Dutch Jews had to register with the Zentralstelle for "voluntary emigration."

On December 11, 1941, following the bombing of Pearl Harbor by the Japanese, the United States entered the war. For many of Europe's Jews, having the United States fighting against Germany provided a glimmer of hope in a distressing year, but for others it meant that their one possible means of escape had now been closed to them.

■

ON JANUARY 29, 1942, AFTER MONTHS of pain and an operation in late 1941, Rosa Holländer died of cancer. Otto and Edith had decided not to tell Anne that her grandmother was fatally ill, and she was deeply upset by her death. She writes about Oma Holländer from time to time in her diary and confides to "Kitty": "No one will ever know how much she is in my thoughts and how much I love her still."[65] Rosa's death was announced in the pages of the *Joodse Weekblad*, and she was buried in the Jewish cemetery, Gan Hashalom, in Hoofddorp, just outside Amsterdam.

Edith's sorrow was aggravated by the distance between herself and her brothers. There had been no postal service to Europe from the United States since Pearl Harbor, and Edith's only contact with Julius and Walter was through her mother-in-law in Switzerland.

On April 12, Alice Frank sent Otto and Edith a food parcel and a letter explaining the situation: "Julius is longing for news, which I can very well understand. I write to him as often as possible and hope for an answer, but you have to be very patient."[66] Although Switzerland was able to retain its neutrality, there were plenty of Nazi sympathizers in the country, and as a result, Erich Elias lost his job. On April 27, Erich was ordered by the German consulate in Basel to hand in his passport after being deprived of his German citizenship. His son Buddy remembers entering the consulate with him that day. Erich, dressed in his best suit and hat, stalked furiously up to the desk, where he flung his passport at the bewildered official without a word before marching out again.

On June 2, 1942, together with the rest of the family in Amsterdam, Otto wrote to congratulate Buddy on his seventeenth birthday. His letter was distinctly melancholy: "We can see from our children how time has gone by and sometimes I feel more like a grandfather when I think of my grown-up daughters. Well, let's hope that we will be able to see each other again soon, peacetime must come again, after all."[67] Ten days later, on June 12, Anne celebrated her thirteenth birthday. Among the gifts from her parents was the diary she had chosen from the local bookstore a few days before. Around this time, Otto told his daughters that preparations had been made for them to go into hiding, and he tried to soften the blow by reassuring Anne, "Don't you worry about it, we shall arrange everything. Make the most of your carefree young life while you can."[68]

Otto's plans to go into hiding could not have been more timely. Although concentration camps had been in existence since 1933, for years they were not used specifically for systematic murder, although inmates died frequently from their mistreatment. The plot to destroy the Jews of Europe in a new network of concentration camps was finalized at the Wannsee Conference in Berlin in January 1942. Adolf Eichmann, as head of Section IVB4 in Berlin,

92   led the operation. By then the camp—whether concentration camp, work camp, transit camp, or ghetto—had become part of life in occupied territory. Poland was transformed "into a vast slave plantation"[69] with almost six thousand camps spread across it. In Germany, the camps were more visible and more numerous yet. In the region of Hessen alone, over six hundred camps existed, and Berlin had a similar number for forced labor.

In preparation for the deportations from the Netherlands, the German administration had taken over Westerbork refugee camp, surrounding it with barbed wire and installing armed SS men throughout. Westerbork was eventually used as a holding camp for Jews awaiting deportation from the Netherlands, and it became, as Abel Herzberg wrote,

> another word for purgatory. There was nothing to sustain one, materially or spiritually. Each was thrown on his own resources, utterly alone. Desperation, total and absolute, seized everyone. People sought help but seldom found it, and, if they did, knew that it could not possibly prevail. Deportation to Poland might at best be postponed—for a week, perhaps, or for a few weeks at most. Husbands were powerless to protect their wives, parents had to watch helplessly while their children were torn away from them for ever. The sick, the blind, the hurt, the mentally disturbed, pregnant women, the dying, orphans, new-born babies—none was spared on the Tuesdays when the cattle-trucks were being loaded with human freight for Poland. Tuesdays, week in, week out, for two interminable years.[70]

In return for exemption from the transports, a number of German Jews remained in charge of the actual administration. This bred resentment among Dutch Jews, who accused them of being better Nazis than the SS.

In Amsterdam, the offices of the Joodse Raad overflowed with people fighting for "Bolle" exemption stamps, which offered, quite literally, a stay of execution. Few of those eligible for the stamps actually received them, and in the end they, too, were deported, first to Westerbork and then on to the concentration camps of Auschwitz or Sobibor. Trains left Westerbork every month between July 1942 and September 1944; passenger numbers peaked in October 1942 (11,965) and in May (8,006) and June 1943 (8,420). Responsibility for the ruthlessly smooth operation of the trains lay with the Reichsbahn, part of the transport ministry, where 500,000 clerical and 900,000 operating staff performed their duties without a word. For the purposes of the Reichsbahn's budget, deported Jews were classified as normal passengers and children under four years of age as traveling free.

The Dutch largely considered the growing rumors about concentration camps unpleasant propaganda: "Dance-halls were full, cinema attendances were higher than ever, the beaches were as popular as always. Sports events in general, soccer in particular, drew large crowds to the stadiums."[71] The official line was that Jews would be sent to work camps, but only the foolish or deluded could have believed that when the deportations began. The Dutch Jewish historian Jacob Presser fumed to a university colleague: "It is not the villain who is our problem, but the 'common man' who demeans himself in the execution of atrocious acts."[72] In full view of the local Dutch population, families wearing the yellow star and carrying rucksacks walked in long rows through Amsterdam's streets, and trams loaded with devastated Jews trundled along to Muiderpoort Station and Centraal Station.

The Netherlands has the worst record of Jewish deaths during the Holocaust in Western Europe. In Belgium, 60 percent of Jews survived; in France, 75 percent. In the Netherlands, only 25 percent of Jews survived. What explanation can be given? There are several possible reasons.

By the 1930s, Dutch Jews were fully integrated into Dutch

94   society, unlike Eastern European Jews, who were familiar with pogroms and aggressive anti-Semitism. The German administration of the Netherlands was largely Austrian, and this may have made for easier working relationships with the authorities (mostly Austrian themselves) in Berlin. The geography of the Netherlands did little to help the Jews, since there were few natural hiding places and little chance of escape over the borders, which led into occupied territory, or the North Sea. Furthermore, unlike France and Belgium, where the trains came to a halt, more or less, between March and July 1943, the deportations from the Netherlands ran continuously. Most damaging of all was Dutch bureaucracy, which fully and efficiently registered Jews and non-Jews, thus equipping the Germans with valuable information. There were never more than two hundred German policemen operating in Amsterdam, but the occupying forces were able to perform their duties without wide-scale interference. The Dutch underground press gave relatively little coverage to the plight of the Jews; the newspaper *Vrij Nederland* admitted: "Unnoticed, the poison of propaganda has affected us, and its after-effects will be felt for a long time, especially in our children, who have been used to it and do not know any better. For them, being a Jew means being a constant exception."[73]

On July 4, Otto Frank wrote to his family in Switzerland. His letter hints that they would soon go into hiding: "Everything is fine here too, although we all know that day by day, life is getting harder. Please don't be in any way concerned, even if you hear little from us. When I'm not at the office there's still a lot to do and a lot to think about, and one has to come to terms with decisions that are very difficult to take on board. . . . We haven't forgotten you and know that you're thinking of us constantly, but you can't change anything and you know you have to look after yourselves."[74] A brief letter written for Julius and Walter, but sent to Otto's mother, implies again that the disappearance was about to take

place: "Everything is difficult for us these days, but we have to take
things as they come. I hope peace will come this year and that we
will be able to see each other once again. I regret that we're unable
to correspond with I [Alice] and her family but there's nothing we
can do. I'm sure she will understand."[75]

Ultimately, the Franks did not go into hiding on the date they
had intended. On Sunday, July 5, 1942, sixteen-year-old Margot
Frank was ordered to report to the SS for deportation to a German
labor camp.

five OUT OF SIGHT

MARGOT FRANK WAS AMONG THOUSANDS
of young German Jews targeted by the Nazis in the first weekend of
July 1942 to be deported from the Netherlands. The aim was to
send four thousand Jews to "Germany" during three days in mid-
July. The lists of deportees were drawn up by the Zentralstelle für
Jüdische Auswanderung. Among the Dutch staff there was Tonny
Ahlers's best friend, Peters, and Ahlers himself was a frequent vis-
itor to the Zentralstelle.

Margot's friend Laureen Nussbaum recalls:

It was agony. Some of my friends wanted to go when the call-up
came because they did not expect anything too bad, but their parents begged them to stay and hide, while the parents of other
friends made them obey the call-up in order to save the rest of the
family. My sister Susi was also sent a card, but my mother discovered a loophole in the law, which saved her. That period was hell.
It was the beginning of summer vacation, and when we went back
to school, hardly anyone was left. I became one of six in a class; my
sister was the only child in her class. The teachers were allowed to
remain until all the students were gone. They watched with in-

creasing apprehension, how the classes dwindled by the day, but
they did not desert their posts. Eventually, they, too, were deported to the death camps.[1]

In her diary, Anne described the emotional events of July 5: the
shock, the fear, and the panic. The decision to go into hiding the
following day was taken immediately. Otto recalled: "It was said
that life in the camps, even in the camps in Poland, was not so bad;
that the work was hard but there was food enough, and the persecutions stopped, which was the main thing. I told a great many
people what I suspected. I also told them what I had heard on the
British wireless, but a good many still thought these were atrocity
stories."[2] By evening, all those who had pledged to help the Franks,
together with the van Pels family, were aware that the building on
the Prinsengracht was about to hold a perilous secret. Otto sent a
final coded postcard to Switzerland, wishing his sister a happy
birthday months in advance: "We wanted to be sure that you received our thoughts for you on the right day, as later we'll have no
opportunity. We wish you all the best from the bottom of our
hearts. We are well and together, that's the main thing. Everything
is difficult these days, but you just have to take some things with a
pinch of salt. I hope we'll find peace this year already so that we can
see each other again. It's a pity that we can no longer correspond
with you, but that's how it is. You must understand. As always, I
send you all my best wishes, Otto."[3]

Following the first deportation from the Netherlands, a Dutch
protest leaflet was circulated that issued an eerily prophetic
warning:

During the night of July 15, 1942, around 1:50 A.M., the first group
[of called-up Jews] had to report at Amsterdam's Centraal Station.
Thereafter, every day 1,200 Jews will have to do likewise. From
Westerbork in Drenthe where the unfortunate people are being
screened, approximately 4,000 Jews altogether are being de-

98 ported each time. The trains for this purpose stand ready. Specialists from Prague well versed as executioners have gone there in order to expedite the deportations as much as possible. In this manner, a total of approximately 120,000 Jewish Dutch citizens will be taken away.

Such are the sober facts. They compare in brutality and matter-of-factness only with the instructions of the Egyptian Pharaoh who had all Jewish male children killed, and with Herod, that anti-Semite who had all infants in Bethlehem killed in order to kill Jesus. Now, several thousand years later, Hitler and his henchmen have found their place in this company. Official Polish reports name the figure of 700,000 Jews who have already perished in the clutches of the Germans. Our Jewish fellow citizens will suffer a like fate. . . . We are dealing with the realization of threats which the Nazis have hurled at the Jews again and again—their destruction and annihilation.

The Dutch people have taken note of the anti-Jewish measure with disgust and outrage. To be sure, our people must pay heavily for the fact that they did not refuse to sign the Declaration on Jews so ingenuously presented to them. It is our joint guilt—that of the Jewish Council not excepted—that our enemies now dispose of a complete Jewish administration.

All prior German measures had aimed at isolating the Jews from the rest of the Dutch, to make contact impossible, and to kill our sentiments concerning living side by side and in solidarity. They have succeeded much better than we know ourselves or are probably willing to admit. The Jews have to be killed in secrecy and we, the witnesses, must remain deaf, blind, and silent. . . . God and history will condemn us and hold us partly responsible for this mass murder if we now remain silent and simply look on. . . .[4]

The Frank family entered their hiding place on July 6, 1942; they were joined by Hermann, Gusti, and Peter van Pels on July 13,

1942, and on November 16, after having asked Miep if she knew of "somewhere safe," Fritz Pfeffer arrived. For two years, eight people lived in the strict confinement of five rooms, remaining behind the gray door of the annex (concealed by a movable bookcase) exclusively through the day and going only as far as the offices at night. Apart from their protective friends, no one was supposed to know they were there. Neighbors from the Merwedeplein believed a story begun by a letter deliberately left behind by Otto to put people off the track; they thought the Franks had escaped to Switzerland, helped by Otto's old army friend Crampe. Otto's family in Switzerland, who believed they had gone into hiding but did not know where they were, began to realize that they were safe through hints dropped by Kleiman in letters to Erich Elias.

The survival of the eight in hiding was dependent upon observing a set of rules regarding security and retaining their sanity and a belief that they would eventually regain their freedom, but most of all, it was dependent upon their helpers. Miep and Jan, Bep and her father, Kleiman and his wife, Johanna, and Kugler (who did not tell his wife the secret) provided them with food and the necessary articles of day-to-day living, kept up their spirits, and protected them in every sense. In a letter to Israel's Holocaust museum Yad Vashem, Otto described their duties:

> Miep and Bep had the extremely difficult task to provide food. To nourish eight people while most of the food-stuff was rationed, was a hard job. They had to buy in different shops, so that it would not raise suspicion if they bought big quantities in one. Mr. Gies and Mr. Kleiman bought ration cards on the black market for us, and after some time we became short of money, they sold parts of our jewelry. Besides Mr. Kugler sold spices without booking sales to help finance our needs. All these activities were risky and they always had to be careful not to be trapped by German collaborators or agents provocateurs. Apart from food there were lots of other

items which we needed in the course of the twenty-five months of our hiding, such as toilet-articles, medicine, clothes for the growing children, etc., as well as books and other materials to keep us busy.[5]

Miep later admitted that she almost enjoyed the challenge of shopping for her hidden friends: "I would go to all the shops, and I would try things out a little with the man in the shop. How far I could go, how much I could ask, to what extent I could pretend to be in such a terrible situation. Yes, that was like playing in a theater."[6] Miep purchased meat from a friend of van Pels who had a butcher's shop on Rozengracht and groceries from a shop on nearby Leliegracht. The latter was run by Hendrik van Hoeve, a resistance worker who was himself hiding a Jewish couple in his home. Kleiman's friend Siemons, who had a bakery on the Raamgracht, provided them with bread. Bep was responsible for setting aside bottles of milk from the office staff's allowance, and Jan Gies bought ration cards through the National Relief Fund, a resistance group. As time wore on, the advantage of having hoarded dried and canned food in the attic of the annex became increasingly clear.

The helpers' aid went beyond such practicalities, however. In his memoir, Otto explained: "Nobody could imagine what it meant for us that my four employees proved to be sacrificial helpers and genuine friends in a time when bad powers had the upper hand. They demonstrated a true example of humane cooperation, while taking a huge personal risk in looking after us. As time went by, this became more and more difficult. Their daily visits above gave us an enormous lift."[7] In a radio interview granted after the war, Kleiman said: "The reason I offered to help Otto Frank and his family during the hiding period is because I knew him as a sincere businessman and a very decent and helpful person, qualities for which he is generally respected."[8] Kugler's attitude was much the same: "What else could I do? I had to help them; they were my friends. Life changed completely for the people in hiding. They had to remain completely silent, especially during the day. But it was also a tense and frightening time for us, the helpers. Our greatest fear was that the hiding place would be discovered. I had to put on an act for Otto Frank's former business associates, for clients, and for the neighbors."[9]

It was difficult for the helpers to keep their double lives a secret. Willy Voskuijl, one of Bep Voskuijl's sisters, recalled: "We knew nothing about the Frank family being in hiding. What we did notice is that after dinner Bep and father often sat together talking very quietly."[10] In a rare interview, Bep spoke about the people in hiding: "I ate dinner with the Franks every night. . . . Once I stayed and slept in the secret annex. Honestly speaking, I was terribly frightened. When I heard a tree creaking or when a car drove along the canal, I became frightened. I was thankful when morning came and I could once again just return to my work. I can still see Anne crouching under my desk trying to get a glimpse of the outside world, the street, the canal. Naturally we had to be careful because nobody was supposed to know that there were other people in this building besides the group of us in the office."[11] Jan recalled: "People who looked after those in hiding also had a particular kind of life. They might have become somewhat withdrawn. They weren't as free to express themselves. . . . Because it is actually a terrible life in such a small community. Having to be silent about those things, and cope with them, and keep everyone at arm's length—while acting as if everything is normal."[12] In contrast to her reply about the dismissal of her Jewish coworker Esther, Miep said she had no fear when taking the risk of hiding the Franks and their friends: "That was not a word in our vocabulary: scared. Especially not at first, in the beginning. Yes, later, you were worried sometimes. You would think. 'How can this go on?' . . . But the care for these people—and really, the compassion for what these people went through—that was stronger. That won out."[13]

The need to go into hiding changed the balance of the relationship between Miep and Otto. Miep remembers: "He didn't like that, because after all he was the director, and in normal life whatever he said would happen. But now he depended upon us. Well, just imagine the situation. That change. He had to wait to see whether we agreed with everything, whether we approved, whether we did everything according to his requests." Miep and Jan also had a non-Jewish fugitive hidden in their home, something they deliberately did not tell Otto. Miep explains why: "Otto would never have approved of that. I know just what he would have said, 'Miep, if anything happens to you. . . .' We lived in separate worlds, also toward our friends. They knew nothing about it. That was the rule: don't tell."[14] Jan confirmed: "We knew, for example, those people on the other side of the street, they are good. Why? That is hard for us to say. You see things . . . you hear things. You hear people talking, and this is how you figure out the value of certain individuals. It's not a 100 percent rule but in general it worked for me. I was lucky."[15]

Since the helpers were also Otto's employees, they kept the firms running on his behalf, and Kleiman and Kugler discussed business with him every day. There were some difficulties arising from Kugler's new responsibilities; Anne wrote of van Pels working himself "into a rage again because of some blunder on Mr. Kugler's part," and on October 20, 1942, she recorded: "A big row here . . . Mr. van Pels and Pim were so angry that both of them slept badly. Kugler is really being silly. Now he wants to employ a girl but obviously he can't for our sake and for his own as well."[16] Nonetheless, Kugler used money from the business to aid those in hiding. After the invasion of 1940, Otto and Kleiman had purchased the apparatus with which to make substitute spices, since goods from the Netherlands East Indies were no longer available owing to the worldwide conflict. There was demand enough for the products manufactured by Otto's business, and Gies & Co. showed a small profit during the war. Opekta was left alone by the Germans: on July 1, 1944, the BEI informed the company that they had approved the resignation of the "Jewish director Otto Frank" and that "Jews no longer exert any personal or financial influence" on the company.[17]

The eight in hiding were not ignorant about the fate of the Netherlands' Jews. They had a radio, which they listened to daily, and heard reports from England that Jews were being "regularly killed by machine-gun fire, hand-grenades—and even poisoned by gas."[18] Although the news disturbed them deeply, they continued to listen to the broadcasts, for, as Otto later wrote, "through the wireless we could feel connected with the outside world."[19]

The news and their own confinement took a toll on each of them. There were frequent arguments, as each of them despaired and grew depressed, retreated, and lost faith in the future at some point. Yet there was also humor during the hiding period, a strong sense of community, and celebrations of birthdays and holidays. Otto quickly realized that boredom would be among the worst of their personal demons: "Only with a certain time allocation laid down from the start and with each one having his own duties, could we have hoped to live through the situation. Above all the children had to have enough books to read and to learn. None of us wanted to think how long this voluntary imprisonment would last."[20] Through the day, they followed a timetable of reading, writing, and studying languages. In the evening, when absolute silence was no longer a necessity, they listened to classical music on the radio, played board games, recited poetry, and discussed politics. They were all enthusiastic readers, and in the evening Otto read aloud to his family from the favorites of his youth: Heine, Goethe, Schiller, and Körner. Religion was also a part of their lives in hiding: on Friday nights, they observed the Sabbath, led by Edith Frank and

104   Fritz Pfeffer, and they cooked from Jewish recipes and honored the High Holy Days. They also celebrated Christmas, but from Anne's diary it appears that the festivities included no actual religious feeling but were simply a means of having fun.

After the war, Otto revealed how they kept up their spirits: "I remember to have once read a sentence: 'If the end of the world would be imminent, I still would plant a tree today.' When we lived in the secret annex, we had the device 'fac et spera,' which means 'Work and Hope.' "[21]

■

WHILE THE FRANK FAMILY AND THEIR friends were cut off from the rest of the world, Tonny Ahlers enjoyed a period of good fortune. Petoma was still going strong; according to a postwar statement, Ahlers claimed to have earned 70,000 guilders through the company during the years 1942–43. How long the business between Otto's company and his own went on during this time, and how this was organized, is uncertain. In an interview with a family friend conducted on the author's behalf, Miep Gies conceded that it was possible there were deliveries, and that these would have been dealt with by Kleiman.[22] Presumably, Ahlers had hoped the arrangement would continue; that could explain why, as he wrote to former SS Oberscharführer Silberbauer in 1964, he "permitted" Otto and his family to go into hiding for a time.[23] Aside from his companies Petoma and PTM (the Wehrmacht agency), Ahlers kept himself busy in other ways. Since August 1941, Ahlers had been in the paid employ of the SD.[24] He reported Jews, and people breaking the Nazi laws of the land, to Untersturmführer Kurt Döring, who appreciated Ahlers's ability to exert "a certain influence over people."[25] He tried to betray Josef van Poppel, in whose network of spies he worked, for reasons known only to himself. Van Poppel had been unexpectedly thrown out of the NSNAP, owing, he believed, to "the activities of Ahlers."

In 1942, van Poppel began to suspect that the SD had asked Ahlers to keep an eye on him: "I constantly had people come to my home asking trick questions. For instance they would say the SD were looking for them and could I help." He recalled that sometime in 1942 Ahlers banged on his door and shouted that he was under orders to arrest him: "I asked Ahlers for proof, but the only thing he could show me was a document which said he was an SD agent. I told him that I would throw him down the stairs if he didn't go away. Ahlers said he was arresting me because he knew that I was hiding someone who was wanted by the SD, a piece of gossip he had picked up at Café Trip. Ahlers went away with the two men in WA uniforms who were downstairs during our argument. He came back about three hours later and apologized for his behavior. And actually, I *did* have someone in my home, a man called Geri. . . . Through Ahlers, Geri was arrested that same afternoon and received a three-year prison sentence."[26] Van Poppel also confirmed Ahlers's involvement in the arrest and execution of two men whom he knew.

In February 1943, Tonny Ahlers betrayed his own family. A man named Aloserij was visiting Ahlers's mother and stepfather, as he often did, to play cards. Ahlers was also present, and he and Aloserij started to argue about the Russian advance. Aloserij remembered: "The next day I was arrested. They took me to the Doelenstraat police station and kept me there for four days before releasing me. . . . Undoubtedly, Ahlers informed the SD about the debate and betrayed me—and his stepfather—to the SD. Exactly a year later I was arrested again. . . . They informed me that this was due to my 'attitude' at Ahlers's stepfather's home. I was sent to Vught concentration camp."[27] The Aloserij affair had other repercussions: Ahlers's stepfather was also deported to Vught, and Ahlers's brother Huibert had his house searched by the SD for Communist propaganda and was placed under surveillance. Ahlers tried to betray another family friend, but the man was able to escape through a window as the Gestapo arrived downstairs. The man's wife recalled, "Ahlers was known around here as a member of the NSB and as an SD man."[28] "Here" was the Jordaan district of Amsterdam, and specifically, the area around the secret annex.

At the start of 1943, two young men evading forced labor went into hiding in Ahlers's apartment. Why he offered them protection is unclear, although he immediately set them to work for him and did not pay them wages. The two men soon realized they were "anything but safe" in Ahlers's home. After the war, one of the men recalled that Ahlers "had a buying agency for the Wehrmacht and strong ties with the SD. He was, among others, very close with a certain Döring . . . we soon left for another address."[29] Ahlers himself moved on in November 1943, to a spacious apartment at 22 Jan van Eyckstraat, where he lived with his wife and baby son. The house became available when the Jewish owners were deported; a document from the Amsterdam Telephone Service shows that Ahlers was given permission from the SS to occupy the house. Ahlers's previous home had cost him only ten guilders per month in rent; the apartment on Jan van Eyckstraat cost almost seven times that amount, but the difference was in all probability paid by the SD. With his contacts at the Zentralstelle, Ahlers was able to furnish the apartment with beautiful belongings stolen from other deported Jewish families. Two of Ahlers's Petoma employees visited him in his new home. He showed them "photographs in which he appeared in his black [NSB] uniform during parties. In his living room there was a large portrait of him next to Mussert. On his door there was a sign with the text: 'When absent call at the Sicherheitsdienst, Euterpestraat' . . . When we wanted to quit Petoma he did not accept this and told us that if we did not go to work he would fetch the Grüne Polizei."[30]

Following the move to Jan van Eyckstraat, Ahlers's life took a yet more malevolent turn. His association with the SD became stronger, unsurprisingly so, since his luxurious apartment was located in the dark heart of Nazi Amsterdam, a stone's throw from the SD headquarters on the Euterpestraat. The SD offices were in a requisitioned school; the clock tower of the redbrick building dominated the immediate skyline and cast long shadows down the much-feared street. Jan van Eyckstraat was bordered at one end by the Zentralstelle and at the other by the Expositur department of the Joodse Raad. This department of the Jewish Council was responsible for liaison with the German authorities. Headed by Dr. Edwin Sluzker, the staff of the Expositur determined who was eligible for exemption from deportation.

Almost all of Ahlers's neighbors were members of the SD. Karel Wolters, who had taken charge of the liquidation of Otto's business, lived directly opposite, and next door lived Ahlers's boss, Kurt Döring, together with two highly feared German officials, Emil Rühl and Friedrich Christian Viebahn.[31] Ahlers rented out a room to the Nazi spy Herman Rouwendaal, who specialized in infiltrating resistance groups and betraying Allied pilots. It was probably through Rouwendaal that Ahlers first came into contact with Maarten Kuiper, a detective with the SD.[32] Kuiper had known Rouwendaal since August 1943, when they worked for the same police bureau in Amsterdam-East. On January 27, 1944, Kuiper visited Rouwendaal in Ahlers's apartment. A witness at Kuiper's postwar trial described him with revulsion: "One is reminded of a pike, which can still bite resolutely into a finger even after having been on dry land for hours."[33]

Maarten Kuiper, born in The Hague in November 1898, joined the Amsterdam Municipal Police in 1925, conducting himself with "a fixed, almost exaggerated professional zeal." In 1941, he became a member of the NSB and was given the task of pursuing Communists. He joined the SD headquarters on the Euterpestraat "at his own request," and within a short time he was executing members of the resistance and other enemies of the Reich in cold blood. He also established a formidable reputation as an anti-

108 Semite, "hunting down Jews as industriously as he had at first hunted Communists"; he "murdered and tortured like a medieval executioner." By the mid-war years, he was one of the most prolific betrayers of Jews in hiding, estimating "the number of arrests he made during the first years of the war minimally at 250 persons. In the following years he lost count."[34] Ahlers and Kuiper became friends, moving in the same corrupt circles, united by their hatred of Communists and Jews. Ahlers idolized the older man and even began to tell people that Kuiper, the notorious Jew-hunter, was his father-in-law.[35]

Throughout his "evil career," Kuiper received a bonus for every Jew he arrested.[36] And among those arrests would be one that took place in the summer of 1944, in the annex of a spice company on the Prinsengracht.

■

IN HIS MEMOIR, OTTO WROTE NOTHING of his emotions during the hiding period and instead chooses to focus on one of the very few positive aspects:

> I have to say that in a certain way it was a happy time. I think of all the good that we experienced, while all discomfort, longing, conflicts, and fears disappear. How fine it was to live in such close contact with the ones I loved, to speak to my wife about the children and about future plans, to help the girls with their studies, to read classics with them, and to speak about all kinds of problems and all views about life. I also found time to read. All this would not have been possible in a normal life, when all day long you are at work. I remember very well that I once said, "When the Allies win, and we survive, we will later look back with gratitude on the time that we have spent here together."[37]

About his role as peacemaker among the individual members of the annex, Otto said: "We had thought that communal life hiding with the family of my partner would make life less monotonous. My main task was to ensure as happy a communal life as possible, and when I compromised, Anne reproached me for being too yielding."[38] He did confide in Miep that he felt "overwhelmed" by the responsibility of keeping the peace, and that he also worried constantly about "the danger" his friends were in, caring for them.[39]

From the first day, it was Otto who oversaw the small details of life in hiding. While Margot and Edith were still in shock, he and Anne tacked strips of material to the windows to frustrate prying eyes across the courtyard. After that, it was he who decided the rules regarding safety and personal space. In other areas, too, it was Otto who took charge: he suggested subjects to study and books to read, conducted the children's lessons, decided how they would manage their rations and resources, determined what security measures they should take, joined in with all the games, and, outwardly at least, maintained a positive perspective on their situation. Miep describes Otto as "the most logical, the one that balanced everyone out. He was the leader, the one in charge. When a decision needed to be made, all eyes turned to Mr. Frank."[40] He was quite different from the Otto they had known before. Miep recalls: "I noticed a new composure, a new calm about Mr. Frank. Always a nervous man before, he now displayed a veneer of total control, a feeling of safety and calm emanated from him. I could see that he was setting a calm example for the others."[41] Sometimes his nerves were bad, though Miep may not have seen it; Anne occasionally commented on his bad moods, during which he kept whatever was troubling him to himself. On October 17, 1943, she commented: "Daddy goes about with his lips tightly pursed, when anyone speaks to him, he looks startled, as if he is afraid he will have to patch up some tricky relationship again." His one means of escape was reading, either "serious, rather dry descriptions of people and places," German classics, or, most commonly of all, Dickens.[42]

"The one person who visibly meant something to Anne was her

father. That was always apparent."[43] Miep's observation of the relationship between Otto and Anne strikes all readers of the diary and was often cited by young people as one of their primary reasons for writing to Otto. In her revised diary, Anne opens her biographical sketch of life up to that point by describing Otto as "the dearest darling of a father I have ever seen,"[44] though Otto removed this reference from the published version. Initially, Otto worried about how his youngest daughter would adjust to life in hiding: "From the start it was clear to us that a life in total seclusion would be much harder for the lively Anne to put up with than for us. We knew that she would miss greatly her many friends and school. Margot, who was more mature, would come to terms with our situation."[45] Otto tried to bolster Anne's morale: soon after their arrival in the annex, Anne wrote in her diary: "It is as if the whole world had turned upside down, but I am still alive, Kitty, and that is the main thing, Daddy says." He told her that the Dutch people were not to blame for their predicament, and declared that "you could fill a whole diary saying how fantastic the Dutch are."[46] When Anne's fears overcame her, it was usually Otto who was the one to comfort her. His friend Jean Grossman recalled how, after the war, "Otto told me how inadequate he felt to meet all of Anne's emotional needs in hiding. Cut off from friends her own age, often she tried to find in him a substitute for the normal companionship she missed."[47] In an attempt to combat Anne's loneliness, he tried to keep her as occupied as possible. Otto spoke to Anne when her behavior seemed unreasonable, sometimes losing his temper, which he did not do often.

Otto urged Anne on in her search for self-discovery, and when she was thirteen, he told her the facts of life, going further than most parents of his generation, although still not completely satisfying her curiosity: "Daddy told me about prostitutes, etc., but all in all there are still a lot of questions that haven't been answered yet."[48] Otto was the only one who noticed when Anne withdrew into herself during her infatuation with Peter: "I desperately want to be alone. Daddy has noticed that I'm not quite my usual self, but I really can't tell him everything."[49] Otto was reluctant to say anything to either Anne or Peter, despite the discomfort and amusement their romance aroused among the other fugitives. In his memoir, Otto explained how the relationship "brought a few problems, but because I had trust in both Anne and Peter, I could speak openly with the two of them. I could see that this friendship would make life easier for Anne in the annex."[50] Peter was extremely fond of Otto and would later prove to be a brave and thoughtful friend to him.

Otto told Anne, during her adolescent struggle to establish her independence, that "all children must look after their own upbringing."[51] He published almost intact Anne's penultimate entry in the diary about how distanced she felt from him; he cut from the published version, however, several sections in which she criticizes him personally—for instance, his indifference to her idea that each person in the annex should give a talk on a given subject, and his apparently scatological sense of humor. Gone, too, was the entry: "I used to be jealous of Margot's relationship with Daddy before, there is no longer any trace of that now; I still feel hurt when Daddy treats me unreasonably because of his nerves, but then I think: 'I can't really blame you people for being like that, you talk so much about children—and the thoughts of young people, but you don't know the first thing about them!' I long for more than Daddy's kisses, for more than his caresses. Isn't it terrible of me to keep thinking about this all the time?"[52] It is unclear exactly what Anne meant from this entry; she removed it herself from her second version, and Otto chose not to restore it. She retained her comment that "Daddy would never become my confidant" in her rewrites,[53] but in the published diary Otto changed the line to "my confidant over everything," a subtle but meaningful difference.[54]

Otto's relationship with his eldest daughter appears to have

112   been untroubled and tranquil. His postwar recollections about Margot referred only to her innate goodness. Margot also kept a diary during the period in hiding, but it has never been found: it would have been intriguing to read, since her personality in Anne's diary, and from Otto's comments, is one-dimensional. Otto admitted to Father John Neiman, one of his closest and most trusted friends during the 1970s, that he had not even been aware that Margot, like Anne, was recording her thoughts. Father Neiman explains: "Otto never spoke much about Margot, but he did say that one of the most surprising things to come out of his reading of Anne's diary was the discovery that Margot had also been keeping a diary. The two girls sometimes read parts of their journals to each other. He had had no idea about Margot's need to confide in someone, or rather, something. She was always so reserved. None of them, apart from Anne, had known about it. And I think, of course, that he was very disappointed Margot's diary had not been preserved."[55]

Whether Margot was ever plagued by insecurities, depressions, and jealousies, as her young sister was, will probably never be known. Her relationship with Anne was not always easy, but Otto devised a way in which the two sisters could become closer. He told Margot: "Have some secret with Anne. Something you do not tell your mother or me."[56] Margot suggested to Anne that they write to each other, and Anne kept their notes in her diary. Through them, a fraction of Margot's emotions are revealed. She wrote that Anne and Peter should enjoy their friendship, commenting, "I only feel a bit sorry that I haven't found anyone yet, and am not likely to for the time being, with whom I can discuss my thoughts and feelings . . . one misses enough here, things that other people just take for granted. . . . I have the feeling that if I wished to discuss a lot with anyone, I should want to be on rather intimate terms with him. I would want to have the feeling that he understood me through and through without my having to say much, but for that reason it would have to be someone whom I felt to be my superior intellectually." In a second letter, she wrote wistfully: "In my heart of hearts I feel I have the right to share mutual confidences with someone."[57] Margot did confide to some extent in her mother, and the relationship between them was always good-natured, in contrast to the conflict between Anne and Edith.

Otto was disturbed by the friction between his wife and youngest daughter. In his memoir, he recalled:

> I was concerned that there was no particularly good understanding between my wife and Anne, and I believe my wife suffered more from this than Anne. In reality she was an excellent mother, who went to all lengths for her children. She often complained that Anne was against everything that she did, but it was a consolation for her to know that Anne trusted me. It was often hard for me to mediate between Anne and her mother. On one hand, I didn't want to hurt my wife, but it was often difficult for me to point Anne in the right direction when she was cheeky and naughty to her mother. Usually I would wait until after such a scene, would take Anne aside, and would speak to her as if she were an adult. I explained to her, that in the situation we were in, each one of us had to control himself, even when there were grounds to complain. That often helped for a while.[58]

In her diary on October 3, 1942, Anne wrote: "I told Daddy that I'm much more fond of him than Mummy, to which he replied that I'd get over that. . . . Daddy said that I should sometimes volunteer to help Mummy, when she doesn't feel well or has a headache; but I shan't since I don't like her and I don't feel like it. I would certainly do it for Daddy, I noticed that when he was ill. Also it's easy for me to picture Mummy dying one day, but Daddy dying one day seems inconceivable to me."[59] Otto cut this entry considerably. Edith was often upset by Anne's attitude toward her and confided to her husband, "I know how she feels about me, but I'm glad she has you."[60]

The recently discovered pages from Anne's diary are interesting in that they show how over time Anne began to consider her mother's feelings more, but her closing paragraph indicates the gulf that still existed: "What do we know of one another's thoughts? I can't talk to her, I can't look lovingly into those cold eyes, I can't. Not ever! If she had even one quality an understanding mother is supposed to have, gentleness or friendliness or patience or something, I'd keep trying to get closer to her. But as for loving this insensitive person, this mocking creature—it's becoming more and more impossible every day!"[61] Nonetheless, Edith was often supportive of Anne when Otto was not. She understood her daughter's fear of discovery when they were listening to the wireless in the private office, and returned to the annex with her while Otto stayed below, uncomprehending. It was Edith, too, who sympathized with Anne at night when she wanted a light switched on during the battles between German and Allied aircraft: Anne had "begged Daddy to light the candle again. He was relentless, the light remained off. Suddenly there was a burst of machine-gun fire, and that is ten times worse than guns, Mummy jumped out of bed and to Pim's great annoyance lit the candle. When he complained her answer was firm: 'After all, Anne's not exactly a veteran soldier,' and that was the end of it."[62] Anne herself remarked that "Mummy and Daddy are always on my side"[63] and changed her entry of September 27, 1942, from, "Daddy at least defends me, without him I would honestly be almost unable to stand it here," to, "Mummy and Daddy always defend me stoutly, I'd have to give up if it weren't for them."[64]

The relationship between Otto and Edith during the time spent in hiding has not been given a great deal of attention. Otto never spoke of it, and Anne's diary gives only brief insights, though the newly discovered pages have focused attention upon it. For those outside the family, the relationship seemed admirable. Anne records how Gusti van Pels liked to taunt her husband by remarking, "Mr. Frank always answers his wife, doesn't he?"[65] In addition to those comments already quoted from the missing pages, Anne also noted that her parents' marriage had always been presented to her as ideal, "never a quarrel, no angry faces, perfect harmony, etc. . . . Daddy accepts Mummy as she is, is often annoyed, but says as little as possible, because he knows the sacrifices Mummy has had to make. Daddy doesn't always ask her opinion—about the business, about other matters, about people, about all kinds of things. He doesn't tell her everything, because he knows she's far too emotional, far too critical, and often far too biased. . . . He looks at her teasingly, or mockingly, but never lovingly."[66]

Anne's judgment is harshly phrased, but behind it lay the truth. It was Edith who ultimately found the enforced seclusion harder to bear than any of them, a possibility Otto had not considered. Before her marriage to Otto, she had shown signs of being an emancipated woman, but afterward she took on the "precisely defined role" of wife and mother, as she had been brought up to expect from life, drawing her "sense of her own value from performing such 'duties.'"[67] In hiding, this was no longer practicable. Having to share her role as housewife with Mrs. van Pels diminished her standing, and because she and Otto shared their room with Margot after Pfeffer's arrival (Pfeffer moved into Anne's room), it was obvious that she and her husband were not intimate. As the first year in hiding drew to a close, Edith's manner was becoming perceptibly "dismal," and Miep recalls that Edith "began to act oddly." Otto would probably have tried to cheer his wife up by talking about a hopeful future, but all Edith wanted was to admit her misery and fear without being told to pull herself together. She chose to confide in Miep, who simply listened to her confessions that she was "suffering under a great weight of despair . . . she was deeply ashamed of the fact that she felt the end would never come."[68]

The Allied invasion of June 6, 1944, had given new weight to Otto's declarations of optimism. Kleiman sent a postcard to the

116   Eliases in Switzerland on June 22, 1944, implying that Otto and his family were still in safe hands. Otto himself had long been convinced that 1944 would bring them freedom. His belief that the outcome would be positive was given expression in a poem he wrote for Edith's birthday on January 16, 1943. A copy of it was found among Otto's possessions after his death; it has never been published before:

> No flowers, and no eel,
> No cake, and no scarf,
> No stockings, no purses,
> No, not even something to munch on,
> No sweets, no chocolate,
> Not even a confection from Verkade,
> Nothing to wear, nothing to read,
> How did it use to be?
> If only we had something.
> Stop! Two packets of cigarettes.
> That's all, there's nothing else
> Because the shops, they are empty.
> Furthermore, you wished
> Not to celebrate, to keep it completely quiet
> And that's what will happen,
> And everybody will understand.
> The former friends, the old acquaintances,
> The brothers, those in faraway places,
> I am sure they are thinking of you.
> But there is no letter on the birthday table,
> No telephone can reach you.
> There has never been anything like it,
> And still, even though secluded in the annex,
> We celebrate your birthday today
> Without as much as a bouquet of flowers

To be seen in our room,
But we are not alone, to the contrary,
Money and good words cannot buy
The love and loyalty that we are shown here.
Nobody can measure what it means,
How always again, every morning,
Those good friends look after us,
Bring us news, give us food,
Always ready with head and hands.
What more can you want in life
Than friends who give you everything,
That you have the children with you
—and also Pim—who want to help you
Carry the burden as best they can.
We four are together from early to late,
And if we survive this difficult period in good health,
Then everything else will be fine.
We hope that there will be peace soon,
And that we can spend your next birthday
Free, and without worries.
We hope so—and we *will* succeed.[69]

On August 1, 1944, Anne wrote in her diary before placing it inside Otto's briefcase, where she always kept it, for the last time.

six　BETRAYAL

THERE HAD BEEN MANY REASONS TO worry about discovery during the two years in hiding. In 1943 and 1944, there were several burglaries at the offices and in the warehouse. Each time the danger seemed closer than before; on the evening of April 8, 1944, Otto, Peter, and Hermann van Pels were seen by the burglars in the warehouse downstairs. A hole left in the warehouse door on that occasion was seen by the man who delivered groceries to the office, Hendrik van Hoeve. When van Hoeve saw Jan Gies a day later, he explained why he had not informed the police: "Because with you, I didn't think it was the thing to do. I don't know anything, but I guess a lot."[1] The following month, May 1944, van Hoeve was arrested; the NSB had been tipped off that he was hiding a Jewish couple in his home. This worried the eight in hiding at the Prinsengracht greatly: their food supplies lessened as a result, and they were terrified that van Hoeve would confess their own hiding place under torture. Fortunately for them, van Hoeve withstood his ill treatment silently at the Gestapo headquarters; he was then sent to several concentration camps, including Dora, an underground factory where inmates were worked, often to their death.

During the break-in at the Prinsengracht on April 8, Martin Slegers, the neighborhood night watchman, had also noticed the hole in the warehouse door. Together with a policeman, he inspected the building that night; the families in the annex heard them rattling at the swinging bookcase. Obviously under the impression that the night watchman was trustworthy, Jan Gies spoke to Slegers afterward and asked him to keep an eye on their building. Anne writes in her diary, "Now everyone is going on about whether Slegers is reliable."[2] Perhaps he was not. Among the papers seized in 1945 from the home of Gezinus Gringhuis (one of the men who arrested the Frank family) was a small notebook containing names and addresses of Jews and informants. The author found this book in Gringhuis's file at NIOD (the Netherlands Institute for War Documentation). In the middle of the book appears: "Slegers, Herengracht 100."[3] It was the same Slegers; Otto's voluminous papers included a list of all those mentioned in the diary together with their real names and addresses. Slegers was on that list. Coincidentally, Tonny Ahlers was a former neighbor of Slegers's; in 1940, he had lived for a short time at 5 Herenstraat, which backed onto Slegers's house at 100 Herengracht. Nobody knew about Slegers's connection to Gringhuis; he should also have been questioned about the betrayal. By chance, one of the other men present at the Franks' arrest, Willem Grootendorst, recalled a raid on the evening of April 8, 1944, just a few doors down from where the Franks and their friends were hiding.

There were two other significant causes for concern during the time in hiding: Bep's sister was involved with a German soldier, which could have led to difficulties, and worse yet, the owner of 263 Prinsengracht was a member of the NSB: fifty-two-year-old metal dealer Frederick Peron, who sold the building in February 1943 without the helpers' knowledge. The new owners arrived unexpectedly to inspect the property, and Kleiman had to pretend he had lost the key to the annex. Anne mentions the incident in her diary but does not go into further detail. One wonders why the new owner did nothing with the house after buying it. Why didn't he ask to see the annex at a later date? And how did Kleiman explain the swinging bookcase? These questions remain unanswered.

Shortly after Pieron bought the building, a new head warehouseman was hired to take over from Bep's father, Johan Voskuijl, who was too ill to work. Wilhelm van Maaren, born in Amsterdam on August 10, 1895, was married with three children. During the war, he prepared a hiding place in his own home for his eldest son, in case he should be called up for work in Germany. Very quickly, van Maaren began asking pointed questions about the annex, and about Otto. He set small traps in the warehouse, such as potato meal scattered on the floor to show footprints. When Kugler and Kleiman asked him why he did that, he told them that he hoped to catch the thieves who stole from the stores. One of van Maaren's assistants in the warehouse, J. de Kok, later admitted he had sold some goods that van Maaren himself had stolen. The people in hiding were frightened of him (Anne refers to van Maaren several times in her diary), and the helpers were also nervous of him. He was the first person they suspected of betraying them. Although van Maaren told his assistants of his suspicions that there were Jews hiding on the premises, he was not the only one who had heard such dangerous rumors. With a secret of his own, however, it seems unlikely that he would betray the eight in hiding at the Prinsengracht.

In his 1945 letter to the Dutch authorities about the betrayal, Kleiman writes: "Our accountant van Erp visited a homeopath (Dr. Bangert) after the arrest and told him that a number of Jews had been picked up at one of his business associates' (van Erp), without giving Bangert the name or address. Bangert asked van Erp whether this concerned the premises at 263 Prinsengracht. Extremely surprised, van Erp said it did and asked how Bangert knew this. Bangert replied that he had known a year ago that Jews were hidden at that address."[4] Who told Dr. Bangert about the annex? The Dutch police who interviewed him after the war learned that it was a patient of his who had passed on the information. In a classic example of a missed opportunity, the police merely asked Bangert if van Maaren or his wife was among his clients.[5] Of course, they should have asked to see a complete list of Bangert's patients.

In her 1998 biography of Anne Frank, Melissa Muller claimed that Lena van Bladeren-Hartog, who apparently cleaned the offices at 263 Prinsengracht, betrayed the Franks and their friends. In July 1944, Lena told another woman, Anna Genot, that she had heard a rumor that there were Jews in hiding where she worked. Lena, whose husband, Lammert Hartog, worked as van Maaren's assistant in the warehouse, later insisted she had said this after the arrest. Anna Genot's husband told Kleiman about the conversation, and during the first investigation into the betrayal, Kleiman brought the matter to the attention of the police. Curiously, he did not appear to consider Lena a suspect; instead, he wanted to know who had told her about the hidden Jews. Muller maintains that Lena also confronted Bep Voskuijl about the hidden Jews, adding that she could "no longer just sit by" and allow the situation to continue.[6] According to Muller, Bep told the other helpers about the conversation, yet strangely, none of them mentioned it to the police in charge of the 1948 investigation into the betrayal, despite being asked specifically about the Hartogs. During the second investigation in 1963 and 1964, Kugler wrote privately to Otto about the conversation between Lena and Anna Genot but said nothing about a conversation between Bep and Lena. Nor is there any mention of Lena and her apparent threats in Miep Gies's autobiography. The author asked Cor Suijk, who helped Muller extensively with the research for her book, why none of the helpers told the police about Bep and Lena's discussion. He answered: "Because they were upset and afraid they would be blamed for not doing enough for the Jews in their care."[7] If that was true, then surely

122 their mistaken sense of guilt would have been relieved by helping the police to bring the betrayer to justice.

Muller further asserts that on the morning of the arrest, Lena's husband, Lammert Hartog, who worked in the warehouse below the hiding place, had put on his jacket and disappeared at "the first opportunity."[8] This information she must have from Kleiman's 1945 letter to the Dutch authorities, for he writes that Hartog was panicked by the arrival of the Gestapo—but then explains this was due to Hartog's avoidance of a summons for labor in Germany; he was working for Otto's company "illegally." The last people Hartog would have wanted to see were the Gestapo. Furthermore, Hartog could not have disappeared then because one of the Dutch Nazis remained in the warehouse. When Otto and Kugler left the building at gunpoint, they recalled seeing both warehousemen standing by the front entrance. In her book, Miep Gies remembers Hartog working until the end of the day. Then, according to Muller, Lena and her husband "never went back to work at the building after the Jews' arrest."[9] Muller implies that this was because the Hartogs were guilty of the betrayal, but in fact van Maaren dismissed Hartog following the arrest, an action in keeping with the perception of van Maaren acting then "as if he were the head of the business."[10]

As to motives, Muller claims that Lena was afraid that her husband would be in danger when the hiding place was discovered. Then why call the police when her husband—who was himself wanted by the Gestapo—was in the building? If Lena wished to betray the people in hiding, surely it would have been wiser to do so when her husband was not there. Having no other income, Lammert Hartog needed his job in the warehouse, which Lena had arranged for him. Muller gives Lena a second motive to betray the fugitives: she had lost her only son in the German navy and wanted to avenge his death in some way. This, too, seems highly unlikely, since none of the people in hiding or their helpers could be blamed

for the death of Lena's son. Muller apparently received her information from a relative of the Hartogs, but the Dutch and German
archives reveal a quite different story. Klaas Hartog, Lena's son,
died in May *1945*; more surprising still, it was not until 1952 that a
comrade confirmed the death.[11] Why would Klaas's mother betray a
group of hidden Jews to avenge his death nine months before it occurred? Finally on this issue, Father John Neiman, a close and
trusted friend not only of Otto Frank but also of Miep Gies for many
years (she flew to the United States especially for his ordination to
the priesthood), has a comment to add: "In November 2000, I
stayed with Miep in Amsterdam. I told her I had read Melissa
Muller's book, and I asked, 'Miep, was it Lena? Did she betray
them?' And she looked straight at me and said, 'No. She did not.' "[12]

The detectives in charge of the second investigation into the betrayal confessed that they had no idea who was guilty of calling the
Gestapo on August 4, 1944. They ended their report: "After studying several files . . . it was discovered that two days before the
arrest of the Frank family, two Jews were arrested, also at
Prinsengracht in the immediate surrounding of the annex, after
the two had been betrayed by the Jewish traitors Branca Simons
and Ans van Dijk who were executed after the war."[13] Van Dijk
worked for a man named Pieter Schaap, who led the arrest of
Hendrik van Hoeve, the supplier of groceries to the eight in hiding. Among Schaap's colleagues were Herman Rouwendaal and
Maarten Kuiper, two dangerous men whom Tonny Ahlers knew
well. Rouwendaal was Ahlers's former tenant at the apartment on
Jan van Eyckstraat, and Kuiper was a friend of both Rouwendaal's
and Ahlers's.

■

THE SUMMER OF 1944 MARKED A TURN-
ing point in the life of Tonny Ahlers. After a period of prosperity in
1943, suddenly he found himself in debt and in trouble on a num-

124 ber of counts. His criminal files give few clues about how this occurred. What is clear is that Ahlers's businesses were sinking rapidly, and he was unable to pay his suppliers or the various
authorities to whom he owed money. He was desperate for sugar
for a particular product he was making for the Wehrmacht; that
summer and winter, a large supply of sugar went missing from the
Prinsengracht warehouses. (Van Maaren was blamed but maintained his innocence, and later, when other goods were stolen and
his home was searched, police found nothing.) Perhaps Ahlers was
the thief; he was in the same type of business as Otto Frank, and he
had a record of petty thefts, robberies, and break-ins. Ahlers
moved out of the house on Jan van Eyckstraat and into another in
Amstelveen in an area that was also a Nazi stronghold, populated
by NSB members and employees of the various Nazi agencies. He
and his tenant, the Abwehr spy Herman Rouwendaal, had argued
about rent, and Ahlers, although furious himself, feared that
Rouwendaal would kill him. He told his neighbor, the SD official
Emil Rühl, about the argument and asked if the Gestapo could provide him with protection against the enraged spy. Shortly after the
quarrel, Rouwendaal's wife was anonymously betrayed for anti-
German behavior and sent to a concentration camp.[14]

In early 1944, Ahlers delivered a business associate to the SD
for possession of illegal wirelesses. The man was aware of
Ahlers's sympathies with the Nazis, having seen "documents that
showed he was a confidential agent of the SD." The man explained that, after his arrest, his son-in-law approached Ahlers
for help: "Ahlers then went to visit my wife and told her that he
could do something, but only if he had 200 guilders to bribe the
SD with brandy. My wife gave him the money, but never heard
from him again." The man had known Ahlers for some time but
considered him to be "a very dangerous person for that particular period of the occupation . . . he did not mind hanging somebody if it suited him."[15]

Ahlers's problems seemed to be coming to a head. He needed money badly, his business was failing, and by the end of the year he would be declared bankrupt. Most significantly, he wanted protection against Rouwendaal from the Gestapo and had to demonstrate he was worthy of its protection. Otto Frank was of no use to him now that his own companies, Petoma and PTM, were in the process of collapse. Ahlers's scurrilous postwar letters disclose how he hated Otto Frank, as he hated all Jews. Those same letters reveal that Ahlers knew where Otto and his family were hiding. In the summer of 1944, the reward for betraying Jews was then at its highest: originally the payment stood at two guilders and fifty cents per head, but it rose gradually to forty guilders.[16] The traitor of those hiding in the secret annex would have received 320 guilders—a considerable sum—for his evil deed. After the war, Ahlers declared his motto was always: "There are different ways that lead to one and the same goal."[17] Just over a week before the Franks and their friends were betrayed, the leader of the NSB, Anton Mussert, arrived in Amstelveen to give a pep talk to all the Nazis living in the area. Tonny Ahlers's son is absolutely sure his father and mother would have attended the event to listen eagerly to Mussert's speech.

Maarten Kuiper eventually took over Ahlers's old home on Jan van Eyckstraat. Kuiper, the SD detective with a penchant for hunting down Jews, had "had a hand in hundreds of arrests"[18] and received a premium for his betrayals of Jews in hiding, acting on tip-offs given to him by anonymous informants, colleagues, and friends. Kuiper liked to attend the arrests of the Jews he betrayed. At this point, the postwar testimony of Josef van Poppel, whom Ahlers attempted to betray to the Gestapo, echo down the years: "With a lot of Jewish arrests, Ahlers was the instigator."[19]

Kuiper moved into Ahlers's old house on Jan van Eyckstraat on August 3, 1944—twenty-four hours before the Franks were betrayed.[20]

■

ON THE SUNLIT MORNING OF AUGUST 4,
1944, following a direct telephone call to Julius Dettman at the SD
headquarters, the annex was raided by the Gestapo and a number
of Dutch Nazis.[21] The assault was led by thirty-three-year-old SS
Oberscharführer Karl Josef Silberbauer. Three of his accomplices
were identified by Otto from photographs in 1945: Gezinus
Gringhuis, then fifty-one years old and resident at Marathonweg,
and Willem Grootendorst, born the same month and year as Otto
Frank and resident at Corantijnstraat. Until now, the other man
recognized by Otto and his friends as being present at the arrest on
the Prinsengracht has never been publicly named; in his July 1947
letter to the Dutch authorities, Kleiman stated that the man was not
brought forward following his identification.[22] Kugler explained to
Otto privately years later that this was apparently due to the fact
that the man had already been sentenced to death. His name was
Maarten Kuiper.[23]

Contrary to Muller's statements in her biography of Anne Frank,
the available police records give no clues whatsoever as to whether
the caller was German or Dutch, male or female. The recipient
of the telephone call, Julius Dettman, hung himself on July 25,
1945, before he could be questioned about it, but both Silberbauer
and his Gestapo chief, Willi Lages, were interrogated in 1964. Silberbauer and Lages contradicted each other frequently in their interviews, but agreed absolutely on one aspect of the affair.

In Lages's words, because the denunciation was made directly
to Julius Dettman and the police had gone straight to the hidden
address, the call was not made anonymously at all but "came from
somebody who was known by our organization . . . the tip giver
was known and in the past his information was always based
on truth."[24]

In the summer of 1945, Maarten Kuiper and Tonny Ahlers were
arrested for betraying people to the SD.[25]

■

THROUGHOUT 1942 AND 1943, THOU-
sands of Jews in Amsterdam were arrested in mass raids and sent
to Westerbork to await deportation to the east. A report from the
German authorities in The Hague, dated June 25, 1943, reveals that
102,000 of the Netherlands' 140,000 Jews had been "removed
from the body of the nation."[26] Five days before the report was
drafted, the last "mammoth" round-up in Amsterdam took place:

All of Amsterdam's city districts in the south, including the
Transvaal district (approximately one-third of Amsterdam's total
area), were sealed off, and Security Police together with General
Police, searched apartment after apartment. The Jews found (except for mixed marriages, Jews of foreign nationality, those able to
prove that they were not fully Jewish, and a few special cases) were
prepared for departure and transported to Westerbork the same
night. Success was secured because the preparations for this huge
operation could be kept secret until the last moment. Despite
many rumors, the Jewish lot was taken completely by surprise and
is now depressed, one reason why only few Jews are presently
showing their faces in public.—There were no incidents. The
Dutch population is thoroughly opposed to the deportations but
outwardly displays for the most part an air of impassivity. Large
numbers of people were angry because they could only leave the
sealed off districts with difficulty—Jewish auxiliary police from
Camp Westerbork were used to help with the carting off process.

In the course of the operation we also succeeded in catching
and carting off the core of the former Jewish Council. Those Jews
already in Westerbork, especially emigrants from Germany, reacted to this circumstance by gloating openly. They voiced their
general regret, though, that the top echelon, in particular the Jews
Asscher and Cohen and their retinue, had not been brought in
as well.[27]

■

IN THE SUMMER OF 1944, WHEN THE Nazis increased the reward for turning in hidden Jews, more betrayals were made: "People gave information to the police to settle old scores with those in hiding, or with those who helped them. Some made a lot of money. . . . In the later years of the occupation, when all remaining Jews were in hiding and information from the population registers were effectively worthless, the local knowledge offered by these men [paid informers] was often of great value to the Germans, as was the information offered by the public."[28] There were many motives for betrayals: anti-Semitism, personal dislike, obedience to the Nazi government. Of 25,000 Jews who went into hiding, about 9,000 were caught, and more Jews were captured by Dutch police than by Germans.

Immediately after receiving the telephone call, Julius Dettman rang Abraham Kaper, head of IVB4, the unit assigned to picking up Jews, and told him to send several of his men to 263 Prinsengracht; he had just had a sure tip from a known informer.[29] The details were not as precise as we have been led to believe—the betrayer knew that Jews were in hiding at the Opekta offices, but he did not know exactly where, or how many of them there were. That did not trouble the Gestapo; it was rare enough to hear about hidden Jews, and the informant was a trustworthy source, above all.

Who was that informer? Possibly it was Maarten Kuiper, in an internal call to Julius Dettman's direct line at the SD headquarters. Kuiper had betrayed hundreds of Jews in hiding and was well known to both Lages and Dettman for that reason. Whenever he could, he attended the arrests of the Jews he had betrayed. Tonny Ahlers's son, Anton, has another answer:

In 1952, my father joined the KNSM [Koninklijke Nederlandse Stoomboot Maatschappij—Royal Dutch Steamboat Society] and spent two years traveling the world. We were able to follow his progress in the papers, because we could follow the route of the ship. He went everywhere: Australia, Indonesia—he had always loved traveling. Then when he came back, he bought a telephone. I was very excited by this new element in our lives and I remember it was a white telephone that sat on the windowsill. When I was about seven or eight years old, I heard a conversation on that phone. I was in bed one night, listening to the phone ringing. My father picked it up and he was talking. I heard him mention Otto Frank. And then I heard him say, "I got them into the hiding place and I got them out again."[30]

Tonny Ahlers's brother, too, has no doubts: "Tonny told me he did it. He called the Gestapo and told them there were Jews in that particular building. He was proud of it. Years later, he was still proud to have done that. He did it for the money, and the things he was able to get from the hiding place."[31] Interestingly, Cas recalls having seen his brother with a brass menorah that he said had been taken from the Franks' hiding place. In a 1960s interview for French television, Otto mentioned a brass menorah as being among the items confiscated by the Gestapo and NSB on the day of the arrest. It has never been found.[32]

Unlike the other suspects named as possible traitors of the Franks and their friends, Tonny Ahlers had several incentives to betray the people in hiding: he needed money (having become bankrupt that summer); he hated Jews; he had to prove himself to the Gestapo so that they would protect him against Rouwendaal; he may have wanted Otto Frank out of the way now that the tide of war was turning against Germany; and above all, he was vicious and spiteful enough to want to send people to their deaths.

But that was not the end of the affair, or the relationship between Otto and Ahlers. There were several twists and turns to come, all of which have remained secret, covered up out of Ahlers's desperation, Otto's confusion, and an inability on the part of the postwar authorities to approach the circumstances of August 4, 1944, with an open mind.

■

ASKED ABOUT HIS ARREST DURING AN INterview on French television in the 1960s, Otto said softly, "When the Gestapo came in with their guns, that was the end of everything."[33] Unlike the stage and screen versions of the events of that morning, the arrest took place without banging on doors and shouting from the persecutors and without hysterics from their victims.

The Gestapo and the NSB moved quietly through the building, giving orders to Miep, Bep, and Kleiman to remain seated. When they realized Kugler was in charge, they ordered him to take them to the hidden Jews. Kugler, terrified and aware that the end had come, led them to the secret annex. Otto recalled the moment when the Nazis appeared in front of his own eyes:

> It was around ten-thirty. I was upstairs by the van Pelses in Peter's room and I was helping him with his schoolwork, I didn't hear anything. And when I did hear something I didn't pay any attention to it. Peter had just finished an English dictation and I had just said, "But Peter, in English *double* is spelled with only one *b*!" I was showing him the mistake in dictation when suddenly someone came running up the stairs. The stairs were squeaking, I stood up, because it was still early in the morning and everyone was supposed to be quiet—then the door opened and a man was standing right in front of us with a gun in his hand and it was pointed at us. The man was in plain clothes. Peter and I put up our hands. The man made us walk in front of him and ordered us to go downstairs, and he walked behind us with the pistol. Downstairs everyone was gathered. My wife, the children, the van Pelses stood there with their hands in the air. Then Pfeffer came in, and behind him were

still more strangers. In the middle of the room there was someone from the Grüne Polizei [Silberbauer]. He was studying our faces. They then asked us where we kept our valuables. I pointed to the closet by the wall, where I had stored a small wooden chest. The man from the Grüne Polizei took the box, looked all around him, and grabbed Anne's briefcase. He turned it upside down and shook everything inside it out; there were papers lying all over the wooden floor—notebooks and loose pages. He proceeded to put all the valuable things in the briefcase and shut it. Then he said: "Get ready. Everyone must be back here in five minutes."[34]

Otto continued his account: "The van Pelses went upstairs to get their knapsacks, Anne and Pfeffer went to their room, and I took my knapsack which was hanging on the wall. Suddenly the man from the Grüne Polizei was standing fixated by my wife's bed, staring at a locker that was between the bed and the window and he said loudly, 'Where did you get this?' He was referring to a gray footlocker with metal strips, like all of us had during World War I, and on the lid was written: Reserve Lieutenant Otto Frank. I answered: 'It belongs to me.' 'What do you mean?' 'I was an officer.' That really confused him. He stared at me and asked, 'Why didn't you come forward?' I bit my lip. 'They certainly would have taken that into consideration, man. You would have been sent to Theresienstadt.' I was silent. I just looked at him. Then he said, 'Take your time.' "[35] Theresienstadt, a so-called privileged camp for Jewish war veterans and the elderly, was no less lethal for its inmates than the other camps; the Nazis merely used it as a showcase for public relations purposes. As for Anne's diary, which lay scattered on the floor, Otto remembered that Anne "did not even glance" at it. "Perhaps she had a premonition that all was lost now."[36]

An hour later, the fugitives were taken from their hiding place to the offices below, where Kugler and Kleiman were waiting to be interrogated by Silberbauer. Bep had managed to escape, while Miep sat alone in the front office, having alerted her husband, Jan, to the danger. Kleiman had given her the keys to the building. Silberbauer had already questioned Miep aggressively but decided not to arrest her after discovering that she, like him, was originally from Vienna. However, after barking questions at Kleiman and Kugler and getting nowhere with them, Silberbauer announced that they were also under arrest. The ten prisoners were led down the staircase and out into the street, where a windowless police truck was waiting in front of the warehouse doors. They climbed in, and the doors banged shut behind them.

The journey away from the Prinsengracht took place in silence. It was midday, and in South Amsterdam, the sun glimmered through the trees lining the Euterpestraat. The offices of the Zentralstelle at the end of Jan van Eyckstraat were still and quiet. In contrast, the SD headquarters at 99 Euterpestraat was a hive of activity: German officials and Dutch Nazis gathered on the steps, the street, and the courtyard at the back. The black and white SS flag snapped on its tall pole above them. Inside, the former school was even busier as reports were filed, phone calls were made and taken, meetings were held, and, in the cellars, prisoners were interrogated and tortured.[37]

The new arrivals from the Prinsengracht were shown into a room and locked up. As they sat there in numb shock, Otto tried to apologize to Kleiman for the situation, but his friend interrupted him, "Don't give it another thought. It was up to me, and I wouldn't have done things any differently."[38] Later Kleiman and Kugler were removed from the room. Kugler recalled, "At a distance, in the corridor outside Silberbauer's office, we saw the Franks, the van Pelses, and Pfeffer. All eight looked serious and troubled, not knowing what the future would bring. We waved to each other and that was goodbye."[39]

After a quick interview, during which Otto stated truthfully that he did not know where other Jews were hiding, Silberbauer sent them to the basement cells for the night. The following day they were transferred to the regular prison on the Weteringschans in the city center, and they remained there for two days in filthy, overcrowded conditions. On August 8, they were taken in a large group of people to Centraal Station. The sun shone brightly again, but over the platform hung a heavy, fearful silence as the tense prisoners waited for the train that would remove them from civilization.[40] Among the crowd were two sisters, Lin and Janny Brilleslijper; their resistance work had resulted in their arrest and separation from their husbands and children.[41] Janny noticed the Franks instantly: "A very worried father and a nervous mother and two children wearing sports-type clothes and backpacks."[42] She did not speak to them because no one was talking: "The houses of the city were bathed in gold, and all these people had a sort of silent melancholy about them."[43]

The train to Westerbork was not the dreaded cattle cars. It was a regular train, but the doors were locked and bolted. In an interview, Otto described their mood as surprisingly hopeful:

We were together again, and had been given a little food for the journey. We knew where we were bound, but in spite of that it was almost as if we were once more going traveling, or having an outing, and we were actually cheerful. Cheerful, at least, when I compare this journey with our next. In our hearts, of course, we were already anticipating the possibility that we might not remain in Westerbork to the end. We knew about deportation to Poland, after all. And we also knew what was happening in Auschwitz, Treblinka, and Madjanek. But then, were not the Russians already deep in Poland? The war was so far advanced that we could begin to place a little hope in luck. As we rode toward Westerbork we were hoping that our luck would hold.[44]

It was late afternoon when they arrived in Westerbork, eighty miles from Amsterdam. The flatness of the land, which was like a great plain, caused the summer winds to drive sand and dirt into every eye, every crevice. Flies settled on everything, and particularly on the very young children and babies. In the winter, the area became a swamp when the rains hurtled down and there was no natural shelter. Within the barbed-wire perimeter fence were over one hundred barracks, each containing wooden bunks, and although there was electricity, the lights seldom worked. At night, men and women were housed separately but could meet during the day at work. Like other detention camps, it was a city within itself, offering inmates the possibility of gardening, sports, and theater before they were shipped off to "the undiscovered country."[45] The commandant, Albert Gemmeker, lived in a house near the chicken farm at the edge of the camp and could be friendly to the people in his charge, but he always made sure the transports ran on time. Life in the camp revolved around the schedule of the departures. Everyone tried to avoid the trains by any means available, but few succeeded.

As Otto lined up with his family at the registration desks in the main square, Vera Cohn, who took down their details, was struck by his calmness: "Mr. Frank was a pleasant-looking man, courteous and cultured. He stood before me tall and erect. He answered my routine questions quietly. . . . None of the Franks showed any signs of despair over their plight. Their composure, as they grouped around my typing desk in the receiving room, was one of quiet dignity. However bitter and fearful the emotions that welled in him, Mr. Frank refused to compromise his dignity as a person. His wife and daughters, as though taking a cue from him, acted precisely the same."[46] Rootje de Winter had also noticed the family. She and her husband, Manuel, and daughter, Judith, had been in the camp for a month, having been denounced in their hiding place by a Nazi spy. Judith recalls, "The new transport from Amsterdam came rolling in, and we watched the people getting down from the train. There among them was Otto, and beside him,

Anne. My mother wanted me to go over to her and make friends because we were about the same age. And I did speak to Anne, and to Margot, but I did not want to become real friends. That was a form of self-preservation which I had learned—you never knew what was coming next."[47]

After a visit to the quarantine barracks, where an employee of the Lippmann-Rosenthal Bank robbed them of any remaining possessions, the Franks and their friends, like all Jews who had been in hiding, were assigned to the Punishment Block, barrack number 67. Their freedom, therefore, would be even further limited. Unlike the other prisoners, who were permitted to keep their own clothes and shoes, they had to wear a uniform and clogs. The men had their heads shaved, and the women had their hair cut painfully short. They also had less to eat than everyone else, although their work was harder. Unpaid employment began at five o'clock in the morning in Westerbork's Industrial Department, where they had to chop up old batteries, then sort the tar, the metal caps, and the carbon bars into baskets. It was dirty work, as Rootje confirmed. "We looked like coal miners."[48] Otto wanted to find something else for Anne to do and approached Rachel van Amerongen-Frankfoorder. Rachel was a former resistance worker who was also living in the Punishment Block but had a slightly better job cleaning toilets and handing out clothes to new arrivals. She remembers: "Otto Frank came up to me with Anne and asked if Anne could help me. Anne was very nice and also asked me if she could help me." The decision was not Rachel's to make, but she saw how desperate Otto was to save Anne from the battery shed: "That's the reason he came to me with Anne—not with his wife and not with Margot. I think that Anne was the apple of his eye. Otto Frank was an especially nice and friendly man. You sensed that he had known better times."[49]

Through their work and imprisonment in barrack 67, the Franks met other families who had experiences similar to theirs.

Lenie de Jong-van Naarden and her husband, Philip de Jong, had also been in hiding and ended up in Westerbork, where, Lenie remembers, "my husband quickly made contact with Otto Frank and got along with him very well. They had profound conversations and we had a very good relationship with Mrs. Frank, whom I always addressed as Mrs. Frank. I never called her by her first name; she was really a very special woman. I had less difficulty saying 'Otto.' She worried a lot about her children."[50] Edith and Anne had left their differences behind them when the annex was raided, and survivors of Westerbork and Auschwitz remember them—together with Margot—clinging to each other in the camps. Ronnie Goldstein–van Cleef, another woman who met the family, found them often "pretty depressed. . . . They were very close to each other. They always walked together."[51] Edith was sometimes accompanied on her way to work by Lin Brilleslijper, who recalled: "We spoke much about Jewish art, in which she was very interested. She was a friendly, intelligent person of warm feelings, from a middle-class, German Jewish family. Her open character, her warmheartedness, and her goodness attracted me very much."[52] To others, Edith spoke little; Rootje described her as being almost mute, while Otto "was quiet . . . but it was a reassuring quietness that helped Anne and helped the rest of us, too. He lived in the men's barracks, but once when Anne was sick, he came over to visit her every evening and would stand beside her bed for hours, telling her stories."[53] She remembered Anne comforting a young Orthodox Jewish boy in the same manner. Rootje's daughter, Judith, retains only one clear memory of Otto at that time: "I was lying on my bunk in Westerbork below Anne's bunk. She was sitting up in bed and talking to Otto. They talked on and on. I wanted to go out and jumped up and tore my finger on a nail that was sticking out from the wood. I still have the scar, it's very clear."[54]

Sal de Liema remembers meeting Otto in the Industrial Department while they were "knocking the black stuff out of batteries. . . . We were sitting on top of a huge pile of old batteries, and we were working there. Otto Frank was there, too, and the whole family." Sal and his wife, Rose, went into hiding in early 1942, moving from place to place until they were caught on August 5, 1944. In Westerbork, Sal slept in the same barracks as Otto, and they became close friends: "I was with [Otto] all the time, and we really clicked together. We had nothing. . . . And that's why we held on to each other." Sal hated all things German and insisted that Otto speak only Dutch with him: "I am Dutch. Otto Frank was German, and Dutch people are different to German people. A German Jew is a different person to a Dutch Jew. We had other ideas. . . . I told him, 'Don't talk German to me,' because I hated the German language. Of course, it was his language. He was a German. He was a Jew, but he was a German first." Despite this, they remained friends, for "we really didn't know in the morning if we would live at night."[55] Rose de Liema remembers how they tried to keep up their spirits: "We had long discussions about our experiences. But mainly we tried to encourage each other and hope that the war would soon be over. If we could only hold out long enough. While in hiding, we always listened in secret to the English radio, and we knew that the invasion had been a success. But every day we feared transportation to an extermination camp."[56]

In a speech recorded for schoolchildren many years later, Otto fleetingly recalled his time in Westerbork: "Conditions were not too bad, as the people in charge and the guards were Dutch, of course. The men and the women were living in separate barracks. We could meet in the evening after work. . . . At this time, the Allied armies advanced steadily, and so we hoped that we would not be deported to the concentration camps in Poland. But fate had decided differently."[57] On the warm evening of September 2, 1944, the announcement was made for the following day's transport from Westerbork. The list included 1,019 people. Among them

138   were Otto, his family, the van Pelses, and Pfeffer. It was to be the
final deportation to the east.[58]

That night the camp was in an uproar. Janny Brilleslijper recalls: "Everyone was running around. I knew that Otto Frank
went all over the place. He had the illusion he could go to
Theresienstadt."[59] Otto's efforts were in vain. The 498 women, 442
men, and 79 children listed—Otto and his family included—would
be deported the very next day. It was agony for everyone, but the
anguish was even worse for parents, helpless to protect their children from the unimaginable future. The author Primo Levi gave an
account of the night before his transport left for Auschwitz, turning his attention in particular to the mothers, like Edith Frank,
who were tormented by the knowledge that they were unable to
prevent their children from being led to their probable murder:
"All took leave from life in the manner which most suited them.
Some praying, some deliberately drunk, others lustfully intoxi-
cated for the last time. But the mothers stayed up to prepare the
food for the journey with tender care, and washed their children
and packed their luggage; and at dawn the barbed wire was full of
children's washing hung out in the wind to dry. Nor did they forget
the diapers, the toys, the cushions and the hundred other small
things which mothers remember and which children always need.
Would you not do the same? If you and your child were going to be
killed tomorrow, would you not give him [sic] to eat today?"[60]

■

FOR THREE DAYS AND TWO NIGHTS, THE
nightmare train carrying the Westerbork passengers traveled
through the Netherlands, Germany, and Poland. This time they
were in cattle cars sealed apart from the odd gap in the wood or a
missing plank, without light or sanitation and with hardly any food
or water. Through the day, before they reached Poland, the car-
riages were unbearably hot; after passing the Polish border, espe-

cially at night, they rocked endlessly in a bitter wind. There were many casualties on board the train, but no opportunity to move the corpses from where they lay on the straw-covered floor. The stink of death and bodily waste was overwhelming.

Otto and his family sat squeezed into a carriage of more than sixty people with the van Pelses, Pfeffer, the de Winters, Ronnie Goldstein–van Cleef, Lenie and Philip de Jong, and the Brilleslijper sisters. Before they left the Netherlands, an incident occurred that shook them all even further. Lin remembered: "The train stopped. Six prisoners had sawed a hole in the floor of their truck, and dropped out onto the tracks from the moving train. One was killed, but five managed to save their lives, though one man lost a hand and a girl lost both hands. They still live today: they were helped to safety by the Dutch. The others who had been in the escape truck were crushed into our truck. We could scarcely sit, and the smell was terrible."[61]

When the train stopped at a siding, they were unable to shout to ask anyone where they were. Rootje recalled, "SS guards were patrolling up and down outside the train."[62] They all felt, instinctively, that they were headed for Auschwitz and what seemed to be the edge of the known world. Otto left no record of the journey, except to remark that "each of us tried to be as courageous as possible and not to let our heads drop."[63] Primo Levi, however, wrote of his own deportation to Poland: "We felt ourselves by now 'on the other side.' There was a long halt in open country. The train started up with extreme slowness, and the convoy stopped for the last time, in the dead of night, in the middle of a dark and silent plain."[64]

When the Westerbork train eventually reached "the other side" and stood there, the steam hissing from it, sounds began to penetrate the silence. From beyond the darkness came shouts, screams, the creaking of machinery, and the sharp howling of dogs. Red and white lights illuminated the track on either side of the train.

Rose de Liema recalls with unending horror the moment when the doors were dragged apart: "We stumbled out, and I had the feeling I had arrived in hell. It was night, chimneys were burning with huge bright flames. The SS beat everybody with sticks and guns.

"Then the selection started."[65]

seven   UNFORGETTABLE
MARKS ON MY SOUL

AUSCHWITZ WAS "A WORLD UNLIKE ANY
other because it was created and governed according to the principles of absolute evil. Its only function was death."[1] The exact number of people killed there will never be known because the SS destroyed the appropriate records, but what is certain is that the majority of the victims were Jews.

The camp was created around the remains of an old army barracks in the industrial Polish village of Oświeçim. (The Germans called it Auschwitz.) In the summer of 1941, SS Reichsführer Heinrich Himmler called the future commandant of Auschwitz, Rudolf Höss, to a secret meeting and told him about the Final Solution, adding that "Auschwitz would serve as the center of destruction." At the end of the meeting, Himmler confided, "Every Jew that we can lay our hands on is to be destroyed now."[2] On May 12, 1942, the first Jews transported to the camp were killed in the gas chamber upon arrival.

At the height of its infamy, Auschwitz was a prison empire of twenty-five square miles of barracks, gas chambers, crematories, subcamps, and factories. There were thirty-eight satellite camps, as well as a soccer stadium, a library, a photographic laboratory, a symphony orchestra, and a brothel known as "the puff." Most gassings took place in Birkenau, where the majority of female prisoners were housed. Two thousand armed guards kept discipline in the camp, while eight hundred Jews given the collective title "Sonderkommando" were in charge of ensuring that the gas chambers operated smoothly. Every three months, the Sonderkommando were gassed and replaced by new arrivals. The cost of killing one person in Auschwitz was 0.25 marks.

The majority of trains were timed purposely to arrive in the camp by night to ensure that the prisoners would be even more confused and disoriented. The men and women were separated, and then a selection determined who would work and who would be gassed before sunrise. It was very rare for mothers who refused to be parted from their children, the sick, the disabled, and people aged over fifty or under fifteen to be spared instant death. In his early days as camp commandant, Höss stood outside the gas chambers to learn what happened when the doors had been secured:

> Those who were standing nearest to the induction vents were killed at once. It can be said that about one third died straight away. The remainder staggered about and began to scream and struggle for air. The screaming, however, soon changed to the death rattle and in a few minutes all lay still. . . . The door was opened half an hour after the induction of the gas, and the ventilation switched on. . . . The special detachment now set about removing the gold teeth and cutting the hair from the women. After this, the bodies were taken up by elevator and laid in front of the ovens, which had meanwhile been stoked up. Depending on the size of the bodies, up to three corpses could be put into one oven at the same time. The time required for cremation . . . took twenty minutes.[3]

Sigmund Bendel, a former member of the Sonderkommando, explained the next stage to a British military court: "One hour later, everything is back in order. The men remove the ashes from the pit and make a heap of them. The next convoy is delivered to Crematorium IV."[4]

By the summer of 1944, the crematoria were in prime working order, and the railway track had been lengthened to within two hundred yards of the crematoria. This was done in preparation for the zenith of the Final Solution: the destruction of the Jews of Hungary. Four hundred thousand Hungarian Jews arrived in the camp during two months, and the massacres were so numerous (nine thousand Hungarian Jews were gassed in one day alone) that the crematoria could not cope. Nine gigantic pits were dug and the bodies cremated there. The Nazis worked out that by placing a heavy man alongside a woman or child, the fat running off the man would make the smaller bodies burn faster. The sky flamed red by day and night, and the smoke was visible thirty miles away. On the evening of August 2, 1944, the entire Gypsy camp (four thousand people) was gassed.

As early as 1942, the governments of Britain and the United States had been informed that mass murder was taking place in Europe. In the spring of 1942, two men who had escaped from Auschwitz wrote a report about the gassings. Their sixty-page summary was read in the White House, in the Vatican, and by the Red Cross, as well as by Jewish community leaders in Budapest. On April 4, 1944, "U.S. reconnaissance planes flying over Auschwitz took some remarkably clear photographs that show all the essential evidence—the gas chambers and crematoria, the prisoners standing in line—yet even the experts trained to interpret such photographic evidence apparently saw nothing here but a large prison camp."[5] By July 1944, the Allied armies were in a position to destroy Auschwitz, and Churchill wrote to Anthony Eden that same month about the Final Solution: "There is no doubt that this is probably the greatest and most horrible single crime ever committed in the whole history of the world."[6]

The Allies did nothing, and the gassings went on all summer.

■

ON THE NIGHT OF SEPTEMBER 5, 1944, the Westerbork transport arrived in Auschwitz. As men and women were separated, Otto turned for a last glimpse of his family over the heads of the terrified crowd. He saw Margot and later told his surviving relatives, "I shall remember the look in Margot's eyes all my life."[7]

Five hundred and fifty-nine people, including every child under fifteen, were sent from the searchlight-strafed platform to the gas chamber. Judith de Winter spoke to her father as they left the train: "Despite all the confusion, I saw that my father was apprehensive and very dispirited, so I told him, 'Come on, we have to fight this. Don't lose hope.' But he already had. We were parted, and minutes later he was among those selected for the gas chamber. I didn't see it but found out much later, actually only a couple of years ago. He was fifty-five years old."[8]

Otto Frank was the same age, but he escaped the selection. His bearing and determined spirit saved him, so people who knew him assert. Together with Fritz Pfeffer and Hermann and Peter van Pels, he was among 258 men who were permitted to live. His wife and daughters and Gusti van Pels disappeared into Birkenau with 212 women who were also spared.

Otto and his fellow inmates marched two miles in darkness to the main camp, Auschwitz I. There they were herded into the quarantine barracks, where they would spend their first six weeks of camp life. They were stripped, shaved all over, and sent into the cold showers. Afterward they were given the striped prison uniform and wooden clogs before being tattooed with numbers ranging from B-9108 to B-9365. Otto was branded prisoner B-9174.

After the quarantine period, the men entered the regular camp and were assigned to their huts. Otto and his friends were allocated to Block II. Filled with wooden bunks in narrow tiers of three, the barracks were filthy and freezing. Several people had to sleep in the same bunk on mattresses made of straw but soon turned to pulp by bodily fluids. The floors swam with urine. As the Westerbork Häftlinge (new arrivals) tried to find places on the bunks, one of the senior men in the block approached Otto and his companions. They recognized him as Max Stoppelman, the son of Miep and Jan Gies's landlady in the River Quarter. Through Jan Gies, Stoppelman and his wife had found refuge with a Dutch family, but they were betrayed after only six months. Peter van Pels told Stoppelman that his mother was still alive; Miep had recently visited her in her hiding place outside Amsterdam. From then on, Stoppelman protected Peter and explained to them all how the camp functioned, although the rules were subject to change.

At 4:30 A.M. every day, the men of Block II were ordered out of their bunks for roll call. Prisoners stood for hours to be counted and then put into work groups. Otto, Hermann van Pels, and Fritz Pfeffer were made to dig ditches, but Peter was assigned elsewhere. As Otto recalled, "Peter was lucky to get a job at the post office in the camp which was for SS soldiers and non-Jewish prisoners who got mail and parcels."[9] Peter received more food than the others but would hide it and then share it with them later. Otto and his "comrades," as he called his friends in the camp, were given stale bread and a barely edible soup to eat every day. Their diet resulted in "scurvy and skin diseases, strange afflictions like noma, a gangrenous ulceration that creates gaping holes through the cheek, and phemphicus, whereby large areas of the skin become detached and the patient dies within days."[10] The harsh routine and the terror of sudden execution understandably affected their appearance: "Facial transformations were so rapid among the prisoners that if a few days elapsed without their meeting, it was hard for them to recognize each other."[11] They were beaten frequently by the Kapos ("God Guards") who supervised their work, and punishments were regular and medieval in their cruelty: public floggings by chains, whips, or clubs, fingernail extraction, and

146 imprisonment in cells so small it was impossible to stand, lie, or sit. Thousands of prisoners were chosen for medical experiments. Most of the records were destroyed, but one discovered report shows ninety castrations in a single day. The rare beings who survived such tortures were then sent to the gas chambers.

■

"THE AVERAGE LIFE EXPECTANCY OF A JEW who was not gassed on arrival was between six and seven weeks in Auschwitz."[12] Prisoners had to learn to take the most basic necessities—food, drink, and sleep—where they could. They had to steal food or barter it ("organizing" in camp slang) and be alert to everything around them. It helped if they had faith of some kind, whether religious or emotional: for instance, the belief that a loved one needed them to survive. It was an advantage to speak German, since that was the language of the camps, ruled as they were by the SS and Kapos. "The orders were bellowed in German, and if they were not carried out at once they were repeated in conjunction with a beating, and perhaps an explanation of the beating, because the shouting and the beating were parts of the same speech. Those who did not understand that speech were always the last, always too late, and too easily cheated and deceived. 'Language was the first cause of drowning in the camps.' "[13] German, according to Primo Levi, was life. Prisoners like Otto Frank, who could understand not only regular German but also the "old German of Prussian barracks,"[14] were more fortunate than their comrades. When asked how he had survived Auschwitz, Otto answered, "You needed luck, optimism, and moral strength, but even this did not help if one was starving from malnutrition or caught a disease."[15]

Hermann van Pels's luck ran out after a month in the camp. He injured his thumb while digging a trench and asked his Kapo to give him work indoors instead. The Kapo agreed. The following day there was a selection among those workers, and Hermann van Pels was condemned to the gas chamber. Otto never forgot the moment: "Peter van Pels and I saw a group of selected men. Among those men was Peter's father. The men marched away. Two hours later, a lorry came by loaded with their clothing."[16] The effect on their small group, and upon Peter in particular, must have been devastating, but they still clung to the belief that they would survive. To have friends in that situation was vital. Sal de Liema, who was in the same barracks as Otto, recalled: "I saw [Otto] when we came out of the wagon. And then we walked to Auschwitz. . . . We tried to like each other, to help each other mentally. We couldn't do anything about food or clothes."[17] He remembers Otto's strategy for survival: "He said, 'We should try and get away from these people [prisoners who were obsessed with food] because if you talk all the time about food and stuff, your brain is going to go, we should try to survive mentally. . . . The biggest problem was to save your brain. Don't think about every day. We talked about Beethoven and Schubert and opera. We would even sing, but we would not talk about food."[18] Like other prisoners, Otto and his comrades spent hours discussing art, music, and literature, which gave them a feeling of moral victory over their captors. The knowledge that the SS also took pleasure in arts and music puzzled and revolted the inmates of the camp. One performer in the men's orchestra at Auschwitz spoke of his bewilderment: "Could people who love music to this extent, people who can cry when they hear it, be capable, at the same time, of committing so many atrocities on the rest of humanity?"[19]

Sal remembered one other thing he was able to do to help Otto. One day Otto asked Sal to call him Papa, even though he knew that Sal's real father was hidden in the Netherlands. At first Sal refused, finding it a peculiar request, but then Otto broke down and confessed he found it impossible to live without his children. He cried, "I'm the type of man who needs this, I need somebody to be a Papa for."[20] Sal understood that and was filled with sympathy for

148   Otto, who from then on became "Papa Frank." Otto's morale picked up again; he drew great strength from hearing himself addressed once more as "Papa."

■

AUTUMN BROUGHT MIST AND RAINS TO the vast open expanse of Auschwitz. As the Allies progressed through Europe, Himmler ordered an end to the gassings at Auschwitz. The Nazis gradually began to destroy all evidence of the Final Solution. A group of 1,700 Jews from Theresienstadt were the last to enter the gas chambers, on October 28, 1944.

The following day, there was an announcement in the men's barracks that qualified physicians were allowed to transfer to Sachsenhausen camp in Germany. Fritz Pfeffer applied to leave, feeling that his chances of survival were better there. Otto recalled that he and Pfeffer had grown closer during their time in Auschwitz: "As long as we were together, he discussed more frankly personal matters with me than he had done during the time of our hiding."[21] Pfeffer was one of sixty doctors who boarded the train that day and disappeared into the unknown again.

In November, Otto was sent to work indoors, given the task of peeling potatoes. Joseph Spronz, whom Otto would later befriend, had the same duty for a while and outlines the work in his memoir: "We had to carry up to eighty pans of potatoes to fill the kitchen basin. The potatoes were meant for animals; only the biggest ones were peeled, and the rest were thrown into the machine unpeeled. It was very tiring work but instead of becoming weaker, which we had expected, we grew stronger, thanks to the turnips and other vegetables which we were eating from morning to evening together with some left-over bread. Of course, we only did that when the SS weren't looking. We felt we were living like princes."[22]

The biggest drawbacks were the heavy beatings dealt out and the punishments for stealing: "Those peeling the potatoes were searched three times a day, and those caught stealing something got a horrible beating and were put into the 'Kommando Vollgas,' where they had to work with sewage. All the same, many of us took the risk of smuggling food from the kitchen. . . . The Kapos very often forced us to smuggle in food for them; we were not beaten up for that. We also bartered potatoes for bread."[23] One Kapo took a powerful dislike to Otto and beat him regularly. Otto's health began to fail, slowing his work rate, which resulted in further attacks. At one point, Otto had a fight with another inmate. During an interview conducted with Otto's second wife in the 1980s, it emerged that when Otto returned to Amsterdam after the war, he asked Miep to go with him to visit the owner of a shoe shop. Otto told Miep, "I want to visit this man because I had a fight with him in the camp. I punched him in the face." Miep was shocked by this revelation; it was not the sort of thing she imagined Otto doing. Although worried about the visit, she accompanied Otto to the shop. The owner recognized Otto instantly and walked toward him. There was a brief moment of hesitation, and then he and Otto embraced. Otto explained later, "In the camps, tempers could run high at times because of small, unimportant things."[24] Evidently, the man had done something Otto did not like, but after the war it was forgotten.[25]

Sometime in November 1944, Otto reached the limits of his endurance. Severely depressed, starving, and wracked with diarrhea, he was unable to lift himself from his bunk. He remembered, "On a Sunday morning I could not get up, being exhausted from hard work and little food and having been beaten the day before by the Kapo. . . . That had really affected me, also in terms of my morale. I said, 'I can't get up,' and then my comrades—all Dutchmen, I was the only German, but they totally accepted me—said, 'That's impossible—you must get up because otherwise you are lost.' "[26] Someone sent for the doctor, who happened to be a Jewish man from Amsterdam. Otto recalled, "This Dutch doctor came to my

150   barracks. He said, 'Get up and come to the sick barracks tomorrow morning, and I'll speak to the German doctor and you will be saved.' And this is what happened, and through it I was saved."[27] Dr. S. M. Kropveld, the doctor who admitted Otto to the hospital, remembered visiting Otto in the barracks and finding him "incredibly filthy and covered with lice. He begged, 'Doctor, please help me,' and I went to a Jewish Czech colleague [not a German doctor, as Otto recalled], Fischer, to ask him for advice. Fischer was a neurologist, an extraordinary man, and he was willing to admit Otto Frank for psychological observation. . . . Thus Otto Frank was hospitalized and tucked away in a corner, where he still was when the Russians liberated him."[28]

In the hospital (which Otto accurately described as "a so-called hospital. It was not treatment. It was really that you weren't hit and you had not to work and you had not to be outside"),[29] he met Joseph Spronz, who became a lifelong friend. Spronz arrived in Auschwitz in June 1944 from Budapest. He had been sent to the hospital when his hands were badly burned during an accident in the kitchens. Spronz made friends with a Hungarian doctor who asked him to act as his assistant in the hospital. Spronz's second wife, Franzi, recalls how her husband and Otto met: "In the hospital, my husband formed a circle of people who, despite their illnesses or whatever had brought them there, were interested in music, literature, and art. They each took turns to sing or recite. One evening, my husband was whistling a few bars of Bach's 'St. Matthew's Passion,' and Otto appeared, walking slowly toward him, also whistling the tune. When it was over, Otto said, 'I know that you are Hungarian and I am not, but please, may I join you and your friends?' They invited him to sing or give a speech, and he stood up and recited Heinrich Heine's poem about losing his religion."[30]

In his memoir of Auschwitz, Spronz explained that inmates of the hospital had their footwear and clothes stolen; in return they were given thin nightshirts. The hospital was designed much the

same as the regular barracks, and the food was no better: "In the
hospital, people got less food than the men who worked elsewhere;
this was meant to be a deterrent, otherwise too many people would
have schemed to get there. . . . We had more time to realize how
hungry we were, and to contemplate our low morale, which was
greater in the hospital. We also had more time to become aware of
how precarious fate was for our loved ones . . . and how little hope
our own present situation held for us."[31]

Otto's admission to the hospital coincided with the end of the
gassings, and it was at least somewhat safer than the rest of the
camp. The weather was appalling, and the hospital did offer
slightly more protection from the elements. Snow fell on Auschwitz that December, and thousands of inmates died. In a letter
written a few months later, Otto recounts a sorrowful memory of
Christmas in Auschwitz: "The last music I heard was at Christmas
in the camp, when two comrades played violin and cello very nicely
at the hospital." He added, "I know that they are dead now."[32]

■

IN THE FIRST DAYS OF 1945, THE BOOM
of Russian artillery and the crackling of automatic rifles could be
heard not far from Auschwitz. In mid-January, these sounds were
joined by the rumble on the roads of fleeing Wehrmacht vehicles.
Knowing that the Red Army was closing in, the SS began to destroy
sections of its colossal death factory, Auschwitz. Gas chambers
were blown up, crematoria were demolished, and scores of barracks, electrified fences, and guard towers at Birkenau were torn
down. Clothes, spectacles, suitcases, jewelry, and other belongings
from the dead were sent to Berlin, while in the camp itself, documents and registers were set on fire. Corpses from mass graves
were exhumed and burned in open pits. But the Germans continued to torture and murder prisoners.

On January 12, the Red Army penetrated the inadequate

German defenses at Baranow. The inmates in the hospital heard the news, as Spronz recalled: "When the German lines were pierced at Baranow, we grasped at once that this would mean the evacuation of the camp. Excitement was enormous."[33] On January 16, Russian planes attacked Auschwitz, destroying the kitchen and food depot in Birkenau. On January 17, units of the Red Army approached outlying areas of Kraków from the north and northwest, surprising the German forces. A decision had already been reached about what to do with the Auschwitz prisoners: those who could walk would be evacuated on foot and eventually put to work. Those in the hospital, like Otto, would be abandoned. As fog obscured the roads around the camp and snow continued to fall heavily, Auschwitz itself lay silent, "finally exposed to imminent assault."[34]

■

THE YOUNG MAN WALKED QUICKLY through the snow in Auschwitz I, Main Camp, keeping his head down.[35] Peter van Pels, nineteen years old, had made the journey from his own barracks to the camp hospital almost every evening for two months. Otto later recalled: "Peter acted like a son to help me. Every day he brought me extra food. . . . He never could stay long. We never discussed serious matters, and he never spoke about Anne. I did not have the impression that he matured much."[36] Peter's visit to the hospital on the night of January 18, 1945, would be his last: he was leaving Auschwitz, and he hoped to persuade Otto to do the same.

Otto had heard at noon that day that the camp was to be evacuated. His friend Joseph Spronz remembered: "At midnight, the SS roused physicians and nurses, and me as well. We were deeply frightened by the order to burn the sick-cards of all personnel and the patients then in the hospital; this might have meant the extermination of all unable to walk. It was very painful for both physicians and nurses to abandon the sick, yet we had to do it to prove our fitness."[37] Spronz then found Otto and told him to stay in the hospital if he possibly could. Otto took his advice, hiding in the toilets when he felt the situation was becoming dangerous. He recalled of that evening: "It was twenty below zero. Peter came to me and said, 'We leave.' He was well fed and had a good position, he was young. He told me, 'I am working with them. I'll make it.' I said, 'Peter, hide yourself. You can hide yourself here in the hospital upstairs or somewhere.'" But Peter was too afraid he would be discovered and shot, and felt that his best chance for survival was the march. He and Otto argued about this, and finally Peter left the hospital, alone. Otto cried when he had gone. "Peter was a very good boy, really a good-hearted boy."[38] He was convinced that Peter would not survive the march and knew that his hope of helping the young man to "develop his potentialities, in the future," would now never be realized.[39]

Outside, the snow continued to fall. Shortly after midnight, the first column of prisoners began marching away from Auschwitz. In Birkenau, the temperature had dropped to ten degrees below zero when the SS started pulling the prisoners out of their barracks "onto the snow-covered fields and bullying them into the customary ranks of five. Even then, there were long delays, roll-calls, shouts and confusion. Several thousand prisoners in the camp hospital argued about whether to join the evacuation, and those who wanted to flee fought over the few pairs of wooden clogs that the guards had left them to use in going to the latrines."[40] Groups left at intervals throughout the night and the following day. The women and children from Birkenau left first, then the men from the camp. Sometimes there would be only one hundred prisoners in a column, but there were also groups of over two thousand people who set off on foot "westward toward the cities of Silesia."[41] Reaching the railway stations, prisoners were pushed into open goods-wagons and sent on journeys that sometimes lasted more

154   than a week without food or water. The majority perished, and those who survived "threw the bodies of the frozen dead onto the railway track, and licked snow off the ledges of the wagons to ease their thirst and hunger. There were instances of cannibalism, when starving captives were driven to consume parts of their comrades who died."[42] Prisoners forced to march the entire way into Germany were beaten, shot, starved, and offered little assistance from the ordinary civilians they passed.

At 1:00 A.M. on January 19, the last transport of 2,500 prisoners waited by Birkenau's "Death Gate." Documents and clothing still burned inside the camp. The lights on the main switchboard close to the entrance gate were flicked out, and darkness descended upon the camp. The prisoners marched down to Auschwitz I to await further orders. Six thousand prisoners too sick to march, among them Otto Frank, remained behind, but the camp was once more a silent plain. In the woods, fields, and villages of Upper Silesia, 58,000 former inmates marched through appalling weather, many of them freezing to death, while far below, "the grim and partly gutted ruins of Auschwitz lay abandoned in the snow."[43]

A few hours after the last prisoners who could walk left the camp, Allied aircraft launched an attack on the IG Farben factories in Dwory, very close to Auschwitz I. The heads of IG Farben (employers of slave laborers from the camps and manufacturers of Zyklon B, the chemical used in the gas chambers) set fire to their archives. For Otto Frank and the 1,200 inmates of Auschwitz I, the Allied raid may have helped their morale but was a disaster in immediate, practical terms: it cut the water and electricity supplies to the surrounding area. The camp was plunged into complete darkness. It was like being trapped in a sunken ship: there was no light, food, or drinking water, just starvation and thirst and, outside, a perpetual black fog. The prison compound was buffeted by waves of rain and wind, while the sky above shook with bombs from the Red Army forces.

Otto recalled what followed: "After the Germans left, we were
alone. People from the hospital and quite a number. We found so
much food, cellars of food belonging to the SS, but there was no
water because everything was frozen and broken. There were lakes
in the neighborhood, though, so we went to break the ice and had
water."[44] Spronz remembered: "Every patient who was able to
move was busy carrying water to the kitchen. Only boiled water was
drunk, and black coffee was constantly available."[45] Inmates from
Birkenau, where the SS had set fire to the warehouses containing
prisoners' clothing and belongings and shot two hundred women
at random, also managed to salvage food from the supplies in the
main camp. Aside from this, the fog and rain sustained their chill,
despondent grip, and the rumor spread that the Russians were still
only in the Zakopane Mountains, far away from "the haunted ramp
of Birkenau."[46]

■

IT BEGAN TO SLEET HEAVILY ON JANUARY
25. At two o'clock in the afternoon, a group of SD men strode into
Auschwitz I. Five days earlier, SS-Sturmbannführer Franz Xavier
Kraus, head of the Auschwitz Liaison and Transition Offices, had
received an order to liquidate every last prisoner in the camps of
Birkenau and Auschwitz. Dozens of armed SS entered the hospital
barracks, screaming at the patients and dragging them from their
beds. Otto and his comrades were forced to their feet and marched
down the camp street toward the main gate. Prisoners emerged
from the decaying barracks, stumbling as the SS punched and
kicked them through a path of frozen snow. The SD yelled orders at
the SS, who moved swiftly among the prisoners, pushing them into
line. German Reich prisoners formed the first rows, followed by
Aryans, then other Jews, and finally those inmates unable to stand
were dropped at the back, on the ground. Otto stood in the middle,
knowing exactly "why we were there. We knew we were finished."[47]

Spronz was also among the prisoners: "The SD began to consult one another. We realized that an execution was to come, for leaving the camp in an organized way was out of the question. The Germans were displaying their hand grenades and machine-guns, and we felt the bullets penetrating into our bodies already. Those were moments of mortal anguish."

The SD lined up before the prisoners in a single row, under the black iron gate bearing the maxim: "Arbeit Macht Frei" (Work Brings Freedom). The sleet turned to rain as they raised their machine guns.

An officer stepped forward to give the order to fire.

Suddenly, three loud, snapping explosions echoed in the air. The prisoners in the front row looked at one another in a daze; no one had been killed. There were two further explosions, clearly from outside the camp, and then an armored car appeared from the main road, carrying several SS men. One of them jumped out and addressed the officer in charge of the murder squad. The exchange was brief but plainly urgent. As they were talking, a small convoy of cars pulled up beside the main gate. The conversation between the two men ended, and the officer motioned to the guards. They threw their guns over their shoulders and ran toward the vehicles.[48]

"Return to barracks!" yelled the officer to the bewildered prisoners before climbing into the car nearest him. The guards no longer paid the inmates any attention, and within seconds every vehicle was gone. The stunned prisoners, including Otto, began to walk back to the barracks, helping each other along the windswept camp street. They discussed what they should do. Franzi Spronz recounts the story told to her by her husband: "The Germans had fled and were not coming back. They were cowards, every one. The prisoners wondered what to do next. During the confusion, Otto found my husband and said he was sure that the end must be close and he was determined to survive until the Russians arrived so that he could return home and be with his children again. My husband gave him his address, and then they parted."[49]

■

LIBERATION CAME QUIETLY, TWO DAYS later. On the morning of January 26, the SS returned to Birkenau and dynamited one of the crematoria before leaving in armored cars. In the early hours of January 27, Wehrmacht troops blew up the railway bridge over the Vistula and Sola Rivers and a wooden bridge over the Sola that had been built by prisoners from Auschwitz. At three o'clock in the afternoon, as snow was once more beginning to fall, reconnaissance scouts from the First Ukrainian Front, wearing white capes, made their way out of the woods near Auschwitz and saw the barbed wire of the camp. As they advanced upon the gate, a group of German soldiers appeared. A fierce battle ensued, which ended with the Germans running off and two Russian soldiers being fatally injured. Elsewhere in the area, 231 Red Army soldiers died while fighting to liberate Auschwitz and its subcamps. After removing a number of mines from the area, the Red Army finally entered the compound of Auschwitz I. When the soldiers entered the hospital, Otto Frank was too weak and overcome to stand up to greet them. He could only register his liberators' "snow-white coats. They were good people. We did not care if they were Communists or not. We were not concerned with politics, we were concerned about our liberation."[50]

The Sixtieth Army of the First Ukrainian Front, under the command of General Pawel Kuroczkin, conducted a search of the camp. Lying about the grounds of Auschwitz I they found 48 corpses; at Birkenau there were over 600. All had died in the last few days. Of the millions who had passed through the gates, only 6,000 remained alive at the time of liberation. Fewer than 1 percent of those admitted to the camp survived. In the partially destroyed

158   warehouses, the Russians found 1,185,345 items of women's and men's clothing, 43,255 pairs of shoes, 13,694 carpets, 15,000 pounds of women's hair, and piles of toothbrushes, shaving brushes, artificial limbs, and babies' clothes. A Polish officer reported that the survivors "did not look like human beings: they are mere shadows."[51] The writer Primo Levi, formerly an inmate of Monowitz, was transferred to Auschwitz I and found "innumerable gloomy, square, gray stone edifices, three floors high, all identical; between them ran paved roads, straight and at right angles, as far as the eye could see. Everything was deserted, silent, flattened by the heavy sky, full of mud and rain and abandonment."[52]

On January 28, the thaw began, though it rained heavily on January 29, and the entire main camp of Auschwitz I was transformed into a massive temporary hospital. The sick were bathed by strong Russian nurses who "laid them on the ground on wooden racks, then briskly soaped and rinsed them from head to foot. . . . The Russians split the survivors into national groups. . . . They gave out clean shirts and underwear. . . . The infectious ward, Block 20, [became] a huge dormitory where a single doctor found himself in charge of eight hundred sick and dying patients."[53] There were no drugs or medical equipment, and few real doctors, yet the Russians did what they could, distributing rations and clothing from former SS stores and separating the chronically sick from those likely to survive. Otto fell into this latter category. He was given his own bunk in another barrack, inside a long room where single rows of beds in three tiers reached up to the low ceiling. The hut was packed with mothers, daughters, sisters, and friends who had walked over from Birkenau to search for their menfolk. Otto asked them all if they knew anything about his wife and daughters.

One of the teenage girls who responded was Eva Geiringer, a former neighbor from Merwedeplein in Amsterdam. She describes their meeting: "I saw one face that looked vaguely familiar.

He was middle-aged with hardly any face left at all, just a skeleton's skull out of which stared pale brown inquiring eyes. 'I know you,' I said in Dutch, almost sure in the back of my mind that I had seen him before. He stood up slowly and painfully, tall and dignified still and bowed slightly to me." Eva was unable to tell Otto what had happened to his children, and he knew nothing about her father and brother. They talked further, nonetheless: "I sat on his bunk for a while and told him all the news that I could and he thought it was a good idea that we [my mother and I] move into Auschwitz where the Russians had permanent headquarters and were going to look after the prisoners. I promised to come back and see him."[54]

Gradually, the survivors began to recuperate and move about the camp. Eva recalls how the soldiers organized "able-bodied people to help peel the vast mounds of potatoes to be tipped into heavy black cauldrons for potato and cabbage soup. It was the mainstay food for all, troops included. Large chunks of rough, coarse maize bread were distributed and there was now sufficient food to halt the symptoms of starvation."[55] Water was only available from the blocks of ice cut from nearby lakes and melted down. On Friday evenings, Otto joined a group of his fellow inmates to celebrate the Sabbath. None of the men were religious, but they found comfort in their small congregation.

It began to snow again, but the long camp streets stayed brisk with activity. More Russian soldiers appeared each day, either by truck or on horseback. On the outskirts of the main camp, Russian trucks blocked the roads. Eva remembers "burly fur-clad, fur-capped Russians" who were busy repairing engines and cleaning guns. Everywhere in Auschwitz there was "an air of activity, organization and permanence about the Russian presence. . . . Russians had set up their headquarters and field kitchens and the military appeared to be in complete control. . . . There seemed to be a small permanent band of soldiers who were coping with the problems of the abandoned concentration camp."[56]

One of the most moving discoveries during the research for this biography was the revelation that immediately after his liberation Otto Frank began to keep a diary.[57] It is remarkable not only because it belonged to Otto Frank, but also because it must be one of the very few diaries—if there are any others—that detail an Auschwitz survivor's journey, both spiritual and physical, from liberation until the moment of arrival home. Otto never spoke about the red notebook, which he was given by the Russian soldiers, who handed out pens and paper to those who wanted to write to relatives in safer parts of the world. Although Otto was alive and his mind was intact, unsurprisingly, he was not functioning normally in those early days of liberation. Like a camera, he could only record what he saw; his emotions were kept at bay. His friend Joseph Spronz described his own paralyzed state as "a being without soul, nothing but flesh." Otto's entries between February 11 and February 23, when they left the camp, read starkly:

11.II.45: block 18 (kitchen).
14.II.45: Sal de Liema [reunion with his friend].
16.II.45: Russian cinema.
17.II.45: first stroll outside.
19.II.45: Auschwitz.
23.II.45: day of the Red Army.[58]

Later, the entries become much more descriptive, but Otto focused his attention for the time being on informing his family that he was alive. He wrote many letters, some of which are still in existence. The first was written on February 23, 1945, and was addressed to his mother and sister in neutral Switzerland:

Dearest Mother,
    I hope that these lines get to you bringing you and all the ones I love the news that I have been saved by the Russians, that I am

well, am full of good spirit, and being looked after well in every respect.

Where Edith and the children are, I do not know. We have been apart since 5 September 1944. I merely heard that they had been transported to Germany. One has to be hopeful, to see them back well and healthy.

Please tell my brothers-in-law [Julius and Walter] and my friends in Holland of my liberation. I long to see you all again and hope that this will be possible. If only you are all well. Indeed, when will I be able to receive news from you? All my love, greetings and kisses,

Your son,

Otto[59]

He wrote a similar letter to his brother Robert and sister-in-law Lottie in England, telling them he was "lucky to be saved by the Russians. I am well and in good spirits and well kept. . . . Don't worry about me anymore. I do [worry] about you all but am confident just the same. How much I have to tell you since we met last."[60] Shortly after writing these lines, Otto and his fellow prisoners were told they were leaving the camp. Eva Geiringer, Otto's visitor in the barrack, recalls:

During a night of the third week we heard the crack of gunfire near to the camp. Then the boom of artillery. The barrage continued throughout the night. . . . When we went down next morning the street was full of agitated inmates and soldiers. We gradually realized that the Russians had suffered a severe onslaught from the Germans and had lost ground. Our mutual enemy was advancing toward us once more. We were terrified. Having been through all that suffering and survived, we knew that if they were ever to return they would take bitter revenge and murder us all in cold blood. Eventually, several Russian officers appeared and calmed us down. They indicated in broken German that they were going to move us back behind the lines to Katowitz [Katowice] which was in a safer zone. We had to be ready within the hour.[61]

It did not take long for Otto to pack his possessions. They fitted into one small, striped cloth bag: a needle and thread, and some pieces of paper. He then walked onto the main camp square, where about 150 men and women were standing around, talking nervously. A dozen trucks waited along the street. At a signal from the Russian soldiers, everyone began climbing into the back of the vehicles. It was uncomfortable, but there was plenty of food and water. When the lorries were full, the engines started up, and they made their way out of the camp, driving slowly through the rain along the straight roads toward the main gate.

Less than one month earlier, Otto Frank had stood under that portal, waiting to be shot. Together with everyone else in the Russian-led evacuation, he watched silently as the black iron lettering faded into the mist.

eight EVERYTHING IS LIKE
A STRANGE DREAM

On March 5, 1945, the huge Russian
trains carrying the Auschwitz survivors arrived in Katowice, the
capital of Upper Silesia. Otto and his comrades were housed in a
large public building without any comforts, but he noted in his diary that the local people were "hospitable."[1] On March 12, they
were moved to an empty school in the center of Katowice. Matters
remained uncertain: although Poland was under Russian law,
Hitler's armies in Hungary, Poland, and eastern Germany were
putting up a strong fight. Chaos and distrust were everywhere, and
few resources could be spared for concentration camp survivors.

The Polish people with whom Otto came into contact were kind
and sympathetic, and several invited him to eat with them. On
March 15, he wrote to his mother that he was "fit and well. We are
here now and we are waiting for a transfer to Holland. I know nothing of Edith and the children. Presumably they have already departed for Germany. Do you think we'll see each other again fit and
well? How I do demand everything and anything of you! It's a miracle that I'm still alive—I have had a lot of luck and should be grateful."[2] Another card written that day is straight to the point: "We

164 own nothing more. I hope you are well when you read these lines. I will write more soon. Love, Otto."[3]

Two letters from March 18, the first addressed to his cousin Milly, give a little more detail: "Here we are waiting to be repatriated. . . . Of Edith and the children I know nothing. . . . Now I am a beggar, having lost everything except life. Nothing of my household is left, not a photo, not a letter of my children, nothing, nothing, but I don't want to think what will happen later and if I shall be able to work again. There are as many in the same situation. I long for you all and am so much better now, weighing 60kg [130 pounds] again. How shall I find you all and all my old friends? I always was optimistic and I am still trying my best."[4] The second letter was addressed to his mother:

I still cannot decide, whether to tell you more comprehensively of some of my experiences, the main thing is you know I am alive and well. How the thought always torments me, that I have no idea how Edith and the children are, you no doubt understand. I do however hope to see all well again and I do not want to lose hope. . . . We are being looked after satisfactorily and I will always think of the liberation by the Russians with gratitude. If I hadn't been in hospital due to a weak body—I weighed 52kg—I doubtless would no longer be alive. I have had a lot of luck and a lot of friends. . . . One could never place a value on what our group of friends—Miep Gies, Kleiman, Kugler, Bep—have done to look after us in the hideout. Kleiman and Kugler were arrested with us by the Gestapo and were also taken to a concentration camp. The thought of this pursues me continually—I only hope that these people are now in the meantime free. . . . I can hardly imagine normal circumstances. I don't want to think about the future yet. Here I am a beggar and even look like one. I am still fresh in my mind and my body has recovered, mainly because we don't have to work here. I hope that I can send you further news and that I will hear from you.[5]

On March 19, Otto was able to take his first bath in six months, and he was given fresh clothing to wear: "two shirts and some trousers."[6] On March 22, he discovered the terrible truth about what had happened to his wife. At the Katowice school, Otto was sitting alone at a long table when Rootje de Winter, whom he had met in Westerbork, entered the room. She told him that after arriving in Auschwitz on September 5, she and her daughter, Judith, had been placed in a barrack with Edith, Margot, and Anne. On October 27, there was a selection in the block for the strongest prisoners to be transferred to a munitions factory in Czechoslovakia. Judith was taken, and Rootje had not seen her since. Margot and Anne should have gone, too, but Anne had scabies and was rejected. She was sent to the scabies block soon afterward, and Margot joined her there voluntarily. Edith, Ronnie Goldstein–van Cleef (whom Otto also remembered from Westerbork), and another woman whose daughter was in that block smuggled food in to them every day. On October 30, there was a mass selection in Birkenau. Anne and Margot were selected for a transport to an unknown camp. That was the last Rootje saw of them. She and Edith were sent to await their turn in the gas chambers. As they waited, a woman rushed in and told them they had a chance to escape, by running to another block. Together with twenty other women, Rootje and Edith managed to get away.

Rootje told Otto what happened then, and in her memoir of Auschwitz, she recounts: "Edith falls ill, has a high fever. I want her to go to the hospital. But there is a great fear of being gassed because every week Dr. Mengele goes to the sick barracks to pick out those women who in his eyes are too emaciated to remain alive. Despite everything I bring Edith there. Her fever is higher than 106 degrees and she is immediately admitted to the sick barrack." Rootje also entered the sick barracks but was in another block. A few days later: "New patients arrive. I recognize Edith. She comes from another sick barrack ward. She is but a mere

166 shadow of herself. A few days later she dies, totally worn out."[7] Rootje recalled how Otto reacted to the news of Edith's death: "Mr. Frank did not move when I told him. I looked into his face, but he had turned away. And then he made a movement. I no longer remember exactly what it was, but it seems to me he laid his head on the table."[8]

In his diary, Otto recorded the news numbly, while tormenting himself over his children: "Mrs. de Winter, Zutphen. Told of Edith's death on January 6, 1945, in the hospital, from weakness without suffering. Children October to Sudentenland, very brave, especially Anne, miss special Anne."[9]

■

OTTO WROTE TO HIS MOTHER ON MARCH 28 but was unable to continue, "because Edith's news from January 6, which I now have, affects me so badly that I am not quite all with it. . . . Edith died in hospital with weakness caused by malnutrition, her body could not hold out any longer. In reality she is another person murdered by the Germans. If she had managed to survive another two weeks, everything would have been different after the liberation by the Russians. I have to ask myself, whether we can get to Holland, I do not know. I hope, however, that we can still get there, in spite of the fact that Holland is still not liberated. I do not wish to write any more today."[10] Otto and his comrades waited anxiously for a week as rumors that they were to be transported to Odessa grew, but the transfer failed to materialize. His health was still very poor, and he was in pain from severe diarrhea. At night, they were locked into the school, but during the day and evening he went outside, filled with wonder at the glorious spring weather. In his diary, he notes that he sold his sweater and socks to buy bacon, eggs, and beer.

On March 31, the train that would take them to Odessa arrived at last. Otto wrote to his mother in a more positive mood: "It may be possible that people here can travel onwards, but nobody can say when we will be back in Holland. Indeed it seems that the war is coming rapidly to an end. I am well and am standing up to things well, in spite of the sad news of the death of my wife. I only hope to find my children back at home!"[11] He boarded the train the following day ("thirty-two persons per carriage"),[12] but it was several hours before it began to move, and it made frequent stops for no apparent reason. However, this gave the survivors the opportunity to climb out and exchange information. Otto and Eva Geiringer met again during the journey. She recalls him "standing alone at one of the stops. He looked worn out and sad. Mutti [Eva's mother, Fritzi] was with me then and asked to be introduced to him. She knew he'd just heard from Rootje that his wife had died and she felt great pity for him. I took her over and they exchanged polite words, but there was little to console him and he had no interest in anything. He seemed to want to keep himself apart and remain alone with his grief."[13]

In his diary, Otto recorded the journey and their eventual arrival in Czernowitz. His entries became more detailed as he began to take more interest in his surroundings. After months of starvation, he and his comrades were obsessed with food. Otto listed everything he ate, unable to believe such luxuries as fresh chicken and beer were available. He enjoyed seeing the landscape from the train as it advanced slowly, delayed by cargo trains approaching; at night it hardly moved. During the daytime, passengers climbed down to trade with local farmers. Otto records swapping his shirt for a loaf of bread and a potato dumpling. On April 5, he wrote: "Driving much more regularly. Villages and community houses with straw, much destroyed. We are on our way to Odessa." On the evening of April 6, they arrived in Czernowitz. The following morning, Otto walked three kilometers in the rain to the barracks in the town. He met several Jews who "gave generously bread, eggs, money, liqueur, tea. An enormous reception from all sides, the people seem to be very compassionate." The barracks were new but cold, and the survivors had to sleep on the floor. Food mattered most of all, and that was good. Otto's health had suffered a relapse, and he found it difficult to walk through streets "full of mud because of the rain. . . . My intestines are not okay yet, which depresses my mood. Late bath and disinfecting."[14]

The next day he was still sick and stayed indoors, but the following day he sold some tobacco he had managed to procure to buy bilberries, which he had been told would help his stomach recover. He visited a market where the people were "still compassionate. Invited by lady for tea and cake." He was well enough to join two comrades in getting drunk on double vodkas and wine, which helped him to sleep. The following day, he visited the market again and stood watching the "farmers in old traditional clothes, lots of chickens, eggs, geese, apples, fowl being bought alive."[15] He met many generous people and became skilled at bartering. On April 12, he wanted to find a synagogue but had to collect his thoughts in a park under brilliant sunshine. In an old villa nearby, he met a family who invited him home and made him an excellent meal. They asked him to visit again, but despite his success in leaving the collection center after hours (by slipping under the fence while the guard's back was turned), he was unable to get out of the barracks again.

On April 17, the train was prepared for travel, but Otto was angry when he found that he was not allowed on the transport because he was German. He and several other German-born survivors tried to argue their case but simply had to wait their turn. The following day, it snowed, but Otto sneaked into town to sell his blanket and bought bread and apples. He was seen and brought back to the barracks. He noted, "Was picked up by Russians! It turns out well for me." On April 21, he noted excitedly: "The weather has improved—sun! I was placed on the list, all of a sudden transport in the afternoon. Late in the wagons, the train does not leave yet.

Russians say that Berlin has been taken. In full wagon, did not sleep." Berlin had not surrendered, however, and the train remained in the station until the following afternoon, when people who had hidden in the wagons were discovered. Otto recorded: "Terrible for those people. I was almost among them. In the afternoon the train leaves, slow speed. No sleep, too many people."[16] Diphtheria broke out in one wagon, and a lot of people crowded into Otto's compartment. He had "a very unpleasant night" due to the overcrowded carriage and his diarrhea.

Late in the evening of April 24, the train arrived at the Black Sea port of Odessa. The passengers remained in the train overnight and were taken to their accommodation the following day. It was a five-kilometer walk to the collection center, and one of Otto's shoes split on the way. Around him, the landscape was in ruins: "Everything blown up. Mortar." Otto and his comrades were bathed and deloused. He managed to buy eggs, meat, and red wine and the next day noted that the weather was beautiful. Some Red Cross packages were distributed, and Otto was delighted by the food they were given: "butter, meat, cheese, jam, soap, egg, salmon, chocolate, tea, milk, oatmeal." He and some other comrades were sent to another barracks, less comfortable than the last. On May 2, he wrote: "Tomorrow morning the boat leaves! Exchanged white bread for cigarettes." A moment later, he was told that the transport had been canceled: "Pity. They say that Hitler is dead and Goebbels in the hands of the Russians. In the evening another thirty cigarettes and double chocolate on account of visit by Mrs. Winston Churchill."[17] Hitler had committed suicide in his Berlin bunker on April 30, and Berlin surrendered to the Red Army on May 2; the official German capitulation was announced on May 8. In the Netherlands, the Germans had surrendered two days before.

On May 8, Otto wrote: "Americans enter Utrecht! Impatience increases that we are not getting away yet. Lots of noise and shouting for joy during the night." On May 11, the Auschwitz survivors were moved to a sanatorium twelve miles away. Otto stood in a meadow to take in the "amazing" view of the Black Sea. He was angry that the French were allowed to travel first, but he enjoyed sitting on the beach in the sun. There was "no talk about transportation yet. Everybody is impatient, in spite of daily chocolate and cigarettes." On May 14, they were forced to move on to another house, but Otto and some of his comrades returned in disgust to protest the conditions there. Otto recorded a "sit-down strike. Remained in our room with about thirty men. Others moved." They stayed in the room that night and the following morning were promised "a tent if we are not satisfied with the home. . . . Bath and clean underwear. Wonderful weather. Rain at night." The next day, Otto and his comrades were angry again at their treatment: "The sea is calm, see a ship now and then. The *Nijkerk* is in port, but little hope that we are allowed to go with them. Protest telegram to the embassy because of discrimination of the Dutch people as opposed to the French." On May 19, he wrote: "Talk of transportation aboard an English warship. Tomorrow or the day after. The rumor is confirmed. Great joy, but also still mistrust." A day later, his fears were swept away: "Lay on the beach in the sun. Sword-lilies and tulips are in bloom. [Later] After the meal all of a sudden the order: Pack! With tram and luggage to the harbor. . . . In the harbor large boat about 18,000 tons (English). What a feeling!"[18]

The *Monowai*, a New Zealand ship, had returned from Marseilles with repatriated Russian prisoners of war. The journey from Odessa to Marseilles with the concentration camp survivors would be the second of three trips of its kind, taking former prisoners home. The men slept on hammocks below decks while the women were given cabins. Also on board were French and Italian prisoners of war and a group of voluntary workers. The crew, in their neat uniforms, cared for their passengers well and were keen to see that they received nourishing food. Headwinds delayed their departure until the afternoon of May 21. In the evening sun, Otto ate a meal on the deck, only to find later that his mattress had been stolen. His hammock was comfortable enough, and on the morning of May 22, he woke up with hope for the future, buoyed by the beautiful weather and the substantial breakfast. He spent the afternoon "in the sun on deck, passed Bosporus toward half past five. No war! Streets, minarets, old bastions on the hills, but see also barbed wire." On the evening of May 25, they passed the volcano of Stromboli, which they could see smoking in the distance. The next day, the weather was "a bit stormy, but the boat is excellent. About 3 o'clock, between Sardinia and Corsica. Strong surf, waves came all the way on deck with sunshine. Letters to Mother and Robert."[19]

Otto's letter to his mother has survived. In it, he expresses his longing for his children:

> Tomorrow we will be in Marseilles. . . . We don't know yet whether we can return to Holland or if we'll have to spend a while in England. The main thing for me is that we've left Russia and with this have the possibility to be with our loved ones again. . . . My entire hope lies with the children. I cling to the conviction that they are alive and that we'll be together again, but I'm not promising myself anything. We have all experienced too much to pin our hopes on that kind of thing. Only the children, *only the children* count. I hope continually to find out how they are. . . . Perhaps there are people who have news of the girls. . . . I'll have to stay in Holland, because I don't have any identification—apart from a number—and can only expect to be with you later on. The most important thing now is that we know we'll see each other again soon.[20]

On May 27, the *Monowai* arrived in Marseilles. Otto noted in his diary: "About five o'clock French coast in view. Half past seven an-

chor out. Landing at ten o'clock. Many large ships and large reception for the French with music. Dutch consul takes letters to
Mother and Robert with him. By car to station. Lots of forms, questions. Wine, sandwiches, Red Cross packages. Telegram to Basel.
By car to restaurant. Warm food (cherries). Car-train to Paris eight
o'clock. Joy and help everywhere."[21]

Otto's telegram to his sister in Basel read: "We have arrived
safely in Marseilles and are on our way to Paris, kisses—Otto
Frank."[22] This caused confusion among his relatives when it arrived (it was the first of his letters to reach them), for his mother
assumed he meant that the whole family was together, and overwhelmed with joy and relief, she informed everyone that this was
the case. On May 29, the train arrived, amid torrential rain, in
Lustin, where Otto was billeted for the night in a displaced persons
camp. His registration card has been preserved. Aside from his
name and address, the notes read that he was fluent in Dutch,
English, French, and German, did not claim to be a prisoner of
war, and had almost six hundred French francs on his person
(where he got the money is not clear). The following day, Otto
boarded the train after a breakfast of coffee and marmalade. As
they traveled through Belgium, the weather improved, and Otto
watched the villages decorated with flags to welcome the Allied liberators rush by. At night, he and his comrades disembarked at
"very badly damaged" Roermond and waited through the night for
another train. They traveled a short distance the following day, and
then a few kilometers further the next, spending the night at a
school in Arnhem where "everything is destroyed."[23]

On June 3, 1945, Otto finally arrived in Amsterdam. He ended
his diary: "By car ten o'clock to Utrecht—Rotterdam—
Amsterdam. At eight o'clock everything fine. With car to Miep.
All healthy, Kugler, Kleiman and Lotte Pfeffer. What a joy to see
each other again and how much grief! A load off my mind that all
are here!"[24]

1. Robert, Otto, Herbert and Leni Frank, circa 1895.
Photograph courtesy of Buddy Elias, private collection

2. Otto Frank in 1900.

3. Otto (center) with friends in Frankfurt. The caption on the back reads: "So you won't forget the dancing lessons of winter 1906/07!"
Photograph courtesy of Buddy Elias, private collection

4. Otto and his mother, Alice, on holiday in Granada.
Photograph courtesy of Buddy Elias, private collection

5. Otto around the time of his sojourn in New York.

6. Otto and his siblings shortly before the outbreak of the Great War. *Photograph courtesy of Buddy Elias, private collection*

7. Otto Frank as a German soldier. *Photograph courtesy of Buddy Elias, private collection*

8. Otto being given a haircut while serving on the Somme, 1916. *Photograph courtesy of Buddy Elias, private collection*

9. Edith Holländer, around the time of her engagement to Otto Frank.
Photograph courtesy of Buddy Elias, private collection

10. Otto and Edith's wedding day (and Otto's thirty-sixth birthday), May 12, 1925.
Photograph © AFF/AFS/Archive Photos

11. Otto and his children, Margot and Anne, 1930. Anne captioned this "Papa with his two sprogs."
Photograph © AFF/AFS/ Archive Photos

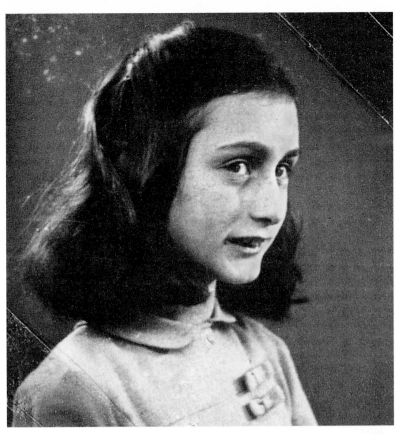

12. Previously unpublished photo of Anne Frank. It was taken shortly before the family went into hiding, and Anne pasted it onto the last page of her first diary. *Photograph © AFF/AFS/Archive Photos*

13. The secret annex during the war years. *Photograph © AFF/AFS/Archive Photos*

14. Three of the helpers (front): Victor Kugler, Bep Voskuijl and Miep Gies. (Back right): Pine; the smiling girl (left) is Esther, who was forced to leave Otto's employ when the anti-Jewish laws came into effect. May 1941. *Photograph © AFF/AFS/Archive Photos*

15. Tonny Ahlers's identity card from the Fokker factory in Amsterdam, 1941.
Photograph © Rijksinstituut, The Hague

16. Tonny Ahlers at the funeral of WA man Hendrik Koot. From *De Telegraaf* newspaper, February 18, 1941. Ahlers is in the white raincoat.
Photograph © De Telegraaf

17. Karl Josef Silberbauer. He led the raid on the secret annex on August 4, 1944.

18. Euterpestraat 99 (now Gerrit van der Veenstraat), the headquarters of the Sicherheitsdienst (German Security Service and Security Police).
Photograph © NIOD

20. Charlotte Pfeffer before the war.
Photograph © AFF/AFS/ Archive Photos

19. Otto Frank, sole survivor of the eight in hiding, reunited with his brothers and sister in Switzerland after the war.
Photograph courtesy of Buddy Elias, private collection

21. Wedding day of Otto and Fritzi, November 10, 1953, in Amsterdam.
Photograph © AFF/AFS/ Archive Photos

22. Otto in his private office at 263 Prinsengracht in 1953. His concentration camp number is visible on his inner arm.
Photograph © Maria Austria Instituut, Amsterdam

23. Otto and his brother Herbert accompany a group of young Japanese readers of Anne's diary around Basel Town Hall.
Photograph courtesy of Buddy Elias, private collection

24. Otto in 1967. His great passion was travel.

25. Otto the grandfather. Otto and Fritzi with Zvi Schloss (left) and Zvi and Eva's three daughters, Jacky, Caroline and Sylvia, whom he loved dearly.
Photograph courtesy of Eva Schloss, private collection

26. Otto a year before his death, with the Orde van Oranje-Nassau medal on his coat. He received the honor on what would have been Anne's fiftieth birthday, June 12, 1979.
Photograph courtesy of Buddy Elias, private collection

SINCE 1943, THE DUTCH GOVERNMENT
in London had been making preparations for the repatriation of
Dutch citizens, estimating that there would be 600,000 returnees,
70,000 of whom would be Jewish.[25] Otto tried to guess how many
would return in a letter to his mother dated June 21, 1945: "Of the
150,000 Jews in this country, I do not believe that there will be
more than 20,000 left."[26] Both estimates fell dismally short of the
actual figures: 5,500 Jews survived the camps and made the journey back to the Netherlands. The Dutch government's treatment of
the concentration camp survivors was nothing short of appalling.
Jews could expect no assistance from the Dutch state; they were
told to apply to Jewish organizations in the Netherlands and abroad
for assistance. Fearing an outbreak of disease and lice when the
survivors returned, the government closed off much of the country
from the east. Jewish survivors kept in centers and camps for displaced persons were often housed in appalling conditions and
treated with disgust. Some survivors were placed in the open yard
of a branch of the Vroom & Dreesman department store, while others were put in former concentration camps alongside members of
the NSB and SS. German Jewish refugees who had lived in the
Netherlands before the war were treated worst of all. On
September 17, 1944, the Dutch government denounced the anti-
Jewish laws and classified German Jews as stateless people of
German origin and therefore "enemy nationals." Only those who
could prove that they had money and homes to return to were allowed to enter the country as regular citizens. (Otto was branded "a
stateless person of German origin," but was able to return to live
with Miep and Jan Gies, nonetheless.) Others were arrested and
imprisoned, and female concentration camp survivors whose hair
had not grown back were assumed to be collaborators whose heads
had been shaved to shame them.

The problems were due not only to the Dutch government but

174   also to the non-Jewish Dutch population, who were waiting anxiously for their own relatives to return from labor camps. The Netherlands had been torn apart during the last months of the occupation, and thousands of Dutch died during the Hunger Winter, when the Germans cut off all food and heating supplies. Returning Jews were often met with a wall of silence from the Dutch, who had no wish to listen to accounts of gas chambers, disease, medical experiments, and death marches that made their own experiences shrink in comparison. Many felt guilty for their lack of support and assistance during the war years, while others decided they had done more than enough to help their Jewish countrymen. The Franks' former neighbor on the Merwedeplein, Laureen Nussbaum, explains: "The general view among the Dutch was, 'We gave you shelter in the 1930s and hid you in the first half of the 1940s, so now go back to where you came from, our job is done.' The Dutch wanted us to fade into the background, they weren't interested in us or what the Jewish people had suffered in those years. They thought their own problems were far more important."[27] The former resistance paper *De Patriot* commented in the summer of 1945:"The re-emerging Jews can thank God for the help they received in that form, and feel humble. Much better people might have been lost because of it. . . . There can be no doubt that the Jews, specifically because of German persecution, were able to enjoy great sympathy from the Dutch people. Now it is appropriate for the Jews to restrain from excess."[28] Some Jewish people returning to their old homes found old acquaintances living there who claimed not to recognize them and refused to move out. Friends who had promised to take care of treasured possessions would not hand them over or swore the items had been taken by the Germans. One survivor of Auschwitz explained, "When I came home to Amsterdam, there was nothing for me. The Dutch had taken everything."[29] The authorities claimed to be powerless in these circumstances and Dutch bureaucracy was equally insen-

sitive, demanding payment of rent and insurance premiums for
the period of deportation.

Anti-Semitism among the Dutch was more apparent after the
war than it was beforehand. In a letter to his brother Robert, Otto
wrote: "The situation of those not yet naturalized is still pretty difficult here. I am sorry to say that the war and Hitler propaganda
have a very bad influence still. There are quite a number of people
coming back from concentration camps who are kept in camps or
not allowed to come back at all."[30] One Jewish woman overheard two
Dutch women commenting, "Look at that, they're wearing their
furs again," while another survivor registering as a repatriate was
greeted by a clerk, "Not another Jew, they must have forgotten to gas
you."[31] Judith de Winter, who had met the Franks in Westerbork, recalls, "I was in a mess, thin as a needle, so when we got home, I was
sent to be examined by a doctor. It was a strange moment. He
looked at me like I came from another world. I could sense a sort of
fear because my experiences were so totally alien to anything he had
encountered. He was not unpleasant, but I could tell by his manner
and the way he touched me that he was frightened of me." Judith was
unable to settle into school and spent a short time in Israel before
deciding to confront "real life" in the Netherlands again: "I came
back to look for a job. I applied for one position at a chemist's in
Amsterdam, and they turned me down—because I was Jewish."[32]

Yet for all those Dutch people who did not welcome Jewish survivors back into the country, there were also many—like the
friends of Otto Frank—who were loyal, sensitive, and caring to the
level of virtuousness. In one of his last interviews, Otto said, "My
greatest support was the five non-Jewish friends who had concealed us in our hiding place. They were friends unto death."[33]

∎

In the summer of 1945, Jan Gies
worked at Amsterdam's Centraal Station registering survivors of
labor and concentration camps. He asked all repatriates arriving in

the city whether they knew anything about the Frank family, the van Pelses, or Fritz Pfeffer. On June 3, a former concentration camp inmate told him that he had seen Otto on the journey back. Just before Jan reached home to give Miep the news, Otto himself appeared at their apartment. Miep recalled: "We looked at each other. There were no words. He was thin, but he'd always been thin. . . . 'Miep,' he said quietly. 'Miep, Edith is not coming back . . . but I have great hope for Anne and Margot.' "[34] Speechless with emotion, Miep guided him indoors.

Later that evening, after Otto had told them his story, he learned what had happened to his Dutch friends. Kleiman and Kugler were imprisoned for a month in Amsterdam before being transferred to Kamp Amersfoort on September 11. Their treatment there was brutal, with frequent roll calls and heavy labor. Kleiman's fragile health deteriorated, and a gastric hemorrhage prevented him from working. On September 18, 1944, the Netherlands Red Cross intervened, and Kleiman was allowed to return home. Kugler remained in Amersfoort until September 26 and was then transferred to the labor camp at Zwolle. On December 30, he was sent to Wageningen, where he was put to work as an electrician and then as a translator for the German army. On March 28, 1945, during a forced march into Germany, Kugler escaped when a group of British Spitfires attacked the area. He hid with a farmer before making his way home to Hilversum. Miep had meanwhile taken charge of the business at Prinsengracht, with Bep working alongside her as usual. Daatselaar, the sales rep who was an NSB member, suggested to Miep that they might be able to bribe the Gestapo into releasing her friends. Miep went twice to the Euterpestraat in the hope that this might work, but it was no use. Van Maaren, the head warehouseman, told Miep that he had been ordered by Silberbauer to act as administrator, which she reluctantly accepted, but when Kleiman returned to work, he dismissed van Maaren as quickly as possible and registered himself as acting director of Gies & Co.

On Monday, June 4, 1945, Otto returned to the Prinsengracht.[35]
His thoughts and feelings must have been in turmoil, but he forced
himself to go up to the former hiding place. When he opened the
door to the annex, the first thing he saw was three brown beans on
the floor: one evening Peter had dragged a sack of supplies up from
the office and it had burst as he tried to carry it to the attic.
Instinctively, Otto picked the beans up and put them in his pocket;
he kept them until his death. In the room he had shared with Edith
and Margot, the dark green paint flaked from the woodwork and
the wallpaper, stained by damp, had begun to peel and bulge. The
map of Normandy, on which Otto had marked the beginnings of
the Allied advance, was still there, and so were the lines indicating
how Anne and Margot had grown. In Anne's room, all her pictures
of film stars, babies, and the classical art that had so appealed to
her lively imagination remained glued to the walls. The thick cur-
tains Otto and Anne had tacked up at the windows to protect their
safety were yellow and ragged, and the smell of neglect hung
throughout the closed-off rooms. When he could bear it no longer,
Otto went downstairs and, out of habit, pushed back the bookcase
to hide the secret door.

Otto had several meetings with old friends that day, including
Kugler, Kleiman, and Lotte Pfeffer. There was no news about
Anne, Margot, Pfeffer, Peter, or Gusti van Pels. In the evening,
Otto had dinner with Miep and Jan again and accepted the offer of
a room in their apartment. Otto insisted that Miep must now address him by his forename, rather than as Mr. Frank, and she
agreed, but only when they were at home. In the office, he would
still be Mr. Frank. "And I never made a mistake in that," Miep recalls. "No. That is maybe why I can handle so many different situ-
ations with different people. That is how I am. I can join in, but in
my heart I may think very differently about things. . . . I am a person who can be silent."[36]

Otto was able to retrieve some of his clothes from friends, along
with a few items of furniture, including the antiques from Edith's

178 dowry. He presented the antiques to Miep, along with a painting that she had always admired, and some real cocoa sent to him from friends in the United States. After months of drinks without any real taste, Miep was so moved by the significance of the gift that she burst into tears. Otto also visited Hendrik van Hoeve, the green-grocer who had provided them with food during the war, and gave him a large basket of fruit, which astonished van Hoeve, who knew how hard it was to come by such delicacies.[37] Otto was more fortunate than most Jews returning to the Netherlands; he was able to find a home with friends, retrieve some of his prewar possessions such as clothes and furniture, and call on friends and family to provide him with money until he was able to repay them. Miep and Kleiman had kept his business running during the months he had been in the concentration camps, and Otto was therefore able to return to work at the Prinsengracht again immediately. There was very little to do, however, since the economy was highly unstable and there were hardly any orders coming in. Occasionally, Otto had to tell his staff that he could not afford to pay them, but they remained as loyal as ever to him. At least Otto could once again take his place alongside Kleiman as a director of Gies & Co. The problems with the Opekta loan resurfaced, however, and Otto wrote to his brother-in-law Erich Elias that, "as regards the Opekta shares, my lawyer takes the standpoint that the old contract between you and me is still in force and that all contracts made under the German oppressor are no longer viable."[38] Nonetheless, as a stateless person of German origin, Otto was seen as an enemy national, and for the next two years, various difficulties arose from the situation.

While Otto was at work on June 8, a postcard his mother had sent to Kleiman in May arrived. For Otto, this was the first sign of life from his mother, sister Leni, brother-in-law Erich, and nephews Buddy and Stephan. Since his friends in Amsterdam had not yet received the letters he sent to them on his journey home,

Otto assumed his mail to Switzerland had not arrived either, although eventually his letters did turn up. He wrote to his mother immediately, condensing all that had happened over the past three years into a few short sentences, unable or unwilling to go into detail. He confessed:

> Everything is like a strange dream. In reality, I can't sort myself out yet. . . . I don't know where the children are, but I never stop thinking of them. . . . Our entire household has been stolen from us. I had kept some things in other places, but not very much. I have neither a hat nor a raincoat, neither a watch nor shoes, apart from those others have lent me, and you can't get anything here, there aren't the supplies. I'm living with Miep Gies. I have enough money at present, I don't need very much anyway. I long to be with you all. . . . I'm waiting to hear from you soon, to learn about everybody—particularly those whom we've heard little about for such a long time. . . . I'm not yet normal, I mean I can't find my equilibrium. Physically, though, I'm fit.[39]

Despite Switzerland's sustained neutrality during the war, the Eliases had also experienced difficulties. After being forced from his job with Opekta, Erich joined another company, Uni-Pectin, which was involved in a similar line of business. Uni-Pectin was based in Zurich, and Erich had to travel the long distance every day by train. The company collapsed during the war, and Erich was again out of work. It was Leni, Otto's flighty younger sister, who saved the family from financial ruin. She began buying shoes and clothes from refugees who needed money and would then sell the goods for slightly more than she had paid. Her small business soon expanded to include household goods and furniture, and before long she had a shop that eventually became a beautiful antiques store. Otto's older brother Robert and his wife, Lottie, were safe in London, while his younger brother

Herbert had spent part of the war in Switzerland, before returning to Paris. He was arrested and imprisoned in the camp at Gurs but managed to survive the starvation and disease that claimed thousands of lives. He returned to his former apartment in the French capital.

Otto's agenda for June 10, 1945, notes, "Dinner at Kleiman's. Moving house."[40] When Miep and Jan's landlady returned from her hiding place in the country, she and her tenants found themselves suddenly incompatible. There was a housing shortage at the time, but Jan's sister who lived on the same street, at 120 Hunzestraat, offered them a home. She gave Jan and Miep her room, and she slept in the sitting room; Otto had a small room at the back of the apartment. Two days after moving into his new home, Otto's thoughts were with his youngest daughter. It was June 12, 1945: Anne's sixteenth birthday. In his agenda, he wrote simply but forcefully, scoring his pen deep into the page, *"Anne."*[41]

■

LIKE THOUSANDS OF JEWS ACROSS EUrope, Otto spent hours trying to piece together the last known movements of his family. He read the lists of victims and survivors printed regularly in the newspapers, called the Red Cross, and placed his own advertisements to inquire for any information about Margot and Anne. His family encouraged him to think positively but grieved and worried with him. His brother Robert wrote, trying to explain their own sorrow at Edith's death and his experiences in Auschwitz:

> How we deplore the loss of Edith, and how we feel with you in your anxiety about your children we cannot describe, just as you have hardly given us a hint of all you have been through during the last few years. May God grant that your children will come back to you soon and in good health. Every other question seems unimportant

compared with this one. You say it's a miracle that you are alive and I believe you and am thankful for it, and that you are in good health and prepared to start a new life. . . . Of course we are longing to see you again and hope that all the restrictions of traveling, etc., will soon be lifted. . . . Tell us as much about you as you feel you can tell us at the moment and believe me that our fondest thoughts are with you all the time.[42]

Missing his children desperately, Otto called upon their friends. On June 14, he visited Anne's friend from the Jewish Lyceum, Jacqueline van Maarsen. She remembers, "He was alone, I didn't understand. I didn't understand the sad eyes on his sunken face either until he told us his story."[43] Laureen Nussbaum and her family had survived, and Otto paid a visit to his former neighbors. Laureen recalls: "Otto came to us not long after his return to Amsterdam. We hadn't moved and that really did delight him, to see us all there, in the same place. I ended up marrying Rudi, a young man who hid in our apartment from September 1944 until the liberation."[44] Otto wanted to talk about his children, but he was eager to help anyone in need. He worked hard to reunite people with their relatives and kept in touch with his former Auschwitz comrades. Max Stoppelman survived the camp, but his wife was dead and he had to build a new life for himself. Sal and Rose de Liema, who had been separated in Auschwitz, found each other again in Amsterdam and were always glad to see Otto. It took a long time for some survivors to return; many were in displaced persons camps and sanatoriums. Otto believed this was the fate of Anne and Margot, as he wrote to his mother: "There is never any communication from Russian-occupied territory and that's why I cannot get any information about the children, since they might be in Germany."[45]

On June 19, Otto's mother wrote of her own distress: "To know that you are alone in your mourning for Edith and still without

182 news of your beloved children is the most terrible experience I have had to bear in a life that has often been very hard. What Edith must have suffered without you and the children, one cannot imagine. We had no news from Czernowitz or Katowice. All the same, my thoughts during that time were always with you. . . . [Edith] was always such a staunch support to you through thick and thin and for the children a devoted mother and the best of friends. I feel the most sorrow for her. . . . Don't lose your courage or hope, and rest assured that deep love embraces you."[46] Alice had contacted the International Red Cross herself to ask if they could trace her granddaughters, but was still waiting to hear from them. On June 21, Otto wrote to Leni and admitted that he was no longer so hopeful that his children had survived: "Up to now I was convinced I'd see them back, but I'm beginning to doubt it. Nobody can imagine how things were in Germany who has not suffered himself. . . . As regards the children, I know that nothing can be done. We have to wait, that's all. I go to the office daily because that's the only way to divert myself. I just can't think how I could go on without the children, having lost Edith already. You don't know how they both developed. It's too upsetting for me to write about them. Naturally I still hope, and wait, wait, wait."[47]

On June 24, Otto visited Eva Geiringer, the young woman he had met in Auschwitz immediately after the liberation. Eva was with her mother, and the two of them were waiting for news of Eva's father and brother. Eva recalls:

> I heard a knock at the front door and found Otto Frank standing there. His gray suit hung loose on his tall, thin frame, but he looked calm and distinguished. "We have a visitor," I said, as I took him in to see Mutti [Eva's mother, Fritzi]. He held out his hand to be introduced to Mutti. "But we've met already," she said, "on the way to Czernowitz." He shook his head. His brown eyes were deep-set and sad. "I don't remember," he said. "I have your

address from the list of survivors. I am trying to trace what has happened to Margot and Anne." He was desolated that he had not yet found them, but he sat and spoke to Mutti for a long time, building up her confidence.[48]

June 28 was Bevrijdingsdag, the official celebration of the liberation. Otto spent the day quietly with Miep, Jan, and Bep. The following day, Edith's brother Julius wrote to Otto: "My last hope is that you will find the children. Walter and I will do everything for you. In case you want to come to the USA we have money saved for you three. Send me a cable when you have found the children. . . . Let me know if you need food. We will send it."[49] On July 7, Otto wrote to Robert and Lottie in London about the difficulty of obtaining accurate information about those still missing:

> As much as I feel the loss of Edith, the sorrow about my children is still prevailing. I *have* to take in the fact of Edith's fate, but I still hope to find my children and that is at the moment all I live for. By chance I heard that a girl returning from Theresienstadt told another girl that she saw Anne and Margot there after the liberation but very ill with typhoid fever. I asked quite a lot of people coming from there but nobody confirmed the news up to now. On the lists their names do not appear, but that does not mean much as the lists are not reliable and very often the names of stateless people are not taken. I do all to find out more about it and I waver between hope and fear. The girl who told the story is not back yet, the girls met at Leipzig, so I can't speak to her myself.[50]

A few days later, Otto received another letter from Julius: "I hope you are doing well in Amsterdam. Every day I expect news from you about the children. Even more than the passing away of Edith, the destiny of the two girls is on my mind day and night. But it is of no use to make life more difficult for you than it is. . . . Please inform

184   us at once and by using the shortest way when you hear of them. Wishing you all luck."[51]

On July 18, 1945, Otto finally found out what had happened to his children. Checking the Red Cross lists once more, he saw at last: Annelies Marie Frank and Margot Betti Frank. But beside their names were the dreaded symbols of crosses, which could mean only one thing. He asked for the name of the woman who had given the information and then traveled to Laren, where he met Lin Brilleslijper, who was renting a small house there with her husband, Eberhard Rebling. Lin, who later wrote and spoke often about her experiences, told Otto everything. She began by telling him that, at the beginning of November, she and her sister Janny were transported from Auschwitz to Bergen-Belsen in Germany. The camp was situated on flat moorland and was wide open to the elements. The Germans had planned to use it originally as a prison for Jews who could be exchanged with German hostages abroad, but the idea was never realized, and in late 1944, thousands of sick prisoners from other camps were evacuated to Bergen-Belsen. There were not enough huts to accommodate the newcomers, so vast tents were erected upon the windswept heath. Immediately after their arrival, wrapped in blankets, Lin and Janny walked to the water pipe on the hill to wash. "Two scrawny threadbare figures emerged," Lin wrote in her memoir. "They looked like little frozen birds. We lay down in the bunkhouse and wept." The frozen birds were Margot and Anne Frank. They told the Brilleslijper sisters that they had been on the Auschwitz transport, and that their mother had been selected. The four of them went over to the tents. "We lay down on some straw and cringed together under our blankets. In the first days it was warm, we slept a lot. It started to rain." Despite their weakened state, the women were forced to work, pulling apart old shoes in a long barracks. A storm broke out one night, and the tents were ripped from their moorings. Barracks were eventually built for them, but more transports arrived each

day: "We were displaced from our bunks. Now we had no roof over
our heads. Every day there was roll-call. But at dusk we had to be
back in the bunks, or we would have been shot."[52]

In the early days of 1945, a typhus epidemic raged through the
camp. Thousands were dying from it, and from hunger and thirst.
The guards deliberately cut off the water supply. Bodies lay everywhere. For a time, the Brilleslijpers did not see Margot or Anne,
but in March, "when the snow was already melting," they found
them in the sick barracks. Both girls had typhus. "We begged them
not to stay there, as people there deteriorated so quickly and
couldn't bring themselves to resist. . . . Anne simply said, 'Here
we can both lie on the bed; we'll be together and at peace.' Margot
only whispered; she had a high fever."[53] Anne and Margot returned
to their usual barracks, where Margot's condition quickly worsened. Seeking to rise from her bunk one day, she fell to the floor.
The shock killed her.

Janny, whom Otto called upon after visiting Lin, recalled later:
"At a certain moment in the final days, Anne stood in front of me,
wrapped in a blanket. . . . She told me that she had such a horror
of lice and fleas that she had thrown all her clothes away . . . during dreadful hallucinations."[54] Without her sister, not knowing that
Otto was alive, but realizing her mother was dead, and suffering
from a violent strain of typhus, Anne died in the camp in late
March 1945. A short while later, Lin and Janny found the bodies of
Anne and Margot and carried them over to one of the mass graves
where up to ten thousand corpses were buried. Bergen-Belsen was
liberated three weeks later.

In the agenda that he kept at the time, and in which he always
recorded any significant events, Otto could find no words for the
worst day of his life. The diary only discloses the fact of his meeting with Lin Brilleslijper, and its magnitude:

"18 July 1945: *Lien Rebling* >!"[55]

Two days after Otto learned of his daughters' agonizing deaths

186   in Bergen-Belsen, the reckless figure who had dominated his life from the shadows during the war emerged again, and began manipulating him once more.

On July 20, 1945, Otto Frank wrote one word in his agenda: "Ahlers."[56]

IN JUNE AND JULY 1945, THE DUTCH AU-
thorities descended on Amstelveen and arrested all those whom
they knew or suspected of having been Nazi sympathizers. Tonny
Ahlers was one of the first to be picked up, on June 6, 1945, less
than two weeks after his second child, another boy, was born.[1] His
brother Cas remembers: "Tonny was stunned when he was arrested. He felt no guilt about his earlier actions. He truly expected
to sail through the liberation without any difficulties—he really had
no idea that he would be arrested and imprisoned."[2] At the end of
June, Tonny Ahlers was sent to the Scheveningen prison, some
distance from Amsterdam, and he was still there on Friday, July 20,
when Otto recorded his name in his agenda.

Did they meet? It is not impossible, but what seems more likely
is that Ahlers's wife, Martha, contacted Otto on her husband's behalf. "Ahlers" appears again in Otto's agenda three days later, on
Monday, July 23.[3] Martha recently told a family member that Otto
had appeared one day on her doorstep, but then one has to ask:
how did Otto know where to find her?[4] This, too, remains a mys-
tery. Martha recalled that Otto had already written a letter in her

188   husband's defense, which he showed to her, saying, "It's terrible, I
        know he is in jail but he's a good man who saved my life. Why are
        they doing this to him?" Martha also claims that Otto invited her to
        visit him at his office, and when she turned up, he showed her
        around the secret annex, which she remembers as very different
        from how it is today.[5] Whatever actually took place on those days,
        the fact is that on July 24, 1945, Otto wrote to the prison authori-
        ties that "in passing" he had heard that Ahlers was "currently in-
        terned" with them and that "I have some information about this
        man and would like to know to which address I should send my in-
        formation."[6] Scrawled across the envelope is Ahlers's cell number.

        The following month, on August 21, 1945, Otto sent a letter to
        the Bureau Nationale Veiligheid (BNV), describing his first meet-
        ing with Ahlers in 1941. He avowed that after two meetings, during
        which he had voluntarily given Ahlers money, "I never saw him
        again." Curiously, Otto had forgotten the date of the encounter
        with Jansen, who tried to betray him to the SS, but he vividly re-
        called when he met Ahlers. Likewise, Otto could not remember
        Joseph Jansen's first name, despite the Jansens being "well known
        to me," and yet he recalled Ahlers's full name and address from
        "one" meeting in 1941. The business arrangement between Otto
        and Ahlers is one explanation, of course, but the additional, very
        precise information presumably came from Ahlers or his wife,
        Martha, during meetings in the summer of 1945. Most astonishing
        of all, Ahlers had the original of Otto's letter to the BNV (a fact that
        emerged a few years later). Only one person could have given it to
        him, since the police would never have done so: Otto Frank. Otto
        ended his letter to the BNV: "I feel that Ahlers saved my life, be-
        cause if [Jansen's] letter had reached the hands of the SS, I would
        have been arrested and executed. . . . I know nothing else about
        this young man."[7]

        Otto's agenda for August reveals two more dates on which the
        name "Ahlers" features: Friday, August 27, and Monday, August

30.[8] Whether the references were to meetings with Ahlers's wife or with Ahlers himself will probably never be known. Otto would write one more letter about the former Dutch Nazi that year, but in the meantime Ahlers was released from prison and attended his brother Huibert's wedding. The shock of "seeing this creature again" impelled one of his brothers-in-law to send a blistering letter to the Dutch authorities. He outlined Ahlers's anti-Semitism, his love of National Socialism, and his violent behavior, and he explained how members of the family had dreaded his visits in wartime: "We were in a state of extreme tension in order to make sure that the people who were in hiding disappeared, or that those who happened not to be at home would not return, that no people came calling to ask for distribution documents or false identity cards and that our children would not let slip who was in our home, or about the wireless. . . . Tonny told us about his good relations with the SD, about his beautiful Jewish home in South Amsterdam and so on, and never missed an opportunity to show us his SD member card. We were always deeply relieved when he left again." In March 1945, Ahlers had apparently visited his sister and brother-in-law to boast about his new work for the resistance: "Knowing his imagination, I asked him for details but he could not respond satisfactorily. If he tried to make himself useful after September 1944, then it was certainly calculated. . . . If he was released [from Scheveningen prison] because of his conduct during the last months of the occupation, then there is something not right about this." Ahlers's brother-in-law ended his letter, "For us he will always be a traitor, someone who collaborated with the Germans."[9]

On November 27, Otto wrote his last letter about Ahlers to the Dutch authorities. It was the same as his letter to the BNV, but with one very interesting addition: "When I found out later that Mr. Ahlers, who had passed himself off as a courier between the NSB and SD, was locked up in the prison on van Alkemadelaan in The

Hague, I felt compelled to write to the BNV to declare what Mr. Ahlers had done for me. When Mr. Ahlers returned from prison some months ago, he came to visit me and told me what had happened. From his remarks I understood that he was very active underground. How it all occurred, I cannot judge, I can only express my gratitude for the great service that Mr. Ahlers has rendered me."[10] We can assume from this letter, then, that at some point during the summer of 1945 Otto and Ahlers did meet. According to Martha Ahlers, Otto visited her husband in prison and gave him a small amount of money to help him out.[11]

On November 28, 1945, the name "Ahlers" appears again in Otto's agenda. Exactly why was Otto so preoccupied with him at such a traumatic point in his own life? Two days before "Ahlers" first appears in Otto's diary in July 1945, Otto had learned that his daughters were dead: when he wrote to the prison authorities in defense of Ahlers on July 24, he also wrote to inform his family that same day that Anne and Margot were never coming home. There was a pattern to the dates and letters concerning Ahlers: the meetings in July, August, and November 1945 always occurred within a few days of the letters Otto wrote in support of him. Equally as telling, Otto was always honest, yet in his letters to the Dutch authorities he was clearly untruthful about his association with Ahlers: he repeatedly changed his story over how often they met, whether money was involved, and whether Ahlers had asked for payment or not. Why did Otto defend him?

At that point, Otto had no reason to suspect Ahlers of his betrayal. As far as he knew, Ahlers had given him Jansen's letter in return for money, and then, according to the Ahlers family, Otto and Ahlers had done business together.[12] But in 1945, when Otto returned to the Netherlands, he did so as "a German," an enemy national, and the persecution he had suffered because he was Jewish meant nothing to the Dutch government. As a German entering the Netherlands, he was due to be investigated for his political allegiances during the war. He had to appeal to people, such as Jan Gies, Johannes Kleiman, and his own lawyer, to speak up for him and confirm to the Dutch government that he "was and is anti-German and anti–National Socialist."[13] When Ahlers wrote to the Dutch authorities in his own defense in 1945, he denied all wrong-doing and claimed to be appalled that "these firms and their own-ers" who had traded with him during the war now spoke "with loathing about the dirty collaborators and traitors of their coun-try." He claimed that his company was "the only one that knows anything about their aspirations to being important during the war."[14] Ahlers wanted Otto to speak up for him, and he had the means of persuading him to do so: in his 1960s letters, Ahlers spun an unpleasant tale about Otto's deliveries to the Wehrmacht, the uses of pectin in the war industry, and the NSB men Otto em-ployed while dismissing the Jewish secretary who once worked for him. Otto's company, which had struggled throughout the 1930s, had made a small but significant profit during the war.[15] He could have said the same things in 1945, with unpleasant consequences for Otto Frank. Miep Gies admits that Otto was worried about the investigations into his past; she explained to a family friend that he was "concerned about his company and the Government, who were considering him still as a 'German' with a 'German' company."[16] Ahlers was unscrupulous, as Otto knew only too well. The letters Otto sent to the authorities on his behalf would ensure that Ahlers kept his silence.

In September 1945, Ahlers was released from jail and returned to his wife and family. According to his Social Services files, he was released because of "certain people, including Jews, declaring that he had helped them" during the war.[17] Yet Otto Frank's letters are the only statements to that effect in Ahlers's files. Ahlers's free-dom did not last long; the POD (Politieke Opsporings Dienst, the Political-Criminal Investigations Department of the Dutch police) remained highly suspicious that somehow Ahlers had managed to

192 engineer matters to his own advantage, and by December he was in prison once more.[18]

■

WHILE OTTO HOPED HIS WARTIME BUSI-
ness dealings would not return to haunt him, his confidence that his children would come back was gone. In his memoir, Otto wrote: "I found two sisters who had been with Margot and Anne in Bergen-Belsen, and they told me about the final sufferings and deaths of my children. . . . My friends, who had been hopeful with me, now mourned with me. . . . It took many months for me to get used to a normal life without my loved ones."[19] He wrote to Herbert in July that he was doing his best "to think of other things and cannot sit still. No one must know how I grieve inside. Who can understand anyway? My wonderful people here, but only these few."[20] His family sent him almost daily letters to offer comfort, condolence, and support. Otto wrote to Robert and Lottie on July 26 but found it impossible to write about his children:

> I'm cared for in every respect. I behave surprisingly calmly. There is so much misery around me that I try to help wherever I can. I feel no bitterness, dear Robert, because I saw so much misery, lived in such wretchedness, and meet all over the same situation. So I cannot say: Why me? Out of the more than 100,000 Jews who were deported, about 2,000 have returned as yet. From the thousands who were forced to flee with the Germans, I met 3 who escaped being shot or frozen to death. I always say again that only those who lived under the oppressor know what it means. I could talk to you for hours about Edith and the girls, but it doesn't help and it's very upsetting for me. So I'll leave it until we meet again.[21]

He began a letter to Milly with the avowal that he would "never be able to bear" the truth about his children's deaths: "Nobody can really help me, though I have many friends. Useless to say much about it, I know quite well those who mean it and those who just only talk."[22] In another letter to Milly, Otto described one positive aspect of life in hiding: "You can have no idea how the girls had developed, because you only knew them as attractive children. Living so close together, we watched them grow into mature human beings and realized their true potentialities. You will hardly believe it, but in spite of the constant strain and tension, the ever-present fear of discovery, we were really happy because we were sharing everything."[23]

In August, letters for Otto came swiftly and in great number from his family. All conveyed their grief over Margot and Anne and expressed their concern for him. Julius and Walter Holländer described their own anguish: "We loved Margot and Anne as if they were our own children. Our life is empty now. Edith and the girls were all we had."[24] Robert expressed sentiments that were often repeated by those who knew Otto: "We admire you greatly for the way you can think and act without a word of bitterness or hatred after all you have been through."[25] The whole family in Switzerland sent him a telegram on August 6: "Received sad news we all mourn our dearest ones fondest love and thoughts keep strong and healthy kisses Mother—Elias Frank."[26] They pleaded with him to visit Switzerland as soon as possible, but as a stateless person Otto was not permitted to travel beyond the Netherlands, even though the war officially ended on August 14, with the surrender of the Japanese government. Although he desperately wanted to visit his family in Switzerland, his time was now occupied with the discovery of a very precious object: Anne's diary.

■

SINCE HIS RETURN TO AMSTERDAM, OTTO had been under the impression that very few of his family's personal belongings remained. He was profoundly shocked to discover that a photo album and Anne's diary had been saved. Miep explained to Otto how, after the police had gone on the day of the arrest at the Prinsengracht, she had been left alone in the offices. The warehousemen were still working below, but she did not see them. Around five o'clock, Jan returned with Bep, and together with van Maaren, who had the keys, they unlocked the door to the annex and went inside. The rooms were in chaos, but among the items scattered on the floor, Miep saw Anne's red checked diary. She picked it up and then sifted through the mess to find the other books and loose pages Anne had used to continue keeping a diary when the original was full. Miep and Bep gathered up all the papers they could find, along with a few other belongings, and deposited them in Miep's desk drawer. The following week, Miep asked van Maaren to check the annex for more papers. He found some and handed them over to Miep, who placed them in her desk with the others. Not long afterward the annex was emptied of its furniture by the Puls removal company.

At first, Miep said nothing to Otto about the diary because she hoped to give it back to Anne, but when Otto told her that his children were dead, she thought of it immediately. She recalls, "I gave what pieces of Anne's writing I had back to Mr. Frank. I gave him everything that I had stored in the desk drawer in my office."[27] Otto's initial reaction to seeing his daughter's cherished diary again is not known, but when he wrote to his mother a few days later, he confessed: "Miep by chance saved an album and Anne's diary. But I don't have the strength to read it. There's nothing of Margot's left anymore, only her Latin work, because our whole household was looted, and that's why everything we used so often and all Edith's and the children's lovely little possessions are lost. I know there is no sense in thinking about them, yet a human being isn't just a mind, but has a heart too."[28] It was several weeks before he could bring himself to open the diary and begin reading.

During that time, Otto learned what had happened to Fritz

Pfeffer and Peter and Gusti van Pels. Pfeffer had been transferred from Sachsenhausen to Neuengamme concentration camp, where his health swiftly began to fail. He died in the Neuengamme sick barracks on December 20, 1944, from enterocolitis, a disease of the intestine. Gusti van Pels arrived on November 26 in Bergen-Belsen, where she was reunited with Anne and Margot, but on February 6, 1945, she was sent to work in an airplane factory in Raguhn, which formed part of Buchenwald camp. She was transferred to Theresienstadt at the beginning of April, but her final whereabouts are unknown; the Red Cross estimates that she died between April 9 and May 8, 1945, in Germany or Czechoslovakia. Peter van Pels survived the death march from Auschwitz. He arrived in Mauthausen, where he was put to work with Melk, the outdoor commando unit that toiled in the camp's rock quarries and underground arms factories. Melk was disbanded at the end of April 1945, and Peter, exhausted and chronically ill, was sent to the sick barracks. He died there on May 5, 1945, the day the camp was liberated.[29]

The news of his friends' deaths affected Otto deeply, and the only way he found himself able to avoid depression was by working and making himself useful to others. In his memoir, he recalled: "I tried to build a new existence in Amsterdam with the helpers who worked for my spice-importing business. I tried to rebuild the firm. I also attempted to reunite orphaned children with their relatives. I visited patients in various sanatoriums. All of this gave me new goals in life."[30] Among those he was able to help were Anne's best friend, Hanneli Goslar, and her young sister, Gabi. Hanneli's mother died in childbirth in 1942, along with the baby she was carrying. The rest of the family were sent to Westerbork and Bergen-Belsen as "exchange Jews" who were never exchanged. Hanneli lost her father and grandparents and put all the energy she had left into caring for Gabi. In February 1945, Hanneli discovered that Anne was in the camp and was able to meet her several times. She

196   recalls: "Anne told me that her father had been killed—her mother, too, she thought. It was a pity she thought her father had died when he had not. The way she idolized him, perhaps she would have had the hope to live if she knew he was still alive."[31] Hanneli and Gabi were sent to Theresienstadt with seven thousand other people, but the train never arrived at its destination; on April 23, 1945, they were liberated by the Russians. Hanneli was taken to a hospital in Maastricht, and Gabi was placed in the care of a family friend.

When he heard where Hanneli was, Otto immediately set out to visit her, traveling fourteen hours in a truck to get there. Hanneli recalls, "I was so excited when Otto came to see me. The first thing I said was, 'Anne is alive, she's in Germany!' He had to tell me the awful truth. We talked for a long time. Otto had me moved from Maastricht to the Joodse Invalide in Amsterdam, which was much better. The sixth floor was for Jews returning from the camps." Otto then arranged for Hanneli to be transferred to a sanatorium in Switzerland, where her uncle lived. Hanneli remembers, "Otto helped me and my sister, Gabi, to get to Switzerland. He sorted out the documents necessary to do that—I couldn't, of course. On December 5, he took me, my sister, and two of my friends to Schipol Airport to see us off, but before we left, he gave us necklaces with Dutch coins on with the date inscribed on the back. I lived in Basel for a while and would sometimes visit Otto's family there. I felt so strange and guilty the first time I had to go to see his old mother; I had survived and her grandchildren had died. In 1947, I emigrated to Palestine, and Gabi followed in 1949. Otto and I stayed in close touch."[32]

Otto also visited Jacqueline van Maarsen again. She recalls: "He cried and cried. He came to see me often, and I was at a loss as to how to console him. The only thing I could do was talk to him about his children, and that was really the only thing he wanted."[33] To his family, such as his brothers-in-law Julius and Walter, Otto wrote about daily practicalities: "Everything seems unimportant, senseless. But life goes on and I try not to think too much and to be angry. We all have to bear our fate. Here all the money I had was taken but it may be that I get a part of it back. I don't need money now, I receive what I need in the firm. I am not working officially and the laws for people not yet naturalized are a handicap in some ways."[34] Business was dismal, and Otto explained why: "I have to build up and work. In poor Holland it is so difficult, especially if you're stateless. Everything is export, not import and then only the most vital of commodities, certainly not pectin."[35] In another letter, he tried to remind himself to be grateful for the little he had: "Luckily I have a base here to start again . . . if the money will be restored the Germans took from me, I needn't complain. . . . There is nothing one can buy anyway. Holland is looted to a great extent."[36] The outstanding amount from the Pectacon liquidation was transferred from the Nederlandse Bank to a company dealing with the repayment of Jewish funds, and in 1947, Otto finally received the credit balance.

Otto was not yet able to find the courage to read Anne's diary, but he did write a little about his lost children to his cousin Milly:

> As the girls grew older they were real friends, especially when we were forced to be together for more than two years in two little rooms. I had time to tell them everything about the family and Anne made a genealogical tree of the family and she wanted to know all about every member. I always impressed on the girls to stick together even if their characters were different and they did. Margot was very good in English, she read *Hamlet* and *Julius Caesar* in the original language; Anne of course only started but worked daily. She read little stories. So great was her interest that she pinned photos of the Royal Family to the wall—they are there still. Of course I know that I shall never get over it and I miss the children far more than Edith. It was the hope and the future and that counts more than the present life. I informed the children about

198   everything, as I thought that we might not return, but I trusted
they would. By chance the friends here could save some photos
and the daybook of Anne. I had it in my hands but I couldn't read
it yet. Perhaps I shall have the force to do so later.[37]

Otto's letters to the family in Switzerland also began to contain
more information about his murdered wife and children. His
emotional state remained very fragile. On September 1, he wrote:

On Monday evening, I went to Hilversum, to the Hofs' house. I
took nearly all our silver cutlery there and it's still there, safe. Mrs.
Hof was always very kind and Edith never forgot her. She helped
Edith in 1933 when Edith didn't know how things worked here, the
schools and so on. . . . I will do all I can to come soon. I'm a bit
afraid of that, though. I'm really on the verge of tears and find it so
easy to cry. . . . Of course, the thoughts of Edith and the children
never leave me, but I'm trying to look more on the positive side of
things than the negative. . . . Sometimes I can't believe that I'm
56 years old. But for me, life does not have meaning anymore.[38]

Otto's delicate composure was almost shattered by the arrival of
a letter from the United States. Otto wrote about the incident to his
mother on September 6, explaining that it was a pen-pal letter for
Anne and Margot: "This girl wanted to start their correspondence
again. I wrote to her in floods of tears. Things like that upset me
very much."[39] The girl was Betty-Ann Wagner, who, together with
her sister Juanita, had exchanged letters with Margot and Anne in
early 1940. She recalls her feelings on receiving Otto's letter. "He
told us how the family had died during the war. I just sat and cried.
I was then teaching, and when I read the details [of Otto's letter], I
read it to my students and tried to impress upon them what had
happened."[40]

At any moment, Otto was liable to break down. He avoided the synagogue on Yom Kippur because there was only an Orthodox service, which "means nothing to me. I know Edith was not so narrow-minded in her thoughts. She never expected or wanted me to fast, and she understood that I went to synagogue only because of her. I would have gone with her or the children, but to go alone makes no sense and would only be hypocrisy."[41] The Liberal Jewish community in Amsterdam had been decimated, but a few who remained wanted to rebuild what was left of their community, and Otto was asked to join them. He immediately accepted and attended regularly on Friday evenings when the Liberal synagogue opened for services. The prayer for the dead that was recited every Friday was one that gave him much strength. Despite his declaration that "I see how much help religion can give, but it's not for me," after the war Otto always carried a notebook in which he had written lines from Jewish prayers and another prayer by Saint Francis of Assisi.[42]

Otto's Saturday evenings were regularly spent with Miep, Jan, Lotte Pfeffer, and some other friends who liked to play canasta. One night, Lotte told him she had received a letter from Werner Peter Pfeffer, Fritz's son, who was living in England. The content of his letter is not known, but whatever he had written upset Lotte greatly, and Otto felt that he should respond. He tried to be as diplomatic as possible, writing:

> I try to place myself in your position. You were about twelve years old when you were separated from your father. You cannot know how he lived in the meantime, what happened in all these years. I on my part know nothing about your mother, your father never spoke about her and he introduced Charlotte as Mrs. Pfeffer to all his acquaintances. Nobody knew that he was not really married to her and it was not his fault that it was not done, but the laws that prevented it being done. For Charlotte this situation is a very difficult one. She did everything possible for your father, she was the

greatest support for him and I know and admire her. I would do anything to help her, she is worth it. And I feel it my duty to tell you that, to inform you. It is impossible for me to judge your feelings toward her but I know it to be in the sense of your father that you respect her for what she is and that you have all the confidence in her and keep in closest connection.[43]

Despite Otto's efforts, Werner Peter and Lotte were never reconciled, and matters only worsened when Lotte had her marriage to Fritz Pfeffer posthumously recognized and received the repatriation payments that Pfeffer's son felt were rightfully his. Werner Peter emigrated to the United States and opened an office furniture and supplies company under the name Peter Pepper. It was many years before he and Otto were in contact again.

On September 24, Otto wrote to his old friend Nathan Straus, who was then president of the New York radio station WMCA: "Dear Charley, you told me once that I am the only one who calls you by this name, but I feel more the old relations between us if I still call you by that name."[44] When Straus replied, he said that he had cabled Otto five hundred dollars, which he hoped would be "some assistance to you in what, despite your unwillingness to speak of it, must be difficult financial circumstances. Don't trouble to acknowledge it. You just forget about it."[45] Otto was overcome by his friend's generous gesture, which he intended to put to good use: "I know you don't like me to speak about it but nevertheless I thank you with all my heart. Even if I am not really in need I don't own much and the amount will help me and others along, as I always use part of what I earn for others, especially orphans at the moment, who want to join their families abroad or to go to Palestine."[46] A few days later, Otto's fragile self-defenses took another blow. He wrote to his mother: "I have just been in the synagogue for a children's festival. Anne and Margot always went to this event together, even when they were in Aachen. On the outside, I was smiling, but inside I was crying bitterly."[47] For parents whose children were killed in the Holocaust, the specter of the lost child or children was ever-present. When Leni's son Stephan fell ill, Otto wrote urging her to be strong for her child: "Human beings can withstand so much when they really must."[48]

In that same letter, Otto revealed that he had at last begun to read Anne's diary. He was both astonished and fascinated by it and in awe of the talent for writing he had never known she possessed: "What I'm reading in her book is so indescribably exciting, and I read on and on. I cannot explain it to you! I've not finished reading it yet, and I want to read it right through before I make some excerpts or translations for you. She writes about her growing up with incredible self-criticism. Even if it hadn't been written by her, it would have interested me. What a great pity that this life had to go."[49] He was enthralled by the diary and the idea of introducing her remarkable gift to friends and family: "I can't put Anne's diary down. It's just so incredible. Somebody has begun copying out the 'fairytales book' that she wrote because I don't want to let it out of my hands for a moment, and it is being translated into German for you. I *never* allow the diary out of my sight because there is so much in it that no one else should read. But I will make excerpts from this."[50]

At the start of November 1945, Otto asked his friend Anneliese Schütz to help him translate some diary passages from Dutch into German for his mother in Switzerland. Schütz, who had worked for the Jewish Council before being deported to Westerbork and Theresienstadt, was living with friends in Amsterdam. She agreed to translate the diary, working from Otto's typed Dutch transcript; he copied the diary out so that he could hold on to the original diaries himself. Miep, who resisted Otto's pleadings that she read the diary, recalls how every night after they had eaten, Otto would work on the translation into German: "Sometimes he'd come walking out of his room holding Anne's little diary and shaking his

202   head. He'd say to me, 'Miep, you should hear this description that
Anne wrote here! Who'd have imagined how vivid her imagination
was all the while?' "[51] In his memoir, Otto recounts how overwhelmed he was by Anne's ability to capture emotions and events,
and the young woman she had become:

> I began to read slowly, only a few pages each day, more would have
> been impossible, as I was overwhelmed by painful memories. For
> me, it was a revelation. There, was revealed a completely different
> Anne to the child that I had lost. I had no idea of the depth of her
> thoughts and feelings. . . . I had never imagined how intensely
> Anne had occupied her mind with the problem and meaning of
> Jewish suffering over the centuries, and the power she had gained
> through her belief in God. . . . How could I have known how im-
> portant the chestnut tree was to her when she had never seemed
> interested in nature. . . . Occasionally she would read humorous
> episodes and stories out to us . . . but she never read out anything
> which was about herself. And so we never knew to what extent she
> went on to develop her character, and she was more self-critical
> than any of us. . . . Through Anne's accurate description of every
> event and every person, all the details of our cohabitation became
> clear to me again.[52]

Otto's family were amazed by the excerpts sent to them, as he
had expected. Exhilarated by the reactions of family and friends
who had read the manuscript, he began to consider whether he
should attempt to have it published. Otto had typed out another
copy of the diary, based not only on Anne's original entries but also
on her own revised version. After hearing a broadcast by the Dutch
minister for education, art, and science on March 28, 1944, in
which the Dutch were told to preserve their diaries, letters, and
documents to show later "what we as a nation have had to endure
and overcome during these years," Anne began to rewrite her diary

with a view to publication.[53] She was never able to complete it; the entries end in March 1944, while the original diary continues until three days before their arrest, August 1, 1944. Otto based his typescript on both versions and added four chapters from Anne's book of "tales." Otto dropped those passages he felt were uninteresting or too intimate and left out some unpleasant remarks Anne had made. On November 16, he explained the process to Milly: "It does not grieve me what she writes and I know quite well that there are several things she did not see right and she would have changed her ideas. In fact she was on very good terms with her mother at the camp later, but it is a disagreeable feeling to publish things against her mother—and I have to do it. There are passages I can scrap, [for instance,] what she thought about my marrying Edith, our marriage, her views on politics as the relationship between England and the Netherlands and others. It keeps my brains busy every day."[54]

Otto visited his friend Kurt Baschwitz, himself a writer, to ask his opinion. Baschwitz's daughter Isa remembers Otto arriving at her father's apartment with a small case containing the diary and various loose sheets: "Otto felt that Anne's diary should be published, that it was important for children, especially German children. He came from a business background and my father was one of his few intellectual friends, and one who also wrote books. Otto wanted to ask me, in particular, whether this would catch on with young people."[55] Isa was unsure, and uncomfortable with Anne's harsh entries about her mother and references to sexual matters. Otto also showed it to his friends Werner and Jetty Cahn; Werner worked for the Dutch publisher Querido. They were deeply impressed, and Otto wrote to his mother in excitement: "Friday I was with Jetty Cahn at her house, and I started to read out some of Anne's diary, to get Werner's opinion about it. He's been with the publisher Querido for ages, where Jetty was too. Next Friday is the big decision, but already I have the impression: publish without a

204 doubt—quite a big item! You can't imagine what this means. The diary would come out in German and English, telling everything that went on in our lives when we were in hiding—all the fears, disputes, food, politics, the Jewish question, the weather, moods, problems of growing-up, birthdays and reminiscences—in short, everything."[56]

Werner Cahn submitted the typescript to Querido, but it was rejected. He approached the German publisher Gottfried Bermann-Fischer (S. Fischer Verlag), which was then based in Amsterdam, and again it was rejected. After a third refusal (from Blitz publishers), Otto asked his friend Ab Cauvern, who worked as a dramatist, to check the typescript for "grammatical errors" and "expressions my daughter had borrowed from the German language and which were therefore bad Dutch."[57] Cauvern did so, then added a simple epilogue: "Anne's diary ended here. On August 4, the Green Police made a raid on the 'Secret Annex.' In March 1945, two months before the liberation of our country, Anne died in the concentration camp at Bergen-Belsen."[58] Isa Cauvern retyped the manuscript. In his December 12 letter to his mother, Otto mentioned the Cauverns' work on the diary: ". . . corrections and copying out. I have got so far with it now, and I would like to have it finished so that I can show it to publishers. . . . I can hardly get away from it all—and do not want to either."[59]

Otto showed the new typescript to several friends, who were divided by his determination to have it published. Anne's friend Jacqueline van Maarsen found it impossible to believe that anyone would be interested: "I thought, how crazy, who would want to read a book written by such a young child? I didn't like the idea because I knew my name was going to be in it, but luckily for me, Anne had changed my name to Jopie, and though I didn't like that either, I was much happier not to have my real name published."[60] Eva and Fritzi Geiringer also saw the diary. (They had recently discovered that Eva's father, Erich, had died on a death march and that her brother Heinz had died in Mauthausen.) Eva recalls, "He showed it to us, and then he read a few pages from it, and he burst into tears. He couldn't carry on. He was very emotional about it and quite shocked by the fact of its survival, and also by what he read. I found reading it very strange myself."[61] Rabbi David Soetendorp recalls that Otto approached his father with the diary: "Otto was lost, in a spiritual wilderness, and so he came to my father, having no rabbi of his own anymore, and asked for spiritual guidance. They got on well together, there was a spark between them. One day, he showed my father the diary manuscript. He asked him if he thought it would be a success if he published it. My father looked at him in amazement. 'Who's going to read that?' Otto, fortunately, decided to ignore him."[62] Most of Otto's friends were encouraging, however, and even Kurt Baschwitz, who had some reservations about publishing certain entries, had no doubt of the diary's power: "It is the most moving document about that time I know, and a literary masterpiece as well."[63]

Amid all the focus on the diary, on December 1, 1945, Otto attended the funeral of his close friend Johan Voskuijl, Bep's father, who had lost his fight against cancer. This new sadness made Otto only more determined that something positive had to come out of all the grief of the past few years, and on December 15, he wrote to his mother: "If for a moment, one looks back, one should only think of the nice things there were and not mourn the past. . . . As sad as much of it was, in the end we were together for a long time, and even though the children were killed for some unknown reason, their spirits remain eternally children."[64]

■

ON DECEMBER 17, 1945, TONNY AHLERS was again arrested by the POD. On Christmas Eve, he wrote to the authorities in a panic, adding a fictitious list of good deeds he had accomplished during the war. He claimed to have saved many lives but could recall only one name: Otto Frank. He wrote how he had "delivered" Otto from "the hands of the SD" and that "this man (Mr. Frank) was 100% for me!" He insisted that Otto had searched for him "so that he could thank me in the highest possible terms. And this man was then unknown to me!"[65] On January 6, Ahlers's wife wrote to the authorities, begging them to free her husband, since she had two tiny children and no income. Ahlers remained in jail, accused of being an "informant for the SD, for betraying people to the SD, and as director of the Wehrmacht Einkauf Buro PTM." Witness after witness confirmed that he had worked for the SD; his own mother told the police, "During the war he has done all kinds of terrible things."[66]

It also emerged that when the police had first tried to arrest Ahlers after the war, he had sent them to an unfortunate man who shared his name and lived nearby. The man's hysterical wife visited Ahlers's father, hoping to convince him to intercede. He merely laughed and said she "could not touch" his son, who had "good papers and was protected by rich Jews." Interviewed in relation to the case, Ahlers's former boss, Kurt Döring, who was due to stand trial for war crimes, was unwilling to incriminate himself. He would only say, "My impression is that Ahlers is a big talker, very ignorant and capable of anything."[67] Listed among the other members of the SD and Zentralstelle staff due to be questioned about Ahlers was Maarten Kuiper. The interview never occurred.

It seems that Ahlers had managed to find himself some influential friends; he was freed from the Levantkade camp (where many former NSB members were being held) for eighteen days while he assisted two detectives in finding out more about Nazi organizations in Amsterdam and its environs. In return, the detectives promised Ahlers that they would do what they could for him in regard to the accusations about his Nazi past. While he was helping them, Ahlers was provided with twenty-five guilders a week and a false identity card. After completing his work with the two detectives, Ahlers was taken back to the Levantkade camp. One very curious piece of information crops up among the notes about this period; one of the detectives, a man named Davids, apparently gave Ahlers some advice about how he could obtain "evidence" that he was politically trustworthy. The person who compiled the notes was puzzled himself, asking, "Is Davids now using Ahlers as a tip-giver, then? It's all very mysterious."[68]

Despite Ahlers's protests to the authorities and his requests to the police that they interview the "Jewish Director of Opekta,"[69] it seems that Otto wanted nothing further to do with him, for there are no more appreciative letters or statements from Otto in Ahlers's file. One explanation, surely, is that Otto had at last been confronted with the evil of which Ahlers was capable: "[Ahlers] was in prison as a political criminal. I went to the commission. . . . They showed me the documents on him, and I saw that I was the only person he had saved. He had betrayed a great many others."[70] If Otto had suspicions that Ahlers was involved in his own betrayal, he kept them to himself for the time being; sometime in the coming months, the investigation into his own political background would begin.

■

TOWARD THE END OF 1945, OTTO FI-nally received all the documents necessary for his journey to Switzerland. Kleiman had intended to accompany him, but he was once again seriously ill with a hemorrhage. Otto traveled alone by train from Amsterdam to Basel, where he arrived in time to celebrate the New Year, 1946. In the beautiful, welcoming house on Herbstgasse, Otto was at last surrounded by the family whom he loved and had not seen since before the war: his mother, Leni, Erich, Stephan, Buddy, and Erich's mother, Oma Ida, who also lived with them, were all there.

Otto returned to Amsterdam in late January, wishing he could

208   have stayed even longer with his family in Switzerland. He wrote to them upon his arrival: "The trip went well. I was the only passenger and Bep met me at the station. I was bombarded with questions. Everything I brought back with me was so gratefully received. There's too much to discuss. I haven't even checked my post yet. . . . It is strange, all these same people and yet so different. . . . It was wonderful to be with you again."[71] They had spoken little of the events of the past year, and Buddy sent Otto a letter to explain why no one had pushed him to tell them more about his experiences: "We didn't have enough time to talk during your stay in Basel to say what is in our hearts. . . . You can't imagine how much I wanted to hear about your life. . . . But to be honest, I was frightened of reopening old wounds."[72] Otto reassured him; he had understood and found it difficult to speak himself of all that had happened without breaking down. He hated to dwell on the tragedy of the past: "There is no point in wasting away in mourning, no point in brooding. We have to go on living, go on building. We don't want to forget, but we mustn't let our memories lead us into negativism."[73]

Following his return from Switzerland, Otto gave the revised typescript of the diary to Werner Cahn, who was keen to have a second opinion on it. He approached Annie Romein-Verschoor, "whose opinion I valued highly. Jan Romein saw the typescript lying there that evening. He read it through that evening in one sitting."[74] Jan Romein, a very well respected Dutch historian, wrote about the diary for the newspaper *Het Parool*. The article, entitled "A Child's Voice," appeared on the front page of the newspaper on April 3, 1946. It began: "By chance a diary written during the war years has come into my possession. The Netherlands State Institute for War Documentation already holds some two hundred similar diaries, but I should be very much surprised if there were another as lucid, as intelligent, and at the same time as natural. This one made me forget the present and its many calls to duty for a whole evening as I read it from beginning to end."[75]

Later that day, publishers began to call Romein, who referred them to Werner Cahn. The most enthusiastic reaction came from Contact publishers in Amsterdam, who wanted the book badly, but difficulties soon arose. Otto recalled the managing director, G. P. de Neve, "telling me that religious advisers had objected to the printing of certain passages (e.g., about menstruation). The proof that I myself did not object to these passages is that they are included in the German and other translations."[76] De Neve also hesitated over Anne's angry outbursts against her mother and the entry where she describes her curiosity about a friend's breasts. A source at Contact believes that passages may have been removed in order to fit the book into Contact's Prologue series, rather than through any religious objections. Whatever the actual reasons were, twenty-five full passages from the typescript were left out, and some lines were rephrased or omitted. The manuscript was then amended for typing errors and its style brought in line with house rules. Otto agreed to the alterations: "The text was edited at the request of the publishing house. Some unimportant changes were made with my agreement. These were entries my daughter made which might cause offense to the readers."[77] In another letter, Otto wrote that the Dutch had "cut out a few parts here as they did not want the book being more than a certain amount of pages. And a few parts they objected (a few lines) on account of the Catholic feeling of the country."[78]

In June, five excerpts from Anne's diary were published in *De Nieuwe Stem*, the left-wing newspaper for which Werner Cahn worked. Otto had found among Anne's papers a list of pseudonyms for all those in hiding and decided to use them in place of real names. Nonetheless, some people strongly objected to Otto publishing his daughter's intimate thoughts and painful experiences of life under Nazi persecution. The Liberal Jewish congregation's Rabbi Hammelburg was against publication, as he recalled in 1981: "Otto Frank was what I call a good man, but also sentimental and weak. He told me for the first time about his daughter Anne's diary

when the manuscript was already with the publisher, Contact. . . .
I didn't read *Het Achterhuis* ["The Back House," the title of the published diary] until it was in the shops. Nor did he ever speak to me
about the whole commercial hullabaloo which went on, and I have
never appreciated the Anne Frank House."[79] Annie Romein-
Verschoor also had misgivings, despite her own involvement (she
wrote the foreword to the first Dutch edition): "Success breeds
success and the desire for money. This is not an imputation against
Otto Frank, who, when he came to tell me that the diary should be
published, with tears in his eyes assured me that he did not wish to
profit from the suffering of his child, and I assumed that he meant
it and has held to that. . . . Otto Frank was certainly opposed to the
success and the formation of myths and the speculative defilement
which inevitably came with it, but he could not stop it."[80]

Otto was convinced that he was doing the right thing: "Anne
would have so much loved to see something published. . . . My
friends' opinion was that I had no right to view this as a private
legacy, as it is a meaningful document about humanity. . . . The
first edition of the diary appeared in 1947. Anne would have been
so proud."[81] Jacqueline van Maarsen was also ultimately in favor of
Otto publishing the book, although she refused his request that she
write something about her friendship with Anne as part of the introduction: "Otto Frank decided to have the diary published for
two reasons: first, to pay homage to his dead daughter, and second,
because he knew that was what she would have wanted."[82] The diary
was originally to have been published in March 1947, as Otto wrote
to a friend, adding, "I take it that later an English and German
translation will come out so you can read it then. It's a unique document, not written to be published, but written from the heart, for
herself alone. It's astonishing how a young girl between thirteen
and fifteen could write how everything affected her. This at least
has survived."[83] To his friend Joseph Spronz, who had lost many
members of his family, including his first wife, in the Holocaust,

Otto wrote that his anguish over his children had not diminished with time and the discovery of Anne's diary: "On the outside I know I seem okay but my life is in fact over. Without children, there is no point in life."[84]

Anne would have been eighteen on June 12, 1947. Despite this, and the belief that his own life was over, Otto knew that June 25 was a momentous day and recorded it in his engagement diary with a single, significant word: *"BOOK."* The diary was issued in a print run of 1,500 copies, with a foreword by Annie Romein-Verschoor. Otto published it under the title Anne herself had chosen: *Het Achterhuis: Dagboekbrieven van 14 Juni 1942–1 Augustus 1944* ("The Back House: Diary Letters from June 14, 1942, to August 1, 1944"). On the spine and on the cover was her name: Anne Frank.

For Otto Frank, a new life was just beginning.

ten

PUBLISH WITHOUT A DOUBT

THE INVESTIGATION INTO OTTO'S BACK-
ground as an enemy national began in 1946. This was done by the
Nederlands Beheers Instituut (NBI)—the body charged with "the
administration of enemy property in the Netherlands, the property of the members of the NSB, and the property of deported
Dutch citizens who had not returned."[1] Otto insisted that the NBI
act quickly to clear his case so that he could travel abroad on business. To satisfy them that he was and had been "politically trustworthy," Otto asked friends, employees, and a few of his
concentration camp comrades to attest to his good character. Jan
Gies, Dunselman, Kleiman, and Aliens Police detective Gerard
Oeverhaus all wrote on his behalf. Oeverhaus stated that Otto was
"100% a friend of Holland, the Dutch people. He was and is anti-
German and anti–National Socialist."[2] Otto also made out his own
declaration. Although the NBI was thorough, it apparently did not
discover Otto's business with the Wehrmacht, and on February 7,
1947, the NBI declared him "no longer an enemy national in the
sense of the Order concerning enemy property."[3]

There had been several changes at the Prinsengracht offices in

1946 and 1947. On May 15, 1946, Bep Voskuijl married Cornelius van Wijk and handed in her resignation. Otto, Miep, Jan, Kleiman, and Kugler all attended the wedding. In May 1947, Miep gave in her notice at the Prinsengracht. She remembers: "At the office real products were again for sale. Since his return Mr. Frank had again become the slightly nervous, soft-spoken man he'd been before the hiding time. The change that had taken place when he'd gone into hiding, the calm authoritative personality he'd assumed, had vanished. But Mr. Frank's interest in the business seemed to be waning."[4] There were difficulties with Opekta; the loan given to Otto by Erich Elias in 1933 was due to be repaid to the NBI under the terms of the order concerning enemy property. Otto was granted permission by the NBI to repay the loan in small installments because profits at Opekta since the end of the war had been so poor. The matter was finally resolved, in 1950, by a decision of the minister of internal affairs. Opekta was removed from the list of enemy nationals, and the money Otto had repaid was transferred to the Nederlandse Bank on behalf of the Swiss company. In the meantime, Otto wrote to his friend Joseph Spronz that he was trying to develop "some import-export business, but just about everything I attempt runs aground on currency regulations and other problems in various countries."[5]

Otto was grateful to still have a home with Miep and Jan, and in 1947 they all moved into a new apartment together. Otto's friend Isa Cauvern had committed suicide, leaving her husband alone in the large apartment he shared only with his daughter Ruth when she was home from boarding school. Ab Cauvern invited Miep and Jan, who had been living with Jan's sister, to move in with him. Miep recalls: "Jan and I discussed the situation with Otto. Otto said that if it was all right he'd like to move along with us to this apartment. . . . 'I prefer staying with you, Miep,' he explained. 'That way I can talk to you about my family if I want.' In fact, Mr. Frank rarely talked about them, but I understood what he meant."[6]

214   Otto was able to visit his family in Switzerland again in 1947. He stayed in Basel for two weeks and wrote to Gertrud Naumann in Frankfurt on January 6: "Today it is two years ago that Edith perished in the camp. You can't allow yourself to give in to your feelings otherwise it would be unbearable. . . . Apart from you and Mrs. Schneider [Otto's former secretary], there are few people in Germany who I care about. . . . In life one must search for the bright spots, so I must be glad to have my mother and to have the opportunity to see her and my brothers and sister again. But there's no substitute for a wife and children. As I'll soon be fifty-eight years old I can't expect much from life anymore."[7] Otto shared his feelings toward his former homeland in a letter to another friend: "In spite of all my experiences, I am not given to hatred. I don't generalize because I know how many injustices occurred through people who generalize. I still have a lot of friends in Germany. Their behavior was correct and they also suffered . . . but there's nothing that would drag me back to Germany."[8] Otto did eventually travel to Germany again to see Gertrud, Kathi Stilgenbauer, and Mrs. Schneider. He admitted, "It was difficult for me, even so."[9]

■

ASKED YEARS LATER ABOUT HIS EDITING of the diary, Otto replied: "Of course Anne didn't want certain things to be published. I have evidence of it. . . . Anne's diary is for me a testament. I must work in her sense. So I decided how to do it through thinking how Anne would have done it. Probably she would have completed it as I did for a publisher."[10] Since the early 1980s, when it became clear that it was *The Diaries of Anne Frank* rather than *The Diary of Anne Frank* that formed the basis for one of the world's best-selling books, people have questioned not only Otto's right to revise his daughter's literary masterpiece but also the extent of his editing. Once asked how much had been omitted,

Otto answered, "Nearly nothing has been withheld. A few letters were withheld which deal with personal affairs . . . of people still living. But these don't affect the diary in the least."[11]

Anne herself never intended to publish her complete diaries. After hearing Bolkestein's broadcast, she wrote: "Just imagine how interesting it would be if I were to publish a novel of the *Secret Annex*. The title alone would be enough to make people think it was a detective story."[12] A month later, she declared: "My greatest wish is to become a journalist someday and later on a famous writer. . . . In any case, I want to publish a book entitled *Het Achterhuis* after the war. Whether I shall succeed or not, I cannot say, but my diary will be a great help."[13] By May, she was ready to begin, using sheets of colored carbon paper from the office supplies. She changed words, removed references, added sentences, deleted whole passages, added scenes from memory, and combined entries to make the writing flow. Among the loose pages recently found were two sheets on which Anne had drafted an introduction:

Writing in a diary is a very new and strange experience for me. I've never done it before, and if I had a close friend I could pour my heart out to, I would never have thought of purchasing a thick, stiff-backed notebook and jotting down all kinds of nonsense that no one will be interested in later on.

But now that I've bought the notebook, I'm going to keep at it and make sure it doesn't get tossed into a forgotten corner a month from now or fall into anyone else's hands. Daddy, Mummy, and Margot may be very kind and I can tell them quite a lot, but my diary and my girlfriend-only secrets are none of their business.

To help me imagine that I have a girlfriend, a real friend who shares my interests and understands my concerns, I won't just write in my diary, but I'll address my letters to this friend-of my-own-imagination Kitty.

So here we go![14]

Otto chose not to use this introduction.

The fact that both of Anne's versions of the diary were incomplete (her original diary for 1943 was lost, and the second draft finishes four months before they were arrested) presented Otto with a problem. For the period from June 1942 until December 1942, Otto had both diaries from which to work, and usually he stuck to the revised version; for the year 1943 he had only the revised version, and for the period from December 1943 until March 1944 he again had both at his disposal. He had to combine these into one consistent whole. Then he had his own ideas about what was permissible to publish. It is commonly thought that Otto removed the sexual references and those where Anne excessively criticized her mother, but by comparing all three texts we can see that this was not so. It was more often Anne herself who eliminated these details from her revised diary: for instance, her original entry for January 6, 1944, begins with a long passage about her mother, then proceeds to a discussion about sexuality before ending with her decision to make friends with Peter. In her revised diary, Anne completely cut the paragraphs dealing with her mother and sexuality and radically reduces the section concerning Peter. Otto split the long original entry into two ("January 5, 1944," and "January 6, 1944") and kept most of the original version intact.[15] Clearly, Otto was astute enough to realize that part of the diary's power lay in entries such as these, and shrewdly suspecting that they would fascinate the reader, he reinstated them. Despite the various constraints, and with no background in writing or publishing, Otto's editing of his daughter's diary was ingenious.

In a private letter, Otto clarified his position: "Anne made an extract of her diaries in which she deleted and changed a great deal of material. . . . But I thought that much of the deleted material was interesting and characteristic . . . so I made a new copy in which I reinserted passages from her diaries."[16] Otto's prologue to the first edition in 1947 read, "With the exception of a few sections, which are meaningless to the reader, the original text has been printed."[17] The first explanation would have made a far more accurate introduction to Anne's legacy. Regardless of this, upon its initial publication, the diary was well received. *De Groene Amsterdammer* praised "the intelligence, the honesty, the insight with which she observed herself and her surroundings." Asserting that "the talent with which she was able to depict what she saw was astonishing," it declared her "a symbol" of all those murdered in the Holocaust.[18] Other reviews were appreciative but whimsical; *De Vlam*'s sentiments would be repeated as often as the Westertoren chimed in the future: "By no means a war document as such . . . but purely and simply the diary of an adolescent girl."[19]

Otto sent copies of the diary to family and friends and to the writers and politicians mentioned in the book. (Gerbrandy, the Dutch prime minister, made a terrible faux pas in addressing his letter of acknowledgment to "Miss Frank.") Otto already felt that the diary could be used in a positive manner; he told Anne's former boyfriend Hello Silberberg that it was "in Anne's spirit that the book should be read as widely as possible, because it should work for people and for humanity. Speak about it, recommend it to others."[20] Laureen Klein, whose wedding to Rudi Nussbaum Otto attended on October 15, 1947, was delighted with the diary's reception: "I read the book as soon as it was published—it really surprised me. I was filled with respect for Anne's literary talent and the way in which she had matured in the intervening years. The fact that she rewrote it with an eye on publication showed that she was destined to be a talented writer. To be honest, I was astounded."[21]

Otto signed a contract with Ernest Kuhn, a New York attorney, who agreed to represent him in negotiations with American and Canadian publishers. Twentieth Century Fox expressed an early interest in the book, but nothing came of it. The diary was in its second printing by the end of the year, and Otto proudly told a relative: "Anne's book is a big success. There have been readings

218 from the book four times already. I hope I can succeed in seeing that English and German editions are also published."[22] Milly visited Otto in Amsterdam that winter and suspected that publication of the diary had been a significant factor in improving his disposition. She recalled: "The country was certainly at its worst, deep snow everywhere, trams few and far between. But the people were so sturdy and uncomplaining that I found it energizing. Otto showed me all over the annex and introduced me to the wonderful group who, for over two years, had risked their lives daily to help them. . . . The rooms were as Anne described them. Her collection of photos still hung on the walls."[23] The secret annex remained exactly as it had been left on the day of the arrest.

In 1948, an investigation was launched to find out who had betrayed them.

■

IN THE LATE 1940S, THE DUTCH POLICE had to investigate hundreds of cases of wartime betrayals. Kleiman had taken the first steps to bring the traitor of his friends to justice by visiting the Politieke Opsporings Dienst (POD) in 1945 with a letter recapitulating the arrest, van Maaren's curiosity in the secret annex, and Lena van Bladeren-Hartog's dangerous gossip to Anna Genot.[24] On December 11, 1945, Otto wrote to his mother:

> I was at the Security Police. We did all we could to try to get out of them who had betrayed us. . . . Yesterday we all went to the police station to study photographs, to see if we could recognize who arrested us and then perhaps learn more from these people about those who betrayed us. The photos were astounding—we could identify two of the men. They're still in prison and we're going to confront them. . . . If only this might work, but quite often the people themselves don't know who the actual traitors were, and simply did what their whiter-than-white superiors told them.[25]

The two men identified from the photographs were Willem Grootendorst and Gezinus Gringhuis. Grootendorst had worked in the Amsterdam police since 1912, first as an agent, then as a detective, before joining the staff of the Zentralstelle. After the war, Grootendorst was tried and imprisoned for "delivering Jews to the SD." He could not remember the arrest at 263 Prinsengracht but admitted having assisted SS Oberscharführer Karl Silberbauer during other arrests and said he had worked with Gringhuis on several occasions. Gringhuis was a policeman when in 1940 he joined the NSB, then the Rechtsfront and the WA. In 1942, he was transferred to the Zentralstelle, working alongside Ahlers's friend Peters. In his declaration about the secret annex, Gringhuis told the police, "I cannot remember anything about an arrest on August 4, 1944, in a house at 263 Prinsengracht in which ten people, among them eight Jews, were taken into custody." Somewhat peculiarly, Gringhuis did say that he had spoken to Otto Frank, who had received an anonymous letter in which a member of the Joodse Raad was named as their betrayer.[26] Otto did not know the man, but Gringhuis did and felt there was no reason to suspect the man's integrity. Interestingly, the letter contained the sentence "Your hiding place in Amsterdam was mentioned at the Zentralstelle."[27] One person who had connections with both institutions was Tonny Ahlers: he occasionally acted as a supervisor at the Expositur department of the Joodse Raad on Jan van Eyckstraat, and he was a familiar face at the Zentralstelle, where his closest friend, Peters, was a staff member. If Ahlers was the writer of the anonymous letter, it would not be the last time he would name another man as the Franks' betrayer. Gringhuis had nothing further to say except: "I have heard the name Silberbauer. I think that he was also employed at the Zentralstelle. I have never been friends with the SD man Kuiper . . . or have I been with him at an arrest?"[28]

Kuiper was not brought forward at either of the two visits to the POD made by Otto and his friends. In 1947, a year before the inves-

220 tigation into the betrayal at 263 Prinsengracht began, Kleiman
made a statement to the POD about Kuiper and the fact that he was
not questioned in relation to the arrest. In a private letter to Otto in
1958, Kugler referred to Kuiper as "a Dutch Nazi with a thick head
. . . about whose deeds a lot has been published in the newspapers," and wished that Kuiper had at least been mentioned publicly
in connection with their case. He then recalled the visit to the POD
to identify Gringhuis and Grootendorst, during which "the civil
servant said that unfortunately the third person [Kuiper] could not
be presented" because he had been sentenced to death.[29] As Kugler
said, the Dutch newspapers were filled with reports about the
Kuiper trial in 1947. The *Elseviers Weekblad* described Kuiper as the
"Criminal of the Euterpestraat . . . a tall man with a sharp nose in a
small face, a short upper lip and a thin mouth. . . . His eyes have the
burning look of a lunatic. Hard throat muscles run under his jaws,
the chin is aggressive." It was impossible to name all those whom
Kuiper had betrayed; he admitted himself that the figures ran into
the high hundreds. On one occasion, he had killed a young man and
his parents, running out into the street to shoot the young man, who
had almost escaped; for this, the press noted, "the bloodhound received fifteen guilders." On December 6, 1947, Kuiper was sentenced to death, whereupon he screamed to the courtroom: "I have
not committed any betrayal, I have not arrested anybody. I have
never denounced Jews! I acted under orders of my superiors!" His
appeal against the death penalty was dismissed. On August 30,
1948, Maarten Kuiper, "the SD detective who arrested numerous
Jews, people in hiding and others," the man whom Tonny Ahlers
had idolized, was executed by firing squad.[30]

The official investigation into the betrayal at 263 Prinsengracht
began in January 1948. Kleiman was the first to be interviewed by
the Politieke Recherche Afdeling (PRA, the Political Investigation
Branch of the Dutch police) on January 12. He told them that
Silberbauer and his men had "seemed to know precisely what they

were doing, for they went straight to the hiding place and arrested all eight persons present there."[31] Kugler and Miep were interviewed two days later but had little to say, unlike van Maaren, who gave the PRA a written declaration in early February. He claimed that the first time he had seen the entrance to the secret annex he had been "dumbfounded by its technical ingenuity . . . the SD would never have been able to find out anything about this secret door without inside information." He added, "I was told that on arrival the SD went straight upstairs to the bookcase and opened the door."[32]

On March 10, Petrus and Anna Genot were interviewed about Lena van Bladeren-Hartog. They confirmed that Lena had told them she had heard there were Jews hiding at 263 Prinsengracht, but Genot himself told detectives that he had worked it out for himself as early as 1942, having noticed the large amounts of food delivered to the offices. On March 18 and 20, Lena van Bladeren-Hartog and her husband, Lammert Hartog, were questioned by detectives. Lena denied mentioning the hidden Jews before they were arrested, but Hartog said that he, too, had been suspicious about the great quantities of food brought in. He declared that van Maaren confided in him "about fourteen days before the Jews were taken away that there were Jews hidden in the building," but did not think van Maaren capable of betraying the fugitives. He had one further comment to add: "I was struck by the fact that the detectives who raided the place were not just on the lookout for hidden Jews but were, you might say, completely in the picture."[33] In other words, he felt sure that the authorities had been tipped off that there were Jews hiding in the building. Van Maaren was questioned on March 31 and admitted that he had known that "something peculiar was going on in the building" for some time, having also noticed the food deliveries. He was adamant that he was not the betrayer.[34]

While the investigation was in progress, a second, almost concurrent inquiry into Otto's attempted betrayal by Joseph Jansen in 1941 began. Jansen's name had come up during inquiries into the secret annex betrayal, but he had spent most of the war years in The Hague and was therefore highly unlikely to have known what was happening at 263 Prinsengracht.[35] Otto never asked for Jansen to be investigated in relation to his family's betrayal, but he did contact the Dutch authorities about the letter of 1941:

> *Concerning Mr. Jansen:* Together with this I send you a copy of my letter concerning Ahlers that I sent to Scheveningen. I do not know if this man whom I refer to as Jansen in my letter is caught already because this is the man who is actually doing the dirty work. I have forgotten his forename initials and I do not know where he lives but there is a woman who lives on the Amstelveensweg and has a flower stall at 72 Amstelveensweg who can tell you all about him. She separated from her husband and she is of Jewish origin and has nothing to do with anything of this. But you can certainly get information from her. I hope that Mr. Jansen is already behind bars or will be caught through this letter.[36]

During the war, Jansen betrayed his own son to the Germans; he wrote to Reich Commissioner Arthur Seyss-Inquart to inform him that his son had said all Germans should be shot. In September 1941, the Jansens' two sons were arrested in the night. Jansen dismissed this to his devastated wife, Jetje, with the words, "Well, there are bound to be victims."[37] Jetje did all she could to have her sons set free—even appealing to Ahlers's neighbor Friedrich Christian Viebahn, who knew her husband—but to no avail. One son was shot in Neuengamme, the other was liberated at Ebensee. On March 31, 1945, Joseph Jansen was arrested. Otto and his employees all gave evidence against him. Jetje recalled: "About the letter to the NSB, which my husband is said to have written concerning Mr. Frank, I cannot tell you anything because I was notified of this fact by Mr. Frank after the war. It is indeed correct, that my husband carried addresses of Jewish people in his wallet during the war. I do not know what he intended to do with them, but out of concern for their safety, I had my children warn the persons concerned, so they could take their measures." She did say that when Otto told her about the letter, "I thought that the ground had disappeared from under my feet."[38] Questioned about his attempted betrayal of Otto, Jansen denied having ever written the letter: "It could not have been my handwriting. I believe that, if I were to stand and look Mr. Frank full in the face, and would tell him that I was not the writer of the letter, that he would certainly believe me. I am not an anti-Semite and I have always respected Mr. Frank and considered him to be a man of high standing. I do not know the solution to this."[39] Jansen was sentenced to four years and six months in jail. His doctor filed a report on him shortly before he was freed, confirming that "now when we go over all this with the accused, everything that he is charged with, it must be said that the accused fully acknowledges it. He knows he has been wrong and he positively feels that denouncing Mr. Frank is a very damaging fact to his name."[40] On March 21, 1949, Joseph Jansen was released. He died a few years later.

During the Jansen inquiry, Miep had a new statement to add to those she had made in the 1946 investigation: "I found out from Mr. Frank that the NSB man who had given said letter to Mr. Frank was Anton Ahlers who lived at Hoofdweg in Amsterdam at the time."[41] When the police arrived to question Ahlers in his prison cell about the matter, they were given unexpected news: he had escaped. It was not the first time Ahlers had broken out; during his multiple prison sentences, he had been transferred from one jail to another and had escaped on several occasions, always returning to his wife, Martha.[42] Once, they were seen together by neighbors, who reported the sighting to the police. Another time, Ahlers actu-

224   ally managed to obtain paid work while he should have been in prison. Eventually, he was captured while committing a theft, but he remained at large during the Jansen inquiry. By the time he was caught and imprisoned once more, the police had apparently forgotten to interview him; he never was questioned by them.[43]

The investigation into the Franks' betrayal was closed on May 22, 1948. In the process of that inquiry, Johannes Kleiman, Wilhelm van Maaren, and Lammert Hartog had all given statements to the effect that the Gestapo and NSB were acting upon inside information, yet the detectives failed to ask how any of them had reached that conclusion. Van Maaren, the main suspect against whom nothing could be proved, was granted a conditional discharge. He was cleared of all charges in an appeal on August 13, 1949.[44]

Tonny Ahlers was released from prison on October 3, 1949, and stripped of his Dutch nationality as a mark of disgrace for his wartime activities.[45]

■

WHEN THE DUTCH EAST INDIES GAINED independence from the Netherlands in 1949, Gies & Co., which depended upon the spices imported from the former colony, experienced a fall in profits. Otto tried to revive the company by inquiring about importing pectin from the United States, but his time was increasingly spent pursuing other publishers who would issue Anne's diary. In July 1949, Otto traveled to London and Paris to meet publishers who had expressed an interest in the book. He signed a contract with Calmann-Lévy, which would publish the diary (Le Journal) in France the following year, and in January 1950, Frank Price, the head of Doubleday's office in Paris, was given an advance copy of Le Journal by the author Manès Sperber, an adviser to Calmann-Lévy. Price's first impression was that "the volume [was] of little importance," and he instructed his assistant Judith Bailey to reject it. Bailey read it, then asked Price to reconsider.[46]

Le Journal was a critical and commercial success upon publication. In August 1950, the American writer Meyer Levin was given a copy of it by his French wife, Tereska Torres. Levin was a forty-four-year-old novelist and freelance writer. During the war, he was employed as a battle correspondent in France. His experience of the liberated camps was firsthand: he helped trace survivors' relatives and friends. In his book *In Search*, he declared: "I realized I would never be able to write the story of the Jews of Europe. . . . Some day a teller would arise from amongst themselves." When reading the diary, he realized that the teller had arisen, and he remembered the dead in Belsen: "I must have gazed down on the body of this young girl. . . . The voice reached me from the pit."[47] He vowed to avenge his murdered co-religionists: "Isn't there something we must do to pay for being alive?"[48]

Levin's struggles to act first as translator of the diary from French to English, then as Otto's agent for American and English rights, and ultimately as the writer assigned the task of writing the stageplay based upon the diary are well documented. Lawrence Graver was the first to chronicle the years of bitter disputes in book-length form in his 1995 study *An Obsession with Anne Frank: Meyer Levin and the Diary*, and in 1997 Ralph Melnick published the more pro-Levin volume *The Stolen Legacy of Anne Frank: Meyer Levin, Lillian Hellman, and the Staging of the Diary*. Levin was one of the first people to see the diary's potential for a stage or film adaptation. Otto responded to his initial letter on September 25, 1950, doubtful that the diary would make the transition to stage or screen well, but he encouraged Levin to make inquiries about the possibility. Otto was more interested in the forthcoming German edition of the diary, which would be published "before Xmas in Heidelberg by the firm Lambert Schneider."[49] He had long hoped that a German publisher would buy the book: "I thought they should read it. But in Germany in 1950, I had difficulty. It was a time when Germans didn't want to read about it. And Schneider of Heidelberg wrote to me. He said, 'I have read the book and feel it has to be published, but I don't think it will be a financial success.' "[50] Part of the problem lay with Anneliese Schütz's translation, which she had based on the Dutch typescript Otto had given to Contact. Otto later admitted that Schütz was "too old for the job, many of her expressions were pedantic and not in a youthful enough style. In addition she . . . misunderstood many Dutch expressions." Nonetheless, he felt that her translation "could by and large be called faithful and in the spirit of the original."[51] His friend Werner Cahn was less certain; for him the translation, "although correct, did not always reflect the style of the young Anne Frank. That is, in any case, a particularly difficult thing to do. But this may well be the reason why well-intentioned German literary circles occasionally expressed doubts about the authenticity of the diary."[52]

There were also some changes "of a more political nature"[53] due to Schütz's attitude that "a book intended after all for sale in Germany cannot abuse the Germans."[54] Anne's description of conditions in Westerbork and the line "We assume that most of them are being murdered" were cut, along with the sentence referring to the secret annex rule that "only exceptionally could one listen to German stations, for instance to hear classical music and the like." Similarly, the secret annex regulation that "only the language of civilized people may be spoken, thus no German" became "all civilized languages . . . but softly!"[55] (Otto insisted that the change was made by the German publisher, but it is clear from the typescript that it occurred at an earlier stage.)[56] Anne's line concerning "heroism in the war or when confronting the Germans" was altered to "heroism in the war and in the struggle against oppression." And her declaration that "There is no greater hostility than exists between Germans and Jews" transmuted into "There is no greater hostility than between *these* Germans and Jews!"[57] Otto admitted that the last change was his doing, and his explanation reveals sentiments akin to Schütz's own: "I made it *these* Germans.

Because there were other Germans too. And I'm sure I thought of discussing it with Anne. It is a matter of character, a matter of responsibility which I feel. We had friends in Germany. Anne had a very good friend in Germany . . . and I had a secretary—we knew these could never have been Nazis."[58] Perhaps Otto would have been less keen to allow alterations to his daughter's diary if he had known the results of polls conducted in Germany. In October 1948, 41 percent of Germans still approved of the Nazi seizure of power. In 1952, 37 percent of the population felt it was better for Germany not to have any Jews, and in the same year, 88 percent said they felt no personal responsibility for the mass exterminations.[59] Removing the German references not only offered to readers of the German edition absolution but also bowed to the idea that Jews could never be German. Anne's original words did not reach the German public until the complete diaries were published in 1986, but by then it was no longer an issue because few people were aware that changes had been made.

The first German printing sold moderately well, though booksellers were reluctant to display it. In a letter dated December 14, 1952, Otto wrote, "In Germany they sold very little, as the newspapers do not cooperate."[60] In 1955, a paperback edition was issued in Germany. It was a runaway bestseller, but by then the diary had already achieved worldwide fame.

■

OTTO LEARNED OF SEVERAL HAPPY events in his friends' lives during 1949 and 1950. Gertrud Naumann married Karl Trenz in 1949, and in 1950 Hanneli Goslar married Walter Pick, an Israeli army major. Otto kept in contact with both women and became close friends with their husbands. On July 13, 1950, Miep and Jan became parents after a pregnancy that came as a surprise to everyone. At the age of forty-one, Miep gave birth to a boy, Paul. She and Jan were ecstatic, and Otto was

228   delighted for them. He continued to share their home after the baby's birth but was increasingly absent to promote the diary.

In England and the United States, most of the big-name publishers had rejected the diary, and Otto recruited his friends, such as Nathan Straus and Werner Cahn, to try to find a publisher willing to take a chance on the book. In late September, the Jewish publishing house Vallentine Mitchell & Co. contacted Otto's Parisian agent, Clairouin, to ask about British rights. When he was in London, Levin visited Vallentine Mitchell, and he advised Otto to let the publisher have the book. Otto held off until he had heard from another publisher, Secker & Warburg, which eventually rejected it. He then began discussions with Vallentine Mitchell. Otto was worried about the English translation: "I *have* an English translation [by Rosie Pool], but my friends in London told me that this translation was not good and advised me not to give it to publishers. So I kept it, but—it certainly is a good base for another translation. . . . I do not know if a translation made for Britain is just as good for USA. An American girl probably uses other expressions."[61] Otto discussed Rosie Pool's translation with Vallentine Mitchell on November 21, concluding, "My New York friend [Straus] wrote me that it was insufficient."[62] Straus later admitted that the translation was "almost incomprehensible," and that he felt "Otto's enthusiasm for the manuscript might be inspired by affection for his lost little daughter rather than based upon any real merit inherent in a child's diary."[63] Otto paid Pool for her work but could not bring himself to tell her that it was useless.

Interest in publishing the diary in the United States was already on the increase when two articles appeared in the American press about the book's success on the Continent. On November 11, Janet Flanner's "Letter from Paris" in *The New Yorker* referred to the diary as "one of the most widely and seriously read books in France,"[64] and Levin's essay about it in the Jewish *Congress Weekly* on November 13, 1950, also helped to raise its profile. The Dutch refugee writer Dola de Jong had seen both articles: "I was what is commonly called 'a scout' for American publishers. . . . I found out about the diary and ordered a copy of the book. But, believe it or not, I couldn't interest the American publishers. I was well connected in those days, but all the publishers I approached rejected the book. In the end, I found a junior editor at Little, Brown in Boston who had the right instincts and feelings. His name was Ned Bradford."[65] On November 22, 1950, Ned Bradford of Little, Brown cabled Otto: "This is definite offer to publish Anne Frank diary in US. Excellent chance simultaneous British publication. . . . Prefer Dola de Jong to translate much enthusiasm for book here. Little Brown & Co."[66] Otto also received an offer from Vallentine Mitchell, which suggested publishing in tandem with America's Random House, which would buy the rights to reproduce the book from them. Otto wrote to them to explain the situation with Little, Brown and followed this up with a visit to London to meet with the publisher.

His companion on the journey was Fritzi Geiringer, who was going to visit her parents and sister in England. He and Fritzi often attended the Friday night services at the Liberal Jewish synagogue together. She recalled: "As time went on I became his confidante and, in turn, I took my problems to him. . . . Having gone through the same experiences, Otto and I found that we had a lot in common and he also took an interest in Eva."[67] Otto and Fritzi traveled to England by train and boat, then parted in London, where Eva was now living and working as a photographer. The meetings with Vallentine Mitchell were favorable, and Otto accepted the British publisher's offer to publish the diary. He told Levin he had also accepted Little, Brown's offer and hoped the two firms could come to some arrangement about an English translation: "This is a difficult question, as London would not accept an American version and USA wanted Mrs. de Jong to translate. I warned Little, Brown to have it translated by someone who was not in school in USA, as the

230   charm of the book could be spoiled."[68] Otto insisted that Dola de
Jong was not the right person to translate the diary and on
December 10 wrote to Levin about his problems with her: "[Mrs.
de Jong] was not satisfied, that I did not want her to translate, as I
know that she is not American and was afraid that she would not
find the right style. . . . I had a pretty sharp correspondence with
her, but I hope that she understood the situation now and that
everything will be settled."[69] Otto later said that he had agreed to de
Jong's "request that she was to be the translator, but never wrote
her to start or urged her to go on with this work. On February 12,
1951, she mentions in a letter that she had started to translate. But
at this date I had not even received contracts."[70] De Jong remembers events very differently but admits that she began the translation without a contract: "Both Ned and I were convinced of the
importance and the eventual success of the diary, so I threw caution to the wind and began the translation. Ned hated to see me
make that commitment, but on the other hand, we trusted Otto
Frank. . . . It was a difficult job because Anne Frank was what in
those days was called a teenager, and this category had its typical
mode of expressing itself. . . . What I'm trying to emphasize here
is that my translation followed Anne Frank in her way of expressing herself. The [other] translation didn't."[71]

Otto's relationship with the American publisher was fraught
with problems. The Little, Brown staff had their own ideas about
production and promotion (with which he did not agree), and they
also tried to wrestle the Canadian rights from Vallentine Mitchell.
The British publisher legally owned those rights, since Canada was
a Commonwealth nation. On January 15, 1951, Otto signed a contract with Vallentine Mitchell that paid him fifty pounds and offered 10 percent of initial sales. He still had not signed a contract
with Little, Brown, and in March, Vallentine Mitchell announced
that it had chosen Barbara Mooyart-Doubleday as the English
translator. Mooyart-Doubleday was a British woman in her twen-

ties who lived in the Netherlands with her Dutch husband and two children. Barry Sullivan, a friend of hers who worked for Vallentine Mitchell, suggested her as the translator and wrote to her in November 1950 about the diary, which he described as "rather a special case. The translator should, I think, be an English woman, with an idiomatic knowledge of Dutch, she should understand the mind of a gay, true and rather sophisticated teenager; she should be able to convey the flavor of the original and not be afraid of a nonliterary translation or of using English schoolgirl expressions."[72]

Mooyart-Doubleday bought a copy of the book and set to work: "I was deeply moved by the diary. I read it in one breath—took it to bed with me and read it through. I did my small bit of translation, and then it must have been a matter of weeks when the publisher came back to me and said they wanted me to do it." The translation took four months:

I sat at the dining room table and wrote it all out in longhand. I had a couple of dictionaries for if I was in any doubt. I would do one page in the afternoon while my little boys slept or played in their playpen, and then I'd get them into bed at seven o'clock and work from seven until nine. My husband told me I had to stop then, otherwise I wouldn't sleep, but I kept a notebook beside the bed because occasionally I would think of things in the night and write them down. Each day I read the three pages I had translated the day before because sometimes after a night's sleep I would think, 'I don't like the way I said that, that could be improved.' My fee was sixty pounds, but when I was halfway through, Vallentine Mitchell wrote to say, 'We are in negotiations and we may be able to sell your translation to Doubleday. If that is the case, we will raise your fee to one hundred pounds.' And fairly soon they told me they were selling it. Later the proofs came, and Otto sat with me out on the balcony of my home, and we read it through.[73]

She vividly remembers her first meeting with Otto: "I was charmed by Otto. He was tremendously courteous, old-worldly in that sense. He showed me around the secret annex, and it was very different then to how it is now. There seemed to be unexpected trapdoors everywhere, creaking wooden stairs, and torn paper on the walls. When he was showing me around, he was not especially emotional because he had something to do, but during lunch, talking one to one, tears came into his eyes several times. He was a very sad man, and at that time, it was all still very close."[74]

Doubleday had come back into the picture through Frank Price, who was more enthusiastic after his second reading of the diary. On March 14, 1951, Price wrote to Otto, offering terms similar to Little, Brown's. Otto replied that he already had an American contract but had refused to sign over difficulties with dramatic rights, which were "more a matter of sentiment on my side than a financial one. I do not want a film to be made based on terror, bombardment, and Nazis spoiling the ideal base of the diary and therefore want to keep these rights under control. He warned Price that his determination to see Anne portrayed correctly meant that he would discuss contract possibilities with Doubleday only when "I know your standpoint about the film question."[75] After receiving a favorable letter from Price on the matter, Otto informed Little, Brown that he would not be signing with them. Dola de Jong was not told of his decision and continued working on her translation, only to find an announcement in the *New York Times* that Doubleday had bought the rights to the diary. She was furious, both with herself and with Otto. On March 30, 1951, Otto met Frank Price in Paris and had lunch with Levin and his wife. When he returned to Amsterdam, Otto found that he had upset his French agent Clairouin by negotiating with Doubleday himself. The agency demanded its fee, arguing that it had provided the initial contact with Price. Otto refused to pay at first but then conceded to paying a third of what they asked. In April, Otto signed a contract with

Doubleday. Frank Price and his colleagues Barbara Zimmerman (the book's editor), Jason Epstein, and Karen Rye, all filled with enthusiasm for the book, "playfully" formed the "Informal Society of Advocates of Anne Frank." Nonetheless, they felt that "the sales potential was small" and decided to "play down the grim aspects of the story" and stress instead the "beauty, humor, and insight of this document of sensitive adolescence."[76]

In July 1951, Otto was in London to deliver to Vallentine Mitchell those passages from the original Dutch typescript that were omitted from the Dutch publication; they included Anne's entries about menstruation and her curiosity about a friend's body. On August 17, the British publisher sent the final translations on to the United States. Barbara Mooyart-Doubleday received a letter from her editor Barry Sullivan: "Today the last batch went on to America. Everyone feels, who has read it, that it's going to be a wonderful book. Some passages go on moving me so deeply though I've read them four or five times now."[77] There had been a great deal of thought given to the title of the book, with suggestions such as *The Hidden Annex*, *The Secret Annex*, *Behind the Hidden Door*, *Families in Hiding*, *Beauty out of the Night*, and *Blossom in the Night*. They finally agreed upon *Anne Frank: The Diary of a Young Girl*.

In October, Doubleday's Barbara Zimmerman wrote to inform Otto that (on his suggestion) they had approached Eleanor Roosevelt to write an introduction. Zimmerman's enthusiastic letter was deeply appreciated by Otto, who responded that he had "the feeling that the matter of Anne's book is not only a commercial question for you but also a personal one."[78] Their friendship rapidly developed through their letters. Twenty-four-year-old Zimmerman was the age that Anne would have been, and she was extremely intelligent and courteous. Otto respected her opinions on everything, often asking her for advice on different matters. Publication in the United States had been postponed until June to coincide with Anne's birthday. On February 11, Zimmerman sent

234 Otto a copy of the introduction signed by Eleanor Roosevelt, adding, "We are enormously pleased, a fine tribute to the book."[79] Otto was very pleased with it himself and wrote to Eleanor Roosevelt to express his gratitude "from all my heart for the interest you are taking in [Anne] and for the help you are giving by your writing in spreading her ideals."[80] Otto never learned that Eleanor Roosevelt had merely given her name to the introduction, which was in fact written by Zimmerman.

On March 6, Levin wrote to inform Otto that he had been assigned to write about the diary for the influential *New York Times Book Review* and that he hoped Otto would still allow him to act as his agent for the stage adaptation of the diary, which he also wanted to write. Otto replied that he was quite happy for Levin to represent him rather than Doubleday, since he preferred "to leave things in your hands, and to pay agent's taxes to you. Why should another earn it when we know best what is in the line of Anne's book and that the ideas prevail?"[81] At Levin's request, on March 31 Otto signed a document authorizing Levin to negotiate all dramatic rights but did not sanction his adaptation of the diary, as Levin later claimed. On April 23, Zimmerman met Levin for lunch and told Otto that she found him "very charming, and he has many fine ideas about the book."[82]

The Diary of a Young Girl was published in Britain in May 1952 by Vallentine Mitchell in an edition of five thousand copies. The critics were unanimously agreed that it was an outstanding work. The *Newcastle Journal* commented: "The chill of Belsen pervades these trivialities. 'She'll grow out of it,' one thinks. And then one stops, and remembers that she was never given the chance." Another reviewer prophesied that "from this one girl's diary a gleam of redemption may arise."[83] However, as the publisher had anticipated, public response was cool; Florence Greenberg's Jewish cookery book far outsold the diary in its first few months. The problem lay partly in the fact that Britain, unlike Germany, had no suppressed memory to confront, and the Holocaust was not part of the general consciousness. In a private letter to Barbara Mooyart-Doubleday, Barry Sullivan explained that it was necessary for the introduction to "dwell a little on the concentration camp angle" because, "in England, Belsen is a hazy, almost 'historical' fact and the word is often used in jokes."[84]

Otto was worried that Doubleday might require his presence in the United States to promote the book and warned them: "It would be terrible for me to have to speak to someone interviewing me. I have to get out of a situation of that kind. I could not stand it."[85] Four days before publication, Zimmerman informed Otto that, "of the great many exciting things that have been happening this week," Levin's review in the *New York Times* was one of the best: "I feel sure the sales will be extremely good. *Anne Frank* will receive a wonderful reception in America!"[86] With hindsight, Zimmerman admits that, despite all the trouble that followed with Levin, "I have to give him credit for that review. It was damn good, very dramatic, and really hit hard. It struck a chord with people and made them race out to read the diary."[87] Levin's "authoritative, dazzling, compelling" review appeared on the first page of the *New York Times Book Review* as "The Child Behind the Secret Door." It begins: "Anne Frank's diary is too tenderly intimate a book to be frozen with the label 'classic,' and yet no lesser designation serves. . . . Anne Frank's diary simply bubbles with amusement, love, discovery. It has its share of disgust, its moments of hatred, but it is so wondrously alive, so near, that one feels overwhelmingly the universalities of human nature. . . . Surely she will be widely loved, for this wise and wonderful young girl brings back a poignant delight in the infinite human spirit."[88] Levin's review in *Congress Weekly* was very different in tone. There he soberly proclaimed: "The Holocaust at long last comes home, and our defenses are shattered. We weep."[89]

On June 16, 1952, *Anne Frank: The Diary of a Young Girl* was pub-

236   lished in the United States. Contrary to initial expectations, and promoted by Levin's impassioned, triumphant review, the first print run of five thousand copies sold out only hours after hitting the shelves. A second printing of fifteen thousand was rushed through, a huge advertising campaign organized, promotional items placed in all the major newspapers across the country, and syndication rights snapped up. By late afternoon, theatrical agents, producers, and television executives had converged upon Doubleday's New York office demanding to know whom they should contact for dramatic rights. In Amsterdam, Otto received the news about his daughter's shoot to literary stardom in a state of shock.

THE QUESTION OF
A JEWISH OR
NON-JEWISH WRITER

IN 1952, THE DIARY WAS PUBLISHED IN
Japan to huge acclaim. To the Japanese public, Anne Frank was "an
acceptable and accessible cultural figure of the war—a young victim, but one who inspired hope for the future rather than a sense
of guilt for the past. Her sex further emphasized the stress on innocence."[1] Anne Frank became a national heroine, and the mid-
1950s became known as the "Anne Frank Years" in Japan.[2] Since
1952, five million copies of the Japanese edition of the diary have
been sold.

Meyer Levin resigned as Otto's agent for dramatic rights when
Doubleday stepped in. His main aim was to adapt the diary for the
stage, and he began putting all his efforts into writing the play and
finding a producer for it. Barbara Zimmerman told Otto that
Doubleday intended to work closely with Levin to ensure that the
adaptation would be handled "suitably and with taste."[3] Otto cabled
the publisher on June 18 with his agreement, adding that Levin
"understands Anne perfectly and therefore I have all confidence in
him."[4] When Zimmerman wrote again, she told him that the diary
was "one of the biggest books that has been published in America

238 in a long time," adding that Doubleday had received offers to adapt the diary for the stage by "some of the most important playwrights in America today!"[5] The producer Cheryl Crawford had a meeting with Doubleday and made Levin an offer: he had two months to write a script, but if she was not satisfied with it, then she retained the right to bring in another author to assist him. Levin agreed to her terms. As a third printing of twenty-five thousand copies of the diary was printed, Zimmerman invited Otto to the United States so that he could meet "producers and playwrights."[6] On June 28, Levin's wife, Tereska, wrote to Otto, angry that Doubleday was evidently hoping "to get rid of Meyer. It's been an incredible and (in a detached way) fascinating thing to watch—the big company against the writer who was not *their* writer!"[7] She implored Otto to name a producer and make a contract with Levin, but in his next letter to Levin, Otto asserted that Levin should work together with another playwright. He admitted that his change of position was due to "long talks" between himself and Doubleday's Frank Price. Regarding Levin's idea that only a Jewish writer could suitably adapt the diary, Otto wrote, "Anne's book is not a war book. War is the background. It is not a Jewish book either, though Jewish sphere, sentiment, and surrounding is in the background. I never wanted a Jew writing an introduction for it. . . . So do not make a Jewish play out of it!"[8]

At the beginning of July, Cheryl Crawford was told by Doubleday that the project was on hold until Otto's visit to New York. Doubleday and Levin were growing increasingly antagonistic to each other, and on July 7, the publisher cabled Otto to resign as his dramatic rights agent. Otto immediately contacted Levin, to ask him if he would represent him again, imploring, "I never lost confidence in your person!!!! . . . I am a terribly nervous man near to a breakdown and *must* be careful not to hasten matters."[9]

Otto was about to make a major change in his life; that month he traveled to Basel to make arrangements to move there permanently. Despite being granted Dutch citizenship, he found Amsterdam too filled with painful memories, as he confided to Zimmerman: "All the past is in some way connected with the city and her inhabitants."[10] He also found the constant stream of diary readers calling at the Prinsengracht "a strain on my nerves," although he appreciated their interest.[11] Most of all, he wanted to be with his family again, and in 1952, he moved into the Herbstgasse house in Basel, where he had his own room on the top floor. Curiously, his area of the house resembled the secret annex. Behind a plain door, a short flight of steps led up to a narrow corridor. To the right was the large attic, and immediately in front, behind another door, was Otto's bedroom, with a low ceiling that made it humid in summer. A long window overlooked the garden and the rear balconies of surrounding houses. Otto took Anne's diaries with him to Basel but kept them in a bank safe. He later explained: "I can no longer live in Amsterdam. I often go there, but I can't stand it for more than three days. Then I go to the Prinsengracht where we hid for two years. . . . Sometimes I look at our hiding place; it has not been changed. . . . I look around and then I leave. I cannot bear the sight any longer."[12]

Otto's life was entering a second new phase: at the age of sixty-three, he was about to marry again. Laureen Nussbaum, who had emigrated to the United States, recalls: "Although it took Otto a long time to recover from his experiences, he was a very handsome man with a lovely, kind personality, and a lot of women liked him—why not! I know that Mrs. van Collem had her eye on him when Anneliese Schütz lived with her during working on the German translation, and Lotte Pfeffer, too, hoped something would happen."[13] Lotte and Otto had been friends for many years, and after the war, Lotte began to rely on him for advice. She had always been admired for her beauty, which had not faded. Every week, she, Otto, Jan, and Miep would play bridge together, and a romantic relationship between the two of them gradually developed. Otto asked her to accompany him to Switzerland to meet his family there; delighted, Lotte bought herself a new outfit for the journey. When they returned, it was obvious that matters had not gone according to plan, for Lotte was upset and the relationship immediately cooled. Otto was already close to Fritzi Geiringer by then, and it may have been that Lotte had expected more from the holiday than Otto had intended. Hilde Goldberg, who was a close friend of them both, recalls, "We were all sure that Otto would marry Lotte. But sometimes things just don't work out. His emigration to Switzerland was partly in response to the situation with Lotte. He really needed to put some space between them. She was madly in love with him, but he wanted Fritzi, who had pursued him to some extent and wasn't going to give him up. Fritzi was an attractive woman, and practical, which was what Otto needed; she was happy to help him with all matters related to the diary. So he made a good match."[14]

Fritzi (Elfriede Markovits) was born into a middle-class Jewish family in Vienna in 1905. At the age of eighteen, she married twenty-one-year-old Erich Geiringer, an Austrian businessman. Erich was very attractive, and unfaithful in the early days of their marriage, which Fritzi was able to forgive but not forget. Nonetheless, their marriage remained strong, and in 1926, their son Heinz Felix was born, followed in 1929 by Eva. Fritzi was a loving, affectionate mother but could also be strict and unyielding. In May 1938, Erich emigrated to the Netherlands to go into partnership with the owner of a shoe factory. When war broke out between England and Germany, Fritzi and the children joined Erich in Amsterdam, at 46 Merwedeplein. Their life there was happy at first, but on July 6, 1942, Heinz received the same call-up notice as Margot Frank. Erich and Fritzi had already made preparations for this eventuality, and the following day they went into hiding. Erich and Heinz disappeared into the Dutch countryside, while Fritzi and Eva found refuge with a teacher in Amsterdam. On May 11,

1944, Fritzi and Eva were betrayed. When they arrived at the Gestapo headquarters, they found Erich and Heinz had also been arrested, and the four of them were sent to Westerbork and then Auschwitz. Fritzi and Eva remained together for much of their time in the camp. Upon their arrival, Fritzi's quick thinking saved her daughter from the gas chambers. She made Eva put on a coat and hat, which made her look much older than her fifteen years. On one occasion, Fritzi herself was selected, but she was saved by a cousin, who intervened on her behalf. After their liberation and journey home, Fritzi and Eva moved back to the Merwedeplein, where Otto was a frequent visitor. Otto helped them with practical problems and supported Fritzi when her betrayer was found and tried. Eva recalls, "My mother attended the trial but came home very upset. Our betrayer had saved a famous Dutch opera singer who testified for her. Our betrayer was acquitted; my mother wanted to kill her."[15]

Eva had known for quite a while that Otto wanted to marry her mother: "Otto came to visit me in England when I was thinking of getting married. I was nervous about leaving my mother on her own, but Otto said, 'Now, don't worry about this, because after you are married and settled, your mother and I are going to marry.' "[16] Otto was a witness at Eva's 1952 marriage to Zvi Schloss, an economics student from Israel who worked for a stockbroker. The couple settled in London and had three daughters. Eva worked as a freelance photographer until 1972 and then started an antiques business in the city.

With Fritzi, Otto discovered the romance that his marriage to Edith had lacked. They addressed each other by pet names: Fritzi was "Putzeli" or "Sugarli," and Otto was "Burscheli." His letters to her from the United States in 1952 reveal his deep affection: "I'm looking forward to seeing you as much as you are with me. In my head you're always with me. I don't think you will have anything to complain about in the future. I haven't experienced real feminin-

242 ity until now. I want to send the letter quickly. Do the kisses do the trick? They're included."[17] Otto's comment about "real femininity" is an intriguing one and presumably means that he felt he had found the right woman at last. Otto's nephew, Buddy, remembers: "Fritzi was terrific for Otto. They were a real partnership in every sense. She helped him so much with the diary—writing endless letters, inviting people to meet them, attending functions, and so on. She was always at his side, and he relied upon her. I liked her—she had a tremendous sense of humor."[18] Father John Neiman, a close friend of the couple, recalls: "Fritzi had great dignity and was as kind as her husband. They were both very easy to get along with, not aloof at all, just the opposite. As husband and wife, they complemented each other perfectly."[19] Their marriage was set for the following year.

■

ON SEPTEMBER 29, 1952, OTTO ARRIVED in New York aboard the *Queen Elizabeth*. He wrote to Fritzi: "My brother-in-law and Miss Zimmerman were waiting for me. A huge Cadillac took me to the hotel. . . . Mr. [Joseph] Marks from Doubleday had left whiskey and flowers at the hotel and he came at six o'clock to greet me. They have opened a bank account for me at the hotel. I only need to give a signature or ask for more money (which I don't do). The thing I wanted most was to talk to my brothers-in-law." Otto's reunion with Julius and Walter was emotional, although Zimmerman was there. Otto described Julius, who had suffered from depression all his life, as "a wreck about the past, very depressed and nervous and I felt deeply sorry for him. The younger one is much better. He arranged to meet with them privately at a later date. His first impression of Zimmerman was that she was "a sweet thing, Anne's age."[20] Zimmerman herself recalls: "Otto turned up with this really beautiful zippered leather notebook which was for a much older person, and I was rather sur-

prised but very touched by the fact that he thought to bring me   243
something. He was a beautiful, tragic man. I didn't know what to
expect when I met him, but he was very spiritual. A lot of people
wanted to meet him."[21]

On October 1, Otto informed Fritzi that since his arrival, "I've
had no peace and quiet and am quite excited although I try to be
calm. . . . Yesterday morning I was at Doubleday. They had just had
a meeting of traveling salesmen and Marks wanted me to say a few
words. I did this but was very nervous. . . . In the afternoon I was
with Levin, who brought me the first script. He said that Miss
Crawford agreed in principle and that only a few changes would be
necessary. . . . This morning I started to read the script. I can read
it only in long intervals because it excites me terribly and I have to
cry all the time."[22] That same day, Otto, Levin, and Crawford met in
Crawford's office. She liked the script, and a discussion about di-
rectors followed. Otto dined with Levin and his wife that evening.
They were joined by William Zinneman, a film executive who had
read Levin's theater script and was full of praise. On October 3,
Crawford sent a letter to Otto at the Madison Hotel and told
him that she had read Levin's script again and now felt it "did not
have enough theatrical potential for Levin to continue working
on it," even with another writer. Levin was "stunned" by her
announcement.[23]

After a drawn-out argument, Crawford agreed to allow Levin to
rewrite his script. On October 3, Otto wrote to Fritzi, telling her
that he had read Levin's first draft and his instinct told him that
"psychologically it's excellent, but I can't judge how it will be on a
stage, that's a matter for Miss Crawford. On Monday we'll have another meeting." Crawford informed Otto that she wanted a second
opinion on the script and proposed the theater producer Kermit
Bloomgarden. After hearing Bloomgarden's and Crawford's
damning views, Otto admitted that his confidence in Levin "was
vanishing"; he found Levin's hope that he could salvage his work

244 "uncomfortable, because this particular knot needs undoing."[24] Otto was introduced to Myer Mermin, a lawyer with much experience of theatrical business matters, through Paul, Weiss, Rifkind, Wharton and Garrison, a firm that Otto's old friend Nathan Straus had recommended. Mermin and Otto liked each other, and Mermin agreed to represent him. Otto wrote to Fritzi that he had had a long talk with Doubleday's vice president Joseph Marks, who was "always suspicious about Levin. Levin doesn't want to give in, as his heart is set on writing the script for the dramatization. It's understandable but I have to rely on the experts. I cannot use my own judgment because it's too important a matter."[25] Otto wrote again on October 24: "Levin came by and declared that although he has no money he wouldn't think of taking a salary for a play that isn't up to standard. His reputation as a writer would be tarnished. I think he should have the opportunity to find other producers if Crawford and Bloomgarden don't like his script. . . . Sometimes I wonder whether I shouldn't just drop the whole 'show business' because there are so many difficulties. I said this yesterday to Levin and explained to him that it's not right for the ideals of Anne to do something that might end up in a court case, and that it's better to do nothing than for that to happen. I think it made an impression on him."[26] On November 11, Otto had a meeting with Zimmerman and Crawford, who had an entirely new proposal: the playwright and novelist Carson McCullers should write the play. Exhausted, Otto agreed. On November 15, he returned to Europe.

On November 21, 1952, Levin signed "under protest" an agreement allowing him one month in which to find a producer from a list compiled by himself and approved by Crawford and Mermin. After that date, he could not perpetrate his own adaptation "in any manner whatever" and Otto would have the right, "free of any claims by you, to engage any other dramatist or dramatists to dramatize the Book and any producer or producers to produce such dramatization."[27] On December 21, having been unable to secure a written agreement to produce his script from any of those on the approved list, Levin renounced all his rights to the play. Otto's thoughts were on more personal matters, as he informed Zimmerman from Basel: "Today I expect Fritzi. She worked up to the fifteenth and we shall stay here together up to the end of the month and go to the mountains in January. . . . Mother was eighty-seven on December 20. She was in good condition and joined us for dinner (she generally is staying upstairs in her room). She rose and made a wonderful speech! My brother came from London, so we were together (her four children). This is an exception we are grateful for."[28] Otto's pleasure did not last long. On December 25, Levin sent him a furious letter, having read in the newspaper that Carson McCullers would probably write the play. He seethed: "I am disgusted and enraged at the thought that a non-Jew has been selected to write this play. . . . I will not stand for this. I will write about it wherever I can. It is adding insult to injury. I will tell the whole story."[29]

Both Zimmerman and Otto's friend Nathan Straus wrote to inform Otto that they disagreed with Levin on "the question of whether a Jew or a non-Jew should write the play." Zimmerman advised going with a non-Jewish writer, otherwise the play might be "limited . . . to simply Jewish experience. The wonderful thing about Anne's book is that it is really universal, that it is a book, an experience, for everyone."[30] Straus agreed: "It would seem to me a distinct advantage if the play were written by a non-Jew. In the first place, it would emphasize the universality of the theme. In the second place, there is, to my mind, little doubt but that the play would be much more readily accepted on its merits if it were written by a non-Jew."[31] When Otto wrote to Levin about the matter a few days later, he actually repeated Straus's words verbatim, hoping that would be an end to the matter, but Levin was still communicating with all those concerned. Zimmerman told Otto that Levin was "impossible to deal with on any terms, officially, legally, morally, personally."[32] Today she reflects: "Levin's play was no good at all. He completely misread the family, turning them into very observant Jews when actually they were upper-middle-class and highly assimilated. It was not so much a play as a series of religious celebrations."[33]

Having heard that Levin was threatening to sue Crawford, Otto wrote to him in exasperation: "I told you that it is against the ideas and ideals of Anne to have disputes and quarrels, disagreements and suing. . . . I would be very much pleased if you would stop with every kind of trouble-making as this is unjust and below your standing. . . . You are a bad loser."[34] Nonetheless, Otto suspected that Levin had not been fairly treated. During his stay in New York, he wrote to Fritzi that "actually it is Doubleday who always warn me off [Levin] and in a certain way agitate me, which I try to resist."[35] Nonetheless, Levin's actions ("wrong and ugly")[36] since his play had been rejected upset Otto, and he told his friend Rabbi Bernard Heller that "I never in my life got so disappointed by the character of any man as Meyer Levin's."[37] Eventually, both the producer Cheryl Crawford and the writer Carson McCullers withdrew from the play and Kermit Bloomgarden stepped in to produce, to the delight of Mermin and Zimmerman. Levin bombarded Otto with aggressive letters after the failure of his most recent attempt to ingratiate himself with Otto and professed that his play meant to him what Anne meant to Otto. Mermin sent Levin a sharp letter, doubting that he could persuade Levin to desist with his battle, "but who knows? I am neither a psychiatrist nor a magician—and again we have to wait to see what will happen."[38]

■

IN MARCH, WHILE STAYING WITH FRITZI and Eva in London, Otto heard that his mother was seriously ill. He flew out to Basel to be with her, then returned to London when she improved, but on March 19 he wrote to Zimmerman: "Today my brother called up and told me that mother died last night after having had a stroke. . . . I am glad to have seen her while she really still enjoyed it."[39] Alice Frank's funeral was the last time Otto, Herbert, Leni, and Robert would all be together. Two months later, on May 23, 1953, Robert Frank, like his father, suffered what was probably a heart attack and died in London.

Otto's method of dealing with grief had always been to keep himself occupied, and following the deaths of his mother and brother, he immersed himself in business connected to the diary. He was troubled by the lack of success of the British edition. Whereas in the United States the book had sold spectacularly well, in Britain, once the current stock had been sold, no further print run had been ordered. Otto's letter to Vallentine Mitchell's Barry Sullivan protesting their decision shows how forceful and determined he could be when roused: "I am convinced that many more books could have been sold. . . . I was influenced by friends from Paris and New York to prefer your firm and to take a Jewish publisher. I honestly and frankly must say that I feel let down by you."[40] Otto was not pacified by a letter from the publisher and fumed: "Had I known that you wanted the book so badly mainly on account of its commercial outlook, I never would have entrusted it to your firm. . . . I am not the only one who regards it as a disgrace that this book is not available on the English market."[41] In the summer of 1954, Pan Books bought the rights to issue it as a cheap paperback, and by the end of the decade, it was one of Pan's best-selling titles.

Otto's other worry was the house at 263 Prinsengracht. The owner intended to sell the building, and Otto wanted to buy it (he retired from Opekta that year) to set up an educational organization relevant to its wartime history. The idea had come from Doubleday's Joseph Marks, as Otto had informed Fritzi the year before: "Marks has this plan whereby all publishers of Anne's book should club together to buy the house at 263 and install a library for

248   young people. That's the way they think here."[42] Otto cherished the idea but could not imagine it being realized. He was delighted when Opekta shareholders, meeting on April 27, agreed to buy the property with the stipulation that "a foundation" appointed by Otto be established there.[43] Unfortunately, the building was literally falling apart, and renovation costs would be enormous. On August 13, Otto received a letter from Kleiman (who still worked for Opekta), urging him to visit Amsterdam immediately. Berghaus, the firm that owned the neighboring house—265—intended to demolish it and rebuild. The structure of the Anne Frank house was so weak that it would probably collapse in the process; even the new roof was leaking. The only solution was to raise more money fast for the renovation. Otto wrote despondently to Barbara Zimmerman: "Mr. Kleiman wrote that he is in favor of selling the house rather than investing another 10,000 guilders—though he knows how I feel about the secret annex." Otto was unable to pay for it himself: "In my present situation living outside of Holland, not earning a salary, I cannot afford it. . . . It hurts me to a great extent to be unable to realize the idea originated by Mr. Marks to have an Anne Frank Foundation in the house and to preserve the secret annex for future generations. . . . I feel it is my duty to let Mr. Marks know the state of this matter. His original idea worked in my mind all this time and became a sort of ideal, trying to make from the secret annex not only a dead monument but to make it a youth center for people from different countries."[44] On September 9, Otto told Zimmerman the latest: "I feel that I should not take the risk of rebuilding if I can avoid it. The experts told me it might just as well get to cost double the amount they originally taxed. So I have to be reasonable. Decision will be taken definitely middle of December if the house next to us will be torn down with the consequences for our lease, and if they want to buy our house, too, or not."[45] His next report was even more dismal: the entire row of houses from 265 to the corner of the street would be torn down.

Berghaus offered a good price for 263 Prinsengracht, and it was ac- cepted. (Curiously, Martha Ahlers worked for the company at the time as a seamstress.) Opekta was permitted to conduct business from the building for one more year. After that, the house would be demolished.

At the end of the year, Otto finally had something to celebrate. On November 10, 1953, he and Fritzi were married at Amsterdam's City Hall. The only guests were Miep and Jan Gies and Kleiman and his wife. After the ceremony, there was a dinner at the Hotel de l'Europe before the newlyweds departed for a small hotel in Arnhem. The following day they traveled to Basel. Erich, Leni, and Stephan continued to live at Herbstgasse (Buddy was frequently abroad in "Holiday on Ice"), and Herbert joined them permanently in 1955. Otto was once more living in the familial atmosphere he had craved, and he loved taking meals at the long table in the front dining room with his wife, brother, sister, brother-in-law, and nephew. They used his parents' silverware for meals and were surrounded by oil paintings and stalwart, rich furniture from the Frankfurt home of his youth. He enjoyed the little displays of familiarity: Leni's scolding of Herbie, who would sit growling in his throat and rapping his fingers on the table when nothing was being said, Erich's quiet, sensible advice, and his wife's ringing laughter at some joke Buddy had passed on in his letters to Stephan. Leni's antiques business was a great success; Erich never had to work again, and each day he would take his newspaper into Leni's shop, where he sat drinking tea and chatting with the customers, to Leni's amused irritation.

■

IN DECEMBER, OTTO LEARNED THAT Frances and Albert Hackett had been suggested to adapt the diary. Their forte was light comedy, such as their award-winning screenplays *Father of the Bride* and *It's a Wonderful Life*. The Hacketts were

250   eager to work on the diary with its "tense drama, the possibility of great intimacy in the scenes. . . . And moments of lovely comedy which heighten the desperate, tragic situation of the people." Bloomgarden reassured them that he did not want to "wring tears out of people" and felt that "the only way this play will go will be if it's funny . . . get them laughing, and that's the way it's possible for them to sit through the show."[46] Zimmerman assured Otto that the Hacketts were ideal for the task, but he was nervous about the choice, confiding in Frank Price: "I am a little afraid, as most Europeans are, of a 'Hollywood' writer for such a serious and delicate subject."[47] As Mermin had suspected, the Hacketts' agent, Leah Salisbury, negotiated a contract much more in her clients' favor than Otto's. By the time it was finalized, Meyer Levin had begun to be active again, placing an advertisement on the theater page of the *New York Post* accusing Bloomgarden of killing his play. He asked the public to contact Otto and demand a test reading. Like Bloomgarden, Otto ignored Levin, who he now felt had "the mind of a psychopath."[48] The Hacketts began work on the script, paying particular attention to a scene that would depict the Hanukkah service in hiding. They consulted a rabbi and "got Jewish prayer books, hymn books," aiming to see "what liberties we could take without offending anyone." At the end of May, they sent copies of their second draft to Bloomgarden, Salisbury, Otto, and their friend author Lillian Hellman, whose opinion they regarded highly and who gave them much advice on the script for the diary adaptation. They were nervous, worried about not only Bloomgarden's reaction but also Otto's: "He may be shocked at the amount of comedy we have in it . . . but I think it is true to the character of Anne . . . and consequently in the spirit of the book."[49]

Otto sent Mermin his opinion on the script on June 2, 1954. He hated it: "Whereas with the Levin play, I felt that the psychological development and the characters were good, but that I could not judge the dramatic value, my first impression of the Hackett version is to be excellent routine work, but giving the spirit of the book . . . I cannot say that the script is against the spirit of Anne but it is not working up to the high spirit of Anne and in its present form would never convey the message which the book contains."[50] He waited three days before sending the Hacketts his views, beginning his letter, "I have a lot to object." Listed as causes for his dislike were the "rather humoristic touch" in the first act, the relationship between Anne and Edith—as well as that between Anne and Peter, which was "too compressed"—and their depiction of Margot as "snappish." What was needed, he told them, was a clear illustration of Anne's "optimistic view" of life. He felt that their play "failed to do justice to the circumstances," and his confidence was so low he was uncertain whether "the points I raised could be corrected."[51] Bloomgarden had several changes himself to suggest. He wanted the Hanukkah scene to be celebratory rather than serious, he proposed a scene in which Pfeffer ("Dussel" in the script) stole bread, and he asked for greater attention to be given to the relationship between Anne and Peter. He also told them to forget Anne's own description of her diary as a chronicle of "how we lived, what we ate and what we talked about as Jews in hiding" and insisted that it should be a depiction of Anne dealing with the normal problems of adolescence under extraordinary circumstances. Neither the Hacketts nor Bloomgarden were inclined to show "a collection of disagreeable people on stage and too much of the depressing atmosphere of nightmare and horror."[52] The Hacketts' close friend, the playwright Lillian Hellman, also had much advice to offer them.

In October, Otto was admitted to the hospital with a nervous breakdown. His fragile state of health had suffered from reviving memories of his time in hiding and his months in Auschwitz, reexperiencing his raw emotions over the loss of his children, and leaving Amsterdam and remarrying. The heavy amount of work on the diary and the constant focus on the past had likewise taken their toll. Hilde Goldberg recalled that he was close to a breakdown when he visited her family in Frankfurt in 1950: "He was still in a great emotional upheaval about having to face the world with this book."[53] Hilde's daughter Ruth told Fritzi years later: "I don't remember a time when I didn't know about Auschwitz and Belsen, or about Anne, or about Otto and his enormous desire to live out his grief publicly."[54] It took him several weeks to recover.

On October 29, 1954, Garson Kanin was appointed director of the play, and it was through him that the script lost some of its most vital elements. In an excessively sentimental article in *Newsweek* in 1979, Kanin compared Anne to the Mona Lisa ("which she strangely resembles") and Peter Pan, among others, and wrote that Otto was "the man who said, a moment before their inescapable discovery, 'For two years we have lived in fear; now we can live in hope.'"[55] Queried on French television about whether he had actually uttered those words, Otto shook his head and laughed. Under Kanin's guidance, Dussel's reports about the ordeals suffered by the Jews and the non-Jewish Dutch disappeared to be replaced by the single sentence: "No one in Holland has enough to eat." Otto's speech about the horrors of the camps was removed, and the arrival of the Nazis at the annex became dramatic: jackboots on the stairs, thundering at the door, and German voices screaming to open up. The specific nature of the Holocaust was obliterated. The lines uttered by the stage Anne (adapted from Anne's own words)— "We're not the only Jews that have had to suffer. Right down through the ages there have been Jews and they've had to suffer"— were changed to: "We're not the only people that have had to suffer. Right down through the ages there have been people that have had to suffer. Sometimes one race, sometimes another."[56] In an effort to secure "better audience identification with the subject and the characters" almost all references to Jews and Jewish suffering were erased. Otto supported Kanin's idea that the play should be

made more universal: "It was my point of view to try to bring
Anne's message to as many people as possible even if there are
some who think it is a sacrilege and does not bring the greatest part
of the public to understand."[57] His friends in Amsterdam also
questioned how Otto could allow certain scenes to be included,
such as the one in which van Pels steals bread. Originally, the
Hacketts had depicted Dussel (Pfeffer) as the thief, but Otto himself advised them to change this to van Pels because of his friendship with Lotte Pfeffer. He then became fearful, however, of a
potential lawsuit from Hermann van Pels's brother, who was living
in New York. (No lawsuit was ever brought.)

On December 6, the Hacketts and Garson Kanin arrived in
Amsterdam. In her diary, Frances recorded that there were "presents from Mr. Frank waiting in hotel room. This is St. Nicholas
Day. Garson, Albert Hackett and I met Mr. Frank for first time."
The following day they visited the annex, and Frances found it
"very harrowing. Stood in Anne's room, stretched out my arms,
touched walls on either side. This is the room she had to share with
the crotchety dentist. Saw Garson looking at one of the photographs Anne had pasted on her wall. It was Ginger Rogers in a picture he had directed—*Tom, Dick, and Harry*." They walked around
the River Quarter and then met the "helpers": Miep, Jan, Bep,
Kugler, and Kleiman. Otto's friend, the Dutch historian Louis de
Jong, offered to read their script to check "for mistakes in documentation." On December 10, Kanin arranged for detailed photographs of the annex, while the Hacketts fired questions at Otto.
The following day was their last, and Frances wrote in her diary: "I
thought I could not cry more than I had. But I have had a week of
tears."[58] Kanin recorded his impressions of the visit in the *New York
Times*, ending: "In all my meetings with [Otto] he was unhurried,
casual, old-worldish. He talked about the hideout and the arrest
without an ounce of emotion. 'This is a cold fish,' I told the
Hacketts. Anyway, after I left for Paris, I had to telephone Mr.

254   Frank. I didn't get him to the phone for days. Finally I learned why. The moment we'd left Amsterdam he collapsed. He had been crushed, but he had not shown it."[59] Otto wrote to Mermin that the week with the Hacketts and Kanin had been "a wonderful experience. . . . They are all working with the greatest devotion and I have every possible confidence in their work." He was satisfied that now they had "undergone the influence of the hiding place . . . the spirit of the script will not be changed."[60]

On December 30, 1954, Otto was told that Levin had begun litigation against him and Cheryl Crawford for the breach of agreements made between 1950 and 1952 permitting him to write or collaborate on the play. For most of 1955, lawyers on both sides explored possible solutions between the parties. In the meantime, Otto would have been deeply hurt to know that his careful suggestions for keeping the play's integrity intact (such as depicting the characters more sensitively and lessening the humor of it all) had been dismissed by Kanin as unimportant. Casting had now begun, and on March 22, 1955, Joseph Schildkraut was chosen to portray Otto. He wrote to Otto of his admiration for the diary and for Anne, who he felt was "as immortal as the Macabeans were—or Joan of Arc—or any other heroine or martyr of history."[61] Schildkraut, born in Vienna in 1896, had been a child actor. In the 1920s, he usually played a rogue, but by the 1930s he was a respected character actor. The role of Anne went to Susan Strasberg, the talented young daughter of the stage impresario Lee Strasberg. The casting of Edith Frank caused rumblings of discontent in the press. The actress chosen, Gusti Huber, was reported to have a "former Nazi affiliation and special friendship with Josef Goebbels."[62] Otto asked Fritzi, who was from Vienna, like Huber, whether she knew anything about her. Fritzi did not but was anxious to know more. A journalist who had survived Dachau sent Bloomgarden a 1935 Vienna newspaper article in which Huber stated her resolve not to "associate with non-Aryan artists [who] would endanger her stature in Nazi Germany."[63] In 1946, she arrived in the United States, after having married a U.S. Army officer. Despite these revelations, Huber held on to the role and also portrayed Edith in the film.

On August 31, Otto wrote to the Hacketts: "I pray that the spirit of Anne's book will be transferred to the public," but admitted, "The whole idea of having all represented on the stage is depressing me always."[64] On September 27, Otto wrote to Barbara Mooyart-Doubleday, translator of the diary from Dutch to English: "The writers used parts of the book as 'bridges' between the scenes having Anne's voice reading between these parts in the dark, while the curtain is down. . . . They ask me now if you have still any rights in the translation which was sold to Doubleday."[65] Mooyart-Doubleday replied that she had no rights as far as she was aware. Nonetheless, the Hacketts pushed Otto to ask her to sign a document renouncing all claims to the diary and the play. Mooyart-Doubleday ignored the request, and it was never mentioned again.

On October 5, 1955, *The Diary of Anne Frank* premiered at New York's Cort Theater. Among the many fur-stole-clad, couture-dressed stars emerging from their limousines was Marilyn Monroe, a close friend of Susan Strasberg's. Backstage, tacked to the bulletin board with small pins, was a letter from Otto Frank: "You will all realize that for me this play is a part of my life, and the idea that my wife and children as well as I will be presented on the stage is a painful one to me. Therefore it is impossible for me to come and see it. My thoughts are with every one of you all the time, and I hope the play will be a success and that the message which it contains will, through you, reach as many people as possible and awaken in them a sense of responsibility to humanity."[66] While the real Otto Frank slept thousands of miles away in Switzerland, the lights in the New York theater dimmed and his alter ego climbed the creaking stairs to a dark and dusty attic.

■

WHEN "OTTO" CLOSED THE DIARY AND
bowed his head, and the curtain fell on that first performance,
everyone in the theater that night was aware that they had just witnessed a resounding success. The reviews were ecstatic. Echoed by
his contemporaries, the critic from the *New York World Telegram*
proclaimed: "The genius of this play is that there is nothing grim or
sensational about it . . . it relates the flowering of a youngster who
was pure in heart . . . in the end they must go to the concentration
camps. And Anne goes, smiling."[67] The Dutch journalists who attended subsequent performances were appalled, however. *Vrij
Nederland* reproached Broadway's contortion of "things which are
sacred." In the United States, the diary was simply "a thing of
amusement" and Anne herself "ridiculous. . . . The entire performance is sacrilege, sacrilege to all those who were tortured."
The idea of "well-fed people entering the theater . . . laughing"
was loathsome.[68] *Het Parool* denounced the play as "kitsch, which I
hope we shall not see here."[69]

Nonetheless, the play made Anne Frank a household name. It
made an overnight star of Susan Strasberg and broke all records; it
ran for 717 performances in the one-thousand-seat Cort Theater
before touring twenty major North American cities. In New York
alone, approximately one million people sat through *The Diary of
Anne Frank*. In November, the Hacketts, keen to repeat their success on the big screen, visited Otto in Basel, staying at the Three
Kings Hotel. The Hacketts' agent, Leah Salisbury, wrote to Otto on
December 1 offering to represent him and assuring him she had
"loved you and suffered with you" and taken "all of you Franks to
my heart" before getting down to the real point: "that the final deal
will assure us the Hacketts as the screen writers and Kanin as the
director."[70]

Otto replied to Salisbury on December 13, thanking her for her
"warm personal interest" but ultimately rejecting her offer. Rather

unpleasantly, Frances wrote to Salisbury that Otto was "a very frugal man . . . and I think he will think twice before paying 10% [Salisbury's fee]." She had found him to be "a curious mixture of great emotion and business" who "gives his money away while taking care to secure its source," and she was intrigued by how he was "unable to speak of the Diary without crying" and yet allowed scenes to be invented and changes made to Anne's words.[71] Otto's aim, of course, was that the "message" of the diary should reach as many people as possible, and he trusted people like the Hacketts and Kanin to know best. For their part, they had long ago realized that they could manipulate him by appealing to him as Anne's father, assuring him that they wanted only what was best "for the diary," "for the play," and now, "for the film." Otto would have been deeply wounded by the cruel letters passing between the Hacketts and Salisbury, who were irritated by his concern over the screen adaptation. On January 9, 1956, in response to Salisbury's spiteful remarks about Otto's emotional state and his intention to travel to the United States, Albert Hackett wrote: "I thought I was the only one who dreaded his visit. He lives in the past and gets talking about the diary, the play or Anne, and very soon he has reduced Frances to tears."[72] The European production of the play was imminent, and Salisbury was worried about Otto having "too much control. Kermit and Garson agreed with me completely—said it was dangerous and must not be allowed to happen." Otto had already suggested changes to the script to make it more realistic, but on January 26, Salisbury told the Hacketts that she had worded the contract so that it would be "impossible for [Otto] to insist upon changes in the American text or . . . to impose his ideas regarding deletions or additions because the play is 'too glamorous' for Europe."[73]

Because of Levin's continual legal combat, Otto's royalties from the play were in limbo. In February, Levin brought a second lawsuit against Bloomgarden and Otto, charging "fraud, breach of contract

258   and wrongful appropriation of ideas."[74] He wanted $150,000 dam-
ages from Otto and $100,000 from Bloomgarden. With this in
mind, Otto decided against traveling to the United States, feeling it
would be "a tremendous strain," not only because of the lawsuit but
also because "I could not escape many people wanting to meet the
real Otto Frank after they had seen the play and this would be very
emotional." He was also concerned about costs: "The business in
Amsterdam does not bring me more than about $1,000 income a
year [as he and Kleiman had agreed] and the capital I have in
Switzerland originates for the greater part from what I received
from Doubleday for the book. All the other countries did not pay
much. I am living here in a very modest way, using two rooms in my
sister's house. I do so because I did not want to use the money from
the play for personal purposes."[75] The play, which had won the New
York Drama Critics Circle Award for the season's best American
production and the 1956 Pulitzer Prize for drama, was grossing
more than $30,000 a week. Traditionally, the Pulitzer Prize–
winning play was performed at the Paris drama festival, but that
year tradition was broken. The U.S. State Department, nervous
about upsetting Franco-German relations, had decided that *The
Diary of Anne Frank* would not be performed.

Otto remained nervous about the Hacketts writing the screenplay. He felt guilty about the portrayals of Pfeffer and van Pels on
the stage, which had caused problems among his friends, and he
was desperate to ensure that the film version did not repeat those
errors: "How could I face the reproaches of my conscience, of my
family, of Miep, Kleiman and the others who never understood
that I gave away the rights to get money without any promise from
the producer to respect the quality of the material."[76] Otto wanted
the film to be more realistic and hoped that the Hanukkah scene
would feature a Hebrew song. The Hacketts were appalled by the
idea, which they felt would "set the characters in the play apart
from the people watching them . . . for the majority of our audi-

ence is not Jewish."[77] Otto was also concerned about Levin, whom he was worried would "break down and commit suicide."[78] Levin's wife begged Otto to find something positive to offer Levin, adding hopelessly, "This case against you has ruined my marriage with Meyer."[79] Otto wanted to help and suggested allowing Levin to have amateur rights in Israel, but the matter remained with lawyers.

In August 1956, the European premiere of the play was held in Sweden, and Otto announced, "This is not a play for me, or even for Jews or Germans—it is a play for all the world."[80] But it was the reception to the play in Germany that caught the headlines of newspapers across the world. One reviewer recalled: "No one was prepared for what actually happened on the evening of October 1, 1956, when seven theaters premiered the German version of *The Diary of Anne Frank*. . . . In Berlin, after the final curtain, the audience sat in stunned silence. There was no applause. Only the welling sound of deep sobs broke the absolute stillness. Then, still not speaking and seeming not to look at each other, the Berliners filed out of the theater."[81] The play "released a wave of emotion that finally broke through the silence with which the Germans had treated the Nazi period."[82] Another review described it as having "the effect of a present day requiem: the audience seemed to be engaged in an act of contrition."[83] Theater playbills included photos, Otto's memories of the period in hiding, accounts of Anne's final days in Belsen, and articles with titles like "Are We Guilty?" It was seen by more than one million people, and Anne was hailed as a national heroine. Schools, streets, and refugee villages were given her name, and a plaque was attached to her former home on Ganghoferstrasse. Two thousand teenagers took part in a pilgrimage to Bergen-Belsen in 1957 to remember her death. Between 1955 and 1960, more than 600,000 copies of the diary were sold in Germany. On its cover were the words: "I still believe in the good of people."

Otto wrote several articles about Germany and ended one with those lines, insisting, "I must keep talking to [the youth of Germany], for like Anne, 'in spite of everything I still believe that people are really good at heart.' "[84] He did not believe in collective guilt and never lost his pride in his German roots. In the 1950s, when the Anne Frank Stichting wanted to ban Germans from visiting the house, Otto vetoed the idea, asking whether that would mean he could no longer set foot in his former hiding place either. He recalled: "I said that you have to get Germans. You don't refuse the Jews of Germany. You don't refuse your own people."[85] Zvi Schloss remembers Otto as "very military in some sense—tidy, punctual, exact. You could see that he had been in the German army. You see, he never had to overcome his hatred, like most German Jewish survivors do. He never hated Germany. He loved his country to the end."[86] Eva Schloss agrees: "He was very proud of having been in the German army and always remained so. He said often, 'I'm a German from a very good family.' My mother, Fritzi, was quite the opposite. She had been born in Austria, but she hated Austrians and never wanted to go back to Austria. I found Otto's attitude difficult, and it caused problems between us for a while. But let me put it this way: Germany was to him like a wayward child to a parent. You love your child but dislike their actions. Otto always loved Germany. He would never abandon Germany, but he was appalled by it just the same. And that hurt him until his death."[87]

Asked in 1959 about how he felt toward Germany, Otto replied: "I realize that at present there are many former Nazis in important positions. Also, anti-Semitism is not diminishing. . . . On the other hand, there are many young people who understand the crimes which have been committed and want to remedy them. So you see, we are not allowed to generalize, and I, for my part, am always ready to help those, no matter where they are, who want to work in the good direction."[88] A year later, he wrote an article for

Coronet magazine, "Has Germany Forgotten Anne Frank?" In it, he
volunteered:

> The older generation of Germans cannot yet face up to past history
> and communicate its lessons to the future. . . . I am intensely in-
> terested in Germany, its future, and its youth. My concern is that
> never again should Germany experience the madness of racial
> prejudice and that Anne's life should not have been empty and
> without meaning. . . . Of all the letters inspired by a reading of
> *The Diary*, I have been most diligent in answering the ones from
> German youth. For their education—in democratic ideals and ways
> of life—is of paramount importance to me. . . . Europeans remain
> concerned about Germany. They are repelled by the past and wor-
> ried about the future. They know that they cannot very well live
> without Germans and never have learned quite how to live with
> them. In that respect I am a typical European, for those are my re-
> actions, too.[89]

On November 27, in the presence of Queen Juliana, the play
premiered in Amsterdam. Otto attended the opening ceremony
with several of his friends and all the "helpers" apart from Kugler,
who was by then living in Canada with his second wife, Loes, whom
he had married in June 1955. (Kugler's first wife died in 1952.)
Miep later reported to Otto how she and Jan had reacted to the play:
"Jan, who usually can stand quite a lot, wasn't able to say a single
word to me during the play and the break. When it was over, I saw
he'd been crying and in the street he told me he was very glad he'd
seen it. And I myself, too, Otto. In spite of the fact that it was devastating. I thought the beginning was scary and I had the feeling I
wouldn't be able to cope but when all the players are onstage it is all
right. And at the end there is this measureless anger, you'd want to
drag the 'Moffen' [Nazis] around the room if you'd seen them, it
doesn't matter that they are not real."[90]

■

IN EARLY 1956, OTTO RECEIVED THE miraculous news that the annex was not going to be demolished. The Dutch press had focused attention on the matter; *Het Vrij Volk* commented: "The Netherlands will be subject to a national scandal if this house is pulled down. . . . There is every reason, especially considering the enormous interest from both inside and outside the country, to correct this situation as quickly as possible."[91] The local historical society Amstelodamum also urged people to "honor Anne Frank's memory . . . by saving this house, which is forever connected to Amsterdam's darkest years of occupation."[92] After Berghaus had taken possession of the building, they gave Kleiman a key so that he could guide around visitors interested in seeing where the diary had been written. In November 1956, Otto spoke to the mayor of Amsterdam about the public interest in the building, and Kleiman spoke to the press about Otto's aim to restore it and to prevent the neighboring houses from being pulled down. Then, in January 1957, the Amsterdam City Council offered Berghaus an alternative location for its offices, and the following month, during the commemoration of the February strike, Kleiman was approached by a group of men who wanted to form the Anne Frank Stichting (Foundation). Otto would be represented on the board of trustees by Kleiman, while other members would include Truus Wijsmuller-Meijer, a former resistance worker; Floris Bakels, a concentration camp survivor and publisher; and Hermann Heldring, the director of KLM. The organization stated its goals as "the restoration of 263 Prinsengracht" and "the propagation of the ideals left as a legacy to the world in the diary of Anne Frank."[93]

In the autumn of 1957, Berghaus presented the building to the Anne Frank Stichting. Berghaus still wanted 350,000 guilders for the house next door and the adjacent properties on the corner of the Westermarkt. When the Anne Frank Stichting announced that it had raised 250,000 guilders, the banking firm Pierson & Co. donated the remainder. Otto was overjoyed; he could at last realize his dream for a museum dedicated in his daughter's memory and embark in earnest upon his mission "to spread her ideals as much as possible."[94]

I HAVE NO SCARS LEFT

AFTER LEARNING THAT OTTO HAD AGREED
to allow the Hacketts to write the screenplay, Lotte Pfeffer wrote to
the authors in fury. She raged against the Hanukkah scene in the
play, in which her husband was portrayed as ignorant of the ceremony and its meaning, when in reality "his religion meant everything to him" and he spoke Hebrew fluently. She objected to their
depiction of him as a bumbling loner, asserting that he was "neither an inveterate bachelor nor a man without relations" but was
survived by a wife, brothers, and a son. She warned, "I do not wish
my husband to be shown in the film as a psychopath. I think it
enough that this had been done already in the play."[1] She also demanded to see a copy of the completed screenplay. The Hacketts'
response was cool; they replied that "a play cannot mirror reality"
and told her that they were not permitted to send her a copy of the
script.[2] Lotte then contacted Otto and threatened him with a lawsuit for libel. Otto tried to defend himself by telling her that she
could not expect "an historical truth" from the film and warned her
"not to be so childish" as to believe that the Hacketts had not taken
legal advice themselves.[3] Among the documents found after Otto's

death was a curious handwritten declaration drawn up in 1956. The stipulations were that Otto "renounces for himself and his heirs repayment of all the sums of money he has given so far to Mrs. Pfeffer," and that Lotte "renounces all former claims to *The Diary of Anne Frank* and the play and the film which have been made from it."[4] Together with the declaration was a letter from Lotte, dated September 5, 1956: "I include the agreement, which I thought I would be able to give you personally, but have so far been unsuccessful. There were no bad intentions, as was assumed." She added wretchedly, "I heard the news that my son has died. So far I still quietly hoped that he would be in Estonia with farmers and I believed I would hear from him one day. Another illusion lost."[5] Lotte had been separated from her son since leaving her first husband; the child remained with him and was later captured by the Nazis.

It was probably the last contact between Lotte and Otto, who had also received an angry letter from a former friend of Fritz Pfeffer's in Germany. Lotte never spoke to Otto, or Miep and Jan, again. She became increasingly isolated and died in her Amsterdam apartment on June 13, 1985. A junk dealer was hired to remove her belongings months later. He found "a complete mess . . . unwrapped packets of lumps of sugar and many old shoes in boxes," as well as "boxes full of buttons and tiny bars of soap . . . and photo albums."[6] Lotte's possessions were deposited at Amsterdam's Waterlooplein flea market, where an employee of the Anne Frank Stichting noticed them. She read the name "Ch. Kaletta" (Lotte's maiden name) in a book and then discovered a folder of yellow newspaper cuttings about Anne's diary. With a shock, she realized what lay before her and bought everything up to preserve it within the Anne Frank Stichting. Lotte's treasured collection of books, letters, and photos documented the warmth and humanity of Fritz Pfeffer and reversed much of the damage done by the Hacketts' ruthless dramatization. Otto himself tried to correct matters when amateur groups wrote to him about staging the play; he advised one

American school: "As to Mr. Dussel, one should realize that he was a single man between two families and therefore felt lonely. There is sometimes the tendency to play this role humorously but it should be played rather in a tragic way."[7]

■

ON APRIL 2, 1957, ELEANOR ROOSEVELT wrote to Otto, having reacted sympathetically to a letter from Levin, who had apparently written to her out of the blue because the introduction to the American edition of the diary was credited to her, not Barbara Zimmerman. She advised Otto to avoid a court case, "which would bring out so many disagreeable things, such as why you moved to Switzerland, [and] would be harmful to the feeling people have for you and for the play and particularly the diary from which the play was written."[8] Levin had implied that Otto moved to Switzerland to avoid high Dutch taxes and asked her to persuade him to settle out of court. Otto was dismayed by the Roosevelt letter. Although he had indeed managed to avoid Dutch taxes for 1952, doing so had not been his reason for emigrating. Otto insisted to her: "I am not led by financial interest. It always has been and still is my intention to give all the net profits of the play and the film to institutions in Holland and Israel in memory of Anne."[9] Otto asked Frank Price and Nathan Straus to write to Mrs. Roosevelt on his behalf. Straus did so, ending his letter with a description of Otto as "an unusually fine, sensitive human being" who had suffered enough "without being forced, in his old age, to endure character assassination, slander—and, worst of all, loss of respect of fine people."[10] Roosevelt apologized to Otto and wished him good luck with the court case.

On December 13, 1957, the Levin trial opened at the Supreme Court of the State of New York before Justice Samuel Coleman. Two weeks later, Levin's charges of fraud and breach of contract were thrown out, but on January 8, 1958, the jury found in his favor on

the issue of whether the Hacketts had plagiarized his work for their
play. Otto and Fritzi had traveled to New York for the trial and
sent a telegram to Switzerland about "this greatest injus-
tice."[11] Bloomgarden suffered a heart attack during the proceedings, and Samuel Silverman, the lawyer who represented Otto and
Bloomgarden in court, said he would consider leaving the bar.
Barbara Zimmerman recalls: "I couldn't attend the trial every day,
but I went a few times, and it was so awful. It was a great strain on
Otto's English. He really couldn't understand the language the
lawyers were throwing at each other. Levin's lawyer would fire
something out, and poor Otto would stand there, blink, and smile,
and the jury just did not get it. They saw him as a slinky for-
eigner."[12] Otto's lawyers appealed the plagiarism charges and succeeded in having the verdict overturned. A new trial was convened,
and talks among the lawyers dragged on.

The Twentieth Century Fox film of Anne Frank's diary began
shooting in the spring of 1958 with a budget of $3 million. Otto,
Kleiman, and Louis de Jong, director of RIOD (now NIOD), were
advisers on the project. The casting of Anne Frank caused great
speculation in the press when it became known that Susan
Strasberg had turned down the role, hoping to move on to new
challenges. (Joseph Schildkraut and Gusti Huber were repeating
their performances as Otto and Edith Frank.) Otto wanted Audrey
Hepburn for the part of Anne.[13] Hepburn, born in Brussels in 1929,
had lived through the war in the Netherlands and recalled how, as
a young girl, she had seen the cattle trucks leaving Arnhem station
"filled with Jews . . . families with little children, with babies,
herded into meat wagons . . . all those faces peering out . . . all the
nightmares I've ever had are mingled with that." In 1947, she read
Het Achterhuis: "It destroyed me. There were floods of tears. I became hysterical." Hepburn was one of the first visitors to the
building on the Prinsengracht. When director George Stevens sent
her the book asking her to audition for the role of Anne, she read it

again "and had to go to bed for the day." Otto then traveled to Bürgenstock to meet Hepburn and her husband, Mel Ferrer. Hepburn recalled: "He came to lunch and stayed to dinner. We had the most wonderful day. . . . He came with his new wife, who had lost her husband and children in the Holocaust. They both had the numbers on their arms. He was a beautiful-looking man, very fine, a sort of transparent face, very sensitive. Incapable of talking about Anne without extreme feeling. I had to ask him nothing because he had a need to talk about it. He struck me as somebody who'd been purged by fire. There was something so spiritual about his face. He'd been there and back." Hepburn kept a photograph of them all taken that day in her copy of the diary, but she told Otto she could not play his daughter. "I didn't want to exploit her life and her death to my advantage."[14]

Natalie Wood was asked to play Anne, but she refused, and after a nationwide search in which ten thousand girls auditioned, nineteen-year-old Millie Perkins, a model from New Jersey, landed the part. George Stevens defended his choice to a cynical press, insisting that he did not want someone who necessarily resembled Anne. (Perkins looked nothing like her, apart from the color of her hair.) The choice of a non-Jewish actress gave rise to questions about whether the Jewish element so lacking in the play would be reinstated for the screen. The answer was unanimously no, with the Hacketts insisting that their chief aim was for the audience to identify with those in hiding: "They see them, not as some strange people, but persons like themselves, thrown into this horrible situation."[15] Stevens announced that his film would be "devoid of Nazi horrors. It will tell the valiant, often humorous story of a wonderful family hiding out in a time of great stress; the story of a teenage girl's magnificent triumph over fear."[16] Stevens filmed a scene depicting Anne in Auschwitz, but it was badly received by the test audience. The film ended with a shot of the Amsterdam sky and "Anne" proclaiming: "In spite of everything, I still believe people are really good at heart." The film was neither a critical nor a commercial success. One New York cinema manager explained that people were "growing tired of the Holocaust."[17] The British *Daily Mail* newspaper thundered: *"The Diary of Anne Frank* is an outstanding instance of a subject being diminished by filming. . . . The girl who wrote the diary must have had something more than the perky charm of a New World Junior Miss. . . . These were European Jews in a European situation. But as presented here, especially by Shelley Winters and Ed Wynn [who played Mrs. van Daan and Mr. Dussel, respectively] they become stock figures from any tragi-comedy of Jewish life in Brooklyn."[18] Nonetheless, the film received eight Oscar nominations and was awarded three.[19]

Otto now realized the dangers inherent in trying to universalize the Holocaust. He was shocked when a Dutch Jewish friend of his related how a woman attending a New York performance of the play expressed "amazement that the characters and events in the play were real." Otto wrote to the Hacketts: "There are a great number of the younger generation who just do not understand what it is all about and that it is a true story. I spoke to youngsters who told me their classmates laughed right at the beginning when the truck came and there were people on it in 'pyjamas.' [The actors were wearing the striped uniforms of the concentration camps at the start of the film.] It seems that some sort of explanation should be given at the beginning—before the film starts."[20] Zimmerman defends the Hacketts: "No one wanted to have a sad, hopeless ending. Okay, so the Hacketts weren't Shakespeare, but it really was not a bad effort. The refrain about people being really good at heart was unfortunate, and it did disguise the real horror somewhat, but the Hacketts helped sell a lot more books."[21] That same year saw the release of the East German film *Ein Tagebuch für Anne Frank*, in which Anne's story served as a background to unmasking former Nazis who were living peaceful lives in Germany. The film received fa-

270   vorable reviews but was given only a limited release. Otto hated it, dismissing it as "mere communist propaganda. Anne's name in connection with it, is used in spite of my strong protest. . . . Of course I am not opposed to an anti-Nazi film, but I objected to using Anne for political propaganda."[22]

By early January 1958, the play had grossed more than $2.6 million, and Otto was keen to use his royalties for the Anne Frank Stichting. The restoration of 263 Prinsengracht was in progress. There were major changes to the front building, where exhibitions about Anne Frank and Nazism would be held. The annex remained empty and forlorn, on Otto's orders: "After the Anne Frank House was restored, they asked me if the rooms should be furnished again. But I answered, 'No!' During the war everything was taken away and I want to leave it like that."[23] Kleiman was displeased with the extensive promotion of the Anne Frank Stichting in the Dutch press and disliked Otto's idea of a collection in the streets. He wrote to Otto: "I do not appreciate this. When there is a disaster, one can say that we must help at any price, and that all means to collect money are permissible, but that is not the case here."[24] Kleiman worked hard at the business side of the Stichting (in addition to his own work) until his death on January 30, 1959. Otto flew to Amsterdam for the funeral and gave a speech that began with a line from Anne's diary: "When Mr. Kleiman comes in, the sun begins to shine."

Otto now became more involved with the Anne Frank Stichting. His greatest dream was to begin an educational foundation in Anne's name, within the museum, and for that he required more money. Kermit Bloomgarden donated $5,000 to the Stichting, and Otto's lawyer, Myer Mermin, wrote directly to those people who Otto thought would be able and willing to contribute, including Edith's brothers, Nathan Straus, and other close friends. Otto had expected the Stichting to receive all monies raised from benefit performances of the Stevens film in the United States, but Spyros

Skouras, president of Twentieth Century Fox, decided that, in keeping with the "universality of the picture," funds would be distributed to various charities.[25] Otto set up an American Anne Frank Foundation (committee members included Senator John Kennedy, Kermit Bloomgarden, Joseph Marks, Myer Mermin, and Nathan Straus; Eleanor Roosevelt was honorary chairman), whose sole task was to generate contributions for the Amsterdam-based Stichting. On March 20, 1959, he and Fritzi arrived in New York for a ten-day stay to generate support for the organization. During a charity dinner, Shelley Winters explained how Otto intended to use his royalties from the film and play: "He will devote approximately half to the Amsterdam Youth Center and related foundations, and half to a memorial to be established in Israel."[26] During their visit to the United States, Otto and Fritzi left their modest hotel to stay with Hilde Goldberg (a former neighbor from Amsterdam who had known Margot well) and her family in Rhode Island. Hilde's daughter Ruth recalled: "Otto used to make surprise appearances in Rhode Island or in New York, whisking me off from school for an intimate chat. He always brought good books that were carefully chosen and much appreciated. He was loving and amusing. And most of all, he always, *always* took me seriously. . . . Otto filled my life, from the very first book of nursery rhymes he gave me to my adult sense of the totality of the diary. . . . For me and I'm sure for others who loved him, his fearful vulnerability was always apparent and astounding. He was strong and brave because he made himself a living testament to his dead family."[27]

Otto was now traveling the world to oversee schools, villages, and charitable organizations set up in his daughter's name. He referred to these events as "step(s) along the road that Anne's diary has sent me traveling in the years since the war."[28] There were other, far less pleasant consequences, however. Neo-Nazis often disrupted performances of the play in Austria and Germany, and in April 1959, Otto had to face the first of several court cases con-

272 cerning the authenticity of the diary.[29] The diary's German publishers heard that Lothar Stielau, an English teacher in Lübeck and former NSDAP and SA member, claimed that the published diary bore little resemblance to Anne Frank's actual diary. Supporting him was Heinrich Buddeberg, who announced in the press that Meyer Levin had written the book. Otto and two publishing houses brought criminal charges against Stielau and Buddeberg, and Stielau was suspended from his job while the trial was conducted. During the proceedings, Stielau asserted that he had been referring to the play rather than the diary, although articles in the press had led him to question the diary's authenticity. For his part, Otto specified the differences between the original diary and the published version and invited experts to examine his daughter's work. The court appointed three women to the task, and in March 1960 they reported that the published diary was "true to its sources in substance and ideas."[30] Stielau's lawyers demanded a second opinion, and the matter limped on until October 17, 1961, when an out-of-court settlement was reached. Stielau's lawyers declared that their client had "no grounds for claiming the diary was a forgery"; the evidence presented had "persuaded him to the contrary."[31] The slander against the diary never abated during Otto's lifetime, although he always fought the accusations and any damages were awarded to the Anne Frank Stichting. Father Neiman recalls, "Stories about the diary being a fake cut him deeply, and though it cost him a lot personally and financially to fight those people, he did it on behalf of all victims of Nazism."[32] Shortly before Otto's death, the Supreme Court in West Germany ruled that Holocaust denial was an offense, and in 1994, following a law passed by the Bundestag, anyone making such claims could face up to five years' imprisonment.

In January 1960, Otto signed the papers to settle the Levin case, hoping to close that matter, too.[33] But a few days later, Levin sent him a vituperative letter: "While the legal phase of our encounter is

over, the moral phase is not done. Your behavior will remain forever as a ghastly example of evil returned for good, and of a father's
betrayal of his daughter's words."[34] Otto was unable to escape
Levin; in March, he visited Israel for the first time and learned that
Levin had recently published a letter in the *Jerusalem Post* claiming
that Otto had rejected his play because it was too Jewish. Despite
this, Otto enjoyed his stay in Israel, and the press was generally
kind. One admiring journalist reported: "I was with Otto Frank
when he dined with the children at the Youth Aliya village of
Nitsanim. Although 71 years old, Mr. Frank had swum in Eilat at 7
o'clock that morning; thirteen hours later he had energy and time
not only to address the children but also to give an interview to two
astute journalists."[35] Otto himself informed Myer Mermin that he
and Fritzi had swum "in the Dead Sea as well as in the Red Sea,
crossed the desert during a heatwave and a sandstorm."[36] He also
saw his old comrade from Auschwitz, Joseph Spronz, his wife
Franzi, and his son Gershon. Franzi remembers: "Otto got very
emotional when he met my husband again—he had a terrible nose-
bleed because of the excitement. He wanted to pay my son's university fees, but there was no need, we could do that ourselves.
Fritzi and I became great friends. During the festival of Purim,
there were parades everywhere, and we all watched them from a
friend's house overlooking the town."[37]

Otto and Fritzi also visited Hanneli Goslar, who was married by
then and had children of her own. "Otto had been on a trip to the
Masada Rock. He told the story in a very amusing way: They went
up in a cable car and it got broken, so they had to do the whole journey on foot. Then when they got back to their hotel, the elevator
wasn't working, so they had to take the stairs to their room on the
eighth floor. Otto found it all very funny. He never complained
about anything because he always said he had lived through the
concentration camps so what was there to worry about now?"[38]
Hanneli was touched to see that Otto kept photos of Fritzi's grand-

274 children, Caroline, Jacky, and Sylvia in his wallet; he clearly regarded himself as their grandfather and spoke of them with deep affection.

At the end of April, Otto and Fritzi flew to Amsterdam for the official opening of 263 Prinsengracht as a museum. At the opening ceremony, Otto could not hold back his tears and cut short his speech, imploring the crowd, "Forgive me for not speaking for longer, but the thought of what happened here is too much for me."[39] The public were then permitted entrance to the Anne Frank House. The house (and its neighbor, 265) had been impeccably restored, with the former warehouse and spice grinding room on the ground floor serving as a lecture hall, while the offices on the second floor and storerooms on the third were used for exhibitions. Otto told journalists that the house was intended "neither as a museum nor a place of pilgrimage. It is an earnest warning from the past and a mission of hope for the future."[40] On the same date, the Anne Frank Stichting Youth Center was launched, with Otto as chairman. The old houses on the Westermarkt corner had been demolished for a new building to house students and provide a base for conferences on discrimination, prejudice, and war. Otto's dream was for the world's youth to join together and strive for peace in his daughter's name, fulfilling his interpretation of her words, "I want to work for the world and mankind."

The following year, Otto told Mermin that he and Fritzi were moving into a home of their own, after years of living with other people. They bought a lovely detached house in the Basel suburb of Birsfelden. There was a spacious basement, above which the Franks lived, and then another floor that they rented out. Surrounding the house was a large garden, which Otto tended himself, growing the "Souvenir d'Anne Frank" rose around the balcony at the rear. Inside the house, one room served as an office in which he and Fritzi replied to the vast correspondence generated by Anne's diary. Above the desk where Fritzi typed while she and

Otto composed their replies was a Star of David created by a nun who had read the diary, and Marc Chagall's lithograph of Anne from a luxury French edition of the book. Later these were joined by a photograph of the Anne Frank statue in Utrecht and a colorful chain of cranes made by Japanese readers.

Otto had many regular correspondents, some of whom became close friends. Among these was Sumi, a Japanese girl who had been placed in a convent by her mother after her father's death; she wrote to Otto after reading the diary and asked to become his "letter daughter." A young American girl, Cara Wilson, started an exchange of letters with Otto in 1960 that continued with Fritzi after his death; she has recently published a book of their correspondence.[41] Another regular writer was John Neiman, now Father Neiman, who began writing to Otto in 1974. He recalls: "I first read the diary in fifth grade. It impressed me hugely, and I decided to write to Otto Frank to tell him how much the book meant to me. In June 1976, after many letters between us, I went to Switzerland at his invitation and stayed at the Hotel Alpha, close to his home. I was most impressed by Otto's humanity, which he had retained after the most terrible experiences. To be honest, he changed my life. In 1979, I was thinking about the priesthood but still had my doubts. I spoke to Otto about it, and he said, 'Your love for Anne is a wonderful thing, but use it, turn your love into doing good for others.' Suddenly everything became clear to me."[42]

Otto took a great interest in all those around him. Every year, he and Fritzi spent Eva's birthday (May 11) and Otto's birthday (May 12) with Eva and her family, either in London or on holiday. Zvi Schloss, Eva's husband, recalls:

Otto wanted to know all about me and about Israel, where I came from. He was a good man. One thing struck me about him immediately: he had a very strong sense of orderliness and cleanliness, which was very German. Eva is very untidy, and he hated it—he used to tell her off a lot. When he came here once, he got dressed in an overall, a gray work-coat, and disappeared. Then we found him cleaning the garage! When we used to lie in bed late, he would come in early with Fritzi and beat on the bed with a walking stick: 'Get up, come on, out of there!' He was very military. You could see that he had been in the German army.[43]

Among the frequent visitors to the Franks' house in Birsfelden was Judith de Winter, who had met Otto in Westerbork, and her husband, Henk Salomon. She remembers: "Otto was always very clear about what he wanted to achieve. He was determined that everyone should know about the Holocaust. He used the money that came from Anne's diary solely for that purpose."[44] Judith's husband agrees: "Otto would never take a taxi when he could walk. It makes me furious when people say, 'Otto Frank lived off his dead daughter.' Nothing could have been further from the truth. He only wanted money to use for the good of others."[45] When Otto was presented with a gold statuette of the god Pan (because the publisher was Pan Books) for one million copies of the diary sold in English in 1971, reporters asked him about his royalties. He replied, "I take the money. I don't give it all to the foundation. There are peace funds and fourteen scholarships in Israel and single scholarships in places like Nigeria. And the tax takes about half."[46] Otto and Fritzi's one extravagance was travel: they liked to see new people and learn about other cultures.

The royalties from the diary were substantial, however, and Otto wanted to protect this income to ensure it was used only for charitable causes. For that reason, on January 24, 1963, he established the Anne Frank–Fonds (foundation) in Basel. To Otto's distress, the Anne Frank Stichting in Amsterdam was not running as smoothly as he had hoped, and he had many disagreements with the board, who he felt did not have enough interest in the educational aspect of the organization. With his faith in his vision of the Stichting shaken, he decided that upon his death the copyright on Anne's diaries and other writings would be inherited by another group, the Anne Frank–Fonds in Basel. He invited a small number of close friends and his nephews Buddy and Stephan to join the Basel-based Fonds. Unlike the Stichting in Amsterdam, Otto wanted the Fonds to remain a small organization promoting "charitable work and to play a social and cultural role in the spirit of Anne Frank."[47] Thus, the Fonds would receive all royalties from the diary and any dramatic adaptations. Unlike the Stichting, the Fonds would have a much closer personal link to the diary.

A few months after the Anne Frank–Fonds was established, the discovery of the Gestapo officer who had arrested the Franks in their hiding place created a furor in the world's press. Tonny Ahlers, who had slunk back into obscurity following his release from prison in 1950, moved swiftly into action, contacting the Vienna authorities involved in the investigation into Karl Josef Silberbauer's wartime past. And from that moment on, Otto Frank publicly avowed that he no longer wanted his betrayer found.

■

THE NAZI HUNTER SIMON WIESENTHAL had been searching for Silberbauer since 1958, when a group of teenagers distributing neo-Nazi leaflets told Wiesenthal that they would be more willing to believe in the authenticity of Anne Frank's diary if he could find the man who arrested her. Wiesenthal was deliberately obstructed in his quest by Otto, who had asked those who knew Silberbauer's real name to call him "Silberthaler." This name was employed in Ernst Schnabel's 1958 book *The Footsteps of Anne Frank*. In that book, Otto said of Silberbauer, "Perhaps he would have spared us if he had been by himself."[48] Wiesenthal could not understand why Otto refused to assist him in his search. Cor Suijk, who knew both men, recalls:

> Wiesenthal knew Otto was trying to prevent him from finding Silberbauer. He said, "If it was up to Otto Frank, we would never have found him." But Otto saw it like this: when Silberbauer discovered that Otto had been an officer in the Great War, he showed respect, giving the family far more time than was usual to pack, and made the NSB men put away their guns. Otto understood him, remembering his own discipline as a German soldier, and so protected the man who arrested his family. Wiesenthal remained angry that Otto respected this man and caused his team so much unnecessary work. And Otto was shocked and far from happy when he heard that Wiesenthal had found Silberbauer. He never wanted that to happen.[49]

Wiesenthal located his man in 1963, when one of the employees of NIOD handed him a telephone directory of the Amsterdam Gestapo. Silberbauer's name leapt out at him; also listed on the same page were several of Ahlers's contacts—including Maarten Kuiper. Wiesenthal was concerned only with Silberbauer, however. He tracked him down: Karl Josef Silberbauer, born to a police officer and his wife in 1911, and a member of the Gestapo since 1938, had been jailed briefly upon his return to Vienna in April 1945. Nine years later, he was given a position with the Vienna police and was working there when the inquiry into his past was launched. On October 4, 1963, Silberbauer was suspended from duties. The story broke in the world's press on November 11, 1963. Silberbauer spoke to one journalist in Vienna and granted an interview for *De Telegraaf*, the Dutch newspaper for which Tonny Ahlers worked as a photographer.

Following Silberbauer's discovery by Wiesenthal, the investigation into the betrayal was reopened. New witnesses were heard, although some of those who had given testimonies before, such as the Hartogs, had died in the intervening years. Otto and his helpers gave the detectives no new leads to follow. The Dutch police involved in the case again concentrated on trying to prove van Maaren guilty, despite Otto's comment: "When we were arrested, Silberbauer was there. I saw him. But van Maaren was not there, and I have no evidence about him."[50] Miep now seemed certain that van Maaren was not the betrayer, while Kugler alone remained convinced that he was the most likely suspect. Extraordinarily, on December 4, 1963, Silberbauer's mother-in-law also wrote to Otto:

> I would like to apologize for bothering you with my writing, Mr. Frank, but . . . it hurts my heart to see how my daughter is suffering. They point after her, the house is often besieged by reporters and photographers. Silberbauer does not even dare to feed the birds in the garden, because there are also people in the back . . . he is not a bad human being. He loves children, animals and flowers, and people like that cannot do the vicious things of which he is accused. What would you have done, Mr. Frank, if one of your soldiers had disobeyed one of your orders? That is what he had to do as well. His step-daughter wrote me a letter full of fear from the U.S. because she has six children and this might hurt them. Thank you, Mr. Frank, for the good things you said about Silberbauer. . . . I would like to ask you, Mr. Frank, if I could lay claim to your goodness, for you to write to Mr. Wiesenthal in order to leave the family finally in peace.[51]

Otto kept her letter, but no response to it has been found.

Tonny Ahlers, meanwhile, had evidently continued his practice of watching from a safe distance before deciding to act. The 1950s had seen Anne Frank's diary grow in acclaim, and Otto Frank was upheld as an example of Jewish resistance and integrity in the face

280   of evil. Ahlers was livid, despite the fact that Otto had defended him when he had been unable to find anyone else willing to do so. Ahlers had again been jailed in 1950 for several months, on a theft charge. Upon his release, he worked for a short time as a security man at Amsterdam's Centraal Station and then traveled abroad for two years with the KSNM. Returning to the Netherlands, he struggled to earn a living as an occasional reporter for *De Telegraaf*. He now had two daughters as well. His son Anton recalls that one day his father simply disappeared: "That was in 1960, and it followed something dramatic happening in his life, although I don't know what it was. There was suddenly this huge panic; he left and we had to get out of our apartment. Some terrible thing. . . . We went to stay with my mother's sister. My brother was in the military then, so it was me, my mother, and two little girls. And then one day, my father reappeared. It was the end of 1961. All our furniture had been packed up and hidden away. Then, when my father came back, we suddenly found ourselves moving into this great new apartment in Amsterdam-Osdorp. In those days, it was very modern and very nice. But I couldn't stand to be in that house. My brother couldn't either." Tonny Ahlers set up a photography business, Photopress International, working from his apartment. Anton recalls that the company never made a profit.

> My father was an amateur in all things. He did everything—all his forms of employment—for a very short length of time. Photopress International was just a front. He never made any money from his photography, not really. My mother was the one who kept us. She worked very hard and had her own dressmaking business. She worked day and night at the sewing machine, and the people who lived downstairs from us used to complain about the noise. It's unbelievable that she stuck to my father for so long. He was very violent toward her. Often at the dinner table, if the food displeased him or his mood was bad, he would just pick up the dish

and fling it across the room. He lied, he cheated, he didn't do any
work. My father made himself a hiding place in the small box
room of our apartment, which was meant for storing bicycles.
When the police came to the house—which they often did—he
would slip in there and then dash out when their backs were
turned.[52]

There had been reference to Otto Frank in the Ahlers household over the years, but in 1963, Ahlers suddenly began to talk
about him constantly; Silberbauer had been found, and the subject
of the betrayal was in newspapers across the world. On December
27, 1963, Ahlers wrote to the authorities in Vienna, explaining that
he had "*exonerating* material about Mr. Silberbauer." He referred
unjustly to Otto's conduct during the war, adding, "Otto Frank cooperated with National Socialists, and should absolutely not be
held to serve as an example of what his co-religionists endured
through Nazi Germany. I can substantiate this with more proof."
He also denounced Anne's diary, referring to "the positive worth
of the diary tales of Anne Frank. Just as fairy tales have a positive
worth." He felt that Silberbauer was "the victim" and "to which extent Otto Frank has betrayed his own cause I leave to the judgment
of others." He offered to act as a witness against Otto, but asked
them not to pass on his letter to NIOD, evidently not wanting his
name to be on file for future researchers. He told them that
Jansen's son was the betrayer; Ahlers almost certainly knew the
young man was dead. He ended his letter: "Otto Frank has very
good reasons to keep silent."[53]

On January 15, 1964, Ahlers wrote to Silberbauer at his home
address. He began his attack on Otto by writing that although the
police were investigating the betrayal, "Otto Frank boldly kept
silent. I know exactly why. But nevertheless this man is referred to
as having 'integrity' and is seen as 'representative.' The question
is: of what?" Ahlers claimed to have many interesting documents

about Otto's conduct during the war in his possession. He closed his letter: "It all boils down to the fact that Otto Frank himself, through the so-called diary of his daughter Anne, has acquired an exceptional social status to which he himself has fervently contributed. . . . It would cost me little trouble to prove that Otto Frank/Opekta delivered to the Wehrmacht in 1941 and was a profiteer and a betrayer of his own kind."[54]

Several months later, Ahlers telephoned a journalist from *Revue*, whose publication had named van Maaren as the betrayer. Ahlers sent the journalist a copy of Otto's August 1945 letter to the authorities on his behalf (which he could only have received from Otto), cleverly omitting the opening lines referring to his own prison sentence. Ahlers wrote in his own letter: "In April 1941 I went to Frank and told him someone wanted to betray him to the SS and he, also by his own declaration, waited until July 1942 to go into hiding. What he did in the meantime is known to me. And his little game with Gies. Frank's oldest daughter was called up for transport to Germany in the summer of 1942, making it clear that the NSB relationships and Wehrmacht deliveries were not a safeguard against being deported." He concluded his letter: "This all happened in 1941–1942, a period in which Jews were involved in a life-or-death struggle and I realize that the behavior of people in that situation must be judged with clemency. I don't judge Otto Frank's actions during the war years. But I think it's insane that Otto Frank is upheld as an example of integrity among Jews after the war." Referring to why the betrayer had never been found (while insisting again that it was Jansen's son), Ahlers claimed that this was due to Otto's guilt about his wartime business transactions: "Because of the understandable fear, he said nothing. Even when he knew someone else could be blamed. It will be difficult to get to the bottom of it all."[55] Clearly, Ahlers was trying to imply that Otto Frank had been a collaborator during the war and had never revealed the name of the betrayer because he was afraid it would lead to the discovery of his own deliveries to the Wehrmacht. The lines "What he did in the meantime is known to me. And his little game with Gies" refer to these deliveries, the NSB men Otto had working for him, and the change of the name of the business from Pectacon to Gies & Co. Ahlers sent a copy of his letter to van Maaren's son.

Anton remembers his father writing those letters: "Yes, I watched him, tapping furiously on his old typewriter. The keys were banging down hard. Those letters were written out of hatred—jealousy and hatred. That was a turning point in our lives. After that, Otto Frank was a subject for daily discussion in our home. My father became obsessed by him. He would talk about him every night before, during, and after dinner. I got sick of him talking about Otto Frank, and I decided I wasn't going to listen anymore and I wasn't going to believe him anymore either. That made him crazy, to think he was talking about all this and no one took him seriously, or even listened to him."[56]

Why did Ahlers write those letters when he knew that his own past could cause him problems if the police chose to confront him? Clearly, he was keen to "exonerate" van Maaren and Silberbauer, while damaging Otto's reputation as far as he could without mentioning his own wartime activities. He was eaten up with hatred for Otto, and probably jealousy as well. But the Dutch authorities did not question Ahlers, seeing him as a peripheral figure, someone who was "not to be trusted with the truth" and therefore not worthy of investigation.[57] They thought him a fool without realizing that, like all fools, Ahlers was dangerous. They did not know about the discrepancies in Otto's letters, his business with Ahlers, Ahlers's friendship with the paid informant, Maarten Kuiper, who had arrested the family, the extent of Ahlers's crimes during the war, or Otto's meetings with Ahlers in 1945. (These meetings become apparent only upon reading Otto's agenda; there are no references to them elsewhere.) Even if Otto

284   himself now suspected Ahlers of his betrayal, he could prove nothing: the people to whom Ahlers probably passed on his fatal information were both dead—Kuiper had been executed, and Julius Dettman had committed suicide.

The Ahlers family believe that Tonny Ahlers continued to exert a hold over Otto Frank until the older man's death. Cas Ahlers (Tonny's brother) is convinced that sometime after Otto emigrated from Amsterdam to Basel, Tonny had begun to blackmail him again, and that he received regular, substantial payments from Otto in Switzerland. Cas claims to have seen a letter from Otto in which was written, "The goods have been delivered again"—an apparently bitter reference to the past.[58] According to Cas, the payments ended with Otto Frank's death in 1980. Could Ahlers have blackmailed Otto after the war? Anton Ahlers believes it is certainly possible: "My father had money that he couldn't account for. I didn't know where it came from, just that he had an income he couldn't explain to us. Every month he received the equivalent of a director's salary into a bank account that he kept separate from his usual business account. With the money, he was able to buy items he could not normally have bought, and we took holidays in places that were very exotic for that time. My father said it was a government benefit on account of his having had polio as a child, but the payments were far too high. He was very proud of this mysterious income, of how large it was. He bought presents for everyone in the family with this money."[59] Anton's wife agrees: "That was really very puzzling to us. A friend of my mother told her that he knew Tonny was receiving a lot of money every month from abroad. When we asked this man about it, he just told us, 'Don't go digging, because a lot of dirt will come out.' "[60] In 1980—the year Otto Frank died—Tonny Ahlers closed his bank account. His lifestyle changed radically; there were no more luxury holidays, no more expensive gifts, and he and his wife were forced to move out of their six-room apartment in Amsterdam-Osdorp into a tiny, rent-assisted flat.

Blackmail and manipulation were typical of his father, Anton explains:

> I had my own business in the early 1980s, and unfortunately, the market for our product plummeted and we went bankrupt. My father sent an anonymous letter to the receivers, telling them that myself and my wife had been drug-running. We were stunned. Later on, I found a copy of the letter in my father's house. He had done it, of course. That was how his mind worked: informing, snitching on people, getting the police involved—for nothing. He was always fighting with neighbors over parking spaces and that kind of thing. And he tried repeatedly to blackmail people. He once wrote to the Albert Heijn supermarket chain, saying he was disgusted with their peanut butter and he wanted hundreds of guilders to keep quiet about it. A madman, really.[61]

On what grounds could Ahlers have blackmailed Otto for so long, and when? The only possibility seems to be the deliveries to the Wehrmacht, which Otto admitted only to the police, never publicly. We can assume from Otto's comments in 1957 (when he said that he was confronted with the fact that Ahlers had betrayed many people) that his contact with Ahlers ended late in 1945.[62] In 1957, Otto still spoke about Ahlers as having saved his life, and thus it is highly improbable that Ahlers was blackmailing him at the time, or when Ahlers was writing the vitriolic letters in connection with the Silberbauer case. So the blackmail must have begun sometime later, clearly after these letters were written. By the 1960s, the diary had become not only world-famous but Otto's life; from his daughter's book, his public persona was that of the perfect father figure. In 1963, Ahlers began demonstrating that he was prepared to talk to anyone about the Wehrmacht deliveries. Otto must have known that despite the fact that he had had no choice in those wartime transactions, to have them made public would have led to unpleasant questions and perhaps accusations against him, which in turn might have reflected badly upon the diary. The sensational manner in which the Dutch press reported these deliveries in 2002 (after the publication of this book) leads one to realize what a storm of criticism Otto would have faced. Otto must have wanted Ahlers to keep his knowledge to himself, and perhaps it is at this point—in the mid-1960s, after Ahlers had written his dangerous letters to the police and one journalist—that the blackmail (if indeed there was blackmail) began.

■

IN 1964, BOTH SILBERBAUER AND HIS wartime commander, Willi Lages, were questioned about the arrest. Both declared that the telephone call was not anonymous, but came from a known betrayer. During his interrogation (mistakenly thinking that Silberbauer had taken the call), Lages told the Dutch detectives, "You ask me whether, given a tip-off, we would have gone straight there and arrested the Jews. It's not logical. In my opinion a tip would first be investigated into whether it was worthy, unless this tip came from somebody who was known by our organization. In the case of the story of Silberbauer's receiving the telephone tip, to go there on the same day, then I conclude from that the tip giver was known and that in the past his information was always based on truth. If that was the case then when Silberbauer received the tip, he must have known the tip giver."[63] Silberbauer explained to the detectives that it was Dettman, and not he, who had taken the call. He then confirmed, "The call had to be from someone well known to Dettman."[64] In his summary, the Dutch detective in charge of the investigation wrote: "Silberbauer also informed us that he was convinced the tip concerning the Franks was made immediately before the arrest. Possibly there is a chance to discover which police officers received a bonus at that time, by making an investigation in the forementioned

'Bundesarchiv.' "[65] It seems that an early attempt to do so was made; there are references to files that the Dutch detectives wanted to view, but then the trail appears to go cold, for no further notes about the "Bundesarchiv" leads have been found. Yet had they followed this lead through, the detectives would surely have at least discovered that Maarten Kuiper, who had been present at the arrest, was paid to betray Jews in hiding. And that discovery might have led them back to Tonny Ahlers.

A number of recently found notes on the investigation process make for interesting reading. There is a reference to Dr. Erich Rajakovic, who was involved with IVB4 (the group charged with finding and deporting Jews) for some time, yet he was not questioned in relation to the Franks' betrayal. Neither was Arno Albani, despite a note that he should have been. Albani worked for the SD and handled Jewish cases A–H (and therefore the Franks) at the Euterpestraat and Zentralstelle. He might have been able to tell the detectives more. For one reason or another, these leads were dropped. The Dutch detective in charge of the Franks' case did investigate eight former SD men who he thought might have been present at the arrest, but met with no success—unfortunately, he did not record the names of the men.[66]

The Dutch police questioned Otto about Ahlers's accusations concerning the Wehrmacht. Otto answered that his company, along with many Dutch businesses—approximately 80 percent—had made deliveries to the Wehrmacht during the war. The detectives compiled a short report on Ahlers but made several mistakes in it. They ended their declaration with an air of vague puzzlement: "It is not clear how Ahlers was familiar with the hiding place."[67] On November 4, 1964, the investigation into the betrayal at 263 Prinsengracht was officially closed.

Otto declared to the police in charge of the Silberbauer case that the former Gestapo officer had acted under orders and had not mistreated anyone during the arrest. And yet, when Miep, Jan, and

288   Bep went up to the annex on the afternoon of August 4, 1944, they found the rooms in complete chaos; the Nazis had clearly been violent in their search of the property for money and other valuables. Otto was merciful toward Silberbauer, in contrast with his antagonistic attitude toward other war criminals.[68] But possibly this act of direct forgiveness was Otto's way of coming to terms with that terrible day in August 1944 and what happened after it.

Otto's statements about Silberbauer's conduct were crucial to the outcome of his case; Silberbauer was acquitted of concealing his past. The former Gestapo officer, who had arrested hundreds of Jews and sent them to their deaths, returned to the Vienna police force.

■

OTTO LOST THREE PEOPLE CLOSE TO HIM in the 1960s. Nathan Straus, his closest friend, died in September 1961 at the age of seventy-two "of natural causes." Newspapers reported on his long and illustrious career, but Otto knew that Straus himself had been an unpretentious man. His funeral was held on September 15, 1961, in New York. Julius Holländer died horrifically on October 4, 1967, when a lift in the New York hotel where he and his brother lived plummeted to the ground from the tenth floor. In January 1968, Otto wrote to a relative: "Walter's desperate loneliness is a source of great pain to me. The two brothers turned their backs on everybody and everything and became recluses. Now Walter is more alone than ever."[69] Walter survived his brother by one year, dying on September 19, 1968, from diabetes. Both brothers had "saved up enough money for a comfortable retirement which they did not live long enough to enjoy."[70] After the heartache of these personal bereavements, Otto's family wanted Otto to celebrate his birthday with enthusiasm. They took a holiday in the Swiss mountains when Otto turned eighty years old on May 12, 1969. Buddy recalls how, after a few glasses of wine, Otto "got

Fritzi up to dance. Instead of adopting the customary dance pose, Otto reeled off a spicy jig. All the young kids were clapping . . . he wasn't showing off, he just jazzed it up a bit. That was Otto. Simple, uncomplicated, with a great sense of humor and dignity."[71]

That same year, a disagreement arose between Otto and Victor Kugler. The Israeli publisher Massada Press wrote to inform Otto that it was planning to publish a book about Kugler's reminiscences of Anne and life in hiding. Because Kugler had said nothing to Otto about this publishing project in his regular letters, Otto felt "astonished and annoyed." He disliked the title, *The Man Who Hid Anne Frank*: "I do not agree with it. *The Man Who Hid Anne Frank* does not exist. There was a group of brave Dutch people to which Mr. Kugler belonged." The other helpers were also dismayed by the news, as Otto wrote to the publishers: "They want to keep in the background and they think that what they did was their human duty. . . . They do not want to be praised or drawn into publicity."[72] In a letter to Otto, Bep Voskuijl confirmed her reluctance to be in the public eye: "I would prefer to stay away from it all, by nature I am already nervous and I cannot take any more stress. Also, the pleasant things, like the invitations here and there, give me nervous breakdowns before and after. . . . I am dead set against publicity."[73] Otto told the co-author of the Kugler book, Eda Shapiro, that he and his helpers were "disappointed about the behavior of Mr. Kugler in this matter."[74] Massada Press eventually canceled the book contract. A few months later, Otto received a letter from Kugler's solicitor, who asked Otto to finance an expensive operation Kugler needed on his eyes. Otto was still angry with Kugler but replied: "If necessary I would of course help him."[75] Kugler was able to pay for his eye operation on his own, however, when the Canadian Anti-Defamation League awarded him $10,000 in 1977 for his wartime heroism. Kugler's wife, Loes, told Otto in a very friendly letter that year that the surgery had been successful. Kugler and Otto remained in contact.

Every month since the Anne Frank Stichting's founding, Otto and Fritzi traveled to Amsterdam. Relations between Otto and the Stichting improved when his friend Henri van Praag took charge of both the Stichting and the Youth Center. Cor Suijk, who subsequently became financial coordinator of the organization, recalls:

> Otto was a keen observer and a good listener. . . . He would seldom overlook mistakes the Anne Frank Stichting staff and I as their director had made. His dissatisfaction regarding our lack of adequate care concerning the archives, correspondence, the museum artifacts, the upkeep of the place, and particularly to preserve the authentic appearance of the house, made the staff fear his regular visits. Not many of these workers were eager to meet him. They usually flew apart, scattering themselves all over the place. His ability to notice shoddy work and sloppy thinking in our publications was distinctly feared. He could be very unrelenting, speaking insistently, but would never shout. His prestige and moral authority resulted from him being absolutely right in his criticism.[76]

The Youth Center, which had been Otto's dream, was disbanded in 1970. The Stichting still had financial difficulties, and to resolve them, Suijk suggested charging people to enter the museum. Otto was opposed to the idea, but when an admission fee was introduced, it saved the house from closure.

On July 30, 1977, Otto's earnest correspondent Cara Wilson arrived in Basel. She met some of Otto and Fritzi's friends and family one evening: "The group of people who gathered into the Franks' cozy front room were all in their late sixties, seventies, and early eighties, but I had never met a group of senior citizens like them before. They were dynamic, teasing, vivacious, very much filled with life and self-esteem. They spoke in rapid German, hands gesticulating, stopping only to briefly translate for me."[77] The following year, Otto met Peter Pepper, Fritz Pfeffer's son, through their mutual friend Father John Neiman. In December 1978, Pepper traveled to Switzerland, and Otto wrote to Father Neiman: "We found him a very sympathetic man. My conversation with him was very cordial and we felt a certain closeness to each other by the link through his father."[78]

Otto's health had begun to fail that year. He suffered from high blood pressure and depression, and on December 15, 1978, he made out his will. He celebrated his ninetieth birthday in style and in public on May 12, 1979, in London, but his health had deteriorated further, and he confided to a friend, "I am suffering frequently from dizziness and circulation-trouble and feel rather weak."[79] Ignoring the advice of his doctor, on June 12, Otto and Fritzi traveled to Amsterdam for the Anne Frank Fiftieth Birthday Tribute in the Westerkerk. Otto received an award from the Dutch queen, whom he then escorted to the Anne Frank House for a private tour. It was Otto's last visit to Amsterdam. On July 9, he wrote to Father Neiman that he and Fritzi were embarking upon "a *very* much needed holiday of three weeks in the Swiss mountains tomorrow. . . . We hope to get new strength during our holiday so that we shall be able to go on with our work though on a much smaller scale. I am feeling my age more and more."[80]

In February 1980, Fritzi contacted Father Neiman: "I have to tell you that Mr. Frank's health is very bad. He is so weak that he has to remain on the couch the whole day, not being able to regain his strength. He is suffering from an obstinate form of pleurisy and we have to go to hospital once a week where much water is taken out of his lung and some medicament put in it."[81] Otto had already admitted the previous November that he was "not in a very good state of health. Though I am not really ill I am feeling miserable most of the time."[82] For the first time in twenty years, he and Fritzi had remained at home during the Christmas holiday period, with Eva and her family visiting them there. Fritzi told friends that on his birthday in May, Otto was too tired to see all those who

292 called to congratulate him. "He stayed on his couch and only wanted to see one person at a time."[83] Father Neiman had visited a few days before and found Otto "very ill then. He was in bed, and I sat with Fritzi for some time. Then Otto woke up and called out that he knew I was there and that he was well enough to see me after all. But he was terribly weak then. It was the last time I saw him."[84]

Suffering from lung cancer, Otto was growing weaker every day. On August 19, 1980, Otto's old Auschwitz comrade Joseph Spronz visited with his wife, Franzi. She recalls:

> The doctors told Fritzi that Otto had only six months to live, but she didn't tell Otto that. He always insisted, "It's not that I am sick, it's just that I am tired!" Leni wanted Otto to have specialist care, but Fritzi preferred to nurse him herself, and she did it wonderfully. When we arrived, Otto was in bed, but he heard us and got up, holding out his arms. He looked into my husband's eyes, and they embraced. Otto murmured against my husband's shoulder, "My dear friend Joseph." He was so weak. The hospital staff arrived to collect him a few minutes later. We followed, and my husband was allowed into Otto's room. They spoke of Auschwitz. Joseph was gone a long time, and when he came out, we told Fritzi we would call the next day. I telephoned the hospital early in the morning. They said, "We're sorry, but Mr. Frank died last night."[85]

■

ANNE'S FRIEND JACQUELINE VAN Maarsen heard the announcement of Otto's death on the Dutch radio, although having seen him the month before, it did not come as a surprise. She was among those who traveled to Basel on an airplane chartered by the Anne Frank Stichting for the funeral on August 22. Fritzi's daughter Eva and son-in-law Zvi flew over from London with their three daughters, who were devastated to lose the man whom they regarded as their beloved grandfather. Otto had wanted to be cremated (which Jewish law does not permit) and asked for his ashes to be interred at the Friedhof Birsfelden, a nondenominational cemetery close to his home. After the funeral, at which poems and prayers of various religions were read, the mourners walked to the house Otto and Fritzi had shared for almost twenty years. Fritzi played a cassette recording of Otto talking about his life; his soft, clear voice filled the room.

Fritzi received hundreds of condolence cards, including a message from an Anne Frank Haven in Israel calling Otto "one of the true humanitarians of the spirit of the nineteenth century," and telegrams from the Judaic Heritage Society in New York and the World Congress of Faiths, for which Otto was vice president. Barbara Mooyart-Doubleday wrote that she would remember Otto for his "great mental and moral force, for his courage in the face of difficulties and sorrow, for his kindness of heart and for his never failing desire to turn ill-will into good," and Barbara Epstein (formerly Zimmerman) was "full of memories and sadness beyond words."[86] Fritzi replied to all the accolades with a small card: "I would like to thank you sincerely for the friendship and heartfelt sympathy shown to me at the occasion of the passing away of my beloved, unforgettable husband, Otto Frank."[87] Otto had stipulated that there should be no gifts for his family, only donations to charities such as the Israel Cancer Association. The only sour note was sounded by the obituary in *Jewish Week*, which condemned Otto's support for those who had "eliminated Anne's poetic tribute to Judaism . . . replacing it with a universalistic observation denigrating the importance of Jewish experience."[88]

On the evenings of October 5 and October 8, respectively, memorial tributes were held for Otto in Basel and New York. The latter was organized by the American Anne Frank Center and featured extracts from the diary, speeches, and music. One of Otto's many young correspondents spoke about visiting him in Basel. "He took me to what he called an authentic English pub. He

294   was eighty-two then, and there wasn't a person in there over thirty, but he was in his element, surrounded by young people from all over the world who crowded around our table, asking questions. He switched effortlessly from language to language." On their way home, she and Otto missed their tram and Otto insisted on running to the next stop, explaining, "I never retrace my steps. I always look ahead. I live with the past every day, but never in it. My place is in the present." Another speaker said simply: "Otto Frank was the creator of Anne Frank's spirit. When she died, he lived for her."[89] At the remembrance evening in Basel, Fritzi spoke about her years with Otto as "among the happiest of my whole life." She recalled that only people mattered to Otto and that his greatest affection was for the young. "He had an innate sense of what it meant to be family and I was very lucky that he viewed my daughter as a blood relative and in her, he had a child again." She remembered, too, that in 1946 Otto had traveled to Frankfurt to find two German friends: "He wanted to show to them that, in his eyes, there was no such thing as collective guilt. Although he believed that Hitler's crimes against the Jews should never be forgotten, he also felt that there was no way forward with hatred."[90] Otto's close friend Rabbi Soetendorp then read a poem Otto had prized:

> Let us commemorate those whom we loved,
> Those who were taken from us and have gone to permanent
>   rest.
> May everything good that they have done,
> Every truth and goodness that they spoke be recognized to
>   the full and may it direct our life accordingly.
> Because through that the living award the dead the greatest
>   honor and they are spiritually united with them.
> May those who mourn find comfort and be uplifted by the
>   strength and trust in this worldly spiritual power
> And the indestructibility of life.[91]

Franzi Spronz remembers a moment later that evening: "A violinist had been hired to play the music Otto loved. My husband was
emotional—after all, he and Otto first met through their love of
classical music. When the violinist began to play, my husband remembered that meeting, and he wept. It was the music Otto had
whistled to him in the hospital in Auschwitz."[92]

thirteen THE LEGACY

FRITZI FRANK OUTLIVED OTTO BY EIGH-
teen years. After his funeral, she returned to London with her
daughter, "totally exhausted, morally and bodily." To Barbara
Epstein she confided that Otto had lost the will to live during the
final months of his life, and that to witness his despair and weakness was "agony to me."[1] She confessed her loneliness to another
friend: "Now my darling Otto has left me and all his friends in the
world. Though I know that he wanted to die after his long and ful-
filled life with the many sad but also happy events, I miss him
terribly."[2]

Otto's marriage to Fritzi had brought him love, companionship—and a new family. He once wrote to a young woman who said
she felt sorry for him to correct her: "All you know about me has
happened twenty-six years ago and though this period was an important part of my life leaving unforgettable marks on my soul, I
had to go on, living a new life . . . think of me not only as Anne's
father as you know me from book and play, but also as a man enjoying new family life and loving his grandchildren."[3] Fritzi supported Otto wholeheartedly in his mission to spread the diary's

"ideals." She recognized its overwhelming importance to her husband and was only half-joking when she told a journalist, "That's the purpose of his life really. All else is an ornament. I am an ornament."[4] Asked whether sharing a similar wartime experience was a factor in the success of their marriage, Otto said, "Oh yes. It makes a big difference. To get married, if my wife had not been in the concentration camps it would be impossible. The same experience: she lost her husband, she lost her son, and if she speaks about it, I understand it. And if I speak about it, she understands."[5]

Fritzi, who often introduced herself as "the second Mrs. Frank," replied with sincerity to Cara Wilson's question about whether she ever felt "upstaged" by Otto: "No. My whole life is Otto. I love to help him, work along with him. There is nothing I want to do more in all the world."[6] Otto's cousin Milly wrote to Fritzi in August 1992, "I am so happy Otto had those lovely years with you and your family, after the storms in the earlier part of his life. You were just perfect for him."[7] After Otto's death, Fritzi stayed in touch with all the "diary" correspondents. It helped stave off loneliness and gave her the feeling that "Otto's spirit is near me."[8] She was determined to continue Otto's work and took a keen interest in everything connected to Anne and the diary. Fritzi was a founding member of the Anne Frank–Fonds and remained actively involved with them until she became ill in 1993. She also tried to remain abreast of what was happening with the Anne Frank Stichting in Amsterdam and was dismayed when she heard that they had paid for a member of the staff to fly to New York to collect Milly Stanfield's papers for their archives. She wrote to Milly of her "astonishment . . . I wonder that they could spend their money making the trip."[9] She also wrote to the Hacketts about new efforts to stage Levin's play in July 1983: "You can see that even after his death Meyer Levin is making trouble."[10]

On December 12, 1984, Fritzi wrote poignantly to Father Neiman about Oliver Elias's (Leni's grandson) bar mitzvah.

298   Although she had enjoyed the ceremony, Fritzi was reminded of her own dead son. Father Neiman visited her each year in Switzerland: "In the 1990s she was becoming remiss, but she still had a wonderful sense of humor and knew exactly what she wanted from life. Shortly after my last trip to Switzerland, I heard that she was knocked over by a tram. Her health never really recovered after that."[11] Following the accident, a Polish woman, Katja Olszewska, was employed as a companion for Fritzi. She recalls: "While I was with Mrs. Frank, she often spoke about Otto. She told me what a wonderful man he was, and how everyone in Birsfelden knew him and admired him. Mrs. Frank rarely spoke about her first husband, though she would talk of her lost son many times. He was very artistic, and she had lots of photos of him. Mrs. Frank told me how unhappy Otto's first marriage had been. He had been forced to marry Edith Holländer and never loved her. Mrs. Frank said, 'The only one he really loved was me.' Then she went over to the big photo of Otto she kept in the room, clasped her hands together, and said sadly, 'Otto! Why did you leave me?' "[12]

As her health worsened, Fritzi's mind began to fail. At the end of 1997, Eva arrived in Basel to take Fritzi to England. Fritzi died in London in October 1998, aged ninety-three.

■

IN HIS WILL, OTTO BEQUEATHED ANNE'S diaries and other writings to the Dutch government. In November 1980, they were taken from the bank safe in Basel, where they had resided ever since Otto emigrated to Switzerland, and presented to the Netherlands Institute for War Documentation (NIOD). In 1986, "to dispel the attacks made upon the book's authenticity coming from hostile circles," NIOD published *The Diaries of Anne Frank: The Critical Edition*. Together with biographical material and the Ministry of Justice's reports testifying to the diary's authenticity, the book included Anne's original diary, her revised version, and the edition published in 1947. Now that Otto's editing could be seen clearly, a backlash against him began, the vanguard being Cynthia Ozick's article "Who Owns Anne Frank?" in *The New Yorker* on October 6, 1997. Ozick condemned the misrepresentations of Anne and her diary and held Otto ultimately responsible for the "shallowly upbeat view" of his daughter and her work: "He had it as his aim to emphasize 'Anne's idealism,' 'Anne's spirit,' almost never calling attention to how and why that idealism and spirit were smothered, and unfailingly generalizing the sources of hatred. . . . The surviving father stood in for the dead child, believing that his words would honestly represent hers." Ozick concluded her piece with a dream of the diary "burned, vanished, lost—saved from a world that made of it all things, some of them true, while floating lightly over the heavier truth of named and inhabited evil."[13] Barbara Epstein (formerly Zimmerman) is furious about such criticism:

> Who do these people think they are? They weren't around at the time, they don't know zip about any of it, they didn't know Otto! Those people are so far off the mark with their wild conspiracy theories. It's absolutely appalling. But that's a lot of American Jews for you—they have a real identity problem and have this need for self-aggrandizement. They're all assimilated Jews who have to have some sort of reinforced identity or something. They don't have any troubled personal experience of their own, and it torments them. I feel so sorry for the way people talk about Otto now. How they rant about what he did to the diary. Otto's impulses in regard to it are so humane.[14]

While Otto undoubtedly promoted the diary in a universal manner, he did so because he believed it to be the most effective method of propagating understanding and tolerance. Readers' letters almost always focused on identification with Anne. The sentiments of one young girl are typical of their reaction: "When I discovered Anne I discovered myself."[15] Otto's nature was to seek out the positive in every situation: "It's my opinion that one should never give up, even in the most extreme circumstances."[16] He was cautious when asked expressly about Anne's belief that "people are really good at heart": "My daughter was at an age of great idealism, but I think she didn't mean that. She thought there is some good in every man and I am an optimist too. I try to find the good in every man, but we know how many bad people exist. You can't forgive those who really are murderers. This is going too far."[17]

Over the years, Otto received thousands of tributes to his daughter, and his willingness to accommodate everyone who showed an interest in her diary brought him both admiration and criticism; Israeli newspapers were gratified when Golda Meir visited the house in 1964, but outraged by Otto's private meeting with the Pope in the Vatican. He was single-minded in his mission, however, and never listened to his detractors. He set up competitions for schoolchildren, offering prizes funded by himself, and invited groups of people into his own home to discuss the diary and the lessons he believed could be learned from it. Otto said of his duty toward his daughter's legacy: "It's a strange role. In the normal family relationship, it is the child of the famous parent who has the honor and the burden of continuing the task. In my case the role is reversed."[18] He also declared: "When I returned from concentration camp alone, I saw that a tragedy of inexpressible extent had hit the Jews, my people, and I was spared as one of them to testify, *one* of those who had lost his dear ones. It was not in my nature to sit down and mourn. I had good people around me and Anne's diary helped me a great deal to gain again a positive outlook on life."[19] In another interview, he stated firmly: "We cannot change what happened anymore. The only thing we can do is to learn from the past and to realize what discrimination and persecution of innocent people means. I believe that it's everyone's re-

sponsibility to fight prejudice."[20] Otto was also enormously proud
of his daughter's gift: "Everyone with ambition is hoping for greatness—or at least success, which is not the same. Even if someone
produces something great, it is frequently not recognized directly.
But a real work of greatness survives generations."[21] When asked to
pinpoint the lessons to be learned from the diary, Otto answered
immediately: "Withhold easy judgment, never generalize, and
don't expect thanks for what you do for people. That doesn't
work. You must have the satisfaction in yourself for having done
something."[22]

Otto never became religious, although those who knew him well
felt that he was an intensely spiritual man. Father Neiman recalls:
"Otto was not at all religious, he told me that, but he often said that
the Nazis had changed that and restored his Jewish identity to him.
That I found intriguing. He cared about Israel very deeply and
could talk about it and the problems it had at length. He gave a lot
of time and money to projects aimed at keeping the peace there."[23]
Asked if he had considered emigrating to Israel after the war, Otto
replied, "No. First of all, I was no Zionist. I am now Zionist, but I
have a task. I couldn't do my task in Israel."[24] Despite one Dutch
journalist's snide remark that it was obvious Israel "did not make
his heart throb," Otto was very interested in politics and in Israel
in particular.[25] On May 27, 1967, he wrote to Cara Wilson: "You can
imagine how excited we are about the situation in the Middle East.
I am deeply worried and depressed [about] the aggression of the
Arab States [and the] behavior of its so-called friends who do not
take any action. For me, Nasser is following the example of Hitler,
both have openly propagated their plans and the world has not reacted until it [is] too late."[26] The following month, he sent a letter
to Arthur Goldberg at the White House, protesting about the
"weakness of counteraction against Arab and Communist false
statements regarding Israel's aggression and American and British military help."[27] Another regular correspondent, Barbara

302   Goldstein, remembers how depressed Otto was in the wake of
the Yom Kippur War in 1973. "They're doing it again!" he cried.
"They're destroying another generation of young Jews!"[28] Later he
told Wilson that he and Fritzi had spent three weeks in Israel. "As
it was our fourth visit to the country we did not do much sight-
seeing. Our purpose was to see relatives and friends and to show
our solidarity with the people still suffering from the consequences of the Yom Kippur war."[29]

Otto always felt that Britain and the United States did not assist
Israel as they should have done, and he declared that "the last thing
I really worked for" at the Anne Frank Stichting was support for
Israel.[30] Although Otto believed in peaceful protest ("problems
cannot be solved by terrorism and violence"), in 1975 he began
writing to a Palestinian prisoner who had advertised in the *Basler
National-Zeitung* for pen friends. After receiving his first letter
from the young idealist who was imprisoned for his violent acts,
Otto told him, "I have answered your advertisement because I am
interested in humanitarian questions. . . . I can understand that
you are writing 'Let my people live.' But you also ought to recognize
the right of Israel to exist and to live in peace. . . . To my idea peace
in the Middle-East can only be established if the Arab States recognize the State of Israel and a solution for the Palestinian question is found. But as long as extreme groups proclaim as their final
aim the destruction of the State, this cannot be achieved."[31] Otto
sent a copy of the diary with his third letter, explaining: "She, my
elder daughter and my wife perished in a Nazi concentration camp
while I miraculously survived. So you see that I am not a bitter man
though of course I never forget what has happened. I am convinced
that nothing can be achieved by hatred and revenge and therefore
I try to work for peace and understanding."[32]

He made a special effort in replying to letters from schoolchildren, although they often asked about one subject he found it hard
to speak about: his time in Auschwitz. He told one class, on the an-

niversary of the camp's liberation, "Though I have been beaten, I have no scars left."[33] He tried to impress upon them the importance of remembrance: "No one, especially we Jews, can ever forget the terrible crimes committed by the Nazis, and the younger generation, that looks upon everything as ancient history, must realize that anti-Semitism and the current form of anti-Zionism are still virulent."[34] The most common question was what Anne would have become had she been permitted to live. Otto usually refused to speculate, but on one occasion he admitted, "I feel that she would have grown into a truly fine writer."[35] Otto was rarely asked about Margot or Edith, and he did not speak of them often himself. A former employee of the Anne Frank Stichting recalls, "He hardly talked about Edith and Margot but you knew when he did that he cherished them in his heart."[36] Father Neiman remembers: "He never spoke about Edith, but that was probably out of respect for Fritzi. The only person who ever said something about Edith was Fritzi. I remember it clearly. It was after Otto had died and we were at the Basel Zoo, chatting about Otto. Suddenly Fritzi said, in her thick Austrian accent, 'Otto loved Edith very much, but he loved me so much more.' That made me laugh—it was so typical of Fritzi."[37]

The diary was the first book to bring the attempted annihilation of European Jewry into the public arena. Otto's friend Rabbi David Soetendorp explains: "Otto was a visionary. In the 1940s and 1950s, you didn't speak about the Holocaust, but for him it was as though his daughter had left him a legacy in which she came back to life. He was a driven man."[38] In recent years, as the Holocaust has flourished as a subject for television, film, and literature, Otto's "universal Anne" has regained some of her Jewishness, becoming a symbol for the one and a half million Jewish children who were murdered. She retains her potency as a universal symbol nonetheless: Hans Westra, the director of the Anne Frank Stichting, promotes her memory as "directly related to a concern

for preserving freedom and maintaining human rights and a plu-
ralistic and democratic society."[39] Hence the title of the current
Anne Frank exhibition, *A History for Today*. Americans account for
a large proportion of the visitors to the Anne Frank House and a
quarter of the diary's twenty million plus sales occurred in the
United States. When *The Definitive Edition* was published in the
States in 1995 it remained on the *New York Times'* bestseller list for
weeks. The accessibility of Anne and the optimistic slant imposed
upon the diary by its earliest dramatizations are the defining factors in these statistics.

■

THERE ARE TWO PARTICULAR CRITICISMS
leveled at Otto Frank that merit attention; both arose during the
controversy surrounding the existence of the "missing pages." The
first concerns the amount of money Otto left his helpers under
the terms of his will, and the second his attitude toward Miep and
Jan Gies. Because he had been unwilling to use the income generated by the diary and the adaptations from it, Otto left behind a substantial amount of money. Understandably, the main beneficiary of
Otto's will was his wife, Fritzi. To her, he bequeathed a sum of
220,000 Swiss francs. He left his sister, Leni, 200,000 Swiss
francs, and his brother Herbert 100,000 Swiss francs, which would
be administered by the Anne Frank–Fonds, since Herbert was
never very good at handling his own money. Otto also named a
number of charities that would benefit specifically under the terms
of his will. The Anne Frank–Fonds in Basel inherited the copyright
to Anne's diaries and all her writings. Otto also charged the Fonds
with the task of administering the royalties from the diaries and
dramatic adaptations. While Fritzi was alive, she would receive
40,000 Swiss francs from the annual royalties, and Leni and
Herbert would receive 20,000 Swiss francs each. Any earnings
above that would go to the Anne Frank–Fonds to administer for

charities and worthy causes, under supervision of the Swiss Federal
Department of the Interior. The Fonds would remain a completely
separate organization from the Anne Frank Stichting in the
Netherlands, which would continue to maintain the house at 263
Prinsengracht as a museum and to disseminate material and educate against racism and prejudice in any form. To those friends who
had protected him during the Holocaust, Otto bequeathed 10,000
guilders to Miep and Jan Gies and 10,000 guilders to Bep Voskuijl.[40]

Cor Suijk, the former finance coordinator and international director of the Anne Frank Stichting, comments: "Miep told me that
Fritzi was behind it. Otto wanted to leave [Miep] more money, and
originally he had, but Fritzi insisted that he change his will, out of
jealousy, Miep felt. She understood it, but that did not make it better. So he left a small amount to each of them, not to show fa-
voritism."[41] Otto's last will and testament was drawn up in
December 1978, replacing an earlier one, but Fritzi's daughter, Eva
Schloss, refutes emphatically that it had anything to do with her
mother's influence: "This business with Miep and the money—it's
ridiculous the way that came out. Otto just would not use the money
he had at his disposal because he felt it did not belong to him. He
was utterly correct in all his dealings. If he had wanted to leave
Miep more, he would have done. My mother could not have
changed his mind if he had felt differently. He didn't leave Miep
much in the end because he felt that the money was not for him and
not for her. It was nothing to do with my mother. Mutti liked Miep
and admired her. She was upset with Miep when she published her
book, but that was because she got some facts wrong there, too."[42]
Eva's husband, Zvi, admits: "It's true that the money he left Miep
was not a lot. And he left his family more. But surely that is understandable? Miep did so much for him, yes, but his family would always come first, especially after his experiences. It was a way of
protecting them for the future—and Miep would never need that
sort of protection. Otto was a bit silly with money, it's as simple as

306   that. He was old-fashioned, and he didn't know the true value of it. It was Anne's money and not his—that was his feeling until the day he died."[43]

Along with the accusations that Otto had disregarded Miep in his will, there was also the issue of Miep and Jan having to stay in a hotel when they traveled to Switzerland to see Otto and Fritzi, despite Otto having lived with them for several years after the war. Suijk contends: "They had to pay for the hotel themselves; Jan's pride would never have allowed Otto to pay their bill. Miep was very hurt by the fact they could not stay in Otto's house, small though the space was. If the situation was the same with them, she would have moved heaven and earth to have Otto and Fritzi stay in their home. She thinks it was jealousy again which meant they could not stay there."[44] Eva replies to this avowal with her own: "This thing about the apartment—look, the space that Mutti and Otto had was small. The only place visitors could have slept was in the sitting room. If I went alone, then I stayed there, but that was different. Remember, this was Miep, Jan, and their son Paul. Otto would not have wanted that because they wouldn't have been comfortable, and it was difficult for them, too. So he asked them to stay at a hotel instead—and I am sure he paid their bill. Sure of it. It's wicked to say otherwise."[45] Cara Wilson, who visited Otto and Fritzi in 1977, affirms that the same explanation was given to her: "Their home was so small, they told me. It was uncomfortable to have guests in such close quarters. They hoped I understood."[46] The author asked Miep Gies, through Cor Suijk, who had offered to put a list of questions to her on the author's behalf, how she felt about the way in which these two issues had been made public and whether she now regretted having brought them out into the open. The reply came back: "This is too personal. Miep chooses not to answer."[47]

Whatever the rights and wrongs of the situation, Miep did benefit, deservedly so, from her help to the Franks and their friends.

She has traveled the world, been received by heads of state, received numerous awards and accolades, written a book, had a film
made from her life story, and in 1995 accompanied Jon Blair to the
podium when he received the Oscar for his documentary *Anne
Frank Remembered*. Like many concentration camp survivors yet
very few of the people who tried to help them, Miep Gies has enjoyed "a greatly heightened public profile" and is treated quite
rightly with "honor, respect, fascination and no small degree of
awe."[48] For the Dutch, she is very much the heroine of the Anne
Frank story, since she represents their wartime ideal.[49] Otto admitted in 1968 that he gave few interviews in the Netherlands and
had to "hold back" there: "You know how it is. In the Netherlands
I can sense a certain resistance, conscious or unconscious. . . .
Here they lived through it all. Thousands of people died here. . . .
Thus, there is a certain feeling: why Anne Frank?"[50] Yet Anne
Frank's story has enabled the older Dutch citizens who were either
bystanders or perpetrators to "alleviate their guilt, and blame the
Nazis for having decimated their Jewish population. . . . The Anne
Frank lore says to the world: 'Look, we Dutch hid her; the terrible
Germans killed her. They were evil and we were virtuous'. . . .
While the Anne Frank story does point to the Netherlands as the
place of refuges, and Dutch sheltering of Jews, it also points to a
more murky side of Dutch wartime collaboration with the German
occupiers."[51] Rabbi David Soetendorp declares: "For Otto and for
all Jewish survivors of the Holocaust, Amsterdam is a town in a
state of bereavement. Although it is vibrant and never sleeps, there
is a sense of something missing. Amsterdam's Utrechtsestraat today is full of very good restaurants and design shops, but before the
war the houses belonged to Jewish people. My mother would tell
me how that street on a Saturday night would be packed with Jewish
people singing. It was their entertainment, and they delighted in
it. All those people are dead now, and nothing can replace them.
What happened there in the war is a scar."[52]

■

IN 2001, *THE DIARIES OF ANNE FRANK:*
The Critical Edition was updated to include five pages from the diary
that had never before been published. The pages in question, written on loose sheets, consisted of an introduction to the diary Anne
had written on June 20, 1942, and an observation about her parents' marriage, dated February 8, 1944 (B), which Anne had
rewritten from her original entry (A). In the winter of 1945, Otto
translated the pages into German when he was in the process of
sending excerpts from the diary to his family in Switzerland, but he
never sanctioned them for publication. After Otto's death and the
return of Anne's writings to Amsterdam, when NIOD set about the
task of authenticating and publishing the complete diaries, it ran
into difficulties. There were some objections from people who did
not wish their full names, or a few personal details, to be made
public; this could be resolved only by the use of initials rather than
names and explanatory footnotes. The greatest objection, however,
came from Otto's widow, Fritzi. She wrote to Father John Neiman,
"I am not at all happy about this book as I think it violates Anne's
right of privacy and my husband's intentions."[53] In another letter
to Bep Voskuijl, Fritzi makes her feelings equally plain: "I want to
try and get the director of the Institute to omit certain passages,
because I do not consider them fit for publication. . . . Anne
writes too openly about sexual matters. I don't know whether I'll
succeed though, but I hope so."[54] One of the passages that caused
Fritzi concern was the entry dated February 8, 1944 (A), in which
Anne discussed her parents' marriage. This was omitted from the
published *Critical Edition,* with a footnote explaining the objections to it.

In early 1998, Cor Suijk contacted the Fonds to inform it that he
had five original diary pages, which he said had been given to him
by Otto Frank. These incorporated Anne's introduction for the diary and her rewritten draft of February 8, 1944 (B). In April 1998,

Suijk wrote to Buddy Elias, claiming to know more about the Stichting, Otto Frank, and the diary than Hans Westra, director of the Anne Frank Stichting, had in his archive, and he declared that the day was soon coming when he would present his knowledge.[55] Suijk asserted that Otto had passed the pages to him during the Bundeskriminalamt investigation of the diary's authenticity in 1980, wanting to save himself and Fritzi unpleasant questions.[56] By handing the pages to Suijk, who was then still working for the Stichting, Otto could legitimately claim to have no further pages in his possession. When Suijk offered to return the pages, he maintained that Otto put out his hands in a silent way of saying, "Keep them." In his 1998 letter to Buddy Elias, Suijk outlined his plans for the diary pages, insisting that, under Swiss law, he had the right to publish them first in Melissa Muller's biography of Anne Frank. They would also form part of a television documentary pertinent to the book's publication; the producer of the documentary intended to give Buddy Elias a prominent role. Once this was achieved, Suijk promised that the Fonds would have the right to copyright.[57]

Suijk had not come forward with the five pages while NIOD was compiling *The Critical Edition*, though that would surely have been the moment to do so when the most extensive inspection of the diary's authenticity was being conducted. The reason he gave for not doing so was the desire to protect Fritzi from being confronted with awkward questions, but he could have informed NIOD about the existence of the pages with the stipulation that they were not for publication; after all, the original version of the entry concerned was omitted at Fritzi's wish. Paradoxically, Suijk was clearly willing for Muller to print the pages in her book while Fritzi was still alive. In May 1998, the Anne Frank–Fonds asked Suijk to honor Otto's will by delivering the diary pages to NIOD. Suijk refused on the grounds that because the pages were not in Otto's possession when he died, they were exempt from the clauses in his will and Otto had not wanted them to form part of the diary. In her book, Muller

310   asserts that Otto stipulated in his will that the original diaries, including 324 of the 327 "loose sheets," were to go to NIOD. Otto
makes no such distinction; his will states that NIOD "will receive
all handwritten notes and the photo album of my daughter Anne
Frank. . . . Whatever other material which has a bearing on Anne
Frank and which is still in my possession at my death . . . should
be given to the Anne Frank Stichting, insofar as the material is not
needed by my wife for continuing the current correspondence."[58]

In August 1998, the news that there were five previously unpublished pages of Anne's diary broke. Press and public interest in the
missing pages was immense, heightened by speculation about what
would happen to the pages, since Suijk had declared that he wanted
a "financial sponsor" for the pages before he would release them to
NIOD. Initially, he was quoted as saying he would donate the
money to the Anne Frank Center in New York, where he was then
working (the center organizes the traveling Anne Frank exhibition
and educates against racism and prejudice); but when Suijk and
the center parted company, he announced his intention to use the
money instead for his own Holocaust Education Foundation, also
based in the United States. Having learned that Muller would be
unable to quote the pages in her biography owing to disputes over
their copyright, Suijk used his platform to attack the Anne
Frank–Fonds, which he accused of squirreling away millions in
Swiss bank accounts. The Fonds did not aid its cause by refusing to
be drawn on the subject under pressure from Suijk. Its support of
various charities and funding of many antiracism-related projects
were largely ignored by a now-hostile press.

Buddy Elias, meanwhile, gave a radio interview in which he discussed visits that Suijk had made to Otto's house in 1996 and 1997.
On one occasion, Fritzi's nurse, Katja Olszewska, had been disturbed by Suijk's interest in reading Otto's will, which lay in a
drawer of the writing desk in the "office." On another occasion,
Suijk appeared with a photocopier. He told Katja he wanted to

make copies from the facsimile diary, which consisted of voluminous loose pages and was kept in the house. Katja telephoned Eva
Schloss to ascertain whether she should permit Suijk to do so and
was told that Suijk had been given permission to copy materials.
The Fonds was angry over such affairs, however, and Katja had
given statements about both incidents to a lawyer. She also told the
author, "Suijk came here often. Once he asked me if I knew where
there were letters, private letters. I said I didn't know."[59] In June
1998, Suijk wrote an astonishing letter to the executor of Otto's
will, in which he inquired which items belonging to Anne were
found to be in Otto's possession after his death. He asked to be informed of whatever had been found, in which way any items had
been registered, and if an inventory had been made.[60] Exactly why
Suijk believed he had the right to be informed of such matters is
puzzling.[61]

The Fonds's attempts to reclaim the pages failed; Suijk was able
to hold on to them because he maintained that Otto had given them
to him as a gift. He placed the pages with Christie's Auctioneers in
New York for one year on the understanding that they would be
used to attract donations to his Holocaust Education Foundation,
which hoped to raise $1.2 million in funds. The Dutch government
bought the pages eventually for $300,000. Initially, the press at-
tacked Suijk for his actions, but in the past year or so, they have
been less antagonistic toward him, particularly in the Netherlands,
where the pages are now stored in NIOD's archives. Public opinion, meanwhile, remains divided. Eva Schloss is vociferous in her
reproach: "I'm sure that Otto would never have wanted those pages
published. And I don't see that they make such a great difference
to the diary. As for the story behind it all—I am sure that Otto gave
them to Cor for safekeeping. That is true. But *not* to keep. They
were not a gift. He just wanted Cor to take them at that moment so
that he was not compromising himself. In May 1980, or around
then, Cor visited Otto with the pages, and he says that Otto put

312 up his hands in a dismissive gesture. That didn't mean 'They're yours,' it meant 'Don't bother me now.' He was a very sick man at that point and found it hard sometimes to deal with even the smallest things. He wasn't thinking right at that time. And Otto would hate Cor for selling them, he would hate him."[62]

Laureen Nussbaum, who has written extensively about Anne's diary, disagrees:

Otto did well to get the diary published in the first place. The Dutch wanted us to fade into the background, they weren't interested in us or what the Jewish people had suffered in those years. So Otto should be congratulated for being probably the first to publish a document from the Holocaust, but when it comes to his editing of it, on that issue I feel that he was headstrong and misled people as to the content. Once he had made certain statements about it, he either could not or would not retract, and as a result those statements have been accepted over the years. As far as the missing pages are concerned, they add an interesting angle, since they show Anne pondering about her mother's situation, but in the end, the whole unpleasant to-do about these pages reveals more about Anne Frank's putative trustees and everyone concerned than about Anne herself. Cor faxed me in early 1998 about them and asked if he could send me copies to translate. This I did, and I kept it secret for as long as he asked. I'm sorry it made such a scandal. In the new *Critical Edition,* Barnouw says nothing about Cor, and that is terrible of him. Cor deserves better than that. Without him, there would be no new version and those pages would still be unknown. He kept them back until the time was right, until Fritzi could not be bothered by the journalists who would surely have come banging on her door. I don't think Otto would be upset at their publication either. He made a present of them to Cor, so in effect he said Cor had the right to do with them what he wanted.[63]

There are a number of questions arising from the "missing pages" affair. In the first place, Suijk claims that Otto removed the pages in 1945 and put them in an envelope, then numbered the remaining pages in sequence as if nothing were missing. The pages must have been removed before Otto's death in 1980, but there is no evidence to confirm that it was in 1945 (or that Otto was the person to number the pages afterward). The Fonds has a copy of Otto's German translation of the pages from late 1945, making it improbable that Otto secreted the pages at that time; he was clearly unfazed by his family and friends reading the pages then. In the second place, Anne's diary—including the entries written on the loose sheets—was examined in 1959 for purposes of establishing its authenticity. Handwriting experts traveled to Basel to inspect her work. What happened to these delicate pages on that occasion? Did Otto entrust them to someone then, as he apparently did with Suijk later? And if so, why did he clearly require the pages to be returned to him then (which he must have done in order to give them to Suijk), while he allowed Suijk to keep them? In the third place, Otto allowed the handwriting experts to view Anne's original version of the entry in question, yet felt that the revised version was too sensitive for them to scrutinize. However, a comparison of both texts reveals that they are quite startlingly similar, and there is certainly nothing that can be deemed disparaging in the second draft that is not present in the first. In effect, Otto was not concealing anything by retaining Anne's revised entry about his marriage. As for the introduction she wrote, although it is different in substance from other passages in the diary, it contains nothing that could be construed as damaging. In it, Anne writes that no one must get their hands on her diary, but the published diary also included the line "I don't intend to show this cardboard covered notebook to anyone."[64]

It seems extraordinarily remiss of Otto to have given them to Suijk, the finance coordinator of the Anne Frank Stichting, in 1980

314   without any form of declaration to confirm that he was making a gift of them to him, to corroborate that they were authentic, and to set out the terms of the bequest (that they could only be released after a certain time). Over the years, Otto had endured many problems with diary-related issues, particularly those involving ownership, rights, and fraud. He knew that he had to be absolutely circumspect in such matters, and to have drawn up some sort of attestation about the pages would also have protected the man he apparently trusted more than any living person—let us not forget, if we ever could, that the diary was Otto's life—against accusations of avarice when he decided to sell them, as Suijk eventually did. In an interview with the Dutch news program *NOVA* in the summer of 2000, Suijk pronounced himself certain that Otto would approve of his conduct regarding the hidden pages.

Otto advocated Holocaust education, unquestionably, but the answer to whether or not he would have sanctioned selling the remains of his daughter's legacy may be found in an interview he gave not long before his death in August 1980. He explained then that he was writing his will and would bequeath all Anne's writings to NIOD. Asked why he was not pledging them to the Anne Frank Stichting, Otto replied, "I'm never sure what the Anne Frank Stichting will be one day. What will become of the Stichting in fifty years? Do we know? You just asked about finances. Maybe some time something will happen. What can I know? It's not safe enough for me." The interviewer pointed out that the pages would be worth a fortune. Otto's response was quiet but confident. "Yes, but they will be with the government so that they won't be sold. You see?"[65]

epilogue THE TELEPHONE CALL

DID TONNY AHLERS BETRAY THE FRANK
family? The evidence we have at the moment is largely circumstan-
tial, and his relatives have only been able to provide us with oral
testimony. These people are witnesses, nonetheless—Ahlers's son
in particular—but whether Tonny Ahlers was telling them the truth
is another matter. His ever-present need to seem important may
be a factor against him, but it may also be one of the reasons why he
informed the Gestapo that there were Jews hiding at 263
Prinsengracht. And although he was indeed a storyteller, his tales
always had some basis in truth.

Born just two weeks before his father was arrested, Anton
Ahlers insists he is not out for revenge, despite the pain his father
inflicted upon him and the rest of the family, physically, emotion-
ally, and mentally. Before he heard his father talking about the betrayal of August 4, 1944, he already knew that he had been a
member of the NSB.

Myself and my brother and sisters suffered terribly because of
that. Hardly any of the other children in the neighborhood would

316   play with us, and we were not allowed to have contact with anyone
             outside the family. Our parents wouldn't allow it, in case some-
             thing was said. If I came home with a letter from school, my par-
             ents wouldn't sign it because someone might recognize the name.
             There were many children in my class, but as far as they were con-
             cerned, I was alone; no one would speak to me because my father
             had been a Nazi. My first relationship with a girl ended because
             her father couldn't stomach the idea of her marrying the son of an
             NSB man. The same thing happened to my sister. We suffered
             a lot.

He is convinced that his father betrayed the Franks: "I know it. I've
always known it."[1]

Cas Ahlers is equally adamant that his brother was the traitor,
but his testimony is problematic on two counts. First, he is clearly
confused about certain issues; he claimed, for instance, that the
Franks had been picked up on the Euterpestraat, which is patently
untrue, although this misconception can perhaps be explained by
the fact that the Franks were taken there immediately after their
arrest. Second, he did not tell the truth about his own past. To the
author he admitted that he had spent much of the war in Germany,
helping to build U-boats in Bremen. It was forced labor, he said.
However, the archives in Amsterdam reveal that on June 15, 1942,
Cas Ahlers volunteered to work for the Deutsche Schiff und
Maschinenbau AG in Bremen.[2] His then-wife followed him a year
later. What is more, one of Tonny Ahlers's sisters was also a member of the NSB, and his other brother, Huibert, departed from the
Netherlands willingly on June 8, 1942, to work in Germany but became sick and had to return in September 1943.[3] It seems that
Tonny was not the black sheep of the family after all—instead, there
was a small flock.

In September 2002, Tonny's stepsister, Greet, contacted the
author to add her testimony to that of Martha, Cas, and Anton. Her

memories do not conflict with theirs in any significant way; she, too, heard from Tonny that he had been "involved" in the betrayal of the Frank family, although he did not tell her he had made the actual telephone call to the Gestapo, only that he had been "responsible" for the Franks' arrest. She, too, believes that Tonny blackmailed Otto Frank after the war and in the late 1970s, and claims that she saw a letter very similar to the one Tonny showed Cas from Otto Frank. She believed him when he said he was behind the Franks' betrayal because it fitted in with the character she knew. It was her father, after all, whom Tonny had betrayed to the Nazis and who ended up first in Vught and then Amersfoort concentration camp. She remembers Tonny as "a very strange boy. He would do something terrible and then do something good. Nothing he ever did made any sense to anyone but himself. That's what made him so dangerous. He was completely unpredictable."

Certain questions need to be asked before we can know whether Ahlers was the betrayer. When the traitor called the SD on the morning of August 4, 1944, he disclosed only that there were a number of Jews hiding at 263 Prinsengracht. The caller did not know how many or exactly where they were. This fits in with Ahlers as the probable betrayer. He could not have known that the van Pels family and Fritz Pfeffer were hiding with the Franks, and although he knew the building had an annex, he probably did not know for sure that they were in there, although that was the logical assumption. The Nazis who led the raid were surprised by the number of Jews hiding on the premises.[4] But how could Ahlers have known they were in hiding there in the first place? Ahlers himself admitted in a letter that he kept his eye on Otto Frank from the moment of their first meeting until the Frank family disappeared.[5] Indeed, he claimed to have advised Otto to go into hiding. In his 1964 letter to the authorities in Vienna, he wrote that after their first meeting, "I began to urge Otto Frank to go into hiding."[6] This seems absurd, and there can be only three explanations: Ahlers was simply lying; he was telling the truth, but only because there was something in it for him; or he was attempting to deflect suspicion from himself. Whatever the truth of this particular matter, the fact remains that Ahlers did know the Franks were in hiding at the Prinsengracht—as even the Dutch detectives in charge of the 1963–64 investigation were forced to concede.[7]

Ahlers may have discovered the secret of the annex through his own efforts, or he may have heard about it through the very dangerous grapevine that twisted its way through Amsterdam during the war. Through his own curiosity, van Maaren had also come to suspect that there were Jews hiding on the premises where he worked.[8] Ahlers may have come into contact with van Maaren in the course of the business his company did with Gies & Co. Van Maaren was not a Nazi, and he almost certainly was not the betrayer, but he was a gossip. Furthermore, he apparently told Miep Gies that he knew people in the SD who might be able to help the arrested families. Miep recalled: "He did not tell me who or what these people were or if they had any connection with the SD, but he gave me the clear impression that in one way or another he had some influence with the Germans."[9] Could Ahlers have been his contact? If Ahlers and van Maaren did discuss the people hiding at the Prinsengracht, then perhaps that explains why Ahlers was so keen to jump to van Maaren's defense and also why he sent van Maaren copies of all his letters to the authorities.

There is another side to these questions. If Ahlers was not the Franks' betrayer, then why would he lie and say he was? Instead, he could have made quite a name for himself as the former Dutch Nazi who saved Otto Frank from death in 1941. And if he was not the betrayer, then why did he hate Otto so much years after the two of them had last had contact—as is clear from his letters? Otto's favorable words about Ahlers in 1945 must have aided his release from jail. Unlike the other suspects, Ahlers had motives to betray the Franks, and he was well placed to do so. Again and again, when examining the dossiers on the betrayal and those concerning the Nazis who were involved in arresting and deporting Amsterdam's Jews in the years 1942 to 1944, one sees the same names: Albani, Gringhuis, Silberbauer, Schaap, Kaper, Rühl, Viebahn, Lages, Kempin, Dettman, and Kuiper. There was a small circle of men who made it their mission to rid the town of its Jews, and Ahlers knew most of them.

■

AHLERS AND HIS WIFE, MARTHA, DI-vorced in 1985. As the couple had grown older, their relationship had not improved but grew more acrimonious and violent. After the divorce, they lived separately for a time, but then Ahlers became ill; he had serious problems with his heart and lungs. His mind began to fail him, too, and Martha, who had vowed never to allow him back into her life, took him into her home again. His health continued to deteriorate, and at the age of eighty-three, in 2000, Tonny Ahlers died. In a strange twist of fate, his death occurred on the anniversary of the Frank family's arrest: August 4, 2000. Upon hearing the news that their father was dead, the immediate response from the children was one of relief. Anton recalls: "We went to his funeral, but only to make sure he was really dead. My mother was there, of course, but we ignored her when she waved to us.[10] I sat at the back, listening to the music playing as the coffin disappeared to be cremated; first 'We Shall Overcome' and then 'My Way.' "[11] Gone was the man who had overshadowed so many lives, the man whose brother had described him as "an absolute sadist; he could be threatening and charming at the same time."[12]

The author visited Martha Ahlers twice during the course of writing this book. On the first occasion, the ex–Mrs. Ahlers's attitude was one of surprise. She said then that Otto and her husband had worked together and that she had met Otto herself, as had her sons (although she refused to specify when that was). Asked whether her husband and Otto Frank were friends, she hesitated and then replied that they were. Told that the author had letters in which her husband had written about Otto, she said that was quite possible, but when asked whether she would be willing to speak about the matter further, she declined.[13] When the author visited again several months later, the reaction of Ahlers's widow was very different: she was openly aggressive. Despite the author making it clear that she was aware that Ahlers had, in 1941, prevented Otto's arrest by the SS, Martha became extremely agitated and suddenly unleashed a tirade: "My husband never wrote anything about Otto Frank! Otto Frank was my very best friend—I was the first person he took to see the secret annex after the war, and I have photos of him all over my house! You have no idea what that time was like for us, the war was terrible for us, not just the Jews but for us, too. I had Jewish girls working for me all through the war. My husband never betrayed anyone!" Asked then why she was not willing to be interviewed, if she and her husband had helped Jews during the war, Martha did not answer but threatened to call the police.[14] During both visits, the author said not a single word about Ahlers's character—and made no reference to the betrayal of the Frank family.

Her son has since declared that there is not a single photograph of Otto Frank in his mother's house, and never has been. Discussing his mother, Anton states firmly, "What she told you about having Jewish girls working for her is rubbish. And she told you that I met Otto Frank, but I didn't. At least, I was not aware of it, although I know my father told someone close to me that Otto Frank had once been to our house." He paused here, then continued: "My mother always stood by my father, and it's my feeling that whatever he did during the war, she must have known about it."[15]

Of course, Martha's reluctance to speak is understandable. Yet if, as she claims, her husband helped Otto Frank during the war, then it seems a little strange. If Ahlers saved Otto's life, then why is Martha so angry and what is it that she is so frightened of? What does she know?

As the U.S. edition of this book was nearing completion, an answer emerged that is quite extraordinary. The information does not come from the files of collaborators in The Hague, or from the Netherlands Institute for War Documentation, as one might expect. Instead, it comes from the old Social Services files in the Amsterdam city archives. It concerns Martha Ahlers, and her circumstances in 1945.

■

THE LAST MONTHS OF THE WAR WERE ESpecially difficult in Amstelveen, where Tonny and Martha had lived since leaving Jan van Eyckstraat.[16] Because the area was such a hotbed of Nazism, the area had been heavily bombed, and scarcely a house was left standing intact. Most had their windows blown out, while the doors of abandoned houses had been ripped off by the Dutch themselves during the Hunger Winter, when the Germans had cut off all food and fuel supplies; the timber had been set alight to provide warmth and heat on which to cook whatever scraps could be found. Martha hated living there: it was so depressing and frightening. Many of their neighbors, Dutch Nazis and SD men like their friend G. van Donselaar, who lived directly opposite them, had fled, fearing what would happen when the Allies finally reached Amsterdam. Martha knew that their house would be repossessed and that they would lose their home; the Nazis had requisitioned it for sympathizers like themselves in 1942, but as the war dragged to an inglorious end, it was obvious that the owner would reclaim his property—if he was still alive to do so.[17]

Liberation came to the city in May 1945. Now it was the turn of

322 the Dutch Nazis to be terrified; they were no longer the hunters but the prey. In June, there were mass arrests of all those suspected of having been members of the NSB. Martha's husband, Tonny, was among the first to be taken. Neither of them could believe it; both had been so sure that there were bigger fish to catch.[18] Martha had given birth just two weeks earlier and found herself alone in the ruined suburb, which still smelled of smoke and neglect. She had an infant and a toddler to care for and no one to help her. Somehow she managed to get an apartment, far less grand than the house in Amstelveen. It was situated on the Hoofdweg, a long concrete slab of a street that began close to Amsterdam's city center and went on until it reached the polders.[19] But there was still the issue of money; she had absolutely nothing. There was only one solution under such circumstances, and eventually Martha applied to the Social Services for financial assistance.

It was with shock and anger that Martha learned her application had run into difficulties—and why.[20]

■

MIEP GIES HAS OFTEN BEEN ASKED BY reporters and writers over the years whether she knew who had betrayed them. She said nothing, but always held firm to her belief that it was not van Maaren. Cor Suijk declares: "Once I wanted to know something very badly, and I kept asking Miep and asking her. Finally she said, 'Cor, can you keep a secret?' Very eagerly I answered, 'Yes, Miep, I can!' And she smiled and said, 'Me, too.' "[21] In another interview, Miep affirmed, "I am a person who can be silent."[22] Her close friend Father John Neiman attempted to draw Otto on the subject of the betrayal and recalls: "Otto would never talk about that—anything and everything, but not that. Miep also said nothing—for a long time. And then something strange happened. Miep came to America for the Oscars, and we were together at author Alison Leslie Gold's house. Out of the blue, Miep said she knew who had betrayed them. She knew. You could have heard a pin drop. I said, 'Was it someone Otto knew?' She said, 'Yes, it was someone Otto knew.' She thought the person was dead. And then I saw her face change and knew that nothing further could be said."[23]

When articles about the first edition of this book appeared in Germany, a retired journalist named Carole Kleesiek contacted the author. She had interviewed Otto Frank in 1964 for *Die Neue*, the magazine for which she then worked. She was given the assignment after her colleague, the photographer John de Rooy, had spoken to Simon Wiesenthal about the Silberbauer investigation; Wiesenthal told de Rooy that he was absolutely convinced that Otto Frank knew the name of the traitor but for some reason would not reveal it. Although Kleesiek liked and admired Otto Frank after meeting him in London, she was puzzled by his attitude toward the matter of the betrayal: "He was evasive, and yes, I got the feeling that he knew who the traitor was."[24]

On two occasions after 1964, Otto was recorded as saying that they had been betrayed by a Dutch policeman; he told his friend Robert Kempner that a Dutch policeman had received payment for the information that there were Jews hiding at 263 Prinsengracht.[25] In an article for *Life* magazine in 1979, Otto added a curious twist to the story: "We do not know whether we were betrayed because of anti-Semitism or because of money. We never found out who betrayed us. We had our suspicions. A man who'd been in the police during the occupation was suspected and questioned. But we never had proof. I do have a theory though. It was said that a woman made the telephone call that led to our capture. I therefore assume that the policeman who had been cross-examined might have spoken to someone about us."[26] In an interview conducted with Fritzi Frank not long before her death, researchers at the Anne Frank Stichting raised the matter again. Fritzi told them: "[Otto] said all the time that it was a woman's voice on the telephone to the

324 Gestapo. So that went against the idea that it was van Maaren. The Gestapo said it was a woman's voice, whoever it was who knew such a thing. Yes, a female voice called and said they are hiding there, in that house."[27]

"That house" was 263 Prinsengracht, and among the other houses around the courtyard that the annex overlooked was one belonging to a middle-aged couple with several daughters. One daughter they did not see so often anymore. Their relationship with her had broken down after she married a Dutch Nazi known for his violence and criminal record. Everything could have been so different, if only Martha had never met Tonny Ahlers. . . . [28]

■

THE SOCIAL SERVICES FILES ON TONNY Ahlers are kept in the long, cool rooms of the Amsterdam city archives, which are not open to the public. The cardboard covers of the files are dog-eared and dusty, and the papers crammed inside are like fallen leaves. The minute, closely written notes are often hard to decipher, the product of various people having been assigned to Tonny Ahlers's case. The files cover the period when Ahlers was a youth of twenty, just out of jail for the first time, having admitted himself that he had "a difficult character, just like all the Ahlerses," until the 1950s, when he was released from jail yet again, with a wife and two children to support. There are several comments about his wife, one of which reads, "Because her husband previously moved in SD circles, she is very sharp and mistrustful."[29] Another note explains why the Social Services had been unwilling to provide her with a small allowance when she applied for it following her husband's imprisonment.[30]

When the Dutch police flooded Amstelveen to seize former Nazis, suspicion fell not only on Tonny Ahlers but on Martha, too. The slanting handwriting of the clerk is bold and, for once, easy to read: "The wife is as politically untrustworthy as her husband.

During the occupation of our country she was suspected of being in the service of the SD as a betrayer. There have been many telephone calls and letters about her behavior during the war. She was investigated but proved as devious as her husband and no charges could be brought. . . ."[31]

appendix A   CHRONOLOGY OF THE
JEWISH PERSECUTION
IN THE NETHERLANDS[*]

1940

MAY 10: Germany invades the Netherlands.

MAY 15: Surrender of all Dutch forces.

JULY 1: Jews have to leave the air-raid precaution service.

JULY 2: Jews are excluded from labor drafts to Germany.

JULY 31: Bans on ritual slaughter (VO 80/1940), effective August 5.

AUGUST 20: Special regulations on administrative matters (VO 108/1940).

AUGUST 28: College of Secretaries-General is informally instructed not to appoint, elect, or promote anyone of "Jewish Blood" within the civil service.

SEPTEMBER 6: College of Secretaries-General is instructed not to appoint any more Jews to the civil service.

SEPTEMBER 13: Measures concerning the employment of Jews and others in government service (VO 137/1940).

SEPTEMBER 14: Jews are banned from various markets in Amsterdam.

SEPTEMBER 20: Measures for a survey of noneconomic associations and institutions (VO 145/1940).

SEPTEMBER 30: Circular is distributed to local authorities defining a Jew as anyone with one Jewish grandparent who had been a member of the Jewish community.

[*] This table is based upon the one featured in Bob Moore, *Victims and Survivors: The Nazi Persecution of the Jews in the Netherlands 1940–1945* (London: Arnold, 1997), pp. 261–67.

328   OCTOBER 5: Civil servants are forced to sign "Aryan attestation."

OCTOBER 22: Order for the registration of Jewish businesses at the Wirtschaftsprüfstelle (VO 189/1940).

NOVEMBER 21: Circular is sent out banning all Jews from holding public office.

DECEMBER: The creation of the Jewish Coordination Commission.

DECEMBER 19: Bans on Germans working in Jewish households (VO 231/1940).

1941

JANUARY 7: The Dutch Cinema Association bans Jews from all cinemas, publicized in daily newspapers on January 12.

JANUARY 10: Compulsory registration of all persons "wholly or largely of Jewish blood" (VO 6/1941).

FEBRUARY 1: Introduction of *numerus clausus* in education.

FEBRUARY 5: Doctors must declare if they are Jewish.

FEBRUARY 8: WA incite fighting on the Rembrandtplein, Amsterdam.

FEBRUARY 11: Restrictions on Jewish students (VO 27/1941). Decree (VO 28/1941) of Secretary-General of Education, Science, and Culture implementing these restrictions. WA attack on Amsterdam's Jewish quarter, resulting in the death of Nazi Hendrik Koot.

FEBRUARY 12: German authorities seal off the Jewish Quarter and insist on the establishment of a Jewish Council.

FEBRUARY 13: Amsterdam Joodse Raad is set up.

FEBRUARY 19: German police raid Koco, an ice-cream parlor owned by two Jews. Police are attacked.

FEBRUARY 22–23: In reprisal, Germans arrest 425 young men from the Jewish Quarter.

FEBRUARY 25–26: Strike in Amsterdam and beyond in protest of the arrests.

FEBRUARY 27: Decree for the Secretary-General of the Department of Social Affairs on Jewish blood donors.

FEBRUARY 28: Measures against Jewish noncommercial organizations (VO 41/1941).

MARCH 12: Measures for the registration of Jewish businesses and the appointment of Verwalters (VO 48/1941).

MARCH 31: Creation of the Zentralstelle für Jüdische Auswanderung.

APRIL 2: Series of prohibitions for Jews in Haarlem.

APRIL 11: First issue of the *Joodse Weekblad*.

APRIL 15: Commissioner-General Rauter instructs all Jews to hand in their wireless sets on the basis of regulation of February 11 (VO 26/1941).

MAY 1: Ban on Jewish doctors, apothecaries, and translators working for non-Jews. Jews are no longer allowed to own wireless sets. Ban on Jews attending stock and commercial exchanges.

MAY 6: Certain streets in Amsterdam are designated "Jewish Streets."

MAY 15: A synagogue in The Hague is destroyed by fire. Orchestras are "Aryanized."

MAY 27: Decree on declaration and treatment of agricultural land in Jewish hands (VO 102/1941).

MAY 31: Jews are banned from using swimming pools and public parks, and from renting rooms in certain resorts and coastal localities.

JUNE 4: Freedom of movement for Jews is restricted.

JUNE 11: Raids against Jews in Amsterdam.

MID-JUNE: Jewish lawyers are banned from working for non-Jewish clients.

AUGUST 1: Jewish estate agents are banned from working for non-Jews.

AUGUST 8–11: Regulations on the handling of Jewish assets and property. Registration of assets with Lippmann-Rosenthal Bank.

SEPTEMBER 1: Jewish children are forced to attend separate schools (October 1 in Amsterdam).

SEPTEMBER 14: Raid in Twente area (east Overijssel).

SEPTEMBER 15: "Forbidden for Jews" signs appear. Jews are no longer allowed to visit parks, zoos, cafés, restaurants, hotels, guest houses, theaters, cabarets, cinemas, concerts, libraries, and reading rooms (VO 138/1941). Registration of land and property owned by Jews with Lippmann-Rosenthal.

SEPTEMBER 16: Travel permits are introduced.

SEPTEMBER 22: Jews are barred from all noneconomic organizations and associations.

SEPTEMBER 24: Permits are made compulsory for the establishment of certain trades and professions.

OCTOBER 7–8: Raids in Achterhoek, Arnhem, Apeldoorn, and Zwolle.

OCTOBER 20: Further regulations on the establishment of businesses by Jews (VO 198/1941). Joodse Raad sanctions the creation of a card index of Jews in the Netherlands.

OCTOBER 22: Jews are forced to resign from non-Jewish associations (VO 199/1941) and banned from bridge, dance, and tennis clubs, effective November 7.

OCTOBER 27: Germans limit their recognition to Joodse Raad; Jewish Coordination Commission is forced to disband.

NOVEMBER 1: Jews are required to resign from associations with non-Jewish members. Legislation VO 198/1941 used to rescind 1,600 permits for Jews.

330   NOVEMBER 3: Jewish markets are established in Amsterdam.

NOVEMBER 7: Jews are banned from traveling or moving house without permission.

NOVEMBER 10: Final dissolution of the Jewish Coordination Commission.

DECEMBER 5: All non-Dutch Jews are ordered to register for "voluntary emigration."

1942

JANUARY 1: Jews are not permitted to employ non-Jewish domestic servants.

JANUARY 9: Jews are banned from public education.

JANUARY 10: The first Jews from Amsterdam are sent to work camps. The Joodse Raad advises those targeted to obey the summons on the grounds that a refusal will lead to trouble for everyone.

JANUARY 17: Beginning of the concentration of Jews in Amsterdam with the removal of the Jewish community from Zaandam.

JANUARY 20: Wannsee Conference in Berlin outlines practical measures for the extermination of European Jews.

JANUARY 23: Jews are forbidden from using motor cars. Identity cards for Jews are to carry a letter "J."

FEBRUARY 9: 150 stateless Jews from Utrecht are moved to Amsterdam and Westerbork.

MARCH 20: Jews are forbidden to dispose of furniture or household goods.

MARCH 25: Ban on marriage between Jews and non-Jews. Extramarital relations to be severely punished.

MARCH 26: First transport of Jews from occupied Western Europe (Drancy) to Auschwitz.

MARCH 27: Effective introduction of the Nuremberg Laws in the Netherlands.

APRIL 1: Jews are banned from marrying in Amsterdam City Hall.

APRIL 24: Most Jewish butchers are closed down.

MAY 3: Introduction of the Jewish Star. The fate of Jews in the Netherlands is now sealed, for, as the historian Jacob Presser would write, it "marked them out for slaughter."

MAY 12: Jews are no longer allowed to have accounts at the Post Office.

MAY 21: Jews are forced to hand in all their assets and possessions valued at more than 250 guilders to Lippmann-Rosenthal by June 30, 1942. Jews are no longer allowed to rent safety deposit boxes (VO 58/1942).

MAY 29: Jews are prohibited from fishing.

JUNE 5: Total ban on traveling for Jews without prior permission.

JUNE 11: Jews are banned from the fish market.

JUNE 12: Jews are no longer allowed to buy fruits and vegetables in non-

Jewish shops. Bicycles and other transport have to be handed in. All forms of sport are forbidden for Jews.

JUNE 26: The Joodse Raad receives notification of the beginning of the deportations.

JUNE 30: Curfew on Jews after 8:00 P.M. Jews are no longer allowed to ride bicycles. Jews are banned from certain trades and professions. Jews are banned from using public transport.

JULY 4: The first call-up notices are sent out for "labor services in Germany."

JULY 6: Jews are no longer allowed to use telephones or visit non-Jews.

JULY 14: Raids on Jews in south and central Amsterdam.

JULY 15: The first trainload of Jews leaves Amsterdam. Deportations begin from Westerbork to Auschwitz.

JULY 17: Jews may shop only between 3:00 P.M. and 5:00 P.M. and are banned altogether from many streets in The Hague and Scheveningen.

JULY 25: Dutch prime minister Gerbrandy urges help for the Jews via a broadcast from London on Radio Oranje.

AUGUST 2: Arrest of all Catholic Jews, excluding those in "mixed marriages."

AUGUST 6: Raid on Jews in south Amsterdam.

AUGUST 9: Further raid in south Amsterdam.

AUGUST: Series of raids throughout the Netherlands. All Jewish street names are changed.

SEPTEMBER 11: Registration of those in mixed marriages.

SEPTEMBER 15: Jewish students are excluded from education.

SEPTEMBER 16: First issue of exemption stamps.

OCTOBER 2–3: Raids against Jewish work camps.

1943

JANUARY 16: The first Jews arrive in Vught concentration camp.

JANUARY 21: Raid on Jewish asylum Het Apeldoornsche Bos.

FEBRUARY 5: Jews are forbidden from sending requests or letters to the German authorities. All of these are to go through the Joodse Raad.

MARCH 2: Deportations to Sobibor concentration camp begin.

MARCH 27: Amsterdam population registry is attacked and set on fire.

APRIL: All Jews are to leave the provinces and be accommodated at Vught.

APRIL 23: Provincial Netherlands declared free of Jews.

MAY 5: Wilhelm Harster gives the orders for the final phase of Jewish deportations.

MAY 15: Jews in mixed marriages offered choice of deportation or sterilization.

MAY 21: Joodse Raad instructed to select seven thousand of its "exempt" staff for deportation.

MAY 26: Mass raid in Amsterdam to capture remaining Jews.

JUNE 20: Further mass raids in south and east Amsterdam.

JULY 15: Hans Rauter gives instructions for raids in the countryside.

SEPTEMBER 29: Last major raid in Amsterdam. Joodse Raad is wound up.

OCTOBER 5: Reich Commissioner Arthur Seyss-Inquart gives instructions for the treatment of the legally remaining Jews in the Netherlands.

DECEMBER: Those in mixed marriages are called up for service in work camps.

1944

MAY 16: Raids against Gypsies and "asocials."

SEPTEMBER 5, DOLLE DINSDAG (MAD TUESDAY): NSB leader Anton Mussert orders the evacuation of Dutch National Socialists from the west and center of the country to the east.

SEPTEMBER 5–6: Two large transports of inmates from Vught concentration camp are shipped eastward to Germany.

SEPTEMBER 17: Operation Market Garden, the Allied airborne landings around Nijmegen and Arnhem, begins. The Dutch government denounces the anti-Jewish laws and classifies German Jews as stateless people of German origin.

1945

MAY 5: Official liberation of the entire Netherlands.

appendix B　Dramatis Personae

Anton Ahlers: Youngest son of Tonny Ahlers.

Tonny (Anton Christiaan) Ahlers: NSB and NSNAP member and informant for Kurt Döring who entered Otto Frank's life in 1941 and was arrested in 1945 for betraying people to the SD, among other charges.

Casper (Cas) Ahlers: Younger brother of Tonny Ahlers.

Martha Ahlers: Wife of Tonny Ahlers.

Kermit Bloomgarden: Producer of the Hacketts' 1955 stage adaptation of the diary.

Janny Brilleslijper: Together with her sister Lin, she became acquainted with the Franks in Westerbork and was with Anne and Margot shortly before their deaths.

Lientje (Lin) Brilleslijper-Jaldati: In the summer of 1945, she informed Otto that his children were dead.

Werner Cahn: Otto's friend in Amsterdam who tried to find a publisher for the diary in 1945.

Ab Cauvern: Otto's friend who helped revise the diary manuscript; his passing it on to Jan Romein led to the diary's publication in 1947.

Isa Cauvern: Wife of Ab and Otto's secretary before the war. Typed up the manuscript of the diary in 1945.

Cheryl Crawford: Theater producer who showed first interest in bringing the diary to the U.S. stage.

Julius Dettman: Recipient of the telephone call regarding the hidden Jews at 263 Prinsengracht. He killed himself in 1945.

334   Kurt Döring: Tonny Ahlers's boss at SD headquarters and his neighbor (20 Jan van Eyckstraat) from 1943 to 1944.

Anton Dunselman: Amsterdam lawyer who was appointed supervisory director of Otto's company in January 1935. He remained a close friend of Otto's after the war.

Bernhard (Buddy) Elias: Otto's nephew and now president of the Anne Frank–Fonds in Basel.

Erich Elias: Brother-in-law of Otto, married to Leni, and father of Stephan and Buddy. Helped Otto set up the Opekta business in Amsterdam in 1933.

Helene (Leni) Elias (née Frank): Otto's younger sister. Married to Erich Elias and mother of Stephan and Buddy.

Stephan Elias: Otto's nephew who died unexpectedly five days after Otto's death in 1980.

Barbara Epstein (née Zimmerman): The diary's U.S. editor and Otto's close friend to whom he often turned for advice in business matters connected to the diary.

Alice Frank (née Stern): Otto's mother.

Anne Frank: Otto's youngest daughter, who kept the diary that later formed such a large part of Otto's life. Died in Bergen-Belsen at age fifteen.

Charlotte (Lottie) Frank (née Witt): Otto's sister-in-law, married to his brother Robert.

Edith Frank (née Holländer): Otto's first wife and mother of his two daughters. Died in Auschwitz in 1945.

Elfriede (Fritzi) Frank (née Markovits): Otto's second wife, also a survivor of Auschwitz with her daughter, Eva. She lost her first husband, Erich Geiringer, and son, Heinz Felix, in the Holocaust. Fritzi died in 1998.

Herbert (Bitz) Frank: Otto's younger brother.

Jean-Michel Frank: Otto's Parisian cousin and a celebrated furniture designer. Committed suicide in 1941.

Margot Betti (Mutz) Frank: Otto's eldest daughter. Died in Bergen-Belsen at age nineteen.

Michael Frank: Otto's father.

Robert Frank: Otto's older brother.

Jetteke Frijda: Margot's best friend, she remained in contact with Otto after the war and still lives in Amsterdam today.

Jan Gies: Husband of Miep, close friend and "helper" to the Franks during their years in hiding.

Hermine (Miep) Gies-Santrouschitz: First employed as a secretary in the Opekta business in 1933, she became one of Otto's most trusted friends and was one of the Franks' "helpers" during the years in hiding.

HILDE GOLDBERG (NÉE JACOBSTHAL): Friend of Margot Frank and neighbor of the Franks' in Amsterdam's River Quarter. She saw Otto often after the war and her emigration to the United States.

EDITH GORDON (NÉE OPPENHEIMER): Granddaughter of Otto's mother's cousin. Her grandparents and parents saw the Franks often in Frankfurt.

GABI GOSLAR: Younger sister of Hanneli Goslar.

HANNELI PICK-GOSLAR: Anne's best friend in Amsterdam since 1933. Otto helped Hanneli and Gabi to emigrate to Switzerland after the war. She and Otto remained close, and she lives in Israel today.

HANS GOSLAR: Father of Hanneli and close friend of Otto's. Died in Bergen-Belsen in 1945.

RUTH GOSLAR: Mother of Hanneli.

GEZINUS GRINGHUIS: Employed by the Zentralstelle, where he worked alongside Tonny Ahlers's closest friend; he was present at the Frank family's arrest on August 4, 1944.

WILLEM GROOTENDORST: Employed by the Zentralstelle and present at the Frank family's arrest on August 4, 1944.

FRANCES (NÉE GOODRICH) AND ALBERT HACKETT: Writers of the stage and film adaptations of the diary.

LAMMERT HARTOG: Husband of Lena and assistant warehouseman at 263 Prinsengracht. Heard from Wilhelm van Maaren that there were Jews in hiding in the building where they worked.

LENA VAN BLADEREN-HARTOG: Wife of one of the warehouse workers at 263 Prinsengracht, she mentioned to another woman, Anna Genot, that she had heard there were people hiding on the premises.

LILLIAN HELLMAN: Writer to whom Frances Goodrich and Albert Hackett turned for advice about their adaptation of the diary.

HENDRIK VAN HOEVE: Resistance worker and supplier of groceries to the Franks during the period in hiding. Betrayed for hiding a Jewish couple in his home in 1944, he survived four concentration camps.

JULIUS HOLLÄNDER: Otto's brother-in-law, the eldest brother of Edith. Emigrated to the United States with his brother Walter.

ROSA HOLLÄNDER (NÉE STERN): Otto's mother-in-law, who lived with the family in Amsterdam from 1939 until her death in January 1942.

WALTER HOLLÄNDER: Otto's brother-in-law, Edith's brother, who was briefly imprisoned in a concentration camp before escaping to the United States.

GUSTI HUBER: Actress rumored to have Nazi associations who played Edith Frank in both the play and film versions of the diary.

JETJE BREMER-JANSEN: Former sales representative for Opekta and wife of Joseph Jansen.

336   JOSEPH JANSEN: Member of the NSB and former casual employee of Otto's who tried to betray him to the SS in 1941.

GARSON KANIN: Play director whose considerable input omitted almost all references to the fact that the people in hiding were Jews.

JOHANNES KLEIMAN: Otto's friend since 1923, employee, and "helper" during the Franks' two years in hiding.

VICTOR GUSTAV KUGLER: Employed by Otto in 1933 as his right-hand man in the Opekta business, and a "helper" during the Franks' two years in hiding.

MAARTEN KUIPER: Employed by the SD to hunt down Jews, he was present at the Frank family's arrest on August 4, 1944.

WILLI LAGES: Wartime head of the Amsterdam Bureau of the Commander of the Security Police and Security Service.

MEYER LEVIN: Jewish newspaper correspondent and writer who hoped to dramatize the diary for the stage, but who was rejected in favor of the Hacketts. Levin pursued a legal battle with Otto for many years.

ROSE DE LIEMA: Wife of Sal, she met the Frank family in Westerbork and has written an account of her experiences.

SAL DE LIEMA: One of Otto's Dutch comrades in Westerbork and Auschwitz, he retained contact with "Papa Frank" after the liberation. Lives in the United States with his wife, Rose.

WILHELM VAN MAAREN: Warehouseman at 263 Prinsengracht from the spring of 1943 until his dismissal in 1945. He was the main suspect in the betrayal investigations, but nothing could be proved against him.

JACQUELINE VAN MAARSEN: Anne's best friend from 1941 until the Franks went into hiding, she stayed in contact with Otto after the war and wrote a book about her friendship with Anne.

JOSEPH MARKS: Doubleday vice president who was Otto's friend and who first suggested opening the secret annex as a museum.

MYER MERMIN: Otto's lawyer during his legal battles with Meyer Levin.

BARBARA MOOYART-DOUBLEDAY: Original translator of the English-language version of the diary.

GERTRUD NAUMANN-TRENZ: Neighbor of the Franks' in Frankfurt who often baby-sat for Margot and Anne. Remained close to Otto after the war and still lives in Frankfurt.

FATHER JOHN NEIMAN: Began writing to Otto in the early 1970s and became a confidant for Otto, Fritzi, and Miep.

LAUREEN NUSSBAUM (NÉE KLEIN): Margot Frank's friend, and a neighbor of the Franks' in the River Quarter, she stayed in contact with Otto after the war and her emigration to the United States with her husband, Rudi. She has written extensively about the diary.

AUGUSTE (GUSTI) VAN PELS (NÉE RÖTTGEN): Wife of Hermann van Pels.
Died in 1945.

HERMANN VAN PELS: Employed by Pectacon since 1938, he hid in the secret annex alongside the Franks and Fritz Pfeffer with his wife, Gusti, and son, Peter. Died in Auschwitz in 1944.

PETER VAN PELS: Son of Hermann and Gusti. Brought Otto food regularly in Auschwitz until he was forced to participate in a death march. Died in Mauthausen in 1945.

MILLIE PERKINS: Portrayed Anne in the George Stevens film of the diary.

FRITZ PFEFFER: Dentist friend of the Franks' who hid with them in the secret annex. Died in Neuengamme in 1944.

MARTHA CHARLOTTE (LOTTE) PFEFFER (NÉE KALETTA): Wife of Fritz Pfeffer, she had their marriage posthumously recognized after the war. Otto's close friend until the 1950s, when the unfair portrayal of her husband in the dramatic adaptations of the diary led her to break off their friendship.

JOSEF VAN POPPEL: Spy for the Abwehr who employed Ahlers as an agent until Ahlers tried to betray him to the SS.

FRANK PRICE: Head of Doubleday's Paris office, he read the diary in its French translation and eventually recommended it to Doubleday in the United States.

JAN ROMEIN: Author of the first article about the then-unpublished diary, in *Het Parool* in 1946.

HERMAN ROUWENDAAL: Abwehr spy who rented a room from Tonny Ahlers on Jan van Eyckstraat from 1943 to 1944.

EMIL RÜHL: SD official and Tonny Ahlers's neighbor (20 Jan van Eyckstraat) from 1943 to 1944.

LEAH SALISBURY: The Hacketts' agent.

JUDITH SALOMON (NÉE DE WINTER): Met the Franks in Westerbork and remained in contact with Otto after the war.

JOSEPH SCHILDKRAUT: Portrayed Otto onstage in 1955 and in the 1959 George Stevens film.

EVA SCHLOSS (NÉE GEIRINGER): The daughter of Otto's second wife, Fritzi.

ZVI SCHLOSS: Husband of Eva.

ANNELIESE SCHÜTZ: Otto's friend who helped him translate the diary from Dutch into German in 1945.

SS OBERSCHARFÜHRER KARL JOSEF SILBERBAUER: Led the arrest of the Frank family on August 4, 1944. He was traced by the Nazi hunter Simon Wiesenthal in 1963.

RABBI DAVID SOETENDORP: A close friend of Otto's, his parents were also in hiding in the Netherlands during the war, together with his brother.

338 FRANZI SPRONZ: Wife of Joseph, and Fritzi Frank's best friend.

JOSEPH SPRONZ: Husband of Franzi, he met Otto in Auschwitz. He and Franzi were with Otto on the day he died.

MILLY STANFIELD: Otto's cousin who lived in London and became his confidante.

GEORGE STEVENS: Director of the 1959 film *The Diary of Anne Frank*.

LOTHAR STIELAU: Teacher in Germany who charged that the diary was a forgery. Otto fought him in the courts and won his case.

SUSAN STRASBERG: Portrayed Anne in the 1955 stageplay to critical acclaim.

NATHAN STRAUS JR. (FORMERLY CHARLES WEBSTER STRAUS): Otto's closest friend since college in 1908, he offered Otto a job at his father's department store, Macy's, in New York.

COR SUIJK: Former finance director of the Anne Frank Stichting who sold five pages from Anne's diary to the Dutch government in order to fund his own Holocaust educational work.

TERESKA TORRES: Wife of Meyer Levin.

FRIEDRICH CHRISTIAN VIEBAHN: SD official and Tonny Ahlers's neighbor (20 Jan van Eyckstraat) from 1943 to 1944.

BEP VAN WIJK-VOSKUIJL: Employee of Otto's since 1937 and a "helper" of the Frank family during the years in hiding.

JOHAN VOSKUIJL: Father of Bep, he worked for Otto until his illness prevented him from continuing his job. He died in December 1945.

SIMON WIESENTHAL: Nazi hunter who located Silberbauer in the 1960s.

CARA WILSON: American girl who began corresponding with Otto and Fritzi in the 1960s and became a friend, visiting them in the 1970s. Some of their letters have been published.

ROOTJE DE WINTER: Wife of Manuel and mother of Judith (Salomon), she met the Franks in Westerbork and was present at Edith's death in Auschwitz.

KAREL WOLTERS: Lawyer and prosecutor in Amsterdam who oversaw the liquidation of Otto Frank's company Pectacon in 1941. Lived opposite Tonny Ahlers at 31 Jan van Eyckstraat.

appendix C GLOSSARY

ABWEHR: Wehrmacht counterintelligence organization.

ANNE FRANK–FONDS (AFF): Named as Otto Frank's heir in Otto's will. The organization, led by Otto's nephew Buddy Elias, controls the copyright to the diaries and all of Anne's writings and distributes all royalties from those works to various worthy causes.

ARMEE OBERKOMMANDO: German Army High Command in Berlin, headed by Adolf Hitler.

BUREAU NATIONALE VEILIGHEID (BNV): Netherlands Bureau of National Security, based in Scheveningen.

CENTRAAL ARCHIEF BIJZONDERE RECHTSPLEGING (CABR): Located in the Rijksarchief (National Dutch Archive) in The Hague. This is where all the records of those who were suspected of having been (or known to have been) involved in Nazi organizations, or suspected of betraying Jews or committing any crimes specific to the Second World War in Holland are kept.

DEUTSCHE REVISIONS-UND TREUHAND AG: German Audit and Trust Company.

ECONOMISCH FRONT: Economic Front, affiliated with the Nazi Party.

EXPOSITUR: Department of the Jewish Council responsible for liaison with the German authorities. Headed by Dr. Edwin Sluzker, the staff of the Expositur also determined who was eligible for exemption from deportation.

GRÜNE POLIZEI: The German Ordnungspolizei derived their name (Green Police) from the color of their uniforms.

340 HOLLANDSE SCHOUWBURG: Also known as the Joodsche Schouwburg, this former theater was used as a collection point for Jews awaiting deportation to Westerbork, the first stop on the journey to the concentration camps of the east.

JOODSE RAAD VOOR AMSTERDAM: The Jewish Council of Amsterdam, established in February 1941 and headed by Abraham Asscher and David Cohen, functioned as the liaison with the German authorities and passed on the discriminatory decrees to the Jewish community.

NATIONAAL-SOCIALISTISCHE BEWEGING (NSB): The Dutch National Socialist Party, or the Dutch Nazi Party, led by Anton Mussert.

NATIONAAL SOCIALISTISCHE NEDERLANDSE ARBEIDERS PARTIJ (NSDAP): Dutch National Socialist Workers' Party. An even more fanatical branch of the Nazi Party in Holland, known for its violence against Jews and other "political enemies." The group was dedicated to mirroring the ideology and everyday workings of the NSDAP in Nazi Germany.

NEDERLANDS BEHEERS INSTITUUT (NBI): Dutch authority in charge of the administration of "enemy property," the property of NSB party members, and the property of deported Dutch citizens who had not returned.

NEDERLANDS INSTITUUT VOOR OORLOGSDOCUMENTATIE (NIOD, formerly RIOD): Netherlands Institute for War Documentation.

NEDERLANDSCH-DUITSCHE KULTUURGEMEENSCHAP: Dutch-German Cultural Union, affiliated with the Nazi Party.

POLITIEKE OPSPORINGS DIENST (POD): Political-Criminal Investigations Department of the Dutch police.

POLITIEKE RECHERCHE AFDELING (PRA): Political Investigation Branch of the Dutch police.

RECHTSFRONT: Legal Front, affiliated with the Nazi Party.

REFERAT IVB4: Headed by Adolf Eichmann in Berlin, this department of the Gestapo was responsible for the deportation of European Jews to the annihilation camps. In the Netherlands, the office was based in The Hague and run by Willi Zöpf.

REICHSSICHERHEITSHAUPTAMT (RSHA): Reich Security Main Office, controlling intelligence, security, and criminal police work.

SCHUTZSTAFFEL (SS): The NSDAP's security organization, under the command of Heinrich Himmler.

SICHERHEITSDIENST (SD): The Security and Intelligence Service of the German SS.

SICHERHEITSPOLIZEI (Sipo): The German security police.

WEERAFDELING (WA): Defense section (unarmed) of the Dutch National Socialist movement.

WEHRMACHT: German armed forces.

WIRTSCHAFTSPRÜFSTELLE (BEI): German Bureau of Economic Investigation in
the Netherlands.

ZENTRALSTELLE FÜR JÜDISCHE AUSWANDERUNG: The Central Agency for Jewish
Emigration. Run by the German Sipo and SD in Amsterdam, the agency
was charged with the administration of Jewish deportations from the
Netherlands.

NOTES

preface

1. Anton Ahlers, telephone conversation with the author, March 2002.
2. Otto Frank, letter, August 21, 1945 (BE).
3. A. C. Ahlers, letter, December 20, 1966 (photocopy in the possession of the author).
4. All material included in Doc. I., K. J. Silberbauer (NIOD).
5. Dossier A. C. Ahlers (CABR).
6. That journalist was Sander van Walsum, who allowed me to accompany him to meet Cas Ahlers, for which I am grateful.
7. Cas Ahlers, author interview, March 2002.
8. Anton Ahlers, author interview, April 2002.
9. Ibid.

prologue

1. In his letter to the BNV, Otto recalled seeing these letters. Otto Frank, letter, August 21, 1945 (BE).
2. The events and conversations here are based on the following documents: dossier(s) A. C. Ahlers (CABR); A. C. Ahlers, letter, December 20, 1966 (photocopy in the possession of the author); A. C. Ahlers, letter, December 27, 1963, Doc. I., K. J. Silberbauer (NIOD); A. C. Ahlers, letter, January 15, 1964, Doc. I., K. J. Silberbauer (NIOD); Otto Frank, letter, November 27, 1945; dossier J. M. Jansen (CABR); Ernst Schnabel, *The Footsteps of Anne Frank* (London: Pan Books, 1976). It should be noted

344   that there are a number of discrepancies in the different versions, mainly
        owing to lapses in time, memory, and perspective.

3. Paul Gies, e-mail to the author following a conversation with his mother,
   Miep Gies, April 2002. The description of how Ahlers reached Otto's office is taken from this e-mail.

4. The layout of the building has now been slightly changed to accommodate
   the needs of a museum whose visitors number around 800,000 per year.

5. Conversation as detailed by Otto Frank, letter, August 21, 1945 (BE).

6. Except as noted, the account of this encounter is taken from Schnabel, *The
   Footsteps of Anne Frank*, p. 59.

7. Otto Frank, letter, August 21, 1945 (BE).

8. Ibid.

9. Ibid.

10. Miep Gies, declaration in dossier J. M. Jansen (CABR).

11. Otto Frank, letter, August 21, 1945 (BE).

12. Ibid.

13. A. C. Ahlers, Sociaal Dienst (Social Services) files, Gemeente Archief,
    Amsterdam.

14. Dossier A. C. Ahlers (CABR).

15. Otto Frank, letter, August 21, 1945 (BE).

one

1. Otto Frank, letter, February 18, 1916 (BE).

2. Otto Frank, interview transcripts of recorded discussion with Arthur
   Unger, New York, 1977 (AFS).

3. Details of Otto's background and life in Frankfurt can be found in the
   following documents and books: Landau town archives; the pamphlets
   Some Historical Facts About the House and *Facts Relating to the Jews of
   Landau*, available from the Frank-Loeb'sches House; Hermann Arnold,
   "Waren es Vorfahren von Anne Frank?" *Tribüne*, 1990; Dr. Jürgen Steen,
   Esther Alexander-Ihme, Johannes Heil, and Liane Schack, *Früher wohn-
   ten wir in Frankfurt . . .* (Frankfurt: Historisches Museum Frankfurt am
   Main, 1985); "Originally from Frankfurt-am-Main," in David Barnouw
   and Gerrold van der Stroom, eds., *The Diary of Anne Frank: The Critical
   Edition* (London: Viking, 1989) (hereafter referred to as *Diary*); Dr.
   Jürgen Steen and Wolf von Wolzogen, *Anne aus Frankfurt: Leben und
   Lebenswelt Anne Franks* (Frankfurt: Historisches Museum Frankfurt am
   Main, 1996).

4. The street is now called Dantestrasse, and the house, along with several
   other beautiful buildings, has been destroyed. A building affiliated to
   Frankfurt University stands on the site.

5. Edith Gordon (née Oppenheimer), e-mail to author, June 2001.

6. Milly Stanfield, letter, March 29, 1994 (AFS).

7. Otto Frank, undated letter to a former classmate (AFS).

8. Otto Frank, Unger interview, 1977 (AFS).

9. Edith Gordon, e-mail to author, June 2001.

10. Otto Frank, undated letter, in Melissa Muller, *Anne Frank: The Biography* (New York: Henry Holt, 1998), p. 20.

11. *Diary*, May 8, 1944 (a), p. 636. Unless otherwise stated, all quotes from Anne Frank's diary are taken from *The Critical Edition* edited by Barnouw and van der Stroom.

12. Otto Frank, undated letter, in Muller, *Anne Frank*, p. 20. As his daughter Anne would do one day, Otto collected postcards sent to him by relatives from around the world, and after the success of Anne's published diary, travel to exotic locations became his one occasional extravagance.

13. Information about the Straus family from Joan Adler, "Wholedamfam," the Straus family newsletter, February 1998; and Joan Adler, e-mail to author, December 1997.

14. Nathan (Charles Webster) Straus, letter, April 19, 1957 (AFS).

15. Ibid.

16. Otto Frank, letter, September 1909 (BE).

17. Buddy Elias thinks Michael Frank probably died of a heart attack.

18. *Diary*, February 8, 1944 (a), pp. 525–27.

19. *Diary*, December 24, 1943 (a), p. 434.

20. *Diary*, December 24, 1943 (c), p. 434.

21. Milly Stanfield, letter, March 29, 1994 (AFS).

22. Edith Gordon, e-mail to author, June 2001.

23. Jean Schick Grossman, "The Story Within Her Story" (unpublished manuscript), December 5, 1954 (AFS).

24. *Diary*, May 11, 1944 (a), p. 647.

25. Ibid.

26. Otto Frank, letter, December 19, 1909 (BE).

27. Information from Stephen Birmingham, *Our Crowd: The Great Jewish Families of New York* (New York: Dell Publishing, 1967).

28. Information about the Straus family from Adler, "Wholedamfam," and Adler, e-mail to author, December 1997.

29. Milly Stanfield, unpublished memoirs, p. 7 (AFS).

30. Milly Stanfield, letter, November 27, 1995 (AFS).

31. Milly Stanfield, letter, March 29, 1994 (AFS).

32. Milly Stanfield, unpublished memoirs, p. 7 (AFS).

33. Otto Frank, letter, February 2, 1975 (AFS).

34. Milly Stanfield, unpublished memoirs, p. 14 (AFS).

35. Leopold Diego Sanchez, *Jean-Michel Frank* (Paris: Editions de Regard, 1980), p. 50.

36. Milly Stanfield, unpublished memoirs, p. 15 (AFS).

37. Ibid., pp. 15, 16.

38. Daniel Jonah Goldhagen, *Hitler's Willing Executioners: Ordinary Germans and the Holocaust* (London: Abacus, 1999), pp. 81–82.

39. Milly Stanfield, unpublished memoirs, p. 28 (AFS).

40. Otto Frank, letter, August 7, 1915 (BE).

41. Sanchez, *Jean-Michel Frank*, p. 50.

42. Otto Frank, letter, February 13, 1916 (BE).

43. Otto Frank, letter, February 18, 1916 (BE).

44. Otto Frank, Unger interview, 1977 (AFS).

45. Otto Frank, letter, December 24, 1916 (BE).

46. See, for instance, the account of the Battle of the Somme in Brian Moynahan, *The British Century: A Photographic History of the Last Hundred Years* (London: Random House, 1997).

47. Otto Frank, in Ernst Schnabel, *The Footsteps of Anne Frank* (London: Pan Books, 1976), p. 16.

48. Otto Frank, letter, May 19, 1917 (BE).

49. Menno Metselaar, Ruud van der Rol, Dineke Stam, and Hansje Galesloot, eds., *Anne Frank House: A Museum with a Story* (Amsterdam: Anne Frank Stichting, 1999), p. 14.

50. Otto Frank, letter, August 31, 1917 (BE).

51. Otto Frank, letter, June 21, 1917 (BE).

52. Ibid.

53. Otto Frank, letter, June 27, 1918 (BE).

54. Milly Stanfield, letter, March 29, 1994 (AFS).

55. Milly Stanfield, unpublished memoirs, p. 28 (AFS).

56. Ibid.

57. Ibid. See also the account given in Dick van Galen Last and Rolf Wolfswinkel, *Anne Frank and After: Dutch Holocaust Literature in Historical Perspective* (Amsterdam: Amsterdam University Press, 1996), p. 30.

58. Martin Gilbert, *The Holocaust: The Jewish Tragedy* (London: HarperCollins, 1987), p. 23.

59. *Diary*, p. 1.

60. Milly Stanfield, letter, March 29, 1994 (AFS).

61. Milly Stanfield, unpublished memoirs, p. 28 (AFS).

62. Quoted in Goldhagen, *Hitler's Willing Executioners*, pp. 82, 84.

63. The information about Otto's business ventures is taken largely from *Diary*, ch. 1, and from private Frank family letters.

64. Schnabel, *The Footsteps of Anne Frank*, p. 65.

65. *Diary*, pp. 2, 3.

66. Otto Frank, letter, June 27, 1918 (BE).

67. Katja Olszewska, author interview, March 2001.

68. *Diary*, February 8, 1944 (a), pp. 525–27.

69. These pages are fully discussed in chapter 13.

70. Dr. Trude K. Holländer, letter to author, March 25, 1997.

71. Otto Frank, Unger interview 1977 (AFS).

72. The information about Edith Holländer's background and early years is taken mainly from family correspondence, publications of the Anne Frank Stichting, the Holländer family tree, and Muller, *Anne Frank*.

73. *Diary*, May 8, 1944 (a), p. 636.

74. Dr. Trude K. Holländer, letter to author, March 25, 1997.

75. These are now in the archives of the Anne Frank Stichting, donated by the Elias family.

76. *Diary*, February 8, 1944 (a), pp. 525–27.

77. Otto Frank, letter, June 27, 1918 (BE).

78. Otto Frank, letter, May 19, 1917 (BE).

79. *Diary*, May 8, 1944 (a), p. 636.

30. Otto Frank, letter, May 12, 1939, *Anne Frank Magazine 1999* (Amsterdam: Anne Frank Stichting, 1999), pp. 54–55.

two

1. The book is kept in the offices of the Anne Frank–Fonds, Basel, Switzerland.

2. Margot Frank's Baby Book. Courtesy Anne Frank–Fonds.

3. Anne Frank's Baby Book. Courtesy Anne Frank–Fonds.

4. Ibid.

5. Otto gave an extensive interview about early family life to a friend of his, Jean Schick Grossman. See Jean Schick Grossman, "The Story Within Her Story" (unpublished manuscript), December 5, 1954 (AFS).

6. Ibid., p. 12.

7. Ibid.

8. Carl Fussman, "The Woman Who Would Have Saved Anne Frank," *Newsday*, March 16, 1995.

9. Ernst Schnabel, *The Footsteps of Anne Frank* (London: Pan Books, 1976), p. 24.

10. Melissa Muller, *Anne Frank: The Biography* (New York: Henry Holt, 1998), p. 29.

11. Otto Frank, letter, April 2, 1932 (BE).

12. Leopold Diego Sanchez, *Jean-Michel Frank* (Paris: Editions de Regard, 1980), p. 7.

13. Ibid.

14. Otto Frank, letter, June 13, 1932 (BE).

15. Ibid.

16. Otto Frank, letter, June 14, 1932 (BE).

17. David Barnouw and Gerrold van der Stroom, eds., *The Diary of Anne Frank: The Critical Edition* (London: Viking, 1989), p. 4.

18. Mirjam Pressler, *The Story of Anne Frank* (London: Macmillan, 1999), p. 40.

19. Schnabel, *The Footsteps of Anne Frank*, pp. 24–25; and Anna G. Steenmeijer and Otto Frank, *A Tribute to Anne Frank* (New York: Doubleday, 1971), p. 13.

20. Menno Metselaar, Ruud van der Rol, Dineke Stam, and Hansje Galesloot, eds., *Anne Frank House: A Museum with a Story* (Amsterdam: Anne Frank Stichting, 1999), p. 16.

21. Transcript of a tape recording Otto Frank made for an American school group in the 1970s (AFS).

22. Edith Gordon, e-mail to author, June 2001.

23. It would have been logical, surely, for Otto to have contacted the Strauses and emigrated with his family to the United States after finding work with them, but there is no record of whether or not he ever considered such a move.

24. R. Peter Straus, interview with Otto Frank, *Moment*, December 1977.

25. *Diary*, p. 4.

26. Schnabel, *The Footsteps of Anne Frank*, p. 24.

27. Otto Frank, letter, June 19, 1968, in Cara Wilson, *Love, Otto: The Legacy of Anne Frank* (Kansas City, Mo.: Andrews McMeel, 1995), p. 50.

28. Grossman, "The Story Within Her Story."

29. Otto Frank, letter, November 16, 1933, in Muller, *Anne Frank*, pp. 44–45.

30. Elma Verhey, "Anne Frank's World," in Alex Grobman, ed., *Anne Frank in Historical Perspective: A Teaching Guide* (Los Angeles: Martyrs Memorial and Museum of the Holocaust, 1995), p. 18.

31. Edith Frank, letter, December 5, 1935, in Muller, *Anne Frank*, p. 49.

32. Ibid., p. 47.

33. Edith Frank, letter, undated, in *Anne Frank Magazine 1999* (Amsterdam: Anne Frank Stichting, 1999), p. 54.

34. Miep retained contact with her birth family nonetheless.

35. Miep Gies and Alison Leslie Gold, *Anne Frank Remembered* (New York: Bantam, 1987), pp. 13, 15.

36. *Diary*, p. 8.

37. Hilde Goldberg, author interviews, May and June 2001.

38. Laureen Nussbaum, author interviews, May 2001.

39. Ibid.

40. Verhey, "Anne Frank's World," p. 18.

41. Gies and Gold, *Anne Frank Remembered*, p. 22.

42. Hilde Goldberg, author interviews, May and June 2001.

43. Edith Frank, letter, undated, in Muller, *Anne Frank*, pp. 48–49.

44. Verhey, "Anne Frank's World," p. 17.

45. Hilde Goldberg, author interviews, May and June 2001.

46. Edith Frank, letter, undated (BE).

47. Otto Frank, letter, April 9, 1934, in *Diary*, p. 8.

48. Otto Frank, postcard, 1934, from the exhibition "Anne Aus Frankfurt" at the Anne Frank Youth Center, Frankfurt, March 1998.

49. Edith Frank, postcard, 1934, in Muller, *Anne Frank*, p. 66.

50. Edith Frank, letter, 1934 (BE).

51. Information on the Jansen family from dossier J. M. Jansen (CABR), and Otto Frank, letter, August 21, 1945 (BE).

52. Dossier J. M. Jansen (CABR).

three

1. Otto Frank, interviews in *Journal: The Living Legacy of Anne Frank*, September 1967; R. Peter Straus, *Moment*, December 1977; and E. C. Farrell, "Postscript to a Diary," *Global Magazine*, March 6, 1965.

2. Hanneli Pick-Goslar, author interview, June 2001.

3. Stephan Elias, postcard (1), September 1936 (BE).

4. Stephan Elias, postcard (2), September 1936 (BE).

5. Edith Frank, letter, October 1936, in Melissa Muller, *Anne Frank: The Biography* (New York: Henry Holt, 1998), p. 74.

6. Edith Frank, letter, 1936, in Ernst Schnabel, *The Footsteps of Anne Frank* (London: Pan Books, 1976), p. 26.

7. Wolf von Wolzogen, *Anne aus Frankfurt* (Frankfurt: Historical Museum, 1994), p. 102.

8. Edith Frank, letter, 1937, from the exhibition "Anne Aus Frankfurt," at the Anne Frank Youth Center, Frankfurt, March 1998.

9. Report of a conversation with Bep van Wijk-Voskuijl, February 25, 1981 (NIOD).

10. Schnabel, *The Footsteps of Anne Frank*, p. 89.

11. Miep Gies and Alison Leslie Gold, *Anne Frank Remembered* (New York: Bantam, 1987), p. 21.

12. Edith Frank, letter, December 24, 1937, in Muller, *Anne Frank*, p. 91.

13. Edith Frank, letter, December 22, 1937, in Muller, *Anne Frank*, p. 76.

14. Gies and Gold, *Anne Frank Remembered*, p. 27.

15. Julianne Duke, "Anne Frank Remembered," *New York Times*, June 11, 1989.

16. Menno Metselaar, Ruud van der Rol, Dineke Stam, and Hansje Galesloot, eds., *Anne Frank House: A Museum with a Story* (Amsterdam: Anne Frank Stichting, 1999), p. 35.

17. Gies and Gold, *Anne Frank Remembered*, p. 28.

18. Edith Frank, letter, December 22, 1937 (BE).

19. Otto Frank, interview transcripts of recorded discussion with Arthur Unger, New York, 1977 (AFS).

20. Hilde Goldberg, author interviews, May and June 2001.

21. Record of a conversation with Mrs. H. G. Teske-Baschwitz, January 12, 1981 (NIOD); and interview transcripts for the Jon Blair documentary *Anne Frank Remembered* (1995; private collection of Jon Blair).

22. Otto Frank, letter, December 1938 (BE).

23. Dienke Hondius, "The Return," unpublished English translation of *Terugkeer: Antisemitisme in Nederland rond de bevrijding* (The Hague: SDU, 1990). There are no page numbers in this edition.

24. Dossier A. C. Ahlers (CABR).

25. The information on Ahlers's youth is taken from dossier A. C. Ahlers (CABR); A. C. Ahlers, Sociaal Dienst files, Gemeente Archief, Amsterdam; and Cas Ahlers, author interview, March 2002. Because of his lameness, Ahlers was later exempt from forced labor in Germany.

26. Cas Ahlers, author interview, March 2002.

27. Dossier A. C. Ahlers (CABR).

28. A. C. Ahlers, Sociaal Dienst files, Gemeente Archief, Amsterdam.

29. Dossier A. C. Ahlers (CABR).

30. Jean Schick Grossman, "The Story Within Her Story" (unpublished manuscript), December 5, 1954, p. 12.

31. Ibid., pp. 12–13.

32. *Diary*, September 28, 1942 (a), p. 191.

33. Ibid.

34. Otto Frank, Unger interview, 1977.

35. Grossman, "The Story Within Her Story," pp. 10–15.

36. Edith Frank, letter, July 1939, in Muller, *Anne Frank*, p. 92.

37. Quoted in Hondius, "The Return."

38. Milly Stanfield, interview, Carl Fussman, "The Woman Who Would Have Saved Anne Frank," *Newsday*, March 16, 1995.

39. Gies and Gold, *Anne Frank Remembered*, p. 40.

40. Dossier A. C. Ahlers (CABR). Ahlers had in the meantime worked as a hairdresser's assistant again, and then from December 1939 to May 16, 1940, he worked for the KNSM (Koninklijke Nederlandse Stoomboot Maatschappij—the Royal Dutch Steamboat Society), followed, very briefly, by one more stint as a hairdresser's assistant.

41. Dossier A. C. Ahlers (CABR).

42. Emil Rühl, declaration, May 3, 1946, Doc. I, K. J. Silberbauer (NIOD).

43. Dossier A. C. Ahlers (CABR).

44. Schnabel, *The Footsteps of Anne Frank*, p. 50.

45. Milly Stanfield, unpublished memoirs, p. 74 (AFS).

46. Transcript of a tape recording Otto Frank made for an American school group in the 1970s (AFS).

47. Schnabel, *The Footsteps of Anne Frank*, pp. 51–52.

48. Laureen Nussbaum, author interviews, May 2001.

49. Leopold Diego Sanchez, *Jean-Michel Frank* (Paris: Editions de Regard, 1980), p. 64.

50. Ibid., p. 9.

51. *Volk en Vaderland*, February 1941 (NIOD).

52. By coincidence, Ahlers is standing on the steps of the building next door to 400 Singel, where Otto had had his business premises only two months before.

53. The German Ordnungspolizei derived their name (Green Police) from the color of their uniforms.

54. Dossier A. C. Ahlers (CABR).

55. Cas Ahlers, author interview, March 2002.

56. Ibid.

57. Dossier A. C. Ahlers (CABR).

four

1. David Barnouw and Gerrold van der Stroom, eds., *The Diary of Anne Frank: The Critical Edition* (London: Viking, 1989), May 7, 1944 (a), p. 635.

2. Otto Frank, letter, August 21, 1945 (BE).

3. Ernst Schnabel, *The Footsteps of Anne Frank* (London: Pan Books, 1976), p. 59.

4. Otto Frank, letter, August 21, 1945 (BE); Schnabel, *The Footsteps of Anne Frank*, p. 59.

5. Otto Frank, letter, August 21, 1945 (BE).

6. Ibid.

7. Ibid.

8. Schnabel, *The Footsteps of Anne Frank*, p. 59.

9. Otto Frank, letter, August 21, 1945 (BE).

10. Ibid.

11. Ibid.

12. Dossier A. C. Ahlers (CABR). Ahlers sometimes sold the confiscated radios to a shop on the Vijzelstraat, where he received more money for them than he did from the SD. The shop, Aurora, is still there.

13. Otto Frank, letter, August 21, 1945 (BE).

14. Dossier A. C. Ahlers (CABR).

15. Otto Frank, letter, August 21, 1945 (BE); Schnabel, *The Footsteps of Anne Frank*, p. 59.

16. A. C. Ahlers, letter, December 20, 1966 (photocopy in the possession of the author).

17. Pectacon sales ledger, 1940 (AFS).

18. Conversations with Jan A. Gies and Miep Gies-Santrouschitz, February 19 and 27, 1985 (NIOD).

19. Gerlof Langerijs, e-mail to the author, May 2002.

20. Otto did not admit this to the Dutch police until 1964, and never publicly. Report on A. C. Ahlers, February 5, 1964, Doc. I., K. J. Silberbauer (NIOD).

21. W. G. van Maaren, letter, February 2, 1948, Doc. I., W. G. van Maaren (NIOD).

22. Otto Frank, 1947 agenda (AFS).

23. A. C. Ahlers, letter, December 20, 1966 (photocopy in the possession of the author).

24. A. C. Ahlers, Sociaal Dienst files, Gemeente Archief, Amsterdam.

25. Dossier A. C. Ahlers (CABR).

26. Anton Ahlers, author interview, July 2002.

27. Martha's mother had also been pregnant when she married Martha's father. Anton Ahlers, author interview, July 2002.

28. Ibid.

29. Martha Ahlers, author interview, February 2001.

30. Anton Ahlers, author interview, March 2002.

31. Cas Ahlers, author interview, March 2002.

32. Gerlof Langerijs, e-mail to the author, May 2002.

33. Dossier A. C. Ahlers (CABR).

34. *Diary*, p. 11.

35. Otto Frank, letter, October 18, 1955 (AFS).

36. Dossier J. M. Jansen (CABR).

37. Ibid.

38. Ibid.

39. Ibid.

40. Presumably, Jansen did not check to see what became of Otto after he wrote the letter about him; there also seems no reason to assume that he knew Ahlers had managed to get hold of the letter and use it, in his own way, against Otto.

41. Dienke Hondius, "A New Perspective on Helpers of Jews During the Holocaust: The Case of Miep and Jan Gies," in Alex Grobman, ed., *Anne*

Frank in Historical Perspective: A Teaching Guide (Los Angeles: Martyrs Memorial and Museum of the Holocaust, 1995), p. 38.

42. Otto Frank, letter, June 10, 1971 (BE).

43. Hondius, "A New Perspective on Helpers of Jews During the Holocaust," p. 39.

44. Victor Kugler, newspaper cuttings collection (AFS).

45. Otto Frank, letter, June 10, 1971 (BE).

46. A. C. Ahlers, letter, December 27, 1963, Doc. I., K. J. Silberbauer (NIOD); A. C. Ahlers, letter, January 15, 1964, Doc. I., K. J. Silberbauer (NIOD).

47. Hondius, "A New Perspective on Helpers of Jews During the Holocaust," p. 38.

48. Miep Gies and Alison Leslie Gold, *Anne Frank Remembered* (New York: Bantam, 1987), p. 160.

49. Anne Frank, letter, July 1941 (BE).

50. Otto Frank, memoir (BE).

51. Jean Schick Grossman, "The Story Within Her Story" (unpublished manuscript), December 5, 1954, p. 15 (AFS).

52. Otto Frank, newspaper cuttings collection (AFS).

53. Jacqueline van Maarsen, *My Friend Anne Frank* (New York: Vantage Press, 1996), p. 21.

54. Otto Frank, postcard, September 14, 1941 (BE).

55. *Diary*, p. 13.

56. Doc. I., K. O. M. Wolters (NIOD).

57. Ibid.

58. Ibid. In August 1941, Jewish-owned finances were placed under the supervision of the bankers Lippmann-Rosenthal & Co., puppets of the Nazi government. The bank was used by the Nazis as a well for dipping into when they came up with new schemes that needed financing.

59. *Diary*, p. 13.

60. Wolters enlisted in the Waffen SS in February 1943 and was deployed on September 30, 1944, to the Eastern Front, attached to the legal staff. Toward the end of the war, he was wounded and returned to the Netherlands. In 1945, he was imprisoned in Scheveningen. On June 16, 1948, he was sentenced to eight years in prison and forbidden to hold office or serve in the military for the remainder of his life.

61. A. C. Ahlers, letter, December 20, 1966 (photocopy in the possession of the author).

62. Gies and Gold, *Anne Frank Remembered*, pp. 59–60.

63. Ibid., p. 59.

64. Schnabel, *The Footsteps of Anne Frank*, pp. 57–58.

65. *Diary*, June 20, 1942 (a), p. 183.

66. Alice Frank, letter, April 12, 1942 (BE).

67. Otto Frank, letter, June 2, 1942 (BE).

68. *Diary*, July 5, 1942 (b), p. 204.

69. Daniel Jonah Goldhagen, *Hitler's Willing Executioners: Ordinary Germans and the Holocaust* (London: Abacus, 1999), pp. 170–71.

70. Dick van Galen Last and Rolf Wolfswinkel, *Anne Frank and After: Dutch Holocaust Literature in Historical Perspective* (Amsterdam: Amsterdam University Press, 1996), p. 76.

71. Ibid., pp. 68–69.

72. Jacob Presser,

73. Honduis, "The Return," English translation of *Terugkeer: Antisemitisme in Nederland rond de bevrijding* (The Hague: SDU, 1990) (no page numbers in this edition).

74. Otto Frank, letter, July 4, 1942 (1) (BE).

75. Otto Frank, letter, July 4, 1942 (2) (BE).

five

1. Laureen Nussbaum, author interview, May 2001.

2. Ernst Schnabel, *The Footsteps of Anne Frank* (London: Pan Books, 1976), p. 67.

3. Otto Frank, letter, July 5, 1942 (BE).

4. Quoted in Reinhard Rürup, *Topography of Terror: Gestapo, SS, and Reichssicherheitshauptamt on the "Prinz-Albrecht-Terrain": A Documentation* (Berlin: Verlag Willmuth Arenhövel, 1989), pp. 152–53.

5. Otto Frank, letter, June 10, 1971 (BE).

6. Dienke Hondius, "A New Perspective on Helpers of Jews During the Holocaust: The Case of Miep and Jan Gies," in Alex Grobman, ed., *Anne Frank in Historical Perspective: A Teaching Guide* (Los Angeles: Martyrs Memorial and Museum of the Holocaust, 1995), p. 39.

7. Otto Frank, memoir (BE).

8. Johannes Kleiman, in Menno Metselaar, Ruud van der Rol, Dineke Stam, and Hansje Galesloot, eds., *Anne Frank House: A Museum with a Story* (Amsterdam: Anne Frank Stichting, 2000), p. 82.

9. Victor Kugler, ibid., p. 73.

10. Willy Voskuijl, ibid., p. 106.

11. Bep van Wijk-Voskuijl, ibid., p. 85.

12. Dienke Honduis, "The Return," English translation of *Terugkeer: Antisemitisme in Nederland rond de bevrijding* (The Hague: SDU, 1990) (no page numbers in this edition).

13. Miep Gies, in Hondius, "A New Perspective on Helpers of Jews During the Holocaust," pp. 41–42.

14. Ibid., p. 40.

15. Ibid., p. 41.

16. David Barnouw and Gerrold van der Stroom, eds., *The Diary of Anne Frank: The Critical Edition* (London: Viking, 1989), October 20, 1942 (a), p. 286.

17. *Diary*, p. 15.

18. *Diary*, October 9, 1942 (b), footnote, p. 273.

19. Otto Frank, memoir (BE).

20. Ibid.

21. Ibid.

22. Gerlof Langerijs, e-mail to the author, May 2002.

23. Another explanation, of course, could be that Ahlers simply hoped to deflect attention from himself as a suspect. A. C. Ahlers, letter, December 27, 1963, Doc. I., K. J. Silberbauer (NIOD); A. C. Ahlers, letter, January 15, 1964, Doc. I., K. J. Silberbauer (NIOD).

24. A. C. Ahlers, Sociaal Dienst files, Gemeente Archief, Amsterdam.

25. Dossier A. C. Ahlers (CABR).

26. Ibid.

27. Ibid.

28. Ibid.

29. Ibid.

30. Ibid.

31. The three men had adjacent rooms at the SD headquarters on the Euterpestraat, where their reputation for being among the most feared men of the Grüne Polizei arose from the vicious interrogations they conducted in the cellars. All three were later accused and convicted of multiple crimes committed during the war, including several counts of murder.

32. Dossier A. C. Ahlers (CABR); Dossier H. Rouwendaal (CABR); Dossier Maarten Kuiper (CABR).

33. "Maarten Kuiper: The Criminal of the Euterpestraat," *Elseviers Weekblad*, November 29, 1947.

34. Ibid.

35. Dossier A. C. Ahlers (CABR).

36. Ibid.

37. Otto Frank, memoir (BE).

38. Ibid.

39. Jean Schick Grossman, "The Story Within Her Story" (unpublished manuscript), December 5, 1954, p. 7 (AFS).

40. Miep Gies and Alison Leslie Gold, *Anne Frank Remembered* (New York: Bantam, 1987), p. 88.

41. Ibid., p. 78.

42. *Diary*, October 17, 1943 (b), p. 407.

356   43. Undated page of testimony written by Miep Gies (AFS).

44. *Diary*, June 20, 1942 (b), p. 182.

45. Otto Frank, memoir (BE).

46. *Diary*, July 8, 1942 (b), pp. 206, 226.

47. Grossman, "The Story Within Her Story," p. 17.

48. *Diary*, March 18, 1944 (a), p. 545.

49. *Diary*, January 30, 1944 (a), p. 474.

50. Otto Frank, memoir (BE).

51. *Diary*, July 15, 1944 (a), p. 689.

52. *Diary*, January 19, 1944 (a), p. 459.

53. *Diary*, March 7, 1944 (a), p. 515.

54. *Diary*, March 7, 1944 (a), p. 518.

55. Father John Neiman, author interview, April 2001.

56. Grossman, "The Story Within Her Story," p. 20.

57. *Diary*, March 20, 1944 (a), pp. 550–51, 554.

58. Otto Frank, memoir (BE).

59. *Diary*, October 3, 1942 (a), pp. 266–67.

60. Grossman, "The Story Within Her Story," pp. 13–14.

61. *Diary*, February 8, 1944 (a), pp. 525–26.

62. *Diary*, March 10, 1943 (b), p. 340.

63. *Diary*, September 28, 1942 (a), p. 227.

64. *Diary*, September 27, 1942 (a), pp. 249–50.

65. *Diary*, "Tales," August 6, 1943, p. 397.

66. *Diary*, February 8, 1944 (a), pp. 525–26.

67. Mirjam Pressler, *The Story of Anne Frank* (London: Macmillan, 1999), p. 76.

68. Gies and Gold, *Anne Frank Remembered*, pp. 103, 130.

69. Otto Frank, poem, January 16, 1943 (BE). The poem has been translated from German; in the original language it was written in rhyme.

six

1. David Barnouw and Gerrold van der Stroom, eds., *The Diary of Anne Frank: The Critical Edition* (London: Viking, 1989), April 11, 1944 (a), p. 598.

2. Ibid.

3. Doc. I., G. Gringhuis (NIOD).

4. Johannes Kleiman, letter, 1945, Doc. I., W. G. van Maaren (NIOD).

5. Although van Maaren's wife was a patient of Bangert's she only began consulting him after the arrest.

6. Melissa Muller, *Anne Frank: The Biography* (New York: Henry Holt, 1998), p. 229.

7. Cor Suijk, author interview, April 2001.

8. Muller, *Anne Frank*, p. 12.

9. Ibid., p. 284.

10. Harry Paape, quoted in "The Arrest," in *Diary*, p. 26.

11. Bevolkingsregister, Amsterdam. Lammert Hartog died on March 6, 1959. Lena outlived him by only four years; she died on June 10, 1963.

12. Father John Neiman, author interview, April 2001.

13. Doc. I., K. J. Silberbauer (NIOD). One of Ans van Dijk's circle of friends was the woman who betrayed Otto's second wife, Fritzi Geiringer, and her family.

14. Rouwendaal was sentenced to life imprisonment and died July 15, 1964, in Gossel. His wife survived but divorced her husband after the war.

15. Dossier A. C. Ahlers (CABR).

16. Declaration by Abraham Kaper, in dossier Pieter Schaap (CABR).

17. Ibid.

18. "Maarten Kuiper: The Criminal of the Euterpestraat," *Elseviers Weekblad*, November 29, 1947.

19. Dossier A. C. Ahlers (CABR).

20. Address card for Jan van Eyckstraat, Gemeente Archief, Amsterdam.

21. In interviews given after the war, Silberbauer spoke of between six and eight men accompanying him that day, and Miep Gies also stated that there were around six NSBers. Otherwise, the number most commonly given—by Otto, Kugler, and Kleiman—was three or four.

22. Johannes Kleiman, letter, July 16, 1947, in dossier W. G. van Maaren (CABR).

23. Victor Kugler, letter, May 2, 1958 (AFS). Kuiper was executed in 1948.

24. Willi Lages, statement in Doc. I., K. J. Silberbauer (NIOD).

25. Dossiers Maarten Kuiper and A. C. Ahlers (CABR).

26. Reinhard Rürup, *Topography of Terror: Gestapo, SS, and Reichssicherheits-hauptamt on the "Prinz-Albrecht-Terrain": A Documentation* (Berlin: Verlag Willmuth Arenhövel, 1989), p. 153.

27. Ibid., pp. 153–54.

28. Bob Moore, *Victims and Survivors: The Nazi Persecution of the Jews in the Netherlands 1940–1945* (London: Arnold, 1997), pp. 210–11.

29. Doc. I., K. J. Silberbauer (NIOD).

30. Ibid.

31. Cas Ahlers, author interview, March 2002.

32. Otto Frank, French television interview, 1960s. Buddy Elias has a copy of the interview on video, but I have been unable to find further details of this broadcast.

33. Ibid.

34. Menno Metselaar, Ruud van der Rol, Dineke Stam, and Hansje

Galesloot, eds., *Anne Frank House: A Museum with a Story* (Amsterdam: Anne Frank Stichting, 2000), p. 185.

35. Ibid., p. 185.

36. Otto Frank, in Ernst Schnabel, *The Footsteps of Anne Frank* (London: Pan Books, 1976), p. 110.

37. Eva Schloss, author interview, April 2001.

38. Johannes Kleiman, in Schnabel, *The Footsteps of Anne Frank*, pp. 115–17.

39. Victor Kugler, in Eda Shapiro, "The Reminiscences of Victor Kugler, the 'Mr. Kraler' of Anne Frank's Diary," *Yad Vashem Studies* XIII (Jerusalem: Yad Vashem, 1979), p. 360.

40. Janny Brandes-Brilleslijper, in Willy Lindwer, *The Last Seven Months of Anne Frank* (New York: Pantheon, 1991), p. 52.

41. Brilleslijper was their maiden name. To avoid confusion, I have used that name throughout.

42. Janny Brandes-Brilleslijper, in Lindwer, *The Last Seven Months of Anne Frank*, p. 52.

43. Janny Brandes-Brilleslijper, in the Jon Blair documentary *Anne Frank Remembered* (1995).

44. Otto Frank, in Schnabel, *The Footsteps of Anne Frank*, p. 117.

45. Descripton of Westerbork in Jacob Presser, *Ashes in the Wind: The Destruction of Dutch Jewry* (London: Souvenir Press, 1968), p. 432.

46. Vera Cohn, "The Anti-Defamation League Bulletin: The Day I Met Anne Frank," undated.

47. Judith Salomon (née de Winter), author interview, May 2001.

48. Rootje de Winter, in Dick Schaap, "Freedom After Auschwitz: I Knew Anne Frank," newspaper cuttings collection (AFS).

49. Rachel van Amerongen-Frankfoorder, in Lindwer, *The Last Seven Months of Anne Frank*, pp. 92–93.

50. Ibid., p. 144.

51. Ibid., p. 176.

52. Lientje Brilleslijper-Jaldati, "Memories of Anne Frank," in press leaflet for the film *Ein Tagebuch für Anne Frank* (Berlin: VEB Progress Film-Vertrieb, 1959).

53. Rootje de Winter, in Schnabel, *The Footsteps of Anne Frank*, pp. 127–28.

54. Judith Salomon, author interview, May 2001.

55. Sal de Liema, transcript of interview conducted by the Anne Frank Stichting (AFS).

56. Rose de Liema, "So You Will Remember," unpublished memoir, p. 27 (AFS).

57. Otto Frank, transcript of tape recording made for an American school group, 1970s (AFS).

58. One other train left Westerbork, bound for Sobibor.

59. Janny Brandes-Brilleslijper, in Lindwer, *The Last Seven Months of Anne Frank*, p. 54.

60. Primo Levi, in Myriam Anissimov, *Primo Levi: Tragedy of an Optimist* (New York: Overlook Press, 2000), pp. 96–97.

61. Brilleslijper-Jaldati, "Memories of Anne Frank."

62. Rootje de Winter, in Schnabel, *The Footsteps of Anne Frank*, p. 129.

63. Otto Frank, memoir (BE).

64. Primo Levi, in Martin Gilbert, *Holocaust Journey: Traveling in Search of the Past* (London: Orion, 1997), p. 136.

65. De Liema, "So You Will Remember," p. 27.

seven

1. Otto Friedrich, *The Kingdom of Auschwitz* (London: Penguin, 1994), p. 100.

2. Ibid., p. 14.

3. Quoted ibid., p. 32.

4. Quoted in Myriam Anissimov, *Primo Levi: Tragedy of an Optimist* (New York: Overlook Press, 2000), p. 145.

5. Friedrich, *The Kingdom of Auschwitz*, pp. 71–72.

6. Martin Gilbert, *Auschwitz and the Allies* (London: Michael Joseph, 1981), p. 341.

7. Milly Stanfield, letter, undated (AFS).

8. Judith Salomon (née de Winter), author interview, May 2001.

9. Otto Frank, undated letter (AFS).

10. Friedrich, *The Kingdom of Auschwitz*, p. 43.

11. Anissimov, *Primo Levi*, p. 132.

12. Dick van Galen Last and Rolf Wolfswinkel, *Anne Frank and After: Dutch Holocaust Literature in Historical Perspective* (Amsterdam: Amsterdam University Press, 1996), p. 104.

13. Anissimov, *Primo Levi*, p. 121.

14. Ibid.

15. Otto Frank, undated letter (AFS).

16. Otto Frank, in "Anne Frank's Vater: Ich will Versohnung," *Welt am Sonntag*, February 4, 1979.

17. Sal de Liema, transcript of interview conducted by the Anne Frank Stichting (AFS).

18. Sal de Liema, in the Jon Blair documentary *Anne Frank Remembered* (1995).

19. Tzvetan Todorov, *Facing the Extreme: Moral Life in the Concentration Camps* (London: Phoenix, 2000), p. 100.

20. De Liema, in Blair, *Anne Frank Remembered*.

21. Otto Frank, undated letter (AFS).

22. Joseph Spronz, "Auschwitz Memoirs" (unpublished manuscript), p. 21 (AFS).

23. Ibid., pp. 24–25.

24. Interview with Fritzi Frank, conducted by Dienke Hondius for the Anne Frank Stichting (AFS).

25. Dienke Hondius, the interviewer, told this story to Fritzi, after having heard it from Miep. Fritzi knew nothing about it.

26. Otto Frank, undated letter (AFS).

27. Otto Frank, in Blair, *Anne Frank Remembered*.

28. Declaration of Dr. S. M. Kropveld in dossier Westerbork–Auschwitz, September 3, 1944 (NIOD).

29. Otto Frank, interview transcripts of recorded discussion with Arthur Unger, New York, 1977 (AFS).

30. Franzi Spronz, author interview, May 2001.

31. Spronz, "Auschwitz Memoirs," pp. 26–27.

32. Otto Frank, letter, July 27, 1945 (AFS).

33. Spronz, "Auschwitz Memoirs," p. 31.

34. Martin Gilbert, *The Holocaust: The Jewish Tragedy* (London: HarperCollins, 1986), p. 771.

35. Otto Frank, undated letter (AFS).

36. Ibid.

37. Spronz, "Auschwitz Memoirs," p. 32.

38. Otto Frank, Unger interview, 1977.

39. Otto Frank, in Jean Schick Grossman, "The Story Within Her Story" (unpublished manuscript), December 5, 1954, p. 22 (AFS). Peter was sent to Mauthausen.

40. Friedrich, *The Kingdom of Auschwitz*, pp. 87–88.

41. Gilbert, *Auschwitz and the Allies*, p. 335.

42. Anissimov, *Primo Levi*, p. 198.

43. Friedrich, *The Kingdom of Auschwitz*, p. 93.

44. Otto Frank, Unger interview, 1977.

45. Spronz, "Auschwitz Memoirs," pp. 36–37.

46. Friedrich, *The Kingdom of Auschwitz*, p. 97.

47. Otto Frank, Unger interview, 1977.

48. None of the inmates had heard what the officer had been told: that the Red Army was encircling the area and had just liberated Libiąż, less than ten miles northeast of Auschwitz. Otto gave a full account of the terrifying incident in his interview with Arthur Unger and mentioned it in a letter to his mother. However, he always dated the incident wrongly; it occurred on January 25, not the twenty-sixth, as Otto remembered.

49. Franzi Spronz, author interview, May 2001.

50. Otto Frank, "Anne Frank Would Have Been Fifty This Year," *Life*, March 1979.

51. Bernard Wasserstein, *Vanishing Diaspora: The Jews in Europe Since 1945* (London: Penguin, 1996), p. 1.

52. Primo Levi, *If This Is a Man: The Truce* (London: Abacus Books, 1979), p. 194.

53. Anissimov, *Primo Levi*, p. 211.

54. Eva Schloss and Evelyn Julia Kent, *Eva's Story: A Survivor's Tale by the Stepsister of Anne Frank* (London: W. H. Allen, 1988), p. 165.

55. Ibid., p. 173.

56. Ibid., pp. 165, 173.

57. I am especially grateful to Yt Stoker for informing me about the diary, which is kept in the archives of the Anne Frank Stichting.

58. Otto Frank, Liberation Notebook, 1945 (AFS).

59. Otto Frank, letter, February 23, 1945 (BE).

60. Otto Frank, undated letter (BE).

61. Schloss and Kent, *Eva's Story*, p. 174.

eight

1. Otto Frank, Liberation Notebook, 1945 (AFS).

2. Otto Frank, letter, March 15, 1945 (BE).

3. Otto Frank, postcard, March 15, 1945 (BE).

4. Otto Frank, letter, March 18, 1945 (1) (AFS).

5. Otto Frank, letter, March 18, 1945 (2) (BE).

6. Otto Frank, Liberation Notebook, 1945 (AFS).

7. *Anne Frank Magazine 1999* (Amsterdam: Anne Frank Stichting, 1999), p. 55. An American newspaper reported Edith's death quite differently: "A German guard sought to attack Anne's sister Margot. Their mother came to Margot's assistance and, in the struggle, she struck the guard and was immediately dragged away. Her daughters never saw her again." It would appear Rootje told the truth.

8. Ernst Schnabel, *The Footsteps of Anne Frank* (London: Pan Books, 1976), p. 133.

9. Otto Frank, Liberation Notebook, 1945 (AFS).

10. Otto Frank, letter, March 28, 1945 (BE).

11. Otto Frank, letter, March 31, 1945 (BE).

12. Otto Frank, Liberation Notebook, 1945 (AFS).

13. Eva Schloss and Evelyn Julia Kent, *Eva's Story: A Survivor's Tale by the Stepsister of Anne Frank* (London: W. H. Allen, 1988), pp. 196–97.

14. Otto Frank, Liberation Notebook, 1945 (AFS).

362   15. Ibid.

16. Ibid.

17. Ibid.

18. Ibid.

19. Ibid.

20. Otto Frank, letter, May 25, 1945 (BE).

21. Otto Frank, Liberation Notebook, 1945 (AFS).

22. Otto Frank, telegram, May 27, 1945 (BE).

23. Otto Frank, Liberation Notebook, 1945 (AFS).

24. Ibid.

25. For information on Jews returning to the Netherlands, I have relied mainly on Dienke Hondius, "The Return," English translation of *Terugkeer: Antisemitisme in Nederland rond de bevrijding* (The Hague: SDU, 1990) (no page numbers in this edition).

26. Otto Frank, letter, June 21, 1945 (BE).

27. Laureen Nussbaum, author interview, May 2001.

28. Hondius, "The Return."

29. Jack Furth, author interview, April 2001.

30. Otto Frank, letter, July 7, 1945 (BE).

31. Hondius, "The Return."

32. Judith Salomon (née de Winter), author interview, May 2001.

33. Otto Frank, "Anne Frank Would Have Been Fifty This Year," *Life*, March 1979.

34. Miep Gies and Alison Leslie Gold, *Anne Frank Remembered* (New York: Bantam, 1987), p. 184.

35. Otto Frank, agenda, June 4, 1945.

36. Dienke Hondius, "A New Perspective on Helpers of Jews During the Holocaust: The Case of Miep and Jan Gies," in Alex Grobman, ed., *Anne Frank in Historical Perspective: A Teaching Guide* (Los Angeles: Martyrs Memorial and Museum of the Holocaust, 1995), p. 40.

37. Stephan van Hoeve, author interview, May 2001. He does not know where Otto was able to obtain the fruit.

38. Otto Frank, letter, June 21, 1945 (BE).

39. Otto Frank, letter, June 8, 1945 (BE).

40. Otto Frank, agenda, June 10, 1945 (AFS).

41. Otto Frank, agenda, June 12, 1945 (AFS).

42. Robert Frank, letter, June 12, 1945 (AFS).

43. Jacqueline van Maarsen, *My Friend Anne Frank* (New York: Vantage Press, 1996), pp. 51–52.

44. Laureen Nussbaum, author interview, May 2001.

45. Otto Frank, letter, June 21, 1945 (BE).

46. Alice Frank, letter, June 19, 1945 (BE).

47. Otto Frank, June 21, 1945 (BE).

48. Fritzi Frank, in Schloss and Kent, *Eva's Story*, p. 221.

49. Julius Holländer, letter, June 30, 1945 (BE).

50. Otto Frank, letter, July 7, 1945 (BE).

51. Julius Holländer, letter, July 10, 1945 (BE).

52. Lin Jaldati, "Bergen Belsen," in Hyman A. Enzer and Sandra Solotaroff-Enzer, eds., *Anne Frank: Reflections on Her Life and Legacy* (Carbondale: University of Illinois Press, 2000), p. 53.

53. Ibid.

54. Janny Brilleslijper, in Willy Lindwer, *The Last Seven Months of Anne Frank* (New York: Pantheon, 1991), pp. 73–74.

55. Otto Frank, agenda, July 18, 1945 (AFS).

56. Otto Frank, agenda, July 20, 1945 (AFS).

nine

1. This was Anton Ahlers, whom the author interviewed.

2. Cas Ahlers, author interview, March 2002.

3. Otto Frank, agenda, July 23, 1945 (AFS).

4. Anton Ahlers, author interview, July 2002.

5. Ibid.

6. Otto Frank, letter, July 24, 1945 (BE).

7. Otto Frank, letter, August 21, 1945 (BE).

8. Otto Frank, agenda, August 27 and 30, 1945 (AFS).

9. Letter in dossier A. C. Ahlers (CABR).

10. Otto Frank, letter, November 27, 1945, dossier A. C. Ahlers (CABR).

11. Anton Ahlers, author interview, March 2002.

12. Martha Ahlers, conversation with the author, February 2001; Cas Ahlers, author interview, March 2002; Anton Ahlers, author interview, March 2002.

13. Gerard Oeverhaus, letter, February 17, 1946, dossier Opekta, NBI 134994, Rijksinstituut, The Hague.

14. A. C. Ahlers, letter, December 1945, dossier A. C. Ahlers (CABR).

15. A. C. Ahlers, letter, December 20, 1966 (photocopy in the possession of the author); A. C. Ahlers, letter, December 27, 1963, Doc. I., K. J. Silberbauer (NIOD); A. C. Ahlers, letter, January 15, 1964, Doc. I., K. J. Silberbauer (NIOD).

16. Gerlof Langerijs, e-mail to the author, May 2002.

17. A. C. Ahlers, Sociaal Dienst files, Gemeente Archief, Amsterdam.

18. Ibid.

19. Otto Frank, memoir (BE). There is another version of how Otto discov-

ered that his daughters were dead. Miep recalls that Otto received a letter giving him the news, but since the letter is dated November 11, and Otto clearly knew by the end of August that his daughters were dead, this seems unlikely. There may, of course, be an earlier letter to that effect, but I have relied upon the version given in Willy Lindwer's *The Last Seven Months of Anne Frank* and upon Otto's own diary.

20. Otto Frank, letter, July 24, 1945 (AFS).

21. Otto Frank, letter, July 26, 1945 (AFS).

22. Otto Frank, letter, July 27, 1945 (AFS).

23. Quoted in Milly Stanfield, "A Talk: Anne and Otto Frank," April 22, 1990 (AFS).

24. Julius Holländer, letter, July 25, 1945 (BE).

25. Robert Frank, letter, August 1, 1945 (BE).

26. Frank-Elias family, telegram, August 6, 1945 (AFS).

27. Report of a conversation with Miep and Jan Gies, February 18, 1981 (NIOD).

28. Otto Frank, letter, August 22, 1945 (BE).

29. See the relevant individual Netherlands Red Cross dossiers in the archives of NIOD.

30. Otto Frank, memoir (BE).

31. Hanneli Pick-Goslar, author interview, June 2001.

32. Ibid.

33. Jacqueline van Maarsen, *My Friend Anne Frank* (New York: Vantage Press, 1996), pp. 52–53.

34. Otto Frank, letter, August 20, 1945 (BE).

35. Otto Frank, letter, August 1945 (BE).

36. Otto Frank, letter, August 25, 1945 (BE).

37. Otto Frank, letter, August 26, 1945 (AFS).

38. Otto Frank, letter, September 1, 1945 (BE).

39. Otto Frank, letter, September 6, 1945 (BE).

40. Betty-Ann Wagner, "Anne Frank Letter to Iowa Pen-pal to Be Sold," *New York Times*, July 22, 1988.

41. Otto Frank, letter, September 14, 1945 (BE).

42. Otto Frank, letter, September 26, 1945 (BE).

43. Otto Frank, letter, September 20, 1945 (BE).

44. Otto Frank, letter, September 24, 1945 (BE).

45. Otto Frank, letter, October 25, 1945 (BE).

46. Otto Frank, letter, November 14, 1945 (BE).

47. Otto Frank, letter, September 30, 1945 (BE).

48. Otto Frank, letter, September 26, 1945 (BE).

49. Ibid.

50. Otto Frank, letter, September 30, 1945 (BE).

51. Miep Gies and Alison Leslie Gold, *Anne Frank Remembered* (New York: Bantam, 1987), p. 191.

52. Otto Frank, memoir (BE).

53. Gerrit Bolkestein, broadcast on Radio Oranje, March 28, 1944.

54. Otto Frank, letter, November 16, 1945 (AFS).

55. Record of a conversation with Mrs. H. G. Teske-Baschwitz, January 12, 1981 (NIOD).

56. Otto Frank, letter, November 11, 1945 (AFS).

57. "The Diaries, 'Het Achterhuis,' and the Translations," in David Barnouw and Gerrold van der Stroom, eds., *The Diary of Anne Frank: The Critical Edition* (London: Viking, 1989), p. 63.

58. Report of a conversation with Ab Cauvern, January 23, 1981 (NIOD).

59. Otto Frank, letter, December 12, 1945 (NIOD).

60. Jacqueline van Maarsen, author interview, February 1998.

61. Eva Schloss, author interviews, January and May 1998.

62. Rabbi David Soetendorp, author interview, June 2001.

63. Kurt Baschwitz, letter, February 10, 1946, quoted in *Diary*, p. 64.

64. Otto Frank, letter, December 15, 1945 (BE).

65. A. C. Ahlers, letter, December 24, 1945, dossier A. C. Ahlers (CABR). Presumably Ahlers means his "saving" of Otto Frank was even more commendable because there was no personal connection between them. It is curious how, at this point, both Otto and Ahlers seemed at pains to assert that there was no further contact between them. Dossier A. C. Ahlers (CABR).

66. Dossier A. C. Ahlers (CABR).

67. Ibid.

68. Ibid.; A. C. Ahlers, Sociaal Dienst files, Gemeente Archief, Amsterdam.

69. A. C. Ahlers, letter, December 24, 1945, dossier A. C. Ahlers (CABR).

70. Quoted in Ernst Schnabel, *The Footsteps of Anne Frank* (London: Pan Books, 1976), p. 59.

71. Otto Frank, letter, January 25, 1946 (BE).

72. Buddy Elias, letter, February 2, 1946 (BE).

73. Otto Frank, letter, March 16, 1946 (BE).

74. Report of a conversation with Werner Cahn, March 12, 1981 (NIOD).

75. Jan Romein, "A Child's Voice," *Het Parool*, April 3, 1946.

76. *Diary*, p. 68.

77. Ibid., p. 69.

78. Otto Frank, letter, June 19, 1951 (AFS).

79. Report of a conversation with Rabbi I. Hammelburg, February 23, 1981 (NIOD).

366   80. Report of a conversation with Annie Romein-Verschoor, undated (NIOD).

81. Otto Frank, memoir (BE).

82. Van Maarsen, *My Friend Anne Frank*, p. 56.

83. Otto Frank, letter, January 9, 1947 (BE).

84. Otto Frank, letter, June 13, 1947 (AFS).

ten

1. "Imprisonment and Deportation," in David Barnouw and Gerrold van der Stroom, eds., *The Diary of Anne Frank: The Critical Edition* (London: Viking, 1989), p. 56.

2. Gerard Oeverhaus, letter, February 17, 1946, dossier Opekta, NBI 134994, Rijksinstituut, The Hague.

3. *Diary*, p. 56.

4. Miep Gies and Alison Leslie Gold, *Anne Frank Remembered* (New York: Bantam, 1987), p. 195.

5. Otto Frank, letter, June 13, 1947 (AFS).

6. Gies and Gold, *Anne Frank Remembered*, p. 193.

7. Otto Frank, letter, January 6, 1947 (Gertrud Trenz).

8. Otto Frank, letter, January 9, 1947 (BE).

9. Otto Frank, undated letter (AFS).

10. Presumably, Otto means that Anne herself rewrote her diary and omitted certain passages. Otto Frank, interview transcripts of recorded discussion with Arthur Unger, New York, 1977 (AFS).

11. Otto Frank, interview transcript, Westinghouse Broadcasting Co., February 16, 1960 (AFS).

12. *Diary*, March 29, 1944 (a), p. 578.

13. *Diary*, May 11, 1944 (a), p. 647.

14. This introduction has never been published. Anne Frank, diary, June 20, 1942.

15. Laureen Nussbaum's article "Anne's Diary Incomplete" in *Anne Frank Magazine 2000* discusses this entry in particular; she was the first to point out that Otto actually reinstated much of the material Anne herself had deleted.

16. Interview reprinted in "Most Parents Don't Really Know Their Children," *Anne Frank Magazine 1998*, p. 35.

17. Otto Frank, "Introduction," *Het Achterhuis* (Amsterdam: Contact, 1947).

18. "The Diaries, 'Het Achterhuis,' and the Translations," in *Diary*, p. 71.

19. Ibid.

20. Otto Frank, letter, June 1947 (AFS).

21. Laureen Nussbaum, author interview, May 2001.

22. Otto Frank, letter, October 14, 1947 (BE).

23. Milly Stanfield, "A Talk: Anne and Otto Frank," April 22, 1990 (AFS).

24. Van Maaren had been edged out of the business after the liberation.

25. Otto Frank, letter, December 11, 1945 (BE).

26. G. Gringhuis, statement in Doc. I., K. J. Silberbauer (NIOD).

27. Doc. I., K. J. Silberbauer (NIOD).

28. G. Gringhuis, statement in Doc. I., K. J. Silberbauer (NIOD). Gringhuis was sentenced to death but never executed.

29. Victor Kugler, letter, May 2, 1958 (BE). Kugler incorrectly remembered Kuiper's surname, but it is clear from his description, and from Kleiman's letter, that it was Maarten Kuiper to whom he referred. There was no NSB man executed for those crimes under the name Kugler recalled—it is clearly Kuiper whom he means. Kugler also incorrectly remembered Bep's married name—and the name of van Maaren's warehouse assistant.

30. "Maarten Kuiper: The Criminal of the Euterpestraat," in *Elseviers Weekblad*, November 29, 1947. Almost all Dutch war criminals and collaborators received light sentences; few were actually sentenced to death or to long years in jail—and those who were frequently had their sentences considerably shortened. Only thirty-six were executed, "among them not only German Nazis and Dutch collaborators, but also the Jewish woman Ans van Dijk, found guilty of betraying more than 100 Jews."

31. Johannes Kleiman, statement in dossier W. G. van Maaren (CABR).

32. W. G. van Maaren, statement in dossier W. G. van Maaren (CABR). Van Maaren suffered for the rest of his life under the suspicion that he had betrayed Anne Frank. He found it difficult to obtain work and eventually set up his own laundry company. He died in 1971.

33. Lammert Hartog, statement in dossier W. G. van Maaren (CABR).

34. W. G. van Maaren, statement in dossier W. G. van Maaren (CABR).

35. Dossier J. M. Jansen (CABR).

36. Otto Frank, letter, August 21, 1945 (BE).

37. Jetje Bremer, statement in dossier J. M. Jansen (CABR).

38. Ibid.

39. Joseph Jansen, statement in dossier J. M. Jansen (CABR).

40. Dr. Ploegsma, statement in dossier J. M. Jansen (CABR).

41. Miep Gies, statement in dossier J. M. Jansen (CABR).

42. Martha filed for divorce in 1948 but did not follow through with it.

43. Dossier A. C. Ahlers (CABR); A. C. Ahlers, Sociaal Dienst files, Gemeente Archief, Amsterdam.

44. Dossier W. G. van Maaren (CABR).

45. Dossier A. C. Ahlers (CABR); A. C. Ahlers, Sociaal Dienst files, Gemeente Archief, Amsterdam.

368   46. Lawrence Graver, *An Obsession with Anne Frank: Meyer Levin and the Diary* (Berkeley: University of California Press, 1995), p. 21.

47. Ibid., pp. 8–9, 14–15.

48. Ralph Melnick, *The Stolen Legacy of Anne Frank: Meyer Levin, Lillian Hellman, and the Staging of the Diary* (New Haven, CT: Yale University Press, 1997), p. 2.

49. Otto Frank, letter, September 25, 1950 (AFS).

50. Otto Frank, "Postscript to a Diary," *Global Magazine*, 1965.

51. "The Diaries, 'Het Achterhuis,' and the Translations," in David Barnouw and Gerrold van der Stroom, eds., *The Diary of Anne Frank: The Critical Edition* (London: Viking, 1989), p. 72.

52. Ibid.

53. Ibid.

54. Cynthia Ozick, "Who Owns Anne Frank?" *The New Yorker*, October 6, 1997.

55. *Diary*, p. 72.

56. Ibid., p. 73.

57. Ibid.

58. Otto Frank, undated letter (AFS).

59. Robert S. Wistrich, *Anti-Semitism: The Longest Hatred* (London: Methuen, 1991), p. 79.

60. Otto Frank, letter, December 14, 1952 (AFS).

61. Otto Frank, letter, November 18, 1950 (AFS).

62. Otto Frank, letter, November 21, 1950 (AFS).

63. Nathan Straus, letter, April 19, 1957 (AFS).

64. Janet Flanner, "Letter from Paris," *The New Yorker*, November 11, 1950.

65. Dola de Jong, letter to the author, March 2001.

66. Graver, *An Obsession with Anne Frank*, p. 20.

67. Eva Schloss and Evelyn Julia Kent, *Eva's Story: A Survivor's Tale by the Stepsister of Anne Frank* (London: W. H. Allen, 1988), p. 223.

68. Otto Frank, letter, November 29, 1950 (AFS).

69. Otto Frank, letter, December 10, 1950 (AFS).

70. Otto Frank, undated document headed "Comments" (AFS).

71. Dola de Jong, letter to the author, March 2001.

72. Barry Sullivan, letter, November 1950 (Barbara Mooyart-Doubleday).

73. Barbara Mooyart-Doubleday, author interview, April 2001.

74. Ibid.

75. Otto Frank, letter, March 14, 1951 (AFS).

76. Graver, *An Obsession with Anne Frank*, p. 24.

77. Barry Sullivan, letter, August 17, 1951 (Barbara Mooyart-Doubleday).

78. Otto Frank, letter, November 2, 1951 (AFS).

79. Barbara Zimmerman, letter, February 11, 1952 (AFS).

80. Otto Frank, letter, March 25, 1951 (AFS).

81. Otto Frank, letter, March 18, 1952 (AFS).

82. Barbara Zimmerman, May 7, 1952 (AFS).

83. Newspaper clippings (Barbara Mooyart-Doubleday).

84. Barry Sullivan, letter, July 13, 1951 (Barbara Mooyart-Doubleday).

85. Otto Frank, letter, June 2, 1952 (AFS).

86. Barbara Zimmerman, letter, June 12, 1952 (AFS).

87. Barbara Epstein (née Zimmerman), author interview, June 2001.

88. Meyer Levin, "The Child Behind the Secret Door," *New York Times Book Review*, June 15, 1952.

89. Meyer Levin, "Anne Frank: The Diary of a Young Girl," *Congress Weekly*, June 1952.

eleven

1. Tony Kushner, "I Want to Go on Living After My Death: The Memory of Anne Frank," in Martin Evans and Kenneth Lunn, eds., *War and Memory in the Twentieth Century* (London: Berg Publishers, 1997), p. 10.

2. Oddly enough, because the diary was one of the first books to mention menstruation openly in Japan, girls there referred to their periods as "having an Anne Frank."

3. Barbara Zimmerman, letter, June 17, 1952 (AFS).

4. Otto Frank, cable, June 19, 1952 (AFS).

5. Barbara Zimmerman, letter, June 23, 1952 (AFS).

6. Barbara Zimmerman, letter, June 27, 1952 (AFS).

7. Tereska Torres, letter, June 28, 1952 (AFS).

8. Otto Frank, letter, June 28, 1952 (AFS).

9. Otto Frank, letter, July 8, 1952 (AFS).

10. Otto Frank, letter, July 22, 1952 (AFS).

11. Otto Frank, letter, July 28, 1952 (AFS).

12. Otto Frank, "Anne Frank Would Have Been Fifty This Year," *Life*, March 1979.

13. Laureen Nussbaum, author interview, May 2001.

14. Hilde Goldberg, author interview, June 2001.

15. Eva Schloss, author interview, April 2001.

16. Eva Schloss, author interview, May 1998.

17. Otto Frank, letter, October 20, 1952 (BE).

18. Buddy Elias, author interview, April 2001.

19. Father John Neiman, author interview, May 2001.

20. Otto Frank, letter, October 1, 1952 (BE).

21. Barbara Epstein, author interview, June 2001.

22. Otto Frank, letter, October 1, 1952 (BE).

370

23. Lawrence Graver, *An Obsession with Anne Frank: Meyer Levin and the Diary* (Berkeley: University of California Press, 1995), pp. 41–42.

24. Otto Frank, letter, October 3, 1952 (BE).

25. Otto Frank, letter, October 22, 1952 (BE).

26. Otto Frank, letter, October 24, 1952 (BE).

27. Ralph Melnick, *The Stolen Legacy of Anne Frank: Meyer Levin, Lillian Hellman, and the Staging of the Diary* (New Haven, CT: Yale University Press, 1997), p. 63.

28. Otto Frank, letter, December 22, 1952 (AFS).

29. Graver, *An Obsession with Anne Frank*, p. 52.

30. Barbara Zimmerman, January 7, 1953 (AFS).

31. Nathan Straus, letter, January 15, 1953 (AFS).

32. Barbara Zimmerman, January 15, 1953 (AFS).

33. Barbara Epstein, author interview, June 2001.

34. Otto Frank, letter, January 20, 1953 (AFS).

35. Otto Frank, letter, October 29, 1952 (AFS).

36. Otto Frank, February 14, 1953 (AFS).

37. Otto Frank, letter, March 1956 (AFS).

38. Myer Mermin, letter, October 28, 1953 (AFS).

39. Otto Frank, letter, March 19, 1953 (AFS).

40. Otto Frank, letter, March 28, 1953 (AFS).

41. Otto Frank, letter, May 11, 1953 (AFS).

42. Otto Frank, letter, October 1, 1952 (AFS).

43. "Imprisonment and Deportation," in David Barnouw and Gerrold van der Stroom, eds., *The Diary of Anne Frank: The Critical Edition* (London: Viking, 1989), p. 56.

44. Otto Frank, letter, August 14, 1953 (AFS).

45. Otto Frank, September 9, 1953 (AFS).

46. Melnick, *The Stolen Legacy of Anne Frank*, pp. 90, 92.

47. Otto Frank, letter, December 29, 1953 (AFS).

48. Otto Frank, letter, February 15, 1954 (AFS).

49. Melnick, *The Stolen Legacy of Anne Frank*, pp. 100, 105.

50. Otto Frank, letter, June 2, 1954 (1) (AFS).

51. Otto Frank, letter, June 2, 1954 (2) (AFS).

52. Melnick, *The Stolen Legacy of Anne Frank*, pp. 106–7.

53. Hilde Goldberg, newspaper clippings collection (AFS).

54. Ruth Goldberg, letter, 1984 (AFS).

55. Garson Kanin, newspaper clippings collection (AFS).

56. Graver, *An Obsession with Anne Frank*, p. 89.

57. Judith E. Doneson, *The Holocaust in American Film* (New York: Jewish Publication Society, 1987), pp. 70, 71.

58. Frances Goodrich, newspaper clippings collection (AFS).

59. Quoted in Bernard Kolb, "Diary Footnotes," *New York Times*, October 2, 1955.

60. Otto Frank, letter, December 12, 1954 (AFS).

61. Joseph Schildkraut, letter, March 22, 1955 (AFS).

62. Melnick, *The Stolen Legacy of Anne Frank*, p. 125.

63. Ibid., p. 126.

64. Otto Frank, letter, August 31, 1955 (AFS).

65. Otto Frank, letter, September 27, 1955 (AFS).

66. Susan Strasberg, *Bittersweet* (New York: Signet, 1980), pp. 56–57.

67. "The Diary of Anne Frank," *New York World Telegram*, October 6, 1955.

68. Ies Spetter, "Onderduik Pret Broadway," *Vrij Nederland*, November 5, 1955.

69. "The Diary of Anne Frank," *Het Parool*, April 28, 1956.

70. Melnick, *The Stolen Legacy of Anne Frank*, p. 134.

71. Ibid., pp. 134–35.

72. Ibid., p. 135.

73. Ibid., pp. 135, 136.

74. Ibid., p. 136.

75. Otto Frank, letter, March 27, 1956 (AFS).

76. Otto Frank, letter, May 24, 1956 (AFS).

77. Doneson, *The Holocaust in American Film*, p. 70.

78. Otto Frank, letter, July 12, 1956 (AFS).

79. Tereska Torres, letter, July 19, 1956 (AFS).

80. Andrew St. George, "The Diary That Shook a Nation," *Pageant*, July 1958.

81. Ibid.

82. Reader's supplement, in *Anne Frank: The Diary of a Young Girl* (New York: Washington Square Press, 1972), p. 18.

83. Graver, *An Obsession with Anne Frank*, p. 127.

84. Otto Frank, "Has Germany Forgotten Anne Frank?" *Coronet*, February 1960.

85. Otto Frank, interview transcripts of recorded discussion with Arthur Unger, New York, 1977 (AFS).

86. Zvi Schloss, author interview, April 2001.

87. Eva Schloss, author interview, April 2001.

88. Otto Frank, newspaper clippings collection (AFS).

89. Otto Frank, "Has Germany Forgotten Anne Frank?"

90. Miep Gies, letter, December 10, 1956 (AFS).

91. "Anne Frank's Secret Annex Awaits the Wrecker's Ball," *Het Vrij Volk*, November 23, 1955.

92. Menno Metselaar, Ruud van der Rol, Dineke Stam, and Hansje

372   Galesloot, eds., *Anne Frank House: A Museum with a Story* (Amsterdam: Anne Frank Stichting, 1999), p. 248.

93. Ibid., p. 250.

94. Otto Frank, letter, April 14, 1954 (AFS).

twelve

1. Judith E. Doneson, *The Holocaust in American Film* (New York: Jewish Publication Society, 1987), p. 81; Ralph Melnick, *The Stolen Legacy of Anne Frank: Meyer Levin, Lillian Hellman, and the Staging of the Diary* (New Haven, CT: Yale University Press, 1997), p. 168.

2. Doneson, *The Holocaust in American Film*, p. 81.

3. Melnick, *The Stolen Legacy of Anne Frank*, p. 168.

4. Agreement between Otto Frank and Lotte Pfeffer concerning *The Diary of Anne Frank* dramatic adaptations, September 1956 (AFS).

5. Lotte Pfeffer, letter, September 5, 1956 (AFS).

6. Anneke Visser, "Discovery of Letters Written by Man Who Hid in Anne Frank's Secret Annex," *NRC Handlesblad*, November 7, 1987.

7. Otto Frank, letter, 1970 (AFS).

8. Eleanor Roosevelt, letter, April 2, 1957 (AFS).

9. Otto Frank, letter, April 11, 1957 (AFS).

10. Nathan Straus, letter, April 19, 1957 (AFS).

11. Otto Frank, telegram, *New York Times Book Review*, September 28, 1997.

12. Barbara Epstein (née Zimmerman), author interview, June 2001.

13. Audrey Hepburn later became a patron for the Anne Frank Educational Trust UK.

14. Barry Paris, *Audrey Hepburn* (London: Orion, 1996), pp. 20, 136, 311.

15. Melnick, *The Stolen Legacy of Anne Frank*, p. 166.

16. George Stevens, newspaper clippings collection (AFS).

17. Film reviews, newspaper clippings collection (AFS).

18. Majdalany, "Anne Frank Was Never Like This," *Daily Mail*, June 5, 1959.

19. Shelley Winters won Best Supporting Actress for her portrayal of Mrs. van Daan (Gusti van Pels).

20. Doneson, *The Holocaust in American Film*, p. 81.

21. Barbara Epstein, author interview, June 2001.

22. Otto Frank, letter, August 31, 1959 (AFS).

23. Quoted in Menno Metselaar, Ruud van der Rol, Dineke Stam, and Hansje Galesloot, eds., *Anne Frank House: A Museum with a Story* (Amsterdam: Anne Frank Stichting, 1999), p. 250.

24. Johannes Kleiman, letter, June 18, 1958 (AFS).

25. Melnick, *The Stolen Legacy of Anne Frank*, p. 178.

26. "Financial Information Regarding the International Anne Frank Youth

Center," 1959 (AFS). Most of those invited to the dinner made a dona-
tion, but curiously, the list of donors shows that Gusti Huber, the actress
who portrayed Edith Frank, "cannot contribute."

27. Ruth Goldberg, letter, 1984 (AFS).

28. Otto Frank, "Has Germany Forgotten Anne Frank?" *Coronet*, February
1960.

29. I have condensed the various legal battles Otto fought to prove the diary's
authenticity, since the court cases with revisionist historians contain a
great deal of repetitive material that is unlikely to interest the general
reader. This is not to imply that the issue was of little importance to Otto
Frank; on the contrary, it affected him profoundly. Readers wishing to
learn more are directed to "Attacks on the Authenticity of the Diary," in
David Barnouw and Gerrold van der Stroom, eds., *The Diaries of Anne
Frank: The Critical Edition* (London: Viking, 1989).

30. Ibid., p. 87.

31. Ibid., p. 90.

32. Father John Neiman, author interview, April 2001.

33. Otto paid Levin $15,000 and was in turn able to collect his royalties from
the play, which had been tied up during all the legal tussles. Levin relin-
quished any rights to the diary but retained the right to discuss the diary
as a literary issue, as long as such discussion did not touch on the question of whether or not his play should have been produced.

34. Lawrence Graver, *An Obsession with Anne Frank: Meyer Levin and the Diary*
(Berkeley: University of California Press, 1995), pp. 148–49.

35. Otto Frank, newspaper clippings collection (AFS).

36. Otto Frank, undated letter (AFS).

37. Franzi Spronz, author interview, May 2001.

38. Hanneli Pick-Goslar, author interview, June 2001.

39. Anne Frank House, newspaper clippings collection (AFS).

40. Ibid.

41. Cara Wilson, *Love, Otto: The Legacy of Anne Frank* (Kansas City, Mo.:
Andrews McMeel, 1995).

42. Father John Neiman, author interview, May 2001.

43. Zvi Schloss, author interview, April 2001.

44. Judith Salomon, author interview, June 2001.

45. Henk Salomon, author interview, June 2001.

46. John Windsor, "Duty of Dr. Frank," *The Guardian*, June 15, 1971.

47. Anne Frank–Fonds, information leaflet.

48. Ernst Schnabel, *The Footsteps of Anne Frank* (London: Pan Books, 1976),
p. 114.

49. Cor Suijk, author interview, April 2001.

50. Peter Hann, "Arrest Starts New Anne Frank Inquiry," November 1963, newspaper cuttings collection (AFS).

51. Letter, December 4, 1963 (AFS).

52. Anton Ahlers, author interview, March 2002.

53. A. C. Ahlers, letter, December 27, 1963, Doc. I., K. J. Silberbauer (NIOD).

54. A. C. Ahlers, letter, January 15, 1964, Doc. I., K. J. Silberbauer (NIOD).

55. A. C. Ahlers, letter, December 20, 1966 (photocopy in the possession of the author).

56. Anton Ahlers, author interview, March 2002.

57. Report on A. C. Ahlers, February 5, 1964, Doc. I., K. J. Silberbauer (NIOD).

58. Cas Ahlers, author interview, March 2002.

59. Anton Ahlers, author interview, March 2002.

60. Wife of Anton Ahlers, author interview, March 2002 (she does not wish to be named).

61. Anton Ahlers, author interview, March 2002.

62. Schnabel, *The Footsteps of Anne Frank*, p. 59.

63. Willi Lages, statement in Doc. I., K. J. Silberbauer (NIOD).

64. Karl Silberbauer, statement in Doc. I., K. J. Silberbauer (NIOD).

65. Police summary, 1964, in Doc. I., K. J. Silberbauer (NIOD).

66. Dossier W. G. van Maaren, Parket Generaal, The Hague.

67. Report on A. C. Ahlers, February 5, 1964, Doc. I., K. J. Silberbauer (NIOD).

68. In 1967, Otto was co-plaintiff in a war crimes trial, and in a 1965 interview, Otto was asked his opinion about the trials of the Auschwitz criminals conducted in Germany. He answered: "I think they are necessary. At the Nuremberg trials just after the war, the German people thought it was the Allies taking revenge; you could hear that being said in Germany. Now it is the German courts that discover all these beastly acts. They are just as necessary as the Eichmann trial." When questioned about Eichmann's execution, Otto said calmly, "Killing is not the worst. I think he merited killing, but whether he should have been is another matter. I am not an adherent of killing."

69. Otto Frank, letter, January 1968, in Melissa Muller, *Anne Frank: The Biography* (New York: Henry Holt, 1998), p. 288.

70. Dr. Trude K. Holländer, letter to the author, March 25, 1998.

71. Buddy Elias, newspaper clippings collection (AFS).

72. Otto Frank, letter, April 23, 1974 (AFS).

73. Bep van Wijk-Voskuijl, letter, 1957 (AFS).

74. Otto Frank, letter, August 6, 1974 (AFS).

75. Otto Frank, undated letter (AFS).

76. Cor Suijk, letter to the author, March 2001.

77. Wilson, *Love, Otto*, p. 139.

78. Otto Frank, letter, February 24, 1979 (AFS).

79. Otto Frank, letter, June 4, 1979 (AFS).

80. Otto Frank, letter, July 9, 1979 (AFS).

81. Fritzi Frank, letter, February 28, 1980 (AFS).

82. Otto Frank, letter, November 1979 (AFS).

83. Fritzi Frank, letter, May 12, 1980.

84. Father John Neiman, author interview, April 2001.

85. Franzi Spronz, author interview, May 2001.

86. All correspondence is in the archives of the Anne Frank Stichting, Amsterdam.

87. Fritzi Frank, card, August 1980 (AFS).

88. "Otto Frank, Father of Anne, Dead at 91," *New York Times*, August 21, 1980.

89. Cassette recording of "A Memorial Tribute to Otto Frank," October 1980, Anne Frank Center, USA (AFS).

90. Fritzi Frank, "My Life with Otto Frank," 1980 (BE).

91. Ibid.

92. Franzi Spronz, author interview, May 2001.

thirteen

1. Fritzi Frank, letter, October 1980 (AFS).

2. Fritzi Frank, letter, October 1980, in Cara Wilson, *Love, Otto: The Legacy of Anne Frank* (Kansas City, Mo.: Andrews McMeel, 1995), p. 145.

3. Otto Frank, July 20, 1971 (AFS).

4. Otto Frank, interview transcripts of recorded discussion with Arthur Unger, New York, 1977 (AFS).

5. Ibid.

6. Wilson, *Love, Otto*, p. 143.

7. Milly Stanfield, letter, August 1992 (AFS).

8. Fritzi Frank, letter, November 3, 1980 (AFS).

9. Fritzi Frank, letter, November 6, 1994 (AFS).

10. Fritzi Frank, letter, July 1983 (AFS). Levin died on July 9, 1981. Obituaries in the press focused on his thirty-year struggle to have his play recognized and produced. His widow, Tereska Torres, wrote a memoir about being in the eye of the hurricane of Levin's Anne Frank fixation, remembering that during one argument Levin had screamed, "If you really love me, you will take a gun and shoot Otto Frank." His friend Harry Golden commented that suing Otto Frank was the worst public relations

blunder of the twentieth century; it was like suing the father of Joan of Arc. Nonetheless, Levin had been instrumental in bringing the diary to the attention of the American public, and he clearly had a more logical vision of how the Holocaust would be represented in the future than the Hacketts did, for he wrote: "The Final Solution was not a common fate. A new word, genocide, had to be found for this mechanized mass murder that included the hunting down for destruction even of infants confided to non-Jews. Generalizing away the particular Jewish doom falsifies the Holocaust and opens the way for today's campaign of denials. It weakens the warning against genocidal methods that could indeed be directed at other peoples, or again at the Jews." Levin's son, the poet Gabriel Levin, reflects today: "I have no doubt that my father was in a sense 'right' in attacking the Hacketts' play for all the obvious reasons. However, I believe—and I say this with pain—that my father was obstinately, even cruelly wrong in insisting that he had a claim over the play/diaries that somehow superseded Otto Frank's legal and moral rights as the sole survivor to his daughter's literary remains. I may not agree with the way Frank controlled the image of Anne (not only in terms of her Jewishness but also in terms of her sexuality and her relation to her mother), but I do feel strongly that it is not for us to judge the survivors of the camps, and if this is how he decided Anne should be presented to the general public, so be it; after his death a more rounded picture would—and has—come out. I don't believe that Meyer ever lost his mind. But he did lose, I believe, whenever the issue of Otto Frank and the diaries came up, his moral bearings." Despite his father's "battles with the windmills of Anne Frank," Gabriel maintains, Meyer Levin "cared deeply for his family, and he was, strangely enough—for a man with such a temper—rather shy, introverted and 'soft' in his approach to people. He was also driven by a deep sense of justice (again, a paradox, when one considers the fierce insensitivity of his letter to Otto Frank) and was undoubtedly a writer of rare integrity—a writer of the Old School, who lived, passionately, by the word." Gabriel Levin, letter to the author, September 19, 2001.

11. Father John Neiman, author interview, April 2001.

12. Katja Olszewska, author interview, April 2001.

13. Cynthia Ozick, "Who Owns Anne Frank?" *The New Yorker*, October 6, 1997.

14. Barbara Epstein, author interview, June 2001.

15. Barbara Hauptman, essay, "A Visit to Amsterdam," August 1971.

16. *Anne Frank Magazine 1998* (Amsterdam: Anne Frank Stichting, 1998), p. 38.

17. Otto Frank, in "Who Killed Anne Frank?" *Hadassah Magazine*, no. 7, March 1965.

18. Otto Frank, in *Moment*, vol. 3, December 1977 (R. Peter Straus).

19. Wilson, *Love, Otto*, pp. 50–51.

20. Otto Frank, in Anne Frank Stichting, *The Anne Frank House* leaflet, 1999.

21. Otto Frank, letter, February 11, 1966, in Wilson, *Love, Otto*, p. 26.

22. Otto Frank, Unger interview, New York, 1977 (AFS).

23. Father John Neiman, author interview, April 2001.

24. Otto Frank, Unger interview, New York, 1977 (AFS).

25. Elma Verhey, "Anne Frank's World," in Alex Grobman, ed., *Anne Frank in Historical Perspective: A Teaching Guide* (Los Angeles: Martyrs Memorial and Museum of the Holocaust, 1995), p. 17.

26. Otto Frank, letter, May 27, 1967, in Wilson, *Love, Otto*, pp. 38–39.

27. Otto Frank, letter, June 1967 (AFS).

28. Barbara Goldstein, letter, 1974 (AFS).

29. Otto Frank, letter, June 7, 1974, in Wilson, *Love, Otto*, pp. 92–93.

30. Otto Frank, Unger interview, New York, 1977 (AFS).

31. Otto Frank, letter, October 15, 1975 (BE).

32. Otto Frank, December 8, 1975 (BE).

33. Otto Frank, letter, January 26, 1975 (AFS).

34. *Anne Frank Magazine 1998* (Amsterdam: Anne Frank Stichting, 1998), p. 39.

35. Andrew St. George, "The Diary That Shook a Nation," in *Pageant*, July 1958.

36. *Anne Frank Magazine 2000* (Amsterdam: Anne Frank Stichting, 2000), p. 34.

37. Father John Neiman, author interview, April 2001.

38. Rabbi David Soetendorp, author interview, June 2001.

39. Tim Cole, *Images of the Holocaust: The Myth of the "Shoah Business"* (London: Gerald Duckworth & Co., 1999), pp. 40–41.

40. Otto Frank, last will and testament, December 1978 (BE).

41. Cor Suijk, author interview, April 2001.

42. Eva Schloss, author interview, April 2001.

43. Zvi Schloss, author interview, April 2001.

44. Cor Suijk, author interview, April 2001.

45. Eva Schloss, author interview, April 2001.

46. Wilson, *Love, Otto*, p. 128.

47. Cor Suijk, "Questions Put to Miep Gies," letter to the author, 2001.

48. Alvin H. Rosenfeld, "The Americanization of the Holocaust," in *Commentary*, June 1995, p. 38.

49. Miep Gies is the sole survivor of the five helpers. Kugler died in December 1981, Bep Voskuijl-van Wijk in May 1983, and Jan Gies in January 1993.

50. Otto Frank, newspaper clippings collection (AFS).

51. Cole, *Images of the Holocaust*, p. 43.

52. Rabbi David Soetendorp, author interview, June 2001.

53. Fritzi Frank, letter, June 28, 1986 (AFS).

54. Fritzi Frank, letter, n.d. (AFS).

55. Cor Suijk, letter, April 1998 (BE).

56. Details about the Bundeskriminalamt (Federal Criminal Investigation Bureau) investigation can be found in "Attacks on the Authenticity of the Diary," in David Barnouw and Gerrold van der Stroom, *The Diaries of Anne Frank: The Critical Edition* (London: Viking, 1989), pp. 97–98.

57. Cor Suijk, letter, April 1998 (BE).

58. Otto Frank, last will and testament, December 1978 (BE).

59. Katja Olszewska, author interview, April 2001.

60. Cor Suijk, letter, June 1998 (BE).

61. The Anne Frank Center, for which Suijk worked at the time, does not hold archive material on the Frank family.

62. Eva Schloss, author interview, April 2001. Suijk said Otto had given him the pages in May 1980. He had tried to return them several months later, which would be shortly before Otto's death in August 1980.

63. Laureen Nussbaum, author interview, May 2001.

64. *Diary*, June 20, 1942 (B), p. 182.

65. Otto Frank, Unger interview, New York, 1977 (AFS).

epilogue

1. Anton Ahlers, author interview, March 2002.

2. Casper Ahlers, documents relating to his period in Germany, Gemeente Archief, Amsterdam.

3. NSB membership booklet, Gemeente Archief; Huibert Ahlers, documents relating to his period in Germany, Gemeente Archief.

4. Doc. I., K. J. Silberbauer (NIOD); dossier W. G. van Maaren (CABR).

5. A. C. Ahlers, letter, December 20, 1966 (photocopy in the possession of the author).

6. A. C. Ahlers, letter, January 15, 1964, Doc. I., K. J. Silberbauer (NIOD).

7. Report on A. C. Ahlers, February 5, 1964, Doc. I., K. J. Silberbauer (NIOD).

8. Dossier W. G. van Maaren (CABR).

9. Ibid.

10. The relationship between Martha and her children had broken down when she took their father back into her home.

11. Anton Ahlers, author interview, April 2002.

12. Cas Ahlers, author interview, April 2002.

13. Martha Ahlers, conversation with the author, February 2001.

14. Martha Ahlers, conversation with the author, July 2001.

15. Anton Ahlers, author interview, July 2002.

16. The information in this section, unless otherwise stated, is taken from the author's interview with Anton Ahlers, July 2002.

17. The owner was indeed still alive, and he did reclaim the house.

18. Cas Ahlers, author interview, March 2002.

19. Land reclaimed from the sea. It had not yet been built upon.

20. A. C. Ahlers, Sociaal Dienst files, Gemeente Archief, Amsterdam.

21. Cor Suijk, author interview, April 2001.

22. Dienke Hondius, "A New Perspective on Helpers of Jews During the Holocaust: The Case of Miep and Jan Gies," in Alex Grobman, ed., *Anne Frank in Historical Perspective: A Teaching Guide* (Los Angeles: Martyrs Memorial and Museum of the Holocaust, 1995), p. 40.

23. Father John Neiman, author interview, April 2001.

24. Carole Kleesiek, author interview, April 2002.

25. "Anne Frank Betrayed for Ten Shillings," in *Sunday Times* (London), February 5, 1967.

26. Otto Frank, "Anne Frank Would Have Been Fifty This Year," *Life*, March 1979.

27. Interview with Fritzi Frank, conducted by the Anne Frank Stichting (AFS). The author is convinced that there are more documents about the investigation into the betrayal. Otto mentioned a policeman who was suspected and questioned, yet no one fitting that description appears in the known dossiers, and the notion that it was a woman's voice on the telephone—allegedly this information came from the Gestapo—also appears nowhere in the papers.

28. Anton Ahlers, author interview, July 2002.

29. A. C. Ahlers, Sociaal Dienst files, Gemeente Archief, Amsterdam.

30. Eventually, Martha was granted a small allowance.

31. A. C. Ahlers, Sociaal Dienst files, Gemeente Archief, Amsterdam. Many of the old Social Services files have been destroyed, and unfortunately, the one relating to Martha Ahlers is among them. But somewhere there is a dossier containing details of the investigation into Martha's past. And when that is found, we may know far more about the person who dialed the Gestapo headquarters in Amsterdam on that brilliant August morning in 1944. The author is currently trying to track it down.

BIBLIOGRAPHY

books

Anissimov, Myriam, *Primo Levi: Tragedy of an Optimist* (New York: Overlook Press, 2000).

Anne Frank Stichting, *Anne Frank 1929–1945* (Heidelberg: Lambert Schneider, 1979).

Barnouw, David, and Gerrold van der Stroom, eds., *The Diaries of Anne Frank: The Critical Edition* (London: Viking, 1989).

Barnouw, David, and Gerrold van der Stroom, eds., *De Dagboeken van Anne Frank* (Amsterdam: Bert Bakker, 2001).

Birmingham, Stephen, *Our Crowd: The Great Jewish Families of New York* (New York: Dell Publishing, 1967).

Borowski, Tadeusz, *This Way for the Gas, Ladies and Gentlemen* (London: Penguin, 1983).

Brasz, Chaya, *Removing the Yellow Badge: The Struggle for a Jewish Community in the Postwar Netherlands* (Jerusalem: Institute for Research on Dutch Jewry, 1996).

Cole, Tim, *Images of the Holocaust: The Myth of the "Shoah Business"* (London: Gerald Duckworth & Co., 1999).

Colijn, G. Jan, and Marcia S. Littell, eds., *The Netherlands and Nazi Genocide* (New York: Edwin Mellen Press, 1992); includes Nanda van der Zee, "The Recurrent Myth of 'Dutch Heroism' in the Second World War and Anne Frank as a Symbol."

Craig, Gordon A., *Germany 1866–1945* (Oxford: Oxford University Press, 1981).

382   Czech, Danuta, *Auschwitz Chronicle 1939–1945* (New York: Henry Holt, 1990).

Dawidowicz. Lucy S., *The War Against the Jews 1933–1945* (London: Penguin, 1987).

Doneson, Judith E., *The Holocaust in American Film* (New York: Jewish Publication Society, 1987).

Elon, Amos, *Founder: Meyer Amschel Rothschild and His Time* (London: HarperCollins, 1996).

Enzer, Hyman A., and Sandra Solotaroff-Enzer, eds., *Anne Frank: Reflections on Her Life and Legacy* (Carbondale: University of Illinois Press, 2000); includes Bruno Bettelheim, "The Ignored Lesson of Anne Frank," and Lin Jaldati, "Bergen Belsen."

Evans, Martin, and Kenneth Lunn, eds., *War and Memory in the Twentieth Century* (London: Berg Publishers, 1997); includes Tony Kushner, "I Want to Go on Living After My Death: The Memory of Anne Frank."

Ferguson, Niall, *The Pity of War* (London: Penguin, 1998).

Fogelman, Eva, *Conscience and Courage: Rescuers of Jews During the Holocaust* (London: Cassel, 1995).

Frank, Anne, *Tales from the Secret Annexe* (London: Penguin, 1982).

Frank, Anne, *Het Achterhuis* (Amsterdam: Contact, 1947); includes an introduction by Otto Frank.

Friedrich, Otto, *The Kingdom of Auschwitz* (London: Penguin, 1994).

Gies, Miep, and Alison Leslie Gold, *Anne Frank Remembered* (New York: Bantam, 1987).

Gilbert, Martin, *Auschwitz and the Allies* (London: Michael Joseph, 1981).

Gilbert, Martin, *Holocaust Journey: Traveling in Search of the Past* (London: Orion, 1997).

Gilbert, Martin, *The Holocaust: The Jewish Tragedy* (London: HarperCollins, 1987).

Gill, Anton, *The Journey Back from Hell: Conversations with Concentration Camp Survivors* (London: Grafton Books, 1988).

Gold, Alison Leslie, *Memories of Anne Frank: Reflections of a Childhood Friend* (New York: Scholastic Press, 1997).

Goldhagen, Daniel Jonah, *Hitler's Willing Executioners: Ordinary Germans and the Holocaust* (London: Abacus, 1999).

Goodrich, Frances, and Albert Hackett, *The Diary of Anne Frank* (London: Blackie & Son, 1970).

Graver, Lawrence, *An Obsession with Anne Frank: Meyer Levin and the Diary* (Berkeley: University of California Press, 1995).

Grobman, Alex, ed., *Anne Frank in Historical Perspective: A Teaching Guide* (Los Angeles: Martyrs Memorial and Museum of the Holocaust, 1995); includes Dienke Hondius, "A New Perspective on Helpers of Jews During the Holocaust: The Case of Miep and Jan Gies"; Elma Verhey, "Anne Frank's World"; and Elma Verhey, "Anne Frank and the Dutch Myth."

Gutman, Yisrael, and Michael, Berenbaum, *Anatomy of Auschwitz Death Camp* (Bloomington: Indiana University Press, 1994).

Hayes, Peter, ed., *Lessons and Legacies: The Meaning of the Holocaust in a Changing World* (Chicago: Northwestern University Press, 1991); includes Alvin H. Rosenfeld, "Popularization and Memory: The Case of Anne Frank."

Hillesum, Etty, *Letters from Westerbork* (London: Jonathan Cape, 1986).

Hellwig, Joachim, and Gunther Deicke, *Ein Tagebuch für Anne Frank* (Berlin: Verlag der Nation, 1959).

Hondius, Dienke, *Terugkeer: Antisemitisme in Nederland rond de bevrijding* (The Hague: SDU, 1990).

Jong, Louis de, and Simon Schama, *The Netherlands and Nazi Germany* (Cambridge: Harvard University Press, 1990).

Kedward, H. R., *Resistance in Vichy France* (Oxford: Oxford University Press, 1978).

Kolb, Eberhard, *Bergen-Belsen from 1943 to 1945* (Gottingen: Sammlung Vandenhoeck, 1988).

Last, Dick van Galen, and Rolf Wolfswinkel, *Anne Frank and After: Dutch Holocaust Literature in Historical Perspective* (Amsterdam: Amsterdam University Press, 1996).

Levi, Primo, *If This Is a Man: The Truce* (London: Abacus Books, 1979).

Levin, Meyer, *The Obsession* (New York: Simon & Schuster, 1973).

Lindwer, Willy, *The Last Seven Months of Anne Frank* (New York: Pantheon, 1991).

Lipstadt, Deborah, *Denying the Holocaust: The Growing Assault on Truth and Memory* (New York: Free Press, 1993).

Maarsen, Jacqueline van, *My Friend Anne Frank* (New York: Vantage Press, 1996).

Marrus, Michael R., *The Holocaust in History* (London: Penguin, 1989).

Melnick, Ralph, *The Stolen Legacy of Anne Frank: Meyer Levin, Lillian Hellman, and the Staging of the Diary* (New Haven, CT: Yale University Press, 1997).

Metselaar, Menno, Ruud van der Rol, Dineke Stam, and Hansje Galesloot, eds., *Anne Frank House: A Museum with a Story* (Amsterdam: Anne Frank Stichting, 1999).

Middlebrook, Martin, and Mary Middlebrook, *The Somme Battlefields* (London: Viking, 1991).

Miller, Judith, *One by One by One: Facing the Holocaust* (New York: Simon & Schuster, 1990).

Moore, Bob, *Victims and Survivors: The Nazi Persecution of the Jews in the Netherlands, 1940–1945* (London: Arnold, 1997).

384 Moynahan, Brian, *The British Century: A Photographic History of the Last Hundred Years* (London: Random House, 1997).

Mulder, Dirk, *Kamp Westerbork* (Westerbork: Herinneringscentrum Kamp Westerbork, 1991).

Muller, Melissa, *Anne Frank: The Biography* (New York: Henry Holt, 1998).

Paris, Barry, *Audrey Hepburn* (London: Orion, 1996).

Presser, Jacob, *Ashes in the Wind: The Destruction of Dutch Jewry* (London: Souvenir Press, 1968).

Pressler, Mirjam, *The Story of Anne Frank* (London: Macmillan, 1999).

Rittner, Carol, ed., *Anne Frank in the World: Essays and Reflections* (New York: M. E. Sharpe, 1997).

Rürup, Reinhard, *Topography of Terror: Gestapo, SS, and Reichssicherheits-hauptamt on the "Prinz-Albrecht-Terrain": A Documentation* (Berlin: Verlag Willmuth Arenhövel, 1989).

Sanchez, Leopold Diego, *Jean-Michel Frank* (Paris: Editions du Regard, 1980).

Schloss, Eva, and Evelyn Julia Kent, *Eva's Story: A Survivor's Tale by the Stepsister of Anne Frank* (London: W. H. Allen, 1988).

Schnabel, Ernst, *The Footsteps of Anne Frank* (London: Pan Books, 1976).

Steen, Jürgen, Esther Alexander-Ihme, Johannes Heil, and Liane Schack, *Früher wohnten wir in Frankfurt . . .* (Frankfurt: Historisches Museum Frankfurt am Main, 1985).

Steen, Jürgen, and Wolf von Wolzogen, *Anne aus Frankfurt: Leben und Lebenswelt Anne Franks* (Frankfurt: Historisches Museum Frankfurt am Main, 1996).

Steenmeijer, Anna G., and Otto Frank, eds., *A Tribute to Anne Frank* (New York: Doubleday, 1971).

Stoutenbeek, Jan, and Paul Vigeveno, *A Guide to Jewish Amsterdam* (Amsterdam: De Haan, 1985).

Strasberg, Susan, *Bittersweet* (New York: Signet, 1980).

Sulzbach, Herbert, *With the German Guns: Four Years on the Western Front* (London: Leo Cooper, 1998).

Todorov, Tzvetan, *Facing the Extreme: Moral Life in the Concentration Camps* (London: Phoenix, 2000).

Wasserstein, Bernard, *Vanishing Diaspora: The Jews in Europe Since 1945* (London: Penguin, 1996).

Wiesenthal, Simon, *Justice Not Vengeance* (London: Weidenfeld & Nicholson, 1989).

Wilson, Cara, *Love, Otto: The Legacy of Anne Frank* (Kansas City, Mo.: Andrews McMeel, 1995).

Wistrich, Robert S., *Anti-Semitism: The Longest Hatred* (London: Methuen, 1991).

Wolzogen, Wolf von, *Anne aus Frankfurt* (Frankfurt: Historical Museum, 385 1994).

Young, James E., ed., *The Art of Memory: Holocaust Memorials in History* (Munich: Presetel-Verlag, 1994).

articles and other publications

Adler, Joan, "Wholedamfam" (Straus family newsletter), February 1998.

"Anne Frank's Secret Annex Awaits the Wrecker's Ball." *Het Vrij Volk*, November 23, 1955.

"Anne Frank Betrayed for Ten Shillings," *Sunday Times* (London), February 5, 1967.

Anne Frank Stichting, "Anne Frank in the World 1929–1945," exhibition catalog in Dutch and English (Amsterdam: Bert Bakker, 1985).

Anne Frank Stichting, "Anne Frank in the World," exhibition catalog in Japanese (Amsterdam: Anne Frank Stichting, 1985).

Anne Frank Stichting, "Anne Frank: A History for Today," exhibition catalog in English (Amsterdam: Anne Frank Stichting, 1996).

Anne Frank Stichting, *Anne Frank Magazine 1998* (Amsterdam: Anne Frank Stichting, 1998).

Anne Frank Stichting, *Anne Frank Magazine 1999* (Amsterdam: Anne Frank Stichting, 1999).

Anne Frank Stichting, *Anne Frank Magazine 2000* (Amsterdam: Anne Frank Stichting, 2000); includes Laureen Nussbaum, "Anne's Diary Incomplete."

"Anne Frank's Vater: Ich will Versohnung," *Welt am Sonntag*, February 4, 1979.

Ariel, "Testament of Youth," *Huddersfield Weekly Examiner*, October 1954.

Arnold, Hermann. "Waren es Vorfahren von Anne Frank?" *Tribüne*, 1990.

Ballif, Algene, *Commentary*, November 1955.

Baron, Alexander, *Jewish Chronicle*, October 15, 1954.

Brilleslijper-Jaldati, Lientje, "Memories of Anne Frank," in press leaflet for the film *Ein Tagebuch für Anne Frank* (Berlin: VEB Progress Film-Vertrieb, 1959).

Bundy, June, "Anne Frank: The Diary of a Young Girl," *Billboard*, September 27, 1952.

Buruma, Ian, "Anne Frank's Afterlife," *New York Review of Books*, February 19, 1998.

Chapman, John, "Anne Frank Wins Prize," *Sunday News*, May 13, 1956.

Cohn, Vera, "The Anti-Defamation League Bulletin: The Day I Met Anne Frank," undated.

"The Diary of Anne Frank," *Het Parool*, April 28, 1956.

386 "The Diary of Anne Frank," *New York World Telegram*, October 6, 1955.

Duke, Julianne, "Anne Frank Remembered," *New York Times*, June 11, 1989.

Farrell, E. C., "Postscript to a Diary," *Global Magazine*, March 6, 1965.

Fishman, Joel, "The Jewish Community in the Postwar Netherlands 1944–1975," *Midstream* 22 (1976).

Flanner, Janet, "Letter from Paris," *The New Yorker*, November 11, 1950.

Frank, Otto, "Has Germany Forgotten Anne Frank?" *Coronet*, February 1960.

Frank, Otto, "Anne Frank Would Have Been Fifty This Year," *Life*, March 1979.

Frank, Otto, telegram, *New York Times Book Review*, September 28, 1997.

Fussman, Carl, "The Woman Who Would Have Saved Anne Frank," *Newsday*, March 16, 1995.

"Holocaust Survivors Recall Their Hell on Earth," *Watertown Daily Times*, February 5, 1995.

Kolb, Bernard, "Diary Footnotes," *New York Times*, October 2, 1955.

Kramer, Mimi, "Spotlight: Encore, Anne Frank," *Vanity Fair*, December 1997.

"The Living Legacy of Anne Frank," *Journal*, September 1967.

Levin, Meyer, "The Restricted Market," *Congress Weekly*, November 13, 1950.

Levin, Meyer, "The Child Behind the Secret Door," *New York Times Book Review*, June 15, 1952.

Levin, Meyer, "Anne Frank: The Diary of a Young Girl," *Congress Weekly*, June 1952.

Levin, Meyer. "The Suppressed Anne Frank," *Jewish Week*, August 31, 1980.

"Maarten Kuiper: The Criminal of the Euterpestraat," *Elseviers Weekblad*, November 29, 1947.

Majdalany. "Anne Frank Was Never Like This," *Daily Mail*, June 5, 1959.

"Otto Frank, Father of Anne. Dead at 91," *New York Times*, August 21, 1980.

Ozick, Cynthia, "Who Owns Anne Frank?" *The New Yorker*, October 6, 1997.

Pepper, William, "Drama of 'Diary' Is Nonsectarian," *New York World Telegram and Sun*, January 1956.

Puner, Morton, "The Mission of Otto Frank," *ADL Bulletin*, April 1959.

Romein, Jan, "A Child's Voice," *Het Parool*, April 3, 1945.

Rosenfeld, Alvin H., "The Americanization of the Holocaust," *Commentary*, June 1995.

Sagan, Alex, "An Optimistic Icon: Anne Frank's Canonization in Postwar Culture," *German Politics and Society* (Center for German Studies at the University of California Press) 13, no. 3, issue 36 (fall 1995).

St. George, Andrew, "The Diary That Shook a Nation," *Pageant*, July 1958.

Shapiro, Eda, "The Reminiscences of Victor Kugler, the 'Mr. Kraler' of Anne Frank's Diary," *Yad Vashem Studies* 13 (Jerusalem: Yad Vashem, 1979).

Spetter, Ies, "Onderduik Pret Broadway," *Vrij Nederland*, November 5, 1955.

Stocks, Mary, "The Secret Annexe," *Manchester Guardian*, April 28, 1952.

Strang, Joanne, "Stevens Relives Anne Frank's Story," *New York Times Magazine*, August 3, 1958.

Straus, R. Peter, interview with Otto Frank, *Moment*, December 1977.

Stroom, Gerrold van der, "Anne Frank and Her Diaries," paper delivered at the Institute of Jewish Studies, University College, London, June 1997.

Visser, Anneke. "Discovery of Letters Written by Man Who Hid in Anne Frank's Secret Annex," *NRC Handlesblad*, November 7, 1987.

Vuur, Willem, "Anne Frank House in Money Trouble," *Herald Tribune*, April 1, 1971.

Waggoner, Walter H., "New Yorker Aids Dutch Students," *New York Times*, July 26, 1957.

Wagner, Betty-Ann, "Anne Frank Letter to Iowa Pen-pal to Be Sold," *New York Times*, July 22, 1988.

"Who Killed Anne Frank?" *Hadassah Magazine*, March 1965.

Windsor, John, "Duty of Dr. Frank," *The Guardian*, June 15, 1971.

Wolff, Margo H., "Anne Frank Lives On," *Hadassah Newsletter*, May 1958.

*unpublished documents
(excluding correspondence)*

Ahlers, Anton C., dossiers, CABR; report by the Dutch authorities, 1964, Doc. I., K. J. Silberbauer, NIOD; Sociaal Dienst files, Gemeente Archief, Amsterdam.

Baschwitz, Mrs. I., report of a conversation with, January 12, 1981, NIOD.

Cahn, Werner, report of a conversation with, March 12, 1981, NIOD.

Cauvern, Ab, report of a conversation with, January 23, 1981, NIOD.

Döring, Kurt, Doc. I., NIOD; dossier, CABR; newspaper cuttings, NIOD.

Draber, Mrs. R. E., report of a conversation with, February 19, 1981, NIOD.

"Financial Information Regarding the International Anne Frank Youth Center," 1959, AFS.

Frank, Anne, Baby Book, AFF.

Frank, Fritzi, "My Life with Otto Frank," memoir, 1980, BE.

Frank, Fritzi, transcript of interview conducted by Dienke Hondius for the Anne Frank Stichting, AFS.

Frank, Margot, Baby Book, AFF.

Frank, Otto, Liberation Notebook, 1945, AFS.

Frank, Otto, Polish Red Cross declaration regarding his return to the Netherlands, 1945, AFS.

Frank, Otto, Engagement Agenda, 1945, AFS.

Frank, Otto, Engagement Agenda, 1947, AFS.

Frank, Otto, memoir, BE.

388   Frank, Otto, transcript of interview with Westinghouse Broadcasting Co., February 16, 1960, AFS.

Frank, Otto, transcript of tape recording made for an American school group, 1970s, AFS.

Frank, Otto, interview transcripts of recorded discussion with Arthur Unger, New York, 1977, AFS.

Frank, Otto, undated document headed "Comments," AFS.

Frank, Otto, undated document headed "Remarks Regarding Warrant Sent to Me with Your Letter of March 19, 1956," AFS.

Gies, Jan A., and Miep Gies-Santrouschitz, report of two conversations with, February 19 and 27, 1985, NIOD.

Gies, Jan A., and Miep Gies-Santrouschitz, report of a conversation with, February 18, 1981, NIOD.

Gies, Miep, page of testimony written by, AFS.

Gringhuis, Gezinus, dossier, CABR; Doc I., NIOD.

Grootendorst, Willem, dossier, CABR.

Grossman, Jean Schick, "The Story Within Her Story" (manuscript), December 5, 1954.

Hammelburg, Rabbi I., report of a conversation with, February 23, 1981, NIOD.

Hauptman, Barbara, "A Visit to Amsterdam" (essay), August 1971, AFS.

Hondius, Dienke, "The Return," English translation of *Terugkeer: Antisemitisme in Nederland rond de bevrijding* (The Hague: SDU, 1990).

Jansen, Joseph M., dossier, CABR.

Kropveld, Dr. S. M., declaration of, in dossier Westerbork–Auschwitz, September 3, 1944, NIOD.

Kuiper, Maarten, Doc. I., NIOD; dossier, CABR; newspaper cuttings, NIOD.

Landau town archives; and the pamphlets *Some Historical Facts About the House* and *Facts Relating to the Jews of Landau*, available from the Frank-Loeb'sches House.

Liema, Rose de, "So You Will Remember" (memoir), AFS.

Liema, Sal de, transcript of interview conducted by the Anne Frank Stichting, AFS.

Maaren, Wilhelm G. van, Doc. I., NIOD; dossier, CABR.

NSB membership booklet, Gemeente Archief, Amsterdam.

Opekta, dossier, NBI 134994, Rijksinstituut, The Hague; Opekta/Pectacon, dossier, NIOD; Opekta/Pectacon, Delivery Book, 1940, AFS.

Poppel, Josef van, Doc. I., NIOD; dossier, CABR; newspaper cuttings, NIOD.

Romein-Verschoor, Annie, report of a conversation with, undated, NIOD.

Rouwendaal, Herman, Doc. I., NIOD; dossier, CABR; newspaper cuttings, NIOD.

Rühl, Emil, Doc. I., NIOD; dossier, CABR; newspaper cuttings, NIOD.

Schaap, Peter, dossier, CABR.

Silberbauer, Karl, Doc. I., NIOD.

Spronz, Joseph, "Auschwitz Memoirs" (manuscript), AFS.

Stanfield, Milly, "A Talk: Anne and Otto Frank," April 22, 1990, AFS.

Stanfield, Milly, memoirs, AFS.

Viebahn, Friedrich C., dossier, CABR; newspaper cuttings, NIOD.

Wijk-Voskuijl, Bep, van, report of a conversation with, February 25, 1981, NIOD.

Wolters, Karel O. M., Doc. I., NIOD.

INDEX